D0872405

Jewish Philosophers and Jewish Philosophy

Jewish Philosophers
and
Jewish Philosophy

Emil L. Fackenheim

Edited by
Michael L. Morgan

Indiana University Press
Bloomington and Indianapolis

The paper used in this publication meets the
minimum requirements of American National
Standard for Information Sciences—Permanence of
Paper for Printed Library Materials, ANSI Z39.48-1984.

Manufactured in the United States of America

Library of Congress Cataloging–in–Publication Data

Fackenheim, Emil L.
Jewish philosophers and Jewish philosophy / Emil L. Fackenheim ;
edited by Michael L. Morgan.
p.   cm.
Includes index.
ISBN 0-253-33062-9 (cloth : alk. paper)
1. Jewish philosphers. 2. Judaism—20th century. 3. Holocaust,
Jewish (1939–1945)—Influence. 4. Philosophy, Jewish. I. Morgan,
Michael L., date. II. Title.
B5800.F33   1996
181'.06—dc20   95-52976

1   2   3   4   5   01   00   99   98   97   96

To Moshe Davis

In memory
after twenty-five years
of friendship

Contents

Contents

Acknowledgments

The editor would like to thank all those who gave permission to reprint Emil Fackenheim's work in this collection. Many of the essays were written long before the development of computer technology. They had to be scanned and the results prepared to be submitted in WordPerfect. This task was no mean one. The work was done by Bruce Hoffman, Gillian Parker, and Margie Clark. To all of them I convey my deepest gratitude, especially to Bruce, who also produced the index and whose commitment to the study of Emil Fackenheim's work goes far beyond this task. I would also like to thank John Walbridge for help transliterating the Arabic in chapter 1.

This project is one that percolated in Emil's mind and in mine for many years. As we worked on the contents, its shape changed, and it became, I think, more ambitious but also much more satisfying. Hopefully the result is worthy to take its place alongside his many other books as part of one of the most substantial examples of Jewish theology of this century. There is no way that I can adequately thank Emil for his friendship and his work, which has deeply influenced my own in so many ways. Perhaps this volume, like the one published in 1987, will serve as a small token of my regard.

Debbie and Sara, I believe, were aware that this volume was in preparation and may have wondered why I hadn't finished it. Audrey did not have to wonder. As always, she was patient with my delays and tolerant of all the distractions that beset me. Her new career, added to my new responsibilities, has complicated our lives, but our love and mutual support is stronger than ever. Nothing I do could be accomplished without her, nor without the stewardship of our two cats, Blaze and Amanda.

Introduction

Michael L. Morgan

This volume is about Jewish philosophy, Jewish philosophers, and Emil Fackenheim as a Jewish philosopher. That there is such a thing as Jewish philosophy is controversial; that Emil Fackenheim is one is not. Nor is this as paradoxical as it sounds, for there is a sense, clear and uncomplicated, in which a Jewish philosopher is a philosopher who reflects on Judaism and Jewish things, and if this is who a Jewish philosopher is, then Emil Fackenheim is surely one. But there is of course a deeper problem about the possibility of Jewish philosophy, and once this problem arises, it makes problematic anyone being one, Emil Fackenheim included.

The central themes of this collection, one might think, are that this problem is a pseudo-problem, that philosophy itself is a historical phenomenon, that Jewish philosophy is historical as well, and that in our age Jewish philosophy arises out of philosophical encounters with modern realities within a Jewish context. Let me explain a bit more fully these themes.

For much of Western history philosophy has occurred as an attempt to achieve in thought what has been called objectivity or unconditional truth. Generally through the disciplined use of reason, philosophers have sought knowledge or wisdom that is completely general, unqualified, stable, impersonal, and preeminent, and this knowledge is of all kinds, about nature or reality, humankind, morality, and much else. To some, this aspiration is essential to philosophy, a model for which is enshrined in Plato's *Phaedo*, where the physical and the sensory are denigrated in favor of a wholly intellectual, rational attempt to grasp Forms that are incorporeal, pure, eternal, unchanging, and true. This self-portrait of philosophy is old, but it is also persistent, and although modernity has challenged it, from Montaigne to Heidegger, it has a large claim on philosophical inquiry to this day.

Since antiquity, the relationship between this philosophical self-understanding—which is also the self-understanding of what we now call science—and religious life has been problematic. In general, Western religions involve some conception of the divine and a regimen of divine-human relations. In Greek mystery religions and then later in Judaism and Christianity, Scriptural traditions, the divine came to be associated with eternity, perfect wisdom, perfection, and stability. At one level, then, Western religion, like philosophy and science, held out an ideal of absolute, perfect existence. At another, however, each tradition was embedded historically in institutions, practices, and ideas that were concrete, specific, and distinctive. The wholly general or universal features of a tradition were entwined inextricably with wholly particular features.

Moreover, the modes of religious thinking were tied to religious concreteness. In Judaism, for example, the dominant modes of religious thinking were narrative and exegetical. The core of religious expression was the Biblical text and the Talmud, and the primary vehicle of religious thought was Scriptural commentary, either explicitly or implicitly. That is, religious identity was shaped by an original story that undergoes interpretation and revision. The divine-human relation is originally articulated in a revelation, and the goal of religious thought is to clarify and understand that revelation. In one way or other, that revelation is a particular one, and its myriad clarifications are particular as well. The religious life too is particular, the effort to live according to that revelation and to achieve the rewards of such a life.

Philosophy, in contrast, may have models, but it has no such founding story, no revelation. Ever since Parmenides at least, the chief mode of philosophical inquiry has been identified with reason and argument. Perhaps no one more clearly expressed this commitment to open, rigorous, rational analysis than Socrates. As Plato portrays him, Socrates seeks the truth and knowledge of it but disavows having such knowledge; what he recognizes is his own deficiency, his lack of knowledge, and this, the recognition of ignorance, is a prerequisite for philosophical inquiry. The latter then proceeds by dialectic, the asking and answering of questions, that hinges on the disposition to consistency and the aversion to contradiction. Philosophical reasoning, then, is an open-ended, nearly unrestricted pursuit of truth. Unlike the religious thinker, the philosopher does not have the truth. His goal is to find the truth, whatever it may be; it is not to clarify a specific truth already revealed.[1]

Both in content and in method, then, philosophy and religion conflict. One is general, the other specific. One is abstract, the other concrete. One is theoretical, the other practical. One is eternal, the other historical. How, then, given such tensions, can there be such a thing as Jewish philosophy? How can there be a mode of philosophical inquiry that is an open-minded, tolerant, rational search for the truth and that, at the same time, is embedded in Judaism, in the tradition of Jewish revelation, texts, interpretations, practices, and institutions? How can there be philosophical thought that is as particular as it is general, as historical as it is transcendent?

This, then, is the problem which, in these essays, Emil Fackenheim confronts and resolves, both in his writing and in his life. First, he shows it to be a pseudo-problem. Both philosophy and Judaism have transcendent dimensions, but more important both are deeply historical. This is a lesson that Fackenheim learned from two quarters, from the study of Hegel and especially his *Phenomenology* and from his encounter with the evil of Nazism

Introduction

and the horrors of the Holocaust. The latter teaches us modesty and humility, as it teaches horror and shock. It teaches us that not everything can be explained and understood. In reflecting on the significance of the film *Shoah*, Fackenheim quotes Simone de Beauvoir, "when today we see Claude Lanzmann's film, we realize that we have understood nothing."[2] Perhaps this is an exaggeration, but it is surely no exaggeration to say that we have not understood everything, that something is so dark and so extreme that even our most potent thought fails to assimilate it, to bring it under control. Both philosophy and Jewish thought must be exposed to history and to the possibility of the historically real that is beyond our ken. This recognition too comes from Hegel, whose thought travels the road of historical, perspectival experience to its goal in Absolute Thought. When that goal is unachieved, however, and is seen to be unachievable, then what remains is a complex array of historically limited views, each exposed to the vicissitudes of the world in which they occur.[3] If Hegel succeeds, the essence of thought is shown to be transcendent, but if Hegel fails, as Fackenheim comes to realize, then all thought is shown to be historical and finite, situated in a changing, fragile, and contingent world.

For Fackenheim, then, Jewish philosophy is possible, and it is actual wherever a Jewish thinker engages in it. Jewish philosophy is a species of the larger category of Jewish thought; it is that kind of Jewish thought "that involves a disciplined, systematic encounter between the Jewish heritage and relevant philosophy."[4] In an essay dedicated to the memory of his friend Pinchas Peli, Fackenheim elaborates on the nature of this encounter. The Jewish philosopher is one "who exposes his Jewish commitments to general philosophy, and the latter to his Jewish commitments."[5] But even this account, he suggests, is too general; Jewish philosophy is an historical phenomenon. When it occurs, it occurs differently. "What," he asks, "makes a Jewish thinker into a philosopher *today*?"[6] And here he answers that in the age of Auschwitz and a new Jerusalem, the central feature of genuine Jewish philosophy is "reality-connectedness," a set of multiple self-exposures to history and experience. Jewish philosophy, then, involves both the Jewish heritage and the philosophical tradition in dialectical, reciprocal exposures to each other and to the historical situation in which they occur. They are tested against each other and by history, and they are subject to such dialectical reevaluation at every moment. Carrying out this task is the job of Jewish philosophy, and just as this reexamination is embedded in distinct historical situations with different figures in the philosophical tradition, so it itself is historically changing. To a great degree, the character of Jewish philosophy is defined by the historical reality of the Jewish philosopher.

As Fackenheim confronts the problem of Jewish philosophy and hence the problem of his own special identity, a number of distinct dimensions of his life and thought converge. One is a lifelong engagement with Western philosophy that includes the study of great figures in that tradition, from

Plato and the medievals to Spinoza, Kant, Schelling, Hegel, Kierkegaard, Nietzsche, and Heidegger. Another is his devotion to the Biblical text and to Rabbinic Midrash. A final strand is his encounter with Jewish thinkers. When he speaks of Jewish philosophy as a dialectical encounter between "the Jewish heritage and relevant philosophy," he means, by "the Jewish heritage," the Bible and Midrash as well as Halakhic literature, commentaries, poetry, and more. And he means, by "relevant philosophy," the thought of Aristotle and Neoplatonism in the Middle Ages and that of Kant, Hegel, Kierkegaard, Nietzsche, and others in the modern period. But as the contemporary Jewish philosopher, immersed in the Jewish world, seeks to locate the "relevant" philosophical engagement, he turns to others who have already begun the task, other Jewish thinkers who have already initiated the Jewish-philosophical encounter in their own day, from Halevi and Maimonides to Mendelssohn, Hirsch, Cohen, Rosenzweig, and Buber.

The present collection of essays focuses, in part, on this last strand. The other two strands are represented elsewhere.[7] But there has been, until now, no convenient collection of Fackenheim's studies of great Jewish thinkers. This volume is intended to remedy that lack (see part I). I have tried to include here all of his encounters with Jewish thinkers and philosophers, with the exception of his extensive discussion of Spinoza and Rosenzweig in *To Mend the World: Foundations of Post-Holocaust Jewish Thought* (Bloomington: Indiana University Press, 1993). Hence, part I is not a survey of Jewish thinkers or even the rudiments of such a survey. Rather it includes eight very precise engagements with seven different figures on issues that Fackenheim himself was driven to address. They are not scholarly, historical studies, although they arise out of extensive and deep study of the authors' writings. These essays do, then, have historical merit, but their focus is elsewhere, on themes of contemporary relevance that find illuminating expression in the work of a Jewish thinker of the past.[8]

From the late 1960s to this moment, Fackenheim's writing and his thinking have been shaped by the confrontation of thought with the Holocaust. The early expressions of that confrontation are *God's Presence in History* and, before that, the first statement of the 614th commandment in 1967 and the *Commentary* essay, "Jewish Faith and the Holocaust: A Fragment," in 1968. The most probing, important expression is *To Mend the World.* In this last work, there is a section on philosophy after Auschwitz in which the center of attention is our conception of morality and human nature. That set of reflections is extended in the four essays of part II of this collection. I have included these essays for several reasons. First, any authentic Jewish philosophy today must, according to Fackenheim, be self-exposed to history, and in our own day, the critical event is the Holocaust. After the appropriation of the Jewish heritage, the philosophical tradition, and the tradition of Jewish thought and philosophy, the next—not the prior—encounter must be with that dark moment, with the whole of it and with all

Introduction

of its minute details. Here one must turn to central sections of chapter IV of *To Mend the World* and then to these essays, for here Fackenheim begins a general and then a philosophical encounter with the crime, the criminals, the horror, the victims, and indeed the totality of "Planet Auschwitz." Second, a Jewish philosopher is still a philosopher, whose interests are in problems and issues that are genuinely philosophical. As Fackenheim has put it, Jewish philosophy will be recognized as legitimate by philosophers only if there are problems "that, on the one hand, are distinctively Jewish and yet, on the other, are truly philosophical."[9] And surely one such problem is "whether the Holocaust is but one case of the species genocide, or rather, even within that grim category, sui generis and unique."[10] In dozens of places Fackenheim has addressed this problem and its implications.[11] It is a philosophical problem but also a religious, moral, and political one.[12] In the essays in part II Fackenheim turns to it as a philosopher and, in ways unlike those he uses elsewhere, attempts to articulate what makes the death camps unique in history, unprecedented, significant, and epoch-making. Philosophy is not only a mode of response to the Shoah; there is also a philosophical duty to respond, one that arises out of a philosophical encounter with that event.

There would be Jewish philosophy today if Auschwitz had not occurred. But since it did occur, no authentic Jewish philosophy can ignore that event. Part II is about the necessity and character of that encounter; part III is about the result. Fackenheim, especially in chapter 16, "A Political Philosophy for the State of Israel," argues that one component, perhaps at this moment in history the central component, of such a result should be political philosophy for the state of Israel. There is no denying the controversial character of such a claim, but Fackenheim makes it, and reflect on it we must. What is Fackenheim saying? That a genuine, contemporary Jewish philosophy is possible and that for him, given his past and his present, its character must be political, concerned with survival, with power, with human well-being, and with a people's and a nation's historical destiny and role. Furthermore, if Fackenheim is right, the primary political task is not for the Diaspora but rather for the state of Israel. The challenge might be put this way: what is the shape of a genuine Jewish state today, a state that is the venue of political and moral values that we deem necessary and a Jewishness as necessary as these values? Such a state must be possible, but how?

I cannot imagine that Fackenheim would deny other tasks, other problems, for an authentic contemporary, post-Holocaust Jewish philosophy.[13] The breadth of these tasks, for the Jew, is expressed in Fackenheim's reconsideration of his famous 614th commandment, an account that is—it must be noted—a Jewish philosopher's interpretation of what authentic post-Holocaust Judaism requires. In addition, there are specifically philosophical tasks. For example, there surely are epistemological and perhaps even metaphysical problems, about God, religious experience, and more; there are also moral problems, about justice, benevolence, and responsibility; and there are problems about identity, character, and such matters. But, Fackenheim contends, the core of the current philosophical task for Jewish thinkers is about political matters, the nature of the Jewish state, and its Jewishness. Elsewhere he has begun such reflections and here, in a small way, he pursues them.[14]

This volume, then, draws together essays old and new, all of which contribute to clarifying Emil Fackenheim's identity as a Jewish philosopher. Many of the essays are hard to locate in their original form; a few are published here for the first time. I have chosen them and organized them to develop the themes I have discussed above, but they can be read individually and in any order, according to the reader's interests. Of special significance, I imagine, will be the essays in part I, especially Fackenheim's brilliant studies of Cohen and Buber, which provide us with exciting access to central Jewish thinkers of the past, while at the same time exhibiting the mind of one of the most important Jewish philosophers of the present.

PART I

Jewish Philosophers

Introduction to Part I

The essays in this part were published over a period of forty-seven years, starting in 1947. Some are scholarly essays, others more popular pieces. At least two were given originally as lectures. The essay on Hermann Cohen is surely one of the finest essays we have on that important thinker, and the study of Martin Buber's concept of revelation has been hailed as the most penetrating philosophical study we have of Buber's philosophy of dialogue.

If a theme runs through many of these essays, it is the central one of Emil Fackenheim's philosophical work: the relation between philosophy and history, between thought and life. It is the same theme that had formed the framework for his early book *Metaphysics and Historicity*. There Fackenheim had asked whether there was still an element of transcendence in the conception of the self as a self-making process, and he had answered that there was. Even the philosophical view of human existence as historically situated is philosophical in the traditional sense. In these essays, the mingling of philosophical transcendence and religious particularity occurs once more and in several ways. In essence, Fackenheim asks how thinkers as diverse as Moses Maimonides, Cohen, Buber, and Franz Rosenzweig can be both philosophers and Jewish thinkers at once. How can their philosophical thinking be rooted in Jewish experience? This question is not central to all of these essays, to be sure, but it is central to many, and it is in this question that they find their guiding thread. In the work of these figures, the relation between thought and life often is precisely the relation between philosophy and Jewish experience.

In Rosenzweig the issue concerns the role of Yom Kippur in a philosophical system. In Buber it surfaces in a question about the rootedness of Buber's philosophical anthropology, his dialogical conception of the human condition, and its ground in his conception of the Biblical world. And in Cohen it arises on two levels, his treatment of the role of Messianism in ethics and his commitment to the heralded German-Jewish symbiosis. Indeed, in this essay best of all Fackenheim articulates the depth at which history can unsettle the effort to bring philosophical transcendence and religious particularity together. What Fackenheim shows is not only Cohen's attempt to harmonize the two but also the historical reality that dooms the attempt to failure. In other essays he explores the options to this failure, the return to pure philosophical transcendence in Leo Strauss and the honest but serious exposure to history in Pinchas Peli. But if these are the possible outcomes, the fulcrum is Cohen, whose hopes were as noble as his achievement was futile.

In his anecdotal lecture about Strauss, Fackenheim considers Strauss's influence on him and his thinking. He recalls reading Strauss's *Philosophie und Gesetz*, with its attack on Guttmann's antiquarian reading of Maimonides and its challenge concerning Judaism and the Enlightenment. He recalls too his visits to New York, long conversations with Strauss and Strauss's warning that Heidegger needs to be taken with complete seriousness. Finally, he turns to Strauss on Cohen. Here he chastizes Strauss for being at once too optimistic and not optimistic enough. Like Cohen, Strauss was too sanguine about evil, even though he wrote about Cohen after the death camps and all their horrors. And he was also not optimistic enough about what Jewish philosophy could achieve, a recognition of duty that supports a post-Holocaust Jewish will to survive. Fackenheim's scholarly reflection on Cohen and his personal recollections about Strauss converge; Auschwitz challenges both Cohen the teacher and Strauss the student not to underestimate history in favor of eternity.[1]

Reading Strauss's book in Nazi Berlin, Fackenheim had sensed an urgency about revelation and the challenges to it from Enlightenment rationalism. Is it impossible to reconcile the need for revelation with our rational capacities? Is revelation possible in the modern world? (see chapter 7). Strauss's questions became lifelong interests, consuming interests for Fackenheim, signs on a journey to clarify what revelation is and why it is necessary for any authentic Jewish belief.[2] Certainly a prominent stage on that journey occurs in the essay on Martin Buber's conception of dialogue and revelation (chapter 4). There Fackenheim characterizes the modern challenges to revelation, clarifies Buber's doctrine, and defends its nature as a doctrine, as a conception of revelation that meets the challenges of modernity. The result is a powerful defense of Buber's view and of the very notion of a Jewish philosophy that is both existential and philosophical. In the end, for Fackenheim if not so clearly for Buber, the doctrine of dialogue and revelation is neither I-Thou nor I-It knowledge. It is something distinct from both, a thinking that "mediates between I-It and I-Thou knowledge . . . [that] points beyond detached knowledge and thus beyond itself . . . [to] the commitment of the I-Thou standpoint."

The relation between thought and life, philosophy and history, is reflected in the earliest essay in part I, on creation in Maimonides' *Guide* (chapter 1). Elsewhere, Fackenheim summarizes the argument of this chapter in this way:

Jewish Philosophers

Maimonides' crucial departure from "the philosophers", in defense of the foundations of the Law, occurs in his treatment of creation. He grasps this with unsurpassed clarity: given the necessary nexus between God and the world which is asserted by both Aristotle and Neoplatonism, all "arbitrary" divine interference with natural law becomes in principle indefensible. Individual providence and miracles become impossible, above all the crucial miracle of revelation—the very root of the Law itself. Maimonides urges that the philosopher can prove the validity of natural law only *within* the world; that it is therefore philosophically permissible to hold that God has created the laws of nature as well as nature itself; and that if this is the case His act of creation cannot be understood in terms of these laws. He points out certain insuperable difficulties in the emanation-theory which vanish on the assumption of free creation. But he does not hold that creation can be proved philosophically. On strictly rational grounds, the laws of the cosmos may be regarded as either absolute or the product of free creation.

In such a situation religious interest may decide in favor of the latter view. This view saves the foundations of revealed religion: for if God has freely created the laws of nature He is also free to suspend them temporarily, for the purposes of miracles, providence, and, above all, revelation. Revelation is thus rationally possible, and faith may assert its reality without eschewing reason.[3]

Revelation can be defended as compatible with reason and, just as important, thought is shaped to fit history. In the context of exile and persecution, the Law is vital to Jewish survival, and revelation is "the very root of the Law itself." Fackenheim does not here focus on this appreciation of history; like Strauss, he is here exploring the ways in which reason and revelation can live with each other in a premodern world. But the historical ground is there, a premonition of the prominence of history in Fackenheim's later thought.

In these eight essays, we can study Jewish thinkers through the eyes of a Jewish thinker and philosopher. Just as important, we can observe the interplay between "the universal and Jewish aspects" of their thinking. As Fackenheim confronts the *Guide* or Buber's *I and Thou* or Rosenzweig's *Star*, he does so as a philosopher and a Jewish thinker, and in different ways, over a period of nearly five decades, he seeks in these works and in these thinkers his own heritage, the special heritage of Jewish philosophy.

One

The Possibility of the Universe in Al-Farabi, Ibn Sina, and Maimonides

Al-Farabi and Ibn Sina

Possibility Per Se, Necessity Per Se, and Necessity Ab Alio

It is well known that al-Farabi and Ibn Sina introduce into philosophy a concept of "possibility" defined in terms of the indifference of the essence of an entity to existence. "Possible" is that being which requires a cause outside itself in order to exist. "Necessary" is the uncaused which possesses existence as part of its very essence. This distinction is equivalent to a distinction between God (who is uncaused) and all being other than God (which is dependent on a cause outside itself).

Al-Farabi states his view as follows:

> Everything that is belongs to one of two kinds. In the case of beings of the first kind, existence is not involved in their essence. These are called "of possible existence." In the case of a being of the second kind, its essence does involve existence. This is called "necessarily existent." To suppose that which is of possible existence as being nonexistent involves no contradiction; for in order to exist this being requires a cause other than itself. And if it *is* necessary, it has become necessarily existent through something outside itself. It follows therefore that this being is *per se* never other than of possible existence, and that it is necessarily existent *ab alio.* . . .[1]

That Ibn Sina accepts al-Farabi's doctrine is evident from the following statement:

> The necessary being is that which, if assumed to be nonexistent, involves a contradiction. The possible being is that which may be assumed to be nonexistent or existent without involving a contradiction. . . . The necessary being may be so either *per se* or not *per se.* In the former case, a contradiction is involved if it is assumed to be nonexistent. . . . As for the being which is necessary but not *per se,* this is a being which is necessary, provided a certain being other than it is given. . . . Everything that is necessarily existent *ab alio* is possibly existent *per se.* . . . Considered in its essence it is possible; consid-

7

ered in actual relation to that other being it is necessary, and, the relation to that other being considered as removed, it is impossible.[2]

Of the beings which are "possible *per se*," some are or "become"[3] "necessary *ab alio*." With this term al-Farabi and Ibn Sina refer primarily to the mode of existence possessed by the eternal and immaterial beings: although they require a cause outside themselves in order to exist, they yet exist, through their Cause, necessarily and eternally. The sublunary temporal beings are in every respect possible.[4] It would appear to be profoundly significant that the beings making up reality allow, with respect to possibility and necessity, of two different classifications: (1) (a) necessary being—(i) necessary *per se* (God) and (ii) necessary *ab alio* (immaterial and eternal beings other than God) and (b) possible being—(sublunary temporal beings);[5] (2) (a) necessary being *per se* (God) and (b) possible being *per se*—(i) necessary *ab alio* (immaterial and eternal beings other than God) and (ii) possible in every respect (sublunary temporal beings).

Although much valuable work has already been devoted to the exposition and historical background of these notions,[6] there is still a good deal of uncertainty concerning their inner systematic significance within the thought of al-Farabi and Ibn Sina. This is largely due to the difficulty, not adequately appreciated so far, of distinguishing between the exoteric and esoteric doctrines of both these thinkers.[7] Realizing this difficulty, we shall nevertheless advance a suggestion which may shed some light on the inner significance of these notions. This suggestion may not directly enlighten us concerning the real, esoteric teaching of al-Farabi or Ibn Sina in this matter. But it may prove helpful in understanding the reaction to it of Maimonides, who encountered their teaching in its full impact, in both its esoteric and exoteric forms.

Our suggestion takes its clue from Ibn Rushd who charges al-Farabi and Ibn Sina with having attempted to harmonize in this matter the doctrines of the philosophers with those of the *Mutakallimūn*.[8] We cannot dismiss lightly the view of Ibn Rushd, who knew the writings of both the *Falāsifa* and the *Mutakallimūn* better than we may ever know them. Moreover, there is inner philosophical evidence supporting the thesis that al-Farabi's and Ibn Sina's doctrine of necessity and possibility represents an attempt to harmonize the necessity and eternity of the universe, as taught by Aristotle and the Neoplatonists, with *creatio ex nihilo* as taught by the *Mutakallimūn* in accordance with Muslim theology.

Emanation and the Necessity of the Universe

According to Aristotle, the "possible" is that which can be other than it is; and if it can be other than it is, it must *some* time be so.[9] No being which does not some time "not-be" *can* not be: "eternal" and "of necessity" are convertible terms,[10] and the immaterial part of the universe which is eternal

The Possibility of the Universe

is *ipso facto* necessary. To be sure, the immaterial part of the universe is dependent in its movements on the Prime Mover and must therefore have an element of possibility; but it is possible not in respect of substance or even of its movements, but merely in respect of place.[11]

According to the Greek Neoplatonists, the immaterial part of the universe is dependent on God (the One) not only in its movements but in its very existence. Lacking absolute simplicity, it *wholly* derives from the Absolute One, sharing this derivative character with the material changing world. But this "emanation" is eternal and necessary both in its "that" and its "what." The intelligible world emanated from the One can neither "not-be" nor be other than it is: it is as necessary as the One itself. To be sure, Plotinus says, "Isolate anything else, and the being is inadequate. But the Supreme in isolation is still what It is."[12] But metaphysically this means only that the One transcends the series which It necessarily produces. The "isolation" of which Plotinus speaks is of purely logical significance. Metaphysically the analysis of the very nature of intelligible beings leads back to the One; the nonbeing of the *emanata* is as impossible as that of the *emanans*. From the aspect of necessity, Plotinus arrives as little as Aristotle at a basic distinction between God and the universe as a whole; rather does he divide reality into the nonmaterial world (the One, the realms of Intellect and Soul) which exists necessarily and eternally, and the material world whose beings are subject to temporality, change, and destruction.[13]

Such early Muslim works as the so-called *Theology of Aristotle* and the *Encyclopedia* of the Ikhwān as-Safā accept the Neoplatonic doctrine of necessary emanation.[14] And in spite of the necessity of this emanation they show no scruples in identifying it with "creation."[15] In the case of al-Farabi and Ibn Sina, the situation seems at first sight not very different. Without doubt they teach the eternity of the universe, in accordance with both Aristotle and the Neoplatonists.[16] And, though there is legitimate doubt whether this represents their real esoteric teaching, they accept[17] and teach prominently the doctrine of necessary emanation. Both the fact of emanation[18] and the general nature of the emanated universe[19] are of inexorable necessity. For it is part of the very substance of the One to produce the universe actually existing.[20] The One bestows being on what cannot possibly not-be and on what may not-be.[21] Beings of the former kind are *per se* in their state of ultimate perfection;[22] they have no opposites and can neither not-be nor be other than they are.[23] Though absolutely dependent on something other than themselves, they are absolutely necessary. The terminology is adapted to the doctrine of the context: The term "the kinds of the possible" (ajnās al-ashyā' al-mumkina) refers to sublunary beings only, which have opposites and matter, and may therefore not-be or be other than they are;[24] the rational animal is "the most excellent of the possible beings" since those beings which are more excellent are necessary.[25]

In the face of this evidence, in both doctrine and terminology it seems

hardly debatable that al-Farabi and Ibn Sina follow the Greeks in this matter as thoroughly as do the *"Theology of Aristotle"* and the *Ikhwān as-Safā*:
from the viewpoint of "necessity" and "possibility," reality is to be divided
basically not into God and the universe, but into eternal and immaterial
being on the one hand, temporal and material being on the other. The
convertibility of the terms "eternity" and "necessity" appears to be beyond
question.[26] It is certainly significant in this connection that the identification of the heavenly bodies with God is said to have been Ibn Sina's esoteric
teaching.[27]

Creation and the Possibility of the Universe

If al-Farabi and Ibn Sina really teach Neoplatonic emanation, they certainly cannot identify it as simply with Muslim *creatio ex nihilo* as do the
"Theology of Aristotle" and the *Ikhwān as-Safā*. Creation is perhaps the foremost theological problem discussed among their contemporaries.[28] And
where it is discussed, this is done with reference to Qur'an passages such as
Sura xxviii, 88: "Everything goes to destruction except His Face." D. B.
McDonald says of the Muslim commentators on this and other passages:

> With the commentators, the explanation is that all things besides Allah
> are only "possible of existence," while He is "necessary of existence"; they
> may, therefore, be described according to their essential definition as
> "nonexistent," i.e., because they *may* go to destruction, they *are* going to
> destruction.[29]

Al-Farabi may find it easy, with the help of the Aristotelian notion of time,
to show that the act of creation is timeless, the created universe without
beginning and end:[30] in the face of the radical contingency of the universe
implied in the Muslim doctrine of creation, he cannot as easily show that
part of the creation exists by necessity. According to the theological view,
God may never actually annihilate the created world; but to do so cannot
in His very nature be impossible. Even less can the *nature* of part of the
created world exempt it from the possibility of destruction. From the aspect
of possibility and necessity, the theological doctrine of creation requires a
radical division not between eternal and temporal or immaterial and material beings but between the Creator and the created universe.

Al-Farabi is fully aware of this. And in a passage which reads like an
orthodox commentary on the cited verse from the Qur'an he says: "He
dominates, i.e., He has the power to bring about nonbeing and to deprive
of existence those essences which in themselves deserve annihilation; everything vanishes except He."[31] No doubt this passage expresses exoteric doctrine,[32] but even as such it betrays al-Farabi's awareness of the radical possibility of the universe required by the Muslim doctrine of creation. The

The Possibility of the Universe

question which poses itself to the student is: to what extent is his philosophy affected by what he recognizes to be the requirements of *creatio ex nihilo*?

The *Mutakallimūn* accepted without equivocation the radical division of reality into Creator and the created world. To them, creation was both absolute and spontaneous, the will of God dependent on no necessity or law either within or outside of His nature. God could have abstained from creating the world; He could annihilate it at any time; He could create an indefinite number of different worlds. In this sense, the universe was to them absolutely "possible."

Within this general context, the question arose concerning the state of things "before" the creation: does the world become possible because God chooses it, or does He choose it because it is possible?[33] The orthodox, anxious to preserve God's absolute sovereignty, denied even thinkable possibilities apart from the creation: only through God's creation do some things become possible and thinkable.[34] According to their more rationalist opponents, God in His wisdom can create only what is possible.[35] Creation is the imparting of existence to some of the things possible and thinkable independently of the act of creation; it is a selection which implies a differentiation within the realm of nonexistent possibilities.[36]

Both schools agree on the absolute contingency of the created world on the will of God. But the rationalists, who recognize rational relations independently of the actual will of God, can point to a general definition of the character rendering each created thing "possible" in the sense of being the possible object of God's free creation. As ash-Shahrastāni wrote,

> The essential qualities of substance and accidents belong to them *per se*, not because of any connexion with the Creator. He only enters the mind in connexion with *existence* because He tipped the scales in favour of existence. What a thing is in its essence preceded its existence, *viz.* its substantialness and accidentalness, and so it is a thing. What a thing has through omnipotence is its existence and actual occurrence. . . .[37]

The "possible" being is that being whose existence is not implied in its essence. If it exists, its existence comes, essentially, from God. Not everything is possible to God, but whether and for how long any of the possible things are actually to exist depends on nothing but His absolute free will and sovereignty.

Our conclusion, then, is this: Al-Farabi and Ibn Sina do precisely what Ibn Rushd claims they are doing:[38] they combine in this matter Mu'tazilite with philosophical teaching. Attempting to do justice to both theology (which demands the radical contingency of the created universe) and philosophy (which appears to demand the necessity of what is eternal) they combine "possibility," defined as the indifference of the essence of a being to its existence and nonexistence, with necessary emanation. The crucial position is held by the immaterial and eternal beings other than God which are at the same time possible *per se* and necessary *ab alio*. This, then, is their harmonization of theology and philosophy: existence stems from God: hence the primacy of the distinction between the necessary *per se* (God) and the possible *per se* (all caused reality); yet it emanates from Him necessarily: hence the equally fundamental distinction between the necessary, *per se* or *ab alio* (God and all other immaterial and eternal beings), and all being which is simply possible (the material and temporal world).[39] It is profoundly significant that al-Farabi closes one passage dealing with this subject with the previously cited Qur'anic verse:

> The existence of a thing which is due to a cause outside itself is neither impossible, for then it could not exist, nor is it *per se* necessary, for then it could not owe its existence to an external cause: the existence of such a thing is *per se* possible. Given its cause, it is necessary, and with the cause not given, it is impossible. *Per se* it is doomed to destruction; but in relation to the principle of its existence it exists of necessity. "Everything goes to destruction except His Face" (Sura xxviii 88).[40]

Problems arising from the Synthesis

As Maimonides notes, the conception of the possibility of the universe held by al-Farabi and Ibn Sina has a metaphysical significance vastly different from the Mu'tazilite conception by which it is influenced. The "possibility" of a thing may be said to mean in the case of both parties "that there is not more reason why it should exist than why it should not exist."[41] But to the Mu'tazilites this indifference toward existence is absolute, God's imparting of existence being the "tipping of the scales" in a *really* indeterminate situation.[42] For al-Farabi and Ibn Sina the indifference of the essence of a thing toward existence is no more than relative. Absolutely and metaphysically speaking, there is no really indeterminate situation concerning the existence and general nature of the universe.

We have seen that even Plotinus hints at a notion of "possibility" possessed by everything except the One: but the "isolation" on which it was based was purely *logical* in significance.[43] The question on which the significance of al-Farabi's and Ibn Sina's position chiefly depends is this: does their distinction between possibility *per se* and necessity *ab alio* in eternal and immaterial beings caused by God have a logical or a metaphysical status? The answer to this question depends on the status given to the distinction between essence and existence.

Both al-Farabi and Ibn Sina maintain that existence is an accident superadded to the essence of a thing.[44] What does this mean? It may be a distinction of merely *logical* significance indicating the fact that existence is not one of the "constituents" making up the essence of a thing. If that is correct, then the status of the distinction between essence and existence is logical only, and the distinction within one thing between its possibility *per se* and its necessity *ab alio* is not more than logical either. That would mean that al-Farabi and Ibn Sina have not metaphysically parted company with Plotinus, toward a metaphysical distinction between a necessary God and a possible universe. In that case, their more elaborate logical distinctions merely accommodate the religious opinions of their time, without metaphysically yielding one inch.

This, however, is not the only possible interpretation, nor even the one most likely to be correct.[45] It is far more likely that the distinction between possibility *per se* and necessity *ab alio* among eternal beings caused by God is intended to be of not merely logical, but also metaphysical relevance, and that, correspondingly, the status of the distinction between essence and existence is metaphysical also. As in the case of the Mu'tazilites, things would then have their essences *per se* and derive their existence from God. If this is the correct interpretation, it leads to results profoundly precarious for the belief in *creatio ex nihilo*: (1) essences, necessary by reason of the emanation doctrine, are now, in a *metaphysical* sense, possible *per se*. This means that they preserve the metaphysical status possessed in Neoplatonic emanationism but are cut off, *insofar as they are possibles*, from their traditional dependence on the One. The realm of possible essences acquires a metaphysical status completely independent of the One.[46] (2) Existence which *does* come from God is, *metaphysically*, a mere accident.[47] Neoplatonic emanationism implied that the essence of the universe is *not* metaphysically indifferent toward existence, but that derivation from the One is part of the very essence of the emanated being.[48] If the necessity of the emanated universe is to be preserved and yet to be combined with a metaphysical distinction in beings between self-contained possible essences and existence deriving from God, both the independent status of the possibles and the accidentality of existence are a result which appears hardly avoidable.[49] If this is the correct interpretation, it is indeed a paradoxical result of an attempt to do greater justice to Muslim *creatio ex nihilo*.

We must bear in mind that we still know far too little of how to distinguish esoteric from exoteric teaching in either al-Farabi or Ibn Sina to decide where their real teaching lies in this matter, much less to charge them with inconsistency or inadequacy in the solution of their problems. We do not even know, for instance, whether *creatio ex nihilo*, in any sense, was to them an esoteric philosophic problem. Nevertheless, to understand the metaphysical difficulties seen on this level as arising from the position of al-Farabi and Ibn Sina is of great importance: if for no other reason, it is important for the understanding of the position of Maimonides who beyond doubt *does* regard *creatio ex nihilo* as a serious problem, yet has so profound a regard for the teaching of al-Farabi and Ibn Sina that he allows himself to depart from their position only if he can philosophically justify such a departure.

Maimonides

The Doctrine of the Falāsifah as Reflected in Maimonides

In a famous passage Maimonides expresses his respect for the philosophy of al-Farabi in the strongest possible terms.[50] Undoubtedly to him the value of that thinker's writings is second only to that of Aristotle's writings. It is true that the *Guide of the Perplexed* purports to be a "Jewish correction"[51] of the philosophers, its principal aim being not to teach philosophic truth but to defend the roots of religious law;[52] but Maimonides does not yield to the temptation arbitrarily to tamper with their teachings: any departure from the "philosophers" must be justified philosophically.[53] It is a happy result of this position that there is here a more direct interaction between religious inspiration and philosophic reason than had been possible either in *Kalām* proper, where there is no adequate regard for the autonomy of philosophic exigencies, or in the writings of the *Falāsifah* in which religious teaching too readily becomes an exoteric form of philosophy. Maimonides' defense of *creatio ex nihilo* against the philosophic doctrine of the eternity of the universe in itself is nothing uncommon, but his attempt at a philosophically competent defense produces novel solutions of time-honored problems.

In his introduction to the second part of the *Guide*, Maimonides summarizes the doctrines of "the philosophers" in twenty-six propositions. Of these he rejects as invalid only the last, which asserts the eternity and actuality of time and motion. But the position adopted toward that doctrine, in the name of *creatio ex nihilo*, involves important modifications of other philosophic doctrines, evident even in the form in which he restates them. We are here concerned with propositions 19 and 20:

> A thing which owes its existence to certain causes has in itself merely the possibility of existence; for only if those causes exist, the thing likewise exists. It does not exist if the causes do not exist at all, or if they have ceased to exist, or if there has been a change in the relation which implies the existence of that thing as a necessary consequence of those causes.
> A thing which has in itself the necessity of existence cannot have for its existence any cause whatever.[54]

These passages are significant for what they omit as much as for what they state. Al-Farabi's and Ibn Sina's "possibility *per se*" and "necessity *per se*" are fully reflected: a thing is "of possible existence" if it requires a cause outside itself in order to exist: therefore God alone is necessarily existent *per se*, everything else possible *per se*. The difference and omission lie in the meaning of the term "necessity *ab alio*": what Maimonides says here means no more than that any substance, be it material or immaterial, must exist if and when the causes are present which fully determine it toward existence.[55] But to al-Farabi and Ibn Sina "necessity *ab alio*" meant also, and perhaps even primarily,[56] the absolute though derived metaphysical necessity of those immaterial beings which stem from God in eternal and necessary emanation. In the present context, where he states *true* philosophic doctrines, Maimonides is silent on those beings whose necessary existence *ab alio* may itself be an absolute necessity. For he accepts from the philosophers the necessary causes by which the universe functions, but he rejects their ultimate derivation of the universe itself from a Cause connected with its immaterial part in a timeless and necessary relation. Maimonides states:

> As God has necessary existence while all other beings have only possible existence, . . . there cannot consequently be any correlation. . . . How could a relation be imagined between any creature and God, who has nothing in common with any other being?[57]

He goes on to say that a relation can exist only between things which in some respect belong to the same kind. This problem had indeed been obvious to all Neoplatonists also, and they had taken the greatest pains to show not only that the One was wholly unrelated to its derivations,[58] but also that the categories of the realms of Intellect, Soul, and the material world had nothing in common.[59] But the necessity of both the fact of emanation and the general nature of the emanated universe, and the fact that the very essence of immaterial emanated being implied its relation to God, did necessitate some community between God and at least part of the universe. Significantly, al-Farabi's and Ibn Sina's division between "possible being" and "necessary being" allowed two different classifications. In defense of *creatio ex nihilo*, Maimonides struggles for a much more radical division between God and the created universe, and therefore for a universe which is "possible" in a much more radical sense.

The Crucial Departure from "the Philosophers"

With inimitable precision Maimonides grasps the crucial point where he must part company with "the philosophers":

> If the philosopher, in his way of expressing himself, contends: "reality is my evidence; by its guidance I examine whether a thing is necessary, possible or impossible", the religionist replies: "this is exactly the difference between us; that which actually exists has, according to my view, been produced by the will of the Creator, not by necessity; just as it has been created with that special property, it might have been created with any other special property, *unless the impossibility which you postulate can be proved by logical argument.*"[60]

Maimonides yields to no philosopher in emphasis on the rationality of reality: God cannot create what is logically impossible.[61] But that is something quite different from making God's actions subject to the laws governing the actual universe. As for these laws by which the philosophers interpret the functioning of the universe, Maimonides certainly does not deny their validity. In cases where he feels compelled to maintain their suspension, he does so with great reluctance, carefully circumscribing the limits of their suspension.[62] He takes issue with the philosophers only because of their explicit or implicit claim that these laws have *absolute* metaphysical validity encompassing God's act of creation itself. In maintaining that both the fact and the general nature of the actual universe are necessary (i.e., that no other universe is possible) the philosophers assert precisely what Maimonides, in the interest of his religion, feels compelled to deny.

Maimonides regards himself philosophically justified in denying this doctrine of the philosophers; for the proof of the philosophers presupposes its point instead of proving it. The *method* of the philosophers implies the *proton pseudos* of their doctrine: to derive from the nature of things which actually exist what is *absolutely* possible, impossible, and necessary already presupposes the *absolute* metaphysical validity of the laws by which these things are governed. If it is correct philosophical procedure to make the start with an analysis of the actual universe, then this means that the laws it discovers it can prove to be valid only within the actual universe. Their *absolute* validity, "necessary emanation," and "free creation" are questions exceeding the grasp of philosophic proof (see earlier discussion).

Having rejected the method of deriving absolute conclusions from the laws arrived at through a philosophical analysis of the nature of the actual universe, Maimonides finds little difficulty in rejecting the results arrived at on this basis: the eternal and necessary existence of prime matter[63] and of those immaterial beings which have no opposites,[64] and the impossibility of an absolute beginning of the world at a certain point of time.[65] In numerous passages he tries to make it clear that he does not wish to deny what can be philosophically proven: the philosophical interpretation of the functioning of the universe, and the validity of the principles from which this interpretation derives. He holds no brief for those who try to establish *creatio ex nihilo* on an arbitrary suspension of the laws of nature. But he rejects, as an unwarranted dogma, the assumption that these principles and laws can be *proven* to be metaphysically absolute. According to him, not only the universe but also the laws which govern it are the product of God's absolute and free creation:

> We, the followers of Moses our Teacher, and of Abraham our Father, believe that the universe has been produced and has developed in a certain manner, and that it has been created in a certain order. The Aristotelians oppose us, and found their objections on the properties which the things in the universe possess when in actual existence and fully developed. We admit the existence of these properties, but hold that they are by no means the same as those which the things possessed in the moment of their production; and we hold that *these properties themselves have come into existence from absolute non-existence.* Their arguments are therefore no objection whatever to our theory; they have demonstrative force only against those who hold that

the nature of things as at present in existence proves the creation. But this is not our opinion.[66]

Maimonides here achieves a remarkable degree of metaphysical insight. In giving an absolute significance to the categories governing possibility, impossibility, and necessity in the universe, and in arriving on these grounds at a universe absolutely necessary in both its existence and its general nature, "the philosophers," far from exposing the question of the *absolute* origin of existence, in fact presuppose existence and move throughout their discourse merely in the modifications of existence already presupposed in principle. The unqualified necessity of the Aristotelian spheres and the Aristotelian identification of possibility with potentiality, the necessary nexus between the Neoplatonic One and its multiple derivatives, the metaphysical status possessed by the Avicennian possibles,[67] all rest on this procedure. Through a combination of philosophical exactitude with a genuine loyalty to religious doctrine, Maimonides does what neither the *Falāsifah* nor the *Mutakallimūn* had been able to do: he distinguishes sharply between the modifications of actual existence (which are governed by the laws exhibited by "the philosophers") and the absolute origin of existence (which encompasses the origin of these laws also). It is significant but not surprising that he should be among those medieval philosophers who did this lasting service to philosophy, for he followed the inspiration of a religion teaching a God who revealed Himself as "I am who I am,"[68] and whose prime character was not contemplation, absolute simplicity, or the function of being Prime Mover, but the free giving of *existence* to all that is.

Maimonides, then, arrives at a *real* possibility possessed by the universe as a whole without denying, or conflicting with, the philosophical views concerning natural law, and without falling victim to antiphilosophical irrationalism. There *is* natural necessity in the universe: sublunary beings follow as a necessary consequence if their causes are fully given;[69] immaterial beings exist with *natural* necessity, lacking the natural potency for change or destruction. But the universe *as a whole* is in a profounder sense possible—a possibility shared by all created beings alike. For the divine will has given to the universe *existence absolutely*, and this will therefore both can and must be said to transcend all natural necessity.[70] God can *really* annihilate the world[71] and create different worlds.[72] He could have wholly abstained from creating. For al-Farabi and Ibn Sina there is possibility relatively and necessity absolutely: Maimonides makes the Avicennian absolute necessity rest on a profounder possibility.

Maimonides rejects the philosophical position, but he does not claim to be able to refute it.[73] The philosophical position and his own are equally incapable of being proved. Thus the two positions become two opposite faiths: the "philosophical faith" interprets the dependence of the universe on God in terms presupposing actual existence and its categories, and therefore making the universe as a whole coeternal and conecessary with God; the "religious faith" interprets it in terms of an absolute origin of existence, the categories and laws of the actual world becoming applicable only to a world already established.[74] We are confronted here with a scholastic re-enactment of the central Jewish-pagan controversy.

The Possibility of the Universe and Its Temporal Origin

For "necessary emanation," which he rejects, Maimonides substitutes "creation by design."[75] This differs from the former in four respects relevant for our present purpose: (i) the design is freely willed instead of following necessarily from God's nature;[76] (ii) it may be changed according to God's free will; (iii) it is only partly intelligible to man;[77]

> (iv) "the notion of design . . . applies only to things not yet in existence when there is still the possibility of their being in accordance with the design or not."[78]

Only the fourth of these respects contributes an additional element to the understanding of Maimonides' conception of the possibility of the universe. In the opinion of Thomas Aquinas, freely-willed creation may be in time or eternal, either theory being philosophically possible; and it is religious doctrine which decides in favor of creation in time.[79] But to Maimonides creation in time appears to be the sole philosophical alternative to necessary emanation. The student may well find it difficult to account for the fact that Maimonides struggles apparently indiscriminately (i) for free creation against necessary emanation, and (ii) for a temporal origin against the eternity of the universe.[80] He seems to fail to distinguish between the "that" and the "when" of creation,—a failure especially bewildering in view of the facts (i) that Ibn Sina had distinguished these two problems not only in doctrine but also in terminology, (ii) that Maimonides' terminology appears virtually to ignore these distinctions.[81] The resolution of the difficulty, it would appear, lies in the doctrine expressed in the cited passage, implying a concept of "possibility" which Maimonides had already formulated in his *Treatise on Logic*:

> A thing can be "possible" only with reference to the future, before one of the alternatives is realized; when such a realization takes place, the possibility is removed. When Zayd stands near us, his standing is no longer a possibility but resembles something necessary."[82]

The possible thing become actual is necessary in the sense that its causes have determined it toward existence. A world created by design but eternally actual would imply a divine will already determining from all eternity, and therefore no longer free. The question may well be asked whether this really follows, on the basis of Maimonides' limitation of natural necessity to the modifications of the created world. At any rate, he is certainly correct in rejecting what passes among his philosophical predecessors as "eternal creation," as differing from necessary emanation only in name.[83]

The Possibility of the Universe as Philosophical and Theological Problem

Maimonides' novel synthesis of *creatio ex nihilo* and philosophical necessity undoubtedly represents an advance over al-Farabi and Ibn Sina from the viewpoint of theological exigencies, if indeed these thinkers meant to regard these as philosophically serious issues. For Maimonides' synthesis is in conformity with the theological requirements of a radical division between God and the created world bridged by no necessity encompassing them both. Essences are here therefore not preexistent possibles: they are the realm of indefinite logical possibilities which may become the object of the free creative will of God. Existence is not, in a metaphysical sense, an accident:[84] it is each being's mediated participation in the creative act of God. But Maimonides' view would appear to represent an important step from the viewpoint of philosophical exigencies also. Informed by religious inspiration, he begins to seize philosophically the problem of the *absolute* origin of existence. He reaches the metaphysical profundity necessary to bare the insufficient determination of actual reality and its laws *as a whole*. He thus directly contributes to the metaphysical understanding of the ultimate contingency underlying the necessity and rationality of actual reality. With this contribution, he does his share not only in overcoming the "essentialism" inherent in Greek and Muslim emanationism,[85] but also in posing a problem philosophically quite independent of the specific doctrines of creation or emanation.

After the preceding analysis, one final question forces itself upon us: we have assumed throughout this analysis that Maimonides regards it as essential to defend *creatio ex nihilo* against a doctrine implying the eternity and necessity of the universe. It is obvious that this defense is necessary for *theological* reasons,[86] but what precisely are these reasons? The proofs for the existence of God do not depend on the assumption of creation,[87] and Scriptural passages which appear to assert creation need not be taken literally.[88] Why then is creation "a fundamental principle of the Law of our teacher Moses . . . next in importance to the principle of God's unity"?[89] Creation is precisely this: a fundamental principle of the *Law*. On the assumption of the eternity and ultimate necessity of the universe, miracles are *absolutely* impossible,—including the crucial miracle of supernatural revelation.[90] But on the basis of creation, miracles and revelation are possible.[91] They are, to be sure, *relatively* impossible, contradicting natural law: but since natural necessity is not absolute, this is no objection, for a miracle is exactly a temporary supernatural suspension of natural law.

Jewish Philosophers

We can now describe the final relation between philosophy and theology in this matter. Remaining strictly autononous in its methods, philosophy is given the task to prove, if it can, the *possibility* of the principles required by theology. Its achievement for theology is its proof of the *possibility* of a supernaturally revealed Law, deriving from its proof of the *possibility* of *creatio ex nihilo*. Theology then proceeds beyond the reach of philosophy: it "proves" the *reality* of creation through the reality of the revelation and the validity of the Law: "The true miracle is the decisive proof for creation."[92] The universe is so constituted that its laws could be suspended by the Biblical miracles and the Mosaic revelation: this is Maimonides' last word on the possibility of the universe.

Al-Farabi regarded revelation as merely exoterically a starting point.[93] Since theology is thus deprived of autonomy in relation to philosophy, his writings even on religious subjects become, in principle, purely philosophical literature. To Maimonides the "roots of the Law" are an autonomous starting point even in relation to philosophy. His *Guide of the Perplexed* is a *Kalām* rather than a philosophical treatise;[94] its arguments are from the outset devoted to the defense of the Law, and it is philosophical only in that this defense must be philosophically impeccable. In the final analysis, it is this difference which marks Maimonides' departure from the *Falāsifa*.

Two

Samuel Hirsch and Hegel

Man ist nicht mehr Hegelianer: freilich ist das das Trostlose, dass man
noch nichts Anderes ist.

—Samuel Hirsch

I

Hegel's philosophy of religion is virtually unique in the history of Western religious thought.[1] Other philosophers may accept a religious claim to human contact with God; but then they are apt to regard this contact as transcending philosophical comprehension, and to accept the claim on the sacred authority on which it is based. Alternatively, philosophers will reject all religious claims to contact with God. But then they will consider God, if considering Him at all, as a reality requiring philosophy in order to become known, and otherwise unknown; hence as a mere object of thought. And they will view religion as an activity which, whatever its uses, is a mere exercise in human solitariness. If Hegel differs sharply with both these positions it is because of two profound convictions which, jointly, establish the basic objective of his whole philosophy of religion: the belief in the reality of the Divine-human relationship, as attested to by religious immediacy, and the belief that this relationship is capable of being philosophically understood. Because of these two convictions, Hegel's fundamental aim is to comprehend, not God apart from man, nor human religion apart from God, but rather the Divine-human relationship. It is Hegel's proud claim that his philosophy is able to understand that relationship. But this claim rests on the humble admission that the Divine-human relationship itself is real in religious immediacy long before philosophy can attempt to comprehend it and that, if it did not already have reality, philosophy could certainly not give it reality.

In view of the objective of Hegel's philosophy of religion, it is not surprising that Hegel's religious contemporaries—both Jews and Christians—should have regarded his thought as an epoch-making event. The surprising fact is that most of them should have come to see it, not as a powerful ally—rational support analogous to that furnished by thinkers such as

Jewish Philosophers

St. Thomas Aquinas in an earlier age[2]—but rather as a deadly threat, and acceptance of Hegel's system as a whole as radically incompatible with Jewish or Christian religious life. And yet in the long run this reaction was inevitable. This was not because of the Hegelian endeavor to comprehend the religious God-man relationship. It was, rather, because of the particular comprehension of that relationship which Hegel in fact offered.

According to Hegel, the Divine-human relationship, as experienced and lived in religion, is the truth. This truth is present, abstractly and incompletely, even in the most primitive and undeveloped religion. And it is present, concretely and completely, in what for this reason is the absolute religion—modern Protestant Christianity. Indeed, it is only because of this concrete and complete presence of truth in life that philosophy can comprehend it in thought. But given this complete presence of truth in life, philosophical comprehension can then itself be complete.

This fundamental thesis raises, from the outset, a problem crucial for Hegel's entire enterprise. If truth is already wholly present in the absolute religion, then why is there still need for philosophical comprehension? If on the contrary there still is such need, must not religious truth, after all, be incomplete, and the complete philosophy of religion—which presupposes the complete religion—impossible? It may seem that, on the grounds of Hegel's own thesis, the complete philosophical comprehension of the absolute religion is either unnecessary or impossible.

Hegel's reply is that religious immediacy is true in content but falls short of ultimate truth in form. Its form is representation, which, manifesting itself in feeling, cult, and linguistic self-articulation, permeates the totality of its life. Philosophical comprehension must give to the true religious content its ultimately true form. This it does by transfiguring the religious form of representation into the philosophical form of speculative thought.

This transfiguration achieves many things. Primordially, however, it achieves *one* thing. It transforms what for religious immediacy is a relationship between man and a God *other* than man, into a single, dynamic, self explicating reality from which all appearance of radical otherness has vanished. This transformation, to be sure, cannot *simply* be a product of autonomous philosophical thought. Nor can the element of otherness, vital in religion itself, vanish in philosophy of religion without a trace. If the first were the case, philosophy would be, not life comprehended, but a mere arbitrary and lifeless construction.[3] And if the second were true, the wealth of religious Divine-human relationships would collapse, in philosophical comprehension, into an empty unity.[4] The philosophical transformation is possible only because religion *itself* manifests, in varying degrees, an inner bond between man and God, and because philosophy, instead of simply rejecting the element of otherness which vitally remains even in the absolute religion, internalizes and absorbs it. A difference remains, however, between religious immediacy and its philosophical comprehension. For religion lives, even in its highest form, with the distinction between a God worshiped and human worship, Divine Grace and its human reception. It is this remaining distinction which philosophy internalizes, and it does so by reenacting the religious reality in the form of thought. But in this reenactment the religious relationship between man and God is transfigured into a single, self-developing Whole.

This outline, however brief and even superficial, suffices to disclose a grave dilemma, posed by Hegel for his Jewish and Christian contemporaries. Either their religious life had to remain a meeting of man with God—a meeting in which God is other than man, and man other than God. But then that life remained fettered to an illusion which had now been disclosed, and the immediacy of religious existence could not survive this disclosure. The owl of Minerva had spread its wings, and the dusk in which it had done so was the dusk of all religious life.[5] Or else the religious life of Christians and Jews alike could transfigure itself into a higher, speculative life, rising above the illusion of the otherness of God.[6] But then this new form of life was in radical conflict with the old, for the new God required man for His self-realization, being incompletely real without him. And the new man was a mere phase in the Divine self-realization. Man's freedom was no longer human freedom, free to turn to or against God. It was a mere moment of Divine freedom, and what had always been taken for a radical human choice between obedience to and rebellion against God were both, in the new religion, part of the process of Divine self-realization.[7]

Confronted with this dilemma, then, could the Jewish or Christian believer simply reject the Hegelian comprehension of religion, by a straightforward and immediate reaffirmation of his relationship to the other God? If he were vitally affected by the philosophical tradition culminating in Hegel, he could not, for he had then accepted from Kant the idea that an externally legislating God is incompatible with autonomous morality,[8] and from Schleiermacher the thesis that true religiosity finds God within, refusing to accept Him on Scriptural authority without.[9] Indeed, by the time Hegel appeared on the scene, this believer may well have been close enough to either a mystical reduction of the human to the Divine or—more likely—to a humanistic reduction of the Divine to the human, to be on the verge of simply rejecting the God of his tradition, who remained other than man. And if he was reluctant to go past this verge, it is to Hegel, above all, that he must have looked for guidance, for it was Hegel, more than any other idealistic thinker, who took seriously the otherness of God proclaimed by religious immediacy and who, when finally sublating it into thought, avoided the reduction, either of man to God or of God to man.

Such, then, were the reasons why the philosophically minded among Hegel's Jewish and Christian contemporaries could not simply dismiss the

Hegelian comprehension of their religion. And yet, because of the dilemma described above, they were also unable to accept it.

II

We have thus far dealt with Hegel's challenge to Judaism and Christianity, the two religions taken jointly. We must now turn to his specific additional challenge to Judaism alone. For there is such an additional challenge, and it is grave enough to explain why, whereas there were Christians who, after all, could seek to reconcile acceptance of Hegel's system with a continued Christian life, no analogous attempt was possible within Judaism. Loyalty to Judaism was compatible with acceptance of Hegelian fragments. It was not compatible with acceptance of the system as a whole.

Superficially, this was because Hegel had an unexalted image of Judaism. To be sure, the mature Hegel had abandoned his earlier prejudice—shared, among many others, by Kant—that, bound in blind obedience to barren, external laws, Judaism is a mere "positive" religion, without spirit and inward power.[10] Recognizing Judaism as indeed a religion of the spirit, he had made a serious effort to comprehend that spirit. And he had found it to consist in "sublimity"—the awe-filled, single-minded, and uncompromising Jewish dedication to the One God. But while crediting Judaism with an advance toward truth, Hegel nevertheless viewed sublimity as a mere aspect of total religious truth, and Judaism, because confined to that aspect, as left with a fragmented world. Geared to its God who is One, Judaism finds the world—which is manifold—barren and undivine. Its God is the "Lord" of the world, who is "beyond" that world. He is not present here and now.[11]

That this account—one-sided at best—should have been irritating to believing Jewish contemporaries is obvious. But the more thoughtful among them could not regard it as the essence of the Hegelian challenge to their religion. One needed, after all, scant intimate knowledge of Judaism to expose its one-sidedness, and at least one writer—a Christian otherwise sympathetic to Hegelianism—made such an exposure as early as 1843.[12] Why not, then, correct Hegel's account of Judaism and still fit it into the Hegelian system? But merely to fit Judaism into that system was to give a critique of it, and to describe Judaism in terms more adequate than Hegel's own would serve only to make the critique less severe. It is in this circumstance, and in the conditions responsible for it, that the true challenge of Hegel to Judaism is to be found.

Before Hegel appeared on the philosophical scene, the nineteenth-century Jew found himself challenged from two opposite quarters: first, by the Christian testimony on behalf of the risen Christ; second, by the "religion of reason" of deistic or Kantian Enlightenment. Both appraised his religion *ab extra*: the one, in the light of a standard which it did not recognize, the other, in terms of standards too abstract to do it justice. In contrast with both, Hegel tried to understand sympathetically the unique nature of Judaism, and indeed even to incorporate it into his system of total truth. Yet, ironically, it is for this precise reason that his challenge to Judaism was far graver than that of the other two.

As for the ancient Christian challenge, the Jew could do no more than counter the Christian testimony with his own. Nor did he need to do more, for the result was a stalemate which intelligent men of good will had to tolerate. As for the newer "rationalistic" challenge, this exposed, to be sure, the scandal of Jewish particularity. But Jewish particularity was no more—and possibly less—scandalous than the particularity of the incarnate God. A "religion of reason," if abstractable from Christianity, was abstractable also from Judaism. And still today there are Jews who stake all on the belief that the latter abstraction causes less difficulty than the former.

The Hegelian challenge could not be met as cavalierly as this earlier rationalistic challenge. For unlike deistic or Kantian reason, Hegelian reason is saturated with difference, not neutral to it; it achieves universality, not by abstraction from the particular, but by moving through it, allowing to each a partial, and to none more than a partial, place within the whole. This is why, as we have seen, Hegel can at least attempt to enter into Judaism as such. But it is also why, as we see now, he regards it as *in toto* superseded. What ultimately supersedes it can only be a religion which, instead of being particular, is comprehensive of all particulars: according to Hegel, Protestant Christianity. Against this challenge, one could not assert an abstract religion of reason abstractable from Judaism. And while one could assert against it a more adequate concept of Judaism than Hegel's own this was, by itself, of little moment. At least so long as Judaism had a place short of the highest in the dialectical development of religion—albeit one higher than Hegel himself had given it—it was still superseded.[13]

Could one, then, regard Hegel's system as but a new form of the ancient Christian challenge to Judaism, to be countered by the ancient Jewish testimony? At least the system itself claimed that one could not. To be sure, it admitted that *religions* confront each other with conflicting and mutually irrefutable testimonies. But it claimed that *philosophy* of religion has transcended all stalemates of such claims and counterclaims, for it had immersed itself in the life of every religion and appraised that religion by its own standards. It had seen the wealth and coherence sought in one religion found in another, and it had arrived at replacing old dogmatic distinctions between true and false religions with what it claimed to be an undogmatic distinction between less true and more true religions. In its own self-understanding, therefore, the Hegelian challenge to Judaism is quite different from the ancient Christian challenge. The latter regards Judaism as false—in part if not as a whole—in the light of standards which Judaism can refuse to recognize. The former now regards Judaism as superseded, in the light of standards implicit in Judaism itself.

It has now become very plain why the fundamental dilemma posed by the Hegelian comprehension of religion, while grave for both Jew and Christian, was far graver for the Jew than for the Christian. As regards one of its horns, to be sure, there was little if any difference. If Hegel's system was the end of all religious life, it was the end of Jewish no more and no less than of Christian life. The Jew could then but give a "decent burial" to his religion, reproducing in the form of scholarship a form of life which could no longer be lived. But this effort was then paralleled by similar Christian efforts on behalf of Christianity.

It was the other horn of the Hegelian dilemma which found the Jew more exposed than the Christian. If religion could survive its Hegelian comprehension by self-transfiguration into the form of thought, then it was Protestant Christianity which could achieve this feat. As for Judaism, it had long been superseded in life, before Christianity, too, experienced its ultimate transfiguration into thought.

III

Under the circumstances now somewhat lengthily described, more than antiquarian interest is aroused by a Jewish thinker who, writing in the heyday of Hegelianism, tried to face up forthrightly to the Hegelian challenge. There was, to be sure, no lack of Jewish Hegelians with at most marginal commitments to Judaism, or of practicing Jews only superficially affected by Hegelianism. But no writer other than Samuel Hirsch combined a deep commitment to Judaism with a most profound involvement with Hegelianism. And his monumental *Religionsphilosophie der Juden* may be viewed, at bottom, as an attempt to come to terms with this double involvement.[14]

It is as such an attempt that the work will be examined in the present study.[15] Hirsch's book—which has received far less attention than it deserves—might be investigated for many reasons. Thus a study could be made of his use of Hegelian dialectic, which he wields with a skill and sensitivity not infrequently rivaling that of the master himself. It would be worthwhile, as well, to examine his massive use of traditional sources, and it might turn out that, while often arbitrary, Hirsch nevertheless deserves an honored place in the history of philosophic Bible and Midrash commentators. The present study, however, cannot afford the luxury of attending to such topics, for it must concentrate its efforts on the single issue of Hirsch's Jewish response to the Hegelian challenge.

This response would hardly be worth examining if Hirsch were a mere piecemeal apologist. But while it is a matter of course that his intentions are not free of apologetic elements, he is by no means a mere apologist, and his reaction to Hegel is most certainly not piecemeal. He makes basic and radical moves against Hegel, and recognizes them for what they are. Further, these moves are internally connected. Finally, Hirsch's thought as

Samuel Hirsch and Hegel

a whole is consistent and philosophical enough to reflect—for better or worse—the consequences of his fundamental moves.

These facts determine the structure of the present study. This will first seek to elicit the fundamental disagreements with which Hirsch confronts the Hegelian challenge, and the unity by virtue of which they add up to a whole. And it will then consider the effect of these fundamental disagreements, as manifest in the work in its entirety.

IV

It will hardly come as a surprise that Hirsch's first fundamental disagreement with Hegel is concerned with the concept of Judaism. Well armed with Biblical and rabbinic material, he does not find it difficult to contrast the Hegelian concept with the actualities of Jewish religious life. Hegel's Jewish God is "beyond"; the actual God of Judaism dwells in the midst of His people. Hegel's Jew lives in unhappy bondage to an alien law. The actual Jew finds in the Torah joy and salvation. Not wholly without reason can Hirsch on occasion complain that Hegel's view of Judaism is little more than an ancient Christian prejudice, cast into philosophical form.[16]

Along with his concept of Judaism, Hirsch assails Hegel's concept of Greek religion. And the one assault reinforces the other. Hegel himself wavered in his view as to the relative merits of Jewish and Greek religion—a fact which his commentators have failed to stress or even to notice.[17] He was, however, inclined on the whole to compare the Greek gods, who were human and present, with the Jewish God, Whom he thought remote, to the detriment of the latter. Hirsch admits the presence of the Greek gods. But he contends that this is a presence, not of the Divine, but merely of nature deified; and that this deification finds its dialectical nemesis when the Greek gods turn into Fate. He is then able to contrast this blind and impersonal Fate—than which no god is more remote—with the Jewish God Who, from the beginning, is seeing and personal.[18]

From what has thus far been said of Hirsch's approach it may seem that he will take issue, not at all with Hegel's categories, but merely with the Hegelian understanding of Judaism in terms of them. Hirsch contends that it is pagan man who must look for a God "beyond": for the "present" nature which he worships must at length turn into an enemy. And he further contends that it is Jewish man for whom God is "present": for this God is Lord of nature, and the man who worships Him is free to rule it. Does Hirsch, then, wholly accept the Hegelian categories of "present" and "remote" gods? And does his whole argument rest on the empirical material in terms of which he seeks to correct Hegel's concept of Judaism?

While giving much space to empirical material Hirsch knows that his argument cannot wholly rest on it. For he does not give the kind of empirical account of Judaism which, offering a mere multiplicity of beliefs and rituals, indiscriminately mixes the essential with products of chance. As much as Hegel does, he seeks to penetrate behind such external multiplicities to an animating principle which unites them. And to the same extent as Hegel, he is in need of categories if he is to accomplish such a penetration. The very least Hirsch must do, over and above adducing empirical facts about Judaism, is to organize these facts in categories, even if these categories themselves should remain Hegel's own.

But secondly, and far more importantly, even from the brief summary thus far given it is evident that Hirsch's categories cannot remain Hegel's own. For the "presence" ascribed by Hirsch to the Jewish God—Who, being the one transcendent God, must enter into nature if He is to be present— cannot, obviously, be the presence ascribed by Hegel to the Greek gods, which are not transcendent. And as for the latter, their presence is for Hirsch not a presence of the Divine at all.

That this difference will not be minor but fundamental becomes clear on closer inspection of Hegel's concept of "presence." For Hegel, "presence" ultimately turns out to be comprehensiveness. And it is because Christianity comprehends, among much else, the partial truths both of the Greek finite but present gods, and of the Jewish infinite but remote God, that it is the absolute religion. If Hirsch accepted the Hegelian criterion of comprehensiveness he could not, by merely correcting Hegel's image of Judaism, hope to avoid the dialectical sublation of Judaism by Christianity. Nothing less would be required, in that case, than the demonstration that Judaism either replaces Christianity as the absolute religion or else at least shares absoluteness with it.[19]

But can Judaism be regarded as the all-comprehensive religion? We may pass over the objection that the more comprehensive must historically succeed the less comprehensive, since this is a principle not strictly adhered to by Hegel himself.[20] But we must ask whether Judaism can be regarded as a synthesis that includes paganism. Must it not rather be regarded as a radical protest against paganism?[21] Doubt increases on this score as we note the characteristic which, in Hegel's view, enables Christianity to achieve all-comprehensiveness. This is its trinitarianism, which allows all— including pagan—otherness to live its own life while yet absorbing it in a larger whole. But against Hegel's Christian—or pseudo-Christian— trinitarianism, Hirsch must insist on the radical transcendence of the one God of Israel.[22] In sum, then, in order to avoid the dialectical sublation of Judaism in Christianity Hirsch must assail not only Hegel's appraisal of Judaism, but also the categories in which it is made. And this involves him in nothing less than an assault on Hegel's system as a whole.[23]

This assault is necessary, not only on behalf of Judaism against its Hegelian dissolution in Christianity, but also on behalf of all true religion against the threat posed to it by Hegel's philosophy. For Hirsch is well aware of the dilemma we have described above, and he knows that he must escape both from the horn which would be the death of all religion, and from what he takes to be the other horn, the speculative pantheism of a self-realizing God.[24] But he also knows that he can escape both these horns, not by an empirical description of Judaism, however glowing, but only by strategic assaults on Hegel's system as a whole. Failing such assaults, an attempt to correct Hegel's one-sided image of Judaism would be, in the end, but lost labor.

We observe Hirsch, then, proceeding from his first fundamental move against Hegel to a second, no less basic. This concerns the relation between philosophy of religion and the immediacy of religious life.

Hirsch agrees that philosophy, rather than attaining truths otherwise undisclosed, merely comprehends truths already present in life, and that the highest such truth is found in the life of a true religion. He radically denies, however, that in comprehending religious truth, philosophy removes a remaining untruth from it, thus transcending the standpoint of religion itself. No untruth remains in the true religion, and the standpoints of the true religion and of the true philosophy are therefore identical. Thus with a single blow Hirsch wards off the fundamental Hegelian dilemma, which threatens Judaism and Christianity alike.[25]

The all-important question, however, is precisely how this blow is to be struck. Conceivably Hirsch might have insisted that philosophy must remain at what to Hegel is the religious standpoint, for which God remains other than man, for the simple reason that God *is* other than man. Hirsch takes the most fateful of all his steps when, not even considering this possibility, he opts for an alternative. The true religion already *is* at the standpoint reached, according to Hegel, only by the true philosophy. If religious immediacy experienced itself as related to a God other than man, it would, to be sure, stand in need of correction. But the believer in the true religion does not regard himself as standing in such a relation. For the true religious—not merely for the philosophical—standpoint, "there can be no question of a relation to God."[26]

The utterly un-Hegelian nature of this affirmation cannot be overemphasized. Hegel's philosophical comprehension affirms the religious Divine-human relationship but overcomes Divine otherness—and thus religion itself—by transmuting the external into an internal relationship. Hirsch, seeking to deny the transmutation of religion by philosophy, is able to do so only by denying, *in religion*, the Divine-human relationship. At least in the true religion man knows himself related, not to God but only to himself. He experiences his own potential freedom and is gripped by an urge to actualize it. And God enters into this relationship between the potential and the actual self only as the Ground of potential selfhood which man, in actualizing it, acknowledges as a Divine gift. Hirsch does not hesitate to assert that this extraordinary account is in strict conformity with the facts of religious life.[27]

It must be noted, however, that, by itself, this second move escapes from the Hegelian dilemma only in order to be exposed to another. Must all religions somehow be true? If so, Hirsch is either left with a simple pluralism of religious truth which must, on his own view, be self-contradictory. (For if the philosophical is identical with the religious standpoint, each true religion must have its own philosophy, and the philosophy which makes the pluralistic assertion of the truth of *all* religions is then but the philosophy of *one* religion. Yet at the same time, it must claim to be the philosophy of *all* religions.)[28] Or else there are degrees of religious truth. In that case, however, Hirsch has not after all emancipated himself from the Hegelian position, for which comprehensiveness is the criterion of religious truth. But as we have seen, this position must be for him, as a Jew, unacceptable.

This dilemma points to a need, on Hirsch's part, for another utterly un-Hegelian doctrine which would provide an escape from it. This is the distinction between absolutely true and absolutely false religions. But we have as yet found nothing in Hirsch's thought which would justify this distinction.

It is, however, a mark of Hirsch's stature as a thinker that his second move against Hegel, just discussed, directly leads to a third, which provides the needed distinction. Indeed—as was asserted above—his three basic moves against Hegel form a unity on which his whole edifice rests.

We have thus far attended to the fact of Hirsch's denial, in the true religion, of a relationship between man and God. We must now attend more closely to the nature of this denial. Conceivably Hirsch might have asserted, in the true religion, a human-Divine identity, that is, a mystic union. What he in fact asserts is a relationship between the potential and the actual self, God being not a partner of this relationship but only the Ground of it. This assertion is of far-reaching consequence for his concept of freedom. And it also supplies the needed distinction between true and false religions.

In the Hegelian view, freedom, as experienced in religious immediacy, is human freedom, and its primordial choices, for or against God.[29] But for philosophical comprehension this human freedom is a partial manifestation of Divine freedom, and what seems to religious immediacy a radical human choice between obedience to and rebellion against God, is in ultimate truth two phases in the process of Divine self-realization. Thus Hegel not only arrives at religiously unorthodox concepts of sin and freedom. He can also view all religions as partial manifestations of freedom, and the absolute religion—which is the absolutely *free* religion—as totally comprehensive of them. For while in fatalistic religions man may seem to himself the absolutely unfree object of a wholly alien Fate, his apparently absolute unfreedom is in truth but a relative unfreedom; it is less unfree, for example, than forms of existence in which man, wholly devoid of a sense of the Divine, regards himself as master of his human destiny. Thus what seems absolute human unfreedom vis-à-vis God is in truth partial Divine freedom, in man.

Against this complex of Hegelian doctrine, Hirsch takes the radical stand that freedom is human freedom, not only for religious immediacy but also for philosophical comprehension, and hence, absolutely. Consequently, he asserts that what to religious immediacy seems an absolute choice between obedience to or rebellion against God, is in ultimate truth such a choice. And he attacks Hegel's concept of sin—the necessary negative phase in the self-realization of God—as his most ominous error. Sin is a choice which can be made; but it need not and ought not to be made. "In heaven and on earth, there is but one thing which is contingent. . . . Only that is contingent whose very notion is to be either this or that. Only actual sin is contingent."[30] But this one exception to the necessitarianism of Hegel's system is a crucial attack on the system as a whole.

As a result of this attack Hirsch achieves, at one stroke, the needed distinction between absolutely true and absolutely false religions. For it need hardly be said that a true religion rests on a primordial choice for God, and a false religion, on a primordial choice against Him. What needs adding are merely the categories in which these choices are to be understood. These are the categories, if not of Hegel, of contemporary philosophy.[31] To choose for God is to accept him as the Lord of nature, and this choice results in the human freedom to rule over nature. Thus the true religion is a religion of freedom. To choose against God is to deify nature, and this choice results in human self-subjection to nature. Thus the false religion is a religion of unfreedom. But this unfreedom is not, as seems the case to those enslaved by it, an absolute condition externally imposed. It is the product of their own false but free choice.

The true religion, then, is true not by virtue of comprehending all partially true religions. It is true as the radical alternative to absolutely false religions. And the way is found from the latter to the former, not by the dialectical transformation of their partial into a more comprehensive truth, but only by a radical act of conversion or repentance.

V

Hirsch's three fundamental moves against Hegel have now been described in their internal unity. Our remaining task is to consider the consequences of these moves. These, as we have said, are manifest, for better or worse, throughout his work.

We shall begin with Hirsch's account of the false religion, or paganism. No other part of his work is as dependent on Hegel for its material—almost wholly derived from the *Philosophie der Religion*—or for its method, which is thoroughly dialectical. And yet Hirsch's treatment of paganism is wholly independent, and must be so unless his whole case is to fall apart.[32]

Hegel's dialectic, moving positively, shows non-Christian religions to be stages of a process culminating in Christianity. Hirsch's dialectic of paganism is negative, and it culminates, not in the true but rather in the self-refutation of the false religion. This is because, in his view, paganism rests on an original anti-Divine choice, the consequences of which dialectic explicates. The original choice implies the belief that nature is Lord, and subjection to it—that is, sin—man's inexorable fate. But this belief is not a partial truth but rather a total lie. And from this lie there is a dialectical development only to further lies, and at most to a recognition of the vanity of all lies. But the step from this recognition to the truth is not a further dialectical development but rather a radical leap.[33]

Nature worshiped is not God, not even a fragmentary god. Nature gods are mere human projections, and nature itself is undivine. This is why paganism is a lie. Pagan man, moreover, cannot indefinitely remain with this lie. For in worshiping nature gods he is in a state of internal contradiction, and hence is dialectically driven beyond such worship. In nature worship slumbers the knowledge that this subjection is *self*-subjection, and hence that the nature gods projected are exceeded in worth and reality by the man who does the projecting. Deification of nature thus at length gives way to the deification of man. But this too is mere deification; unknown to himself, "the Greek perceived in his gods nothing but the experiences of his own heart."[34] And for this reason Greek religion too carries the seeds of its own disintegration. Because the spirits here worshiped are subject to nature, not, like the true God, sovereign over nature, mortality emerges as the limit of the Greek gods, who are therefore ultimately superseded by Fate. But "a fulfillment and hence transcendence of Fate is impossible on pagan soil."[35]

Paganism finds its ultimate limit when it recognizes its gods as the projections which they are. This occurs in Roman religion, which, withdrawing its god projections, reduces its deities to mere tools of human use. Thus utility itself is deified. But this final pagan deification too finds its nemesis, which constitutes the absolute crisis of paganism in all its forms. "What is the use of use?" With this climactic question paganism is cast into radical despair, ready for what will turn out to be the Christian answer. But it cannot itself produce this answer. Its highest possibility is to be ready to receive it—from elsewhere.[36]

Showing the courage of consistency, Hirsch does not shrink from describing Greek philosophy, too, as confined to the limitations of the pagan world.[37] The Platonic Idea, to be sure, intends the Divine. But because for paganism God is not the Lord of nature, the great pagan philosopher can seek the true God only beyond nature. Hence his Idea, though concrete and alive, fails to encompass the individual, which remains outside, without structure and value. Nor can Aristotle, though recognizing this fault, provide the remedy. His "manifold totalities," to be sure, are intended to animate the individual, but they fail wholly to do so, remaining manifold and fragmentary. And this is why, just as pagan religion culminates in the immediate experience of vanity, pagan philosophy culminates in the rational expression of that experience. This is skepticism.[38] Hirsch concludes, "Philosophy invents no new truth. It only comprehends a spiritual world already present. Hence the decline of the ancient world carried in train the decline of ancient philosophy. It could bring to consciousness the vanity of paganism, but not truth. How then is one to come to truth?"[39]

VI

This question finds its answer, first in Judaism and, secondly, and by way of mediation through Judaism, in Christianity. Judaism does not require a historically prior paganism and is, when preceded by paganism, a revolt against it. For far from being a dialectical development of pagan religion it is its radical alternative. Paganism springs from a primordial self-subjection to nature. Judaism springs from a primordial choice for the true God, who is Lord over nature. The God of Judaism is not nature. But neither is He a spirit who, beyond nature, is powerless to rule it. He is the Creator and Lord of nature, and hence present rather than beyond. And the Jew who worships Him imitates Him by being nature's master rather than its slave. This decisive truth, first abstractly present in Abraham, is the sole content even of the revelation at Sinai.[40]

But as the reader turns from Hirsch's paganism to his Judaism he is struck by a strange irony. The account of paganism is subtle, rich, well integrated, and moving with purpose and clarity. The account of Judaism moves, if at all, unclearly and with hesitation. And while it is filled with rich detail, culled from traditional Jewish sources and ingeniously interpreted, the detail often fits poorly into the overall structure, and the interpretation is apt to be forced and shot through with methodological unclarity. And yet the account of paganism is, after all, merely peripheral, while the account of Judaism must be, and is intended to be, the heart of the whole work!

One need not look far for an explanation of this strange state of affairs. Given Hirsch's concepts of freedom and sin, there can be a Hegelian-style dialectic of unfreedom and sin. But there can be no such dialectic of freedom and virtue. Even of paganism, to be sure, Hirsch—unlike Hegel—can give only a conditional dialectic.[41] For, in the first place, the primordial pagan self-subjection to nature is an absolute act, not a phase in a dialectical movement. And, in the second place, even given this act, nothing can *compel* a pagan to remain tied to its consequences. "For anyone who merely wishes to *know* evil, not to *enjoy* it, paradise is always open."[42] The above dialectic of paganism, then, holds only those pagans in bondage who fail to make a radical choice for paradise.

But of Judaism Hirsch cannot give a dialectic at all. In contrast with the negative pagan dialectic, this would have to be positive, showing how the free acts at earlier stages of Judaism lead to the still freer acts at later stages. But unlike Hegel, Hirsch cannot give such a dialectic. Since man's freedom is human, not a partial manifestation of Divine freedom, Hirsch must refuse to qualify the absoluteness of any individual's freedom for either virtue or sin. "A single vigorous resolution—and a man has broken with sin, dead to its lure."[43] A single lapse, too, and a man has fallen. Lesser representatives of liberal Judaism were ready to accept the belief in necessary human progress, willing to pay the double price of qualifying the freedom for good of earlier generations and, of later generations, the freedom for evil. For Hirsch—who is not a lesser representative of liberal Judaism— the price is too high.

Why should this loss of dialectic be of serious consequence? It endangers, in the first place, a philosophy of Judaism. For Hirsch, philosophy adds to the true religion only reflective self-understanding, which comprehends what religion immediately lives, as a necessary sequence. How then, if the true religion does not possess such a sequence, can it have a philosophy? But the loss of dialectic does not endanger a philosophical understanding of Judaism only. Far more seriously, it endangers any sort of continuous life of Judaism itself. For on the strength of the perennial possibility of the choice between freedom and slavery, Hirsch has rejected the positive dialectic of necessary progress, and he is neither inconsistent nor chauvinistic enough to maintain that, left to themselves, Jews are less inclined than other men to choose slavery. If, then, in the sphere of paganism, revolutionary acts of freedom are too weak to interfere with the negative dialectic of unfreedom, how can they be strong enough in the Jewish sphere to create a vital and positive tradition of freedom? Must not Judaism reduce itself to sporadic acts of an Abraham, a Moses, or an Isaiah, different from similar acts in the pagan sphere only in degree, if indeed at all?

Hirsch is, in fact, confronted at this point with a grave dilemma. Either human freedom is such that, nurtured by antecedent acts of freedom, it can create a vital tradition, relatively immune to unfreedom and sin. But then such traditions should have sprung up within paganism as well as Judaism, and the dialectic of paganism breaks down. Or else, because human freedom has no such power, the pagan dialectic runs its course, relatively unaffected by sporadic revolts against it. But then Judaism too should have become involved in the pagan dialectic, and the teaching of Abraham and Moses, only intermittently coming to life, should be no tradition at all.

It is at this critical juncture that a wholly new element makes its appearance in Hirsch's thought. This is the actual, literal intervention of God in

Jewish—and human—history. It will be remembered that God has thus far appeared in Hirsch's thought only in two capacities—as the Source of human freedom, and as the Lord of nature Whom free man imitates. If God acts at all in either of these two capacities, He does not, at any rate, act upon *man*. But such action now makes its unequivocal appearance. "God is free . . . and wills to *make us free*."[44] He works miracles which are actual miracles, and sends revelations which are actual revelations, reducible to neither philosophy nor poetry nor the voice of conscience, because they are not human creations but actual incursions of God.[45] Indeed, in the history of Israel God has not ceased acting even after prophecy has come to an end. For it is His providence alone which has kept Israel. Had it not been for Divine intervention, Israel would long have abandoned the path of freedom for self-chosen pagan servitude. And as for the purpose of this Divine intervention, it is solely to keep Israel on the path of freedom, forcing it to be the first people to live by a faith by which, in the Messianic age, all men will live.[46] Divine providence, then, at least as thus far described, manifests itself in two ways in the history of man. Leaving paganism to its own inner dialectic, it allows it to refute itself. And intervening actively in the history of Israel, it keeps and promotes the Jewish religion of freedom. But the one ultimate purpose of both these aspects of providence is to bring all men to the living God.

It is by recourse to Divine intervention, then, that Hirsch saves the continuous life of Judaism. And it is by this recourse, too, that he saves his own project of a philosophy of Judaism. Divine intervention in history—which consists of acts of sovereign freedom—is not, to be sure, subject to a dialectical necessity which philosophy might discover. But it does follow a teleological pattern which philosophy can discover after it has taken shape. Hirsch's philosophy of Judaism is, in substance, the discovery of that pattern.[47]

From the manner in which we have introduced Hirsch's intervening God, it may seem that He is a mere *deus ex machina*, invoked in order to save the system from collapse. We hasten to stress that this is far from the case. The careful reader of Hirsch's work can entertain no doubt that he is serious about God. Indeed—although the development of our argument compelled us till now to ignore this fact—the assault on Hegel's philosophical comprehension of religion is double-pronged from the outset. The one prong—thus far alone considered—protects human freedom from reduction to an aspect of Divine freedom. The other prong—thus far ignored—protects the sovereign autonomy of the Divine life from the need of man for self-realization.[48] Nowhere does Hirsch resemble a left-wing Hegelian humanist who, having reduced God to a mere product of human freedom, shrinks from the consequences of this reduction for Judaism.[49]

And yet Hirsch's intervening God is a wholly alien intrusion into his thought, not because he denies God but because he denies the possibility of a Divine-human relationship. For what, one must ask, are the miracles, revelations, and providential acts of his intervening God but part of such relationship? Moving against Hegel, Hirsch has denied a Divine-human relationship. He is compelled to reintroduce such a relationship when attempting to develop a philosophy of Judaism, on the basis of the original denial. On this contradiction, as will be seen, his entire enterprise suffers shipwreck.

As for Hirsch himself, he is curiously oblivious to this fatal contradiction. If aware of a difficulty at all, he considers it, at any rate, resolved by Lessing's doctrine of revelation, to which he has recourse. For both Lessing and Hirsch, revelation is education. It is an action upon man from without, but contains only a content already potentially within. It is an external influence, but its sole purpose is to emancipate man from the need for this influence, and hence from revelation itself. Revelation discloses only what man by himself might find; it but assures that what may be found is in fact found.[50]

But resort to this doctrine cannot resolve Hirsch's difficulties. Not only does it relate the pre-emancipated Israel to the Divine Educator, which on Hirsch's central thesis is impossible; it also frees the emancipated Israel from that relationship only on conditions which to Hirsch are unacceptable. For either the emancipated Israel will live a self-sufficient human life. (But then God is a religious redundancy, and no belief could be more alien to Hirsch, for whom the presence of God is precisely what marks Judaism off from paganism.) Or else the emancipated Israel will live not *in relation to*, but *in* God. (And this is in fact held by Hirsch, who maintains that sin, which is other than God, reduces itself to nothingness, while virtue, which remains real, lives in God, not side by side with Him.)[51] But then there is, once more, a dilemma, for either virtue has its true life in a God eternally complete, but then it suffers loss of its human reality. Or else it retains this reality even in God, but then God is incompletely real without it. Facing up to this dilemma—and echoing rabbinic tradition—Hirsch remarks that "humanly speaking, God is incomplete without man."[52] But while the rabbis could find genuine refuge in this "humanly speaking" Hirsch cannot. Believing man to be related to God, the rabbis could consistently confine human understanding to the human side of that relationship. Denying the God-man relationship, and doing so from a standpoint laying claim to ultimate truth, Hirsch must go beyond the "humanly speaking" to a doctrine claiming final truth. But if that truth is Divine incompleteness Hirsch is, after all, driven back at this late date into Hegelianism, and if it is not, he is driven into a mysticism destructive of human action.

Hirsch's whole Jewish response to Hegel, then, might be summed up as follows. As a Jewish Hegelian correcting Hegel's image of Judaism, Hirsch asserts that the Jewish God is a present God. As a Jew forced to oppose Hegel, he asserts, on the one hand, a transcendent God not dependent for

Samuel Hirsch and Hegel

reality on human action, and, on the other hand, a human freedom which, being human, is free both to turn to and against God. But since he opposes Hegel by denying a God-man relationship in authentic Judaism, he cannot reconcile the present God with the reality of human freedom. Contrary to his own most serious intentions, the life of God and the life of man fall apart.

VII

The difficulties which beset Hirsch's account of Judaism are also, in substance, the difficulties besetting his account of Christianity. This may therefore be more briefly considered.

Denying that Jesus thought of himself as Messiah, let alone the son of God, Hirsch considers him a Jew who meant to be, and was, faithful to Judaism. He even credits Jesus with one "great thought," which, it seems, though thoroughly in the spirit of Judaism, was not yet clearly grasped by Jesus' Jewish contemporaries—that "what all Israel is to be collectively, each Israelite must be, individually"—and having grasped this thought, Jesus exemplified it in his own life. In Hirsch's view, Jesus himself fell prey to but a single error, and even this had a beneficial effect on his followers—the belief in the imminence of the messianic kingdom. For, Jesus having died in a world as yet unredeemed, this belief gave rise to the idea of the resurrected Christ, and in bringing close to Christians the example of the perfect man, this idea inspired them to imitate his perfection. Thus far is Hirsch prepared to go toward asserting identity of spirit between Judaism and what he calls "its dearest child, a beautiful fruit in which the Jew rejoices!"[53] Why then does he nevertheless insist sharply on the need for distinctness of the two religions, not only in the present pre-Messianic era but even in the Messianic age itself?[54]

At least Hirsch's insistence on pre-Messianic separateness is not without firm reasons. First, Christianity did not preserve the pure Judaism of Jesus and his immediate disciples. Second, Christianity has a mission other than that of Judaism in the economy of history. Taken separately, neither of these reasons is new, or interwoven with Hirsch's thought in special intimacy. They assume both these qualities by virtue of being united into a dialectical whole.

As might have been expected, Hirsch views St. Paul as the originator of the break of Christianity with the spirit of Judaism. Going far enough to find even the fourth gospel compatible with Judaism, Hirsch goes on to say, "It needed but a single step—which we shall find taken by St. Paul—to erect an eternal barrier between Judaism and Christianity; and this barrier will not break down until the Church decides to retrace this step."[55]

The step which was of such consequence consisted of the belief that "all men share in Adam's sin, and nobody can free himself of it by his own power," of the consequent belief that the Torah, far from being an aid in the conquest of sin, merely discloses that sin is unconquerable, and of the final consequent belief in the vicarious atonement of a Jesus no longer merely human, but the incarnate son of God. To these three Pauline beliefs, which he recognizes to be aspects of but one belief, Hirsch gives the ancient Jewish reply that the Jew who lives by the Torah is bound, not merely to disagree, but even to fail to understand.[56]

What is not ancient, however, is the philosophical form into which this reply is cast. For Hirsch, the Pauline step must be a partial relapse into paganism. For if unfreedom is the pagan condition, consequent upon self-subjection to nature, then the belief in original sin, and the beliefs which flow from it, cannot but manifest an involvement with that condition.

This is not to say, however, that the Pauline lapse is a simple error which need not and should not have occurred. For while responsible for it, St. Paul is responsible also for initiating the "extensive" mission of Christianity which, in contrast with the "intensive" Jewish mission of remaining true to the God of Israel living in Israel's own midst, is to bring this God to the pagan world. But the one Pauline responsibility is dialectically interwoven with the other.

So far as Judaism is concerned, the Pauline account of the human condition is simply false. However, it describes with complete accuracy the pagan condition at the beginning of the Christian era. Hirsch writes, "The state of the pagans was corrupt and rent in two, and they were aware of this fact. They could not, out of their own power, rise above that condition. They were left only with despair and the yearning for the better. Pauline Christianity thus expressed the complete pagan world-consciousness, which could find help only in a new principle not implicit in it, and hence offered from outside as a miraculous gift. And this was why Pauline Christianity could achieve sole power in the world."[57] The upshot is, then, that while St. Paul erred, it was only in mistaking a specific human condition for a universal, and a relatively true account for an absolute.

Hirsch is now able to assign to Christianity its exact role in the economy of history. Paganism is the dialectic of self-inflicted serfdom, tending toward its own disintegration. Judaism is the life of self-chosen freedom, kept alive—and away from involvement with pagan unfreedom—only by direct Divine intervention. Christianity is, on the one hand, a life of self-chosen freedom, which, on the other hand, can seek to bring this freedom to paganism only by itself becoming involved in the pagan dialectic. Hence, unlike Judaism, it retains an element of unfreedom although, unlike paganism, it possesses within itself the power to overcome this element—both in the pagan world without and in its own internal structure. And when external circumstances are ripe, it rises above the pagan—that is, Pauline—element within. This occurs as Catholicism turns into Protestantism. In

Hirsch's view, the conversion of pagans is the sole prerogative of Catholicism, which can accomplish this task only by remaining Pauline. The task of Protestantism is not to convert pagans, but to "realize freedom in the secular relations" of states already Christian. But this it can do only by emancipating itself from its Catholic-Pauline origins. Hirsch does not fail to note that this image of Protestantism is extraordinary. Nevertheless, he insists on its correctness. The persistence of Pauline elements within Protestantism is due merely to failure of nerve, and they are destined to disappear. "The Protestant Church wants to be Pauline. But this is impossible."[58]

It can hardly be said that this account amounts to a serious Jewish confrontation with what is Christian in Christianity. What must be stressed, however, is that if Hirsch fails it is not because, living in a Christian environment which had long drawn a mere caricature of Judaism, he responds by drawing in turn a caricature of Christianity. Hirsch strains every nerve to reach a fair Jewish appreciation of Christianity. And if his account of it nevertheless comes to grief, it is over exactly the same problem that trips up his account of Judaism. As we have seen, the latter failed to show how, in the absence of a Divine-human relationship, God can live in the midst of Israel. The former account is now driven to conclude that, in the absence of such a relationship, the specifically Christian element in Christianity is at best a dialectically necessary lapse into paganism. But this conclusion on Hirsch's part must not obscure his sincerely held belief that the true God lives in the Christian as well as in the Jewish community.[59] And this belief is dramatically illustrated by a call in which the whole work culminates: the call for a post-Hegelian philosophy which, jointly engaged in by Jews and Protestants, will demonstrate that the true God lives, in a world which Hegel has shown to be free.[60]

VIII

Our overall conclusion is, then, that Hirsch's Jewish confrontation of Hegel ends in failure. It is a heroic failure because his central moves against Hegel are not haphazard but internally connected, because his entire thought allows itself to be permeated by the consequences of these moves, and because, if nevertheless it ends in incoherence, it is driven toward it by an internal inevitability. But because of this incoherence, Hirsch's effort is still a failure.

The present-day Jewish thinker for whom Hegel is still a challenge must wonder whether Hirsch might not have avoided failure had he moved differently against Hegel. What if one asserted against Hegel, not that the true religion eliminates the otherness of God, overcome according to Hegel only in the true philosophy? What if one asserted, instead, that philosophy too must accept the otherness of God, for the simple reason that God is other than the man with whom He yet enters into relationship and that, for this simple reason, philosophy, instead of rising to absoluteness, must remain human?

If Hirsch himself did not even consider this possibility, it was because he shared the conviction of his philosophical contemporaries, for whom a religion accepting a God radically other than man was of necessity a mere "positive" religion, blindly authoritarian, devoid of spirituality, and destructive of human freedom. But this is a conviction which has long been abandoned by present-day religious thinkers. And the possibility which Hirsch dismissed without examination is the possibility which, in any renewed encounter with Hegel—Jewish or Christian—must be explored.

Three

Hermann Cohen—after Fifty Years

I

For a Jew of today to commemorate a fiftieth anniversary in Jewish history is an enterprise fraught with obligation and danger. We are on one side, the event to be commemorated is on the other, and between us yawns an abyss without equal in the annals of history. As we remember, we seek to bridge the abyss, for to save the past for the present is our obligation. Yet no less great is the obligation to remember the abyss itself. And in this double obligation, and the tension between them, lies the danger. We tremble lest, in an effort to save the Jewish past for the present, we pretend, if but for a moment, that the greatest catastrophe in Jewish history never happened. But we also tremble lest, overwhelmed by the catastrophe, we allow the Jewish present to be robbed of its past. To renew the past for present life has always been an essential obligation for the Jewish historian, philosopher, and theologian. Never before has this task been both so indispensable and so difficult.

The task is especially difficult when the event to be remembered lies in the sphere of German-Jewish history. The enormity of the Nazi Holocaust is such as to dwarf all lesser Jewish tragedies which are part of it. Were it not for this fact the tragedy of what once was known as German Judaism would, by itself, have few equals in the annals of history. Nowhere did Jews believe the promise of the modern world more wholeheartedly than in Germany. Nowhere else did they make more thoroughgoing attempts to reconcile their Jewish heritage with the culture that surrounded them. Nowhere did such attempts result in a similar flowering of the spirit. Yet precisely in that country erupted a groundless and demonic hate which is without parallel in the darkest place or time anywhere in history. Without doubt the present-day critic, endowed as he is with hindsight, must reach the inexorable conclusion that the Jewish love which inspired what was once thought of as the "German-Jewish symbiosis" never did have any real counterpart in a German love for things Jewish.[1] But dare he dismiss all the products of this love as mere aberrations, remembered with pain and best forgotten? To do so would be to cut off the Jewish present from the past and, indeed, to rob it of some of its greatest treasures.

Jewish Philosophers

In the case of no other figure in German-Jewish history are the dilemmas of present commemoration so deep and so painful as in that of Hermann Cohen, who died fifty years ago. German history abounds with Jewish personalities—philosophers, poets, artists, scientists—who made invaluable contributions to German culture; none combined as first-rate a contribution to German culture with as forthright and unequivocal a commitment to Judaism as did Hermann Cohen. German-Jewish history is rich in contributions to Jewish thought and scholarship; but neither Zunz nor Moses Hess, neither Geiger nor S. R. Hirsch, neither Buber nor Rosenzweig had at the same time a comparable impact, as Germans, upon German culture. Not even Moses Mendelssohn (who ushered in the era of German Judaism) came anywhere close to Hermann Cohen (who stood at its end), in the degree to which he lived up to Mendelssohn's own advice of living at once in both worlds. And such was Cohen's trust in both these worlds, and in their inherent affinity, that he had no inkling or premonition that disaster was imminent. There are few thoughts to alleviate the pain of the present reader who feels this trust in Cohen's writings. Among these few is that their author was spared the experience of Nazism, which would have broken his spirit.

Without doubt a trust so uncritical, in the mind of a presumably critical philosopher, bespeaks some hidden fault. We must seek out that fault. At the same time, we must guard against the danger of magnifying or misunderstanding it. We are in any case forbidden to judge Jews prior to the Nazi Holocaust in the light of hindsight knowledge, when we, who are after the event, are no more able to understand it than those prior to it could predict it. Moreover, in the case of Hermann Cohen we shall find that, as in a Greek tragedy, the catastrophic events which then seemed impossible, and yet were so soon to become actual, were totally out of proportion to the fault.

We owe this insight less to Hermann Cohen than to ourselves. Such are the momentous events in contemporary Jewish history that an Israeli philosopher can write of Franz Rosenzweig that he was "perhaps the last Jew to argue that an individual's Jewish existence was dependent first and foremost on personal decision, and that history was waiting patiently until each member of this people would discover for himself the grounds for justifying his decision to remain a Jew."[2] This criticism (which would apply far more justly to Cohen than to Rosenzweig) rests on deep insights into contemporary Jewish history. Yet a wide gap exists between these insights and the criticisms one might derive from them. Dare we deny the need for a philosophy of Judaism? Dare we dispense with Cohen and Rosenzweig, who are among its greatest modern representatives? No less a scholar than Julius Guttmann has credited Hermann Cohen with the renewal of the philosophy of Judaism in our time.[3]

But one may give Cohen this credit and still cast him aside. His is the language of an outworn, abstract idealism; we, on our part, if needing the language of philosophy at all, need a language of concreteness which speaks to us of human death and finitude, of the actual world, and of existential decision. Here too, however, caution and discrimination shall be required. It is true that Heidegger thinks of death whereas to Cohen death is not a theme for the moral or the religious consciousness. But it is also true that Heidegger broods on death-in-general and shows no philosophical concern for the murder of children—whereas Cohen rejects the general brooding only because it can result in no action. On his part, Cohen, unconcerned with death, is very much concerned with poverty—which, unlike death-in-general, makes action imperative.[4] But of concern with poverty one finds no trace in Heidegger's writings. One may well ask, then, in this particular instance, who is the "abstract" idealist, and who the "concrete" existentialist, demanding action and commitment.

Questions such as these must be asked by the general philosopher. Additional ones must be asked by the Jewish philosopher. In the premodern world, Jewish thought achieved confrontations *between* Judaism and philosophy. In the modern world its general tendency has been to allow philosophy to be the judge of Judaism. To allow philosophy this role seemed inescapable, for modern philosophy, unlike its medieval predecessors, laid claim to both radical autonomy and total impartiality.

Yet the fact is that this impartiality was rarely extended to Judaism. Despite its claim to autonomy, modern philosophy has not hesitated to confess a need of religious, and in particular Christian, inspiration. The possibility that it might stand in need of Jewish inspiration has been explored only by two major philosophers, both Jewish in origin. Moreover, of these two, Ernst Bloch,[5] who writes during and after the experience of Nazism, dares no more than couple Judaism with Christianity, whereas Hermann Cohen, whose writings precede Nazism, has the moral and intellectual courage to engage in Jewish criticisms of Christianity.

We must conclude, then, that the present-day Jewish critic of Cohen's work is right to view with suspicion any tendency on his part to dissolve existing Judaism into an abstract, philosophically inspired "religion of reason." But he would risk eliminating what is alive, along with what is dead, were he to disregard the possibility that this religion of reason is itself, in part if not as a whole, the product of Jewish inspiration.

II

Seeking out what is alive in Cohen's thought, we do well to begin with what is most obviously dead. During the early period of his career as a Marburg professor of philosophy, Cohen's Judaism had become "mainly a memory of his childhood experiences, not a living and lived reality."[6] After 1912, when he retired from Marburg, began lecturing on Jewish philosophy at the Berlin Hochschule für die Wissenschaft des Judentums, and—above all—was at work on his great book on Judaism, the *Religion der Vernunft aus den Quellen des Judentums,* his celebrated return to Judaism was complete. Yet during that time he was still able to write *Deutschtum und Judentum,*[7] a war-time pamphlet which today seems light-years away.

According to Cohen's pamphlet a unique kinship exists between "Germanism" and Judaism—one which, already partly actualized, is destined to ever fuller actualization. On the one hand, Judaism is one root of Germanism (the other being Hellenism), and these two have found a trans-figured form of modern life in Germanism ever since the Reformation. On the other hand, Judaism, having lost part of its native essence in the me-dieval ghetto, could have regained that essence in its modern form only through German inspiration.

The essence of Germanism is ethical idealism. The Reformation—which has placed the German spirit into the center of world history—is a revolu-tion in behalf of free, inward conscience (a conscience as much moral as religious), and it was only a question of time until this conscience assumed its proper expression of moral autonomy in German philosophy and poetry. The core of the many expressions of Germanism, for Cohen, are Kant and Schiller.

Moral autonomy is universal in validity. It is German, however, in histori-cal origin and location. "What differentiates the German concept of man-kind from the *humanité* of the French revolution is its ethical foundation. The 'mankind' of Germanism alone rests on the grounds of ethics. . . . "[8] Germanism, therefore, has universal significance for all mankind. The future it demands and inspires is universal—peace, socialism, internation-alism; its realization requires the ethical idealism which is the parti-cular product of Germanism. Germanism, therefore, is, in its unique par-ticularity, "the teacher of the world."[9]

Germanism is akin to Judaism: what Germanism has produced in modern art, poetry and philosophy Judaism has possessed since ancient days, in the Messianic expectation. Affirming the uniqueness of the One God from the start, Judaism had achieved total freedom and universalism in the Messianic ideal. All three ideals, to be sure, were obscured if not lost in the medieval ghetto, when the fear of persecution "narrowed and dark-ened"[10] the outlook. "The [Jewish] Messiah was resurrected," however, "in the German spirit."[11] To be sure, Moses Mendelssohn (who began to make "Germanism a life-force for Judaism")[12] failed to bring about this resurrec-tion; for he shrank from affirming a universalistic Messianism and confined Judaism to a narrow, particularistic law. His heirs, however, inspired as they were and are by a German ethical idealism still dormant in Mendelssohn's time, have been enabled to be "as Germans, Jews, and as Jews, Germans."[13] Indeed, so intimate is the kinship between Germanism and Judaism now that it may be said that Germany is the motherland, if not the fatherland, of all modern Jews.

Such, in brief, are the main contentions of *Deutschtum und Judentum*. After fifty years, what shall we say of them? First—and this is in charity as well as justice—the work is a wartime pamphlet, and it is a melancholy fact that, during the First World War, the most foolish utterances were sincerely made by the greatest intellectuals in all the warring countries. Cohen was less foolish than many others. Freud is said to have proclaimed that his libido was with Austria. Cohen could never have made any similar statement. His moral reason, not his libido, was involved, and this is why even in the midst of the war he was able to look beyond it. And what he saw was internationalism, socialism, and peace.[14]

Second—and this is in justice, for charity is not required—in publishing this pamphlet Cohen was not guilty of assimilationist cowardice. On the contrary, the publication was an act of Jewish courage, as was proved when the nationalistic critics did not praise him for his German patriotism but rather accused him of Jewish presumptuousness. When attacked, Cohen did not fail to counterattack. Even though antisemites and Zionists denied the fact, there *was* an "identity of essence" between Germans and German Jews.[15] And if he, Cohen, were ever forced to recognize that he lived within "a people and a state" which were incompatible with his Jewish commitments, then he would refuse to surrender his Judaism, and feel justified in demanding a home in Palestine.[16]

Then why did Cohen, never slow to recognize anti-Semitism or to attack it, possess so uncritical a faith in a German "essence" unsullied by "existence"? And, in seeking out that essence, what made him so sure of his correct identification? Cohen knew that Schopenhauer and Nietzsche were not Kant, Goethe, and Schiller and that Wagner was not Bach, Mozart, or Beethoven.[17] Yet it was not Schopenhauer, Nietzsche, or Wagner that constituted his Germanism. He must have known of Luther, the crass anti-Semite, and Luther, the grim foe of the peasants. Yet the essence of his Luther was free conscience—and socialism![18] In the entire strange pamphlet there is perhaps no stranger passage than the following:

> Despite the universal contrary prejudice I venture to assert that in Germany equal rights for Jews have deeper roots than anywhere else. Everywhere in the world Jews may win a higher share of political rights and government. We German Jews seek this share on the grounds of participation, inwardly recognized, in German morality and religiosity. Hence our road to liberation is harder and more erratic, for it is bound up with the fluctuations of social feelings; but it has deeper historical and cultural roots. And our limited Jewish rights in Germany are of higher value for religious survival than the apparently absolutely equal rights of Jews abroad. . . .[19]

This passage, so indescribably tragic in retrospect, gives us our first clue to a fatal flaw which permeates Cohen's entire thought: a strange abstractness, a shadowy sort of idealism which ascribes to ideas and ideals far greater power and responsibility than they ever can carry. Such abstractness, a grave fault in any case, becomes altogether fatal when it assumes a dream-like quality; when everything is staked on ideas and ideals—in this case, those of Kant, Goethe, and Schiller—which, so far as any historical efficacy was concerned, had long vanished into the past.

This dreamlike unrealism affects Cohen's appraisal of German exist-ence. It affects no less his appraisal of Jewish existence. Cohen recognized the state as a moral necessity. He recognized it as a political necessity as well. As regards a Jewish state, however, he not only denied its necessity but actually went so far as to affirm its impossibility. This was on the grounds that "it would contradict the Messianic idea and the mission of Israel that we [Jews] should be permitted to create a state of our own."[20]

III

It may be thought that a philosophy which permits such wayward views can have no solid foundations. This may well be the view of contemporary philosophers, who do not take philosophical idealism, or any aspect of it, with any kind of seriousness. More justly could it be the view of contempo-rary Jewish philosophers if only because, confronted as they are with un-precedented threats to Jewish survival, they require unprecedented re-sources of realism.

Yet as the contemporary Jewish philosopher looks to all the contempo-rary philosophies he finds little to sustain him in his need. The momen-tous moral crises of the present age require momentous moral resources wherewith to meet them. Yet in one camp of contemporary philosophy—linguistic empiricism—one finds little but trivial responses; and in the other—existentialism—one finds a tendency to exalt the act of commit-ment above any content or purpose. It seems not accidental that any moral strength in either of these philosophical camps appears due to a harking back to earlier, idealistic philosophies, and to Immanuel Kant above all others.

The Jewish philosopher who discovers this fact soon rediscovers an-other. Ever since Kant produced his moral philosophy the theme "Kant and Judaism" has existed in the minds of Jewish philosophers. This theme, many-sided and quite possibly inexhaustible, has nevertheless a cen-tral core: the identity of, and difference between, the categorically com-manding voice of Kant's moral reason, and the no less categorically com-manding voice of the God of Judaism. But Kant's rational autonomy is the core of philosophical modernity, and the categorically commanding God is the core of the divine-Jewish covenant; hence the theme "Kant and Ju-daism" bids fair to remain alive so long as there is both Judaism and modern philosophy.

In his own time Hermann Cohen was the great renewer of the Kantian philosophy. He first produced commentaries whose scholarly value has not diminished with the passage of time. He then produced his own neo-Kantian system, and this rescued the German philosophy of his time from arid positivism and scholasticism. Finally—and this at least for our purposes was his crucial achievement, for we cannot here enter into his general philosophy—there was in his mind throughout an ongoing dialogue between his Kantian and his Jewish commitments.[21]

In this dialogue we will here stress two features. One is further and more philosophical evidence of the weakness which we have already discovered—a dreamlike lack of realism which is not present in Kant himself and which, by itself, suffices to explain why the eighteenth-century master is today more philosophically alive than his nineteenth- and early twentieth-century disciple and expositor. The other feature, however, is a strength, and one which in the end is far more important. Other Jewish thinkers before and after Hermann Cohen have *confronted* Kant *with* Judaism. Probably of Cohen alone can it be said that he showed the boldness and competence to build Jewish commitments *into* Kantianism itself.

We must consider the weakness before considering the strength. Kant makes a well-known distinction between duty and inclination. The distinction is radical, for duty is not duty so long as it subserves inclination and is not for duty's sake. Initially made, this distinction permeates the entire Kantian moral and religious philosophy. The moral will is determined by duty: all concern with ends is shot through with inclination. This will does right for right's sake: it is not moved by hope of reward and fear of punishment even if God is the author of both. The moral will cannot strive even for eternal happiness; it can strive only to be worthy of it. These and other affirmations all rest on the altogether basic faith that the voice of duty is no illusory voice, which commands that which cannot be done. I *can* do what I *ought* to do; the self-determination which is my duty is the essence of my freedom. Here lies the core of Kant's whole ethical idealism.

This ethical idealism, however, is coupled, in Kant himself, with a most remarkable element of critical realism. Kant maintains that duty can and must conquer inclination when the two are in conflict; he does not maintain that inclinations are intrinsically evil, and that their indiscriminate conquest is either possible or desirable. Kant asserts that the good will is determined by duty, and not by consequences; he considers indifference to consequences an existential impossibility. Thus a marked realism is manifest in his analysis of the human moral situation; it is manifest no less in his eschatological expectations. Historically, he looks to a future of perpetual peace; but his hope is as much grounded in a grim political necessity which will compel even the worst of men as in an exalted moral necessity which will compel the best of them. Religiously, he hopes for eternity; but this hope too has an element of realism. Thus his *summum bonum* includes, along with perfect virtue, realizable only by man, also a deserved happiness, irreducible to virtue, such as can only be the gift of God. Hence the Kantian God, though an Idea and an Ideal, is by no means an Idea and Ideal *only*. The God-Idea suffices to inspire moral action. Man being what he is, only an *existing* God can warrant an eschatological hope.

But the Kantian philosophy has had the peculiar fate that whereas, on the one side, empiricists and realists have dismissed his moral idealism, on the other side philosophers inspired by his moral idealism have rejected the realism with which, in Kant himself, the idealism is conjoined. Of such a rejection Fichte is the first great example. Hermann Cohen is the last.

Consider the following examples from Cohen's *Kant Begründung der Ethik*.[22] Kant holds the human will, but not human nature, to be alterable; Cohen affirms the task of "recreating man in accordance with the idea of humanity."[23] Kant maintains that natural necessity, as well as morality, is required for human progress;[24] Cohen stakes his whole faith on the "moral education of the human race."[25] Kant regards the good will as *one* end, but not as *the sole* end; for Cohen "the good will alone is the final end."[26]

Indeed, on this crucial issue he shows his sharpest dissent from his master. As we have seen, for Kant the *summum bonum*, or the highest Good, includes deserved happiness as well as perfect virtue, a doctrine which, in Kant, on the one hand presupposes that sensuousness is as unalterable a part of the human condition as rationality, as well as that, by itself, it is innocent rather than evil; and which, on the other hand, leads him to concepts of God and immortality which correspond to man as a *human* being rather than as an exclusively *rational* one. Taking issue with the Kantian concept of the *summum bonum*, Cohen alters all the concepts bound up with it. Moral law alone, and nothing else, is the end.[27] Personality alone is the object of religion and morality; any additional object—such as happiness—is deleterious to both.[28] Indeed, Cohen goes so far as to reject, in the name of Kant's own ethics and as being inconsistent with that ethics, his entire notion of a *summum bonum*.[29] Kant had inquired into the practical possibility of the *summum bonum*, a question which arises if deserved happiness, as well as moral goodness, is the end. Cohen does not answer the question, but rather rejects it, for the possibility of the sole good (i.e., the good will) lies in the will itself: "Even the [Kantian] question: how is the highest Good practically possible? is deleterious. The question no longer exists."[30]

Thus Cohen eliminates every moral concern with happiness. Others might accept this as a Kantian concession to man's humanity. Cohen rejects it as a moral impurity. According to a well-known story, Cohen is said to have complained that Zionism aimed at normalcy and happiness in behalf of the Jewish people. Perhaps one may ask whether, had he held fast to the realistic as well as to the idealistic elements in the Kantian philosophy, he would have judged any living people, the Jewish included, by so abstractly idealistic, and indeed superhuman, a moral standard.

It is only a consequence of these alterations in Kantian doctrine that any

God, other than the Idea of God, is eliminated. Kant's own doctrine may not be wholly clear, yet the texts give ample warrant for our assertion that Kant's God is not reducible to his Idea of God. Cohen on his part understands (or corrects) Kant as follows:

> God is not author of the moral law; nor the distributor of happiness, nor He who supplies or completes the material conditions of the physical possibility of a final end understood in terms of happiness. . . . According to the critical method, the God-Idea is inescapable as Ground of the harmony between natural and moral teleology, understood as a necessary limiting notion. If the intelligible Ideas [of natural and moral teleology] are already unconditional, then the Idea of God is the Unconditional of these unconditionals, a maxim of a higher degree and of enlarged scope.[31]

IV

The passage just cited leads us to turn from the weakness in Cohen's Kantianism to its strength. This lies in the fact, already referred to, that he builds Jewish moral and religious commitments into Kantianism itself. Perhaps it is not too much to say that it is through these that he regains the contact with reality which, thus far, seems wholly lost.

At first sight it seems that the cited passage does nothing except further emphasize Cohen's weakness, i.e., his lack of realism. Indeed, its content—the God-Idea—may seem to be the ultimate philosophical expression of the weakness. We have thus far found that, unlike Kant himself, Cohen makes no basic concession to human sensuousness, and hence demands nothing less than the recreation of real men in accordance with the idea of humanity. Now we seem to find that in trying to live up to this unrealistic and unreal demand men receive no aid from a real God but merely from the unreal God idea.

But, as Franz Rosenzweig has warned, Cohen's God-Idea is not a *mere* idea:

> Quite apart from the fact that for Cohen an Idea is not a "mere" idea, God Himself is as little a "poetic expression" of the Idea of God as the fact of the mathematical cognition of nature is a poetic expression of the logic of pure cognition. This philosophy avoids strictly any identification of its concepts with its objects, despite the fact that it refers with every step *to* an object.[32]

What is the object referred to by Cohen's God-Idea? The *Ethik des reinen Willens*, Cohen's book in which the God-Idea first finds full philosophical expression, yields a remarkable answer. The work sharply repudiates some varieties of religious experience, notably ancient polytheistic mythology (which, being dead, no longer constitutes a danger) and pantheism (which is very much alive and dangerous), for these, identifying as they do what is with what ought to be, are destructive of genuine morality. At the same time, the work also welcomes other varieties of religious experience, notably Platonism (which is a precursor of sorts of Kantianism) and modern Protestantism (for which, in the interpretation which he gives it, Cohen has a lifelong feeling of affinity). The fact which arrests us, however, and which is altogether without precedent, is that in this purely philosophical modern work a specifically and uniquely Jewish religious experience is assigned an indispensable and indeed foundational role. Cohen writes: "Prophetic Messianism . . . is the most tremendous idea which ethics must borrow and absorb from a reality alien to philosophical methodology."[33]

This "tremendous" idea is and remains Jewish even though Protestantism, as Cohen interprets it, has come to share in it. How does this "borrowed and absorbed" reality manifest its presence in the *Ethik des reinen Willens*? From the aspects of Cohen's thought which we have thus far considered it may appear that he cannot but teach an unworldly ethics in which the will is concerned with nothing other than its own purity, and in which real men and their real moral concerns are neglected in favor of a shadowy idea of mankind. It comes as a surprise that nothing is further from the truth. Cohen attacks any notion that "the earth is ruled by politics while religion is destined for heaven":[34] ethics is to make religion descend from heaven to earth and to transform politics in its own image. The "pure will" is not inapplicable; rather it finds "the deepest confirmation of [its] purity in its applicability."[35] And while there is no moral will without inwardness, a will is merely thought, not will at all, if it is inwardness alone; true will requires "externalization" and action.[36] But all action takes place in the world.

In the context of the *Ethik des reinen Willens* these doctrines seem hardly intelligible except for the "borrowed and absorbed" reality of Jewish Messianism. The gods of pantheism and polytheism are at home in the world; but they dissolve what ought to be into what is. On His part, a transcendent metaphysical God dwells beyond the world; but He inspires philosophers and mystics themselves to rise above the world in order that they might know Him. There is salvation in none of these deities. There is salvation only in the God of the Jewish prophets. These witness to a new God, one, unique, and other than the world, yet a God who announces to men what is good *in* the world. He is a God men will know, not when they explore His essence, but only when they hear His commandments and do His will.[37] And His will must be done in the world.

What is His will? That each man, created in the divine image, be an end in himself.[38] That mankind be one as He is one. That there be international right and justice, socialism and peace.[39]

These are demands which relate to the future. The gods of myth point to the past. Addressing the moral will (which is geared to the future),[40] the prophetic God Himself points to the future.[41] *And since His moral demand is uncompromising, the future pointed to is Messianic.* Here lies the core of the Jewish "reality borrowed and absorbed" by Cohen's moral philosophy.

Here too is the secret which enables Cohen to reconcile an uncompromisingly "idealistic" demand made of the human will with a no less uncompromising concern with the "real"—social, economic and political—world. For if one inquires into the link between ideality and reality—into the ground which prevents the ideal from becoming a mere shadow and the real from being brute fact—there is no doubt as to the answer: it is a moral passion which equals in intensity and source of inspiration, if not in the source of validation, that of the Jewish prophets. Only if this strength is seen in Cohen's thought is his weakness, described earlier, seen in the proper perspective.

As Cohen "borrows and absorbs" Jewish Messianism in his philosophical ethics he is forced to ask an all-important question: "What actuality is guaranteed for the ethical?"[42] Jewish faith has its own answer to this question. Man must work for the Messiah, *and also* wait for him. He can and must do both because the Messianic future is joint work of man *and God.* And such is the dialectical relation between the two that the Messiah may come when men have become good enough to make his coming possible, or wicked enough to make it necessary. Yet even though human goodness or wickedness be extreme, men still may not calculate the end; this is a secret in the keeping of God.

Radical alterations of this Jewish doctrine are forced upon Cohen in the process of philosophical "absorption." This is because a fundamental "gulf" exists between all religion, the Jewish included, and his own neo-Kantian ethics: "ethics can tolerate no external ground."[43] The Reformation has rightly "deified" freedom. The Kantian ethics which has given philosophic form to this deification has recognized that the moral will can have nothing external to it, either to command it or to aid it in its moral performance. The moral will is self-determined (and, in fact, will-to-self); and the Messianic future does not require a togetherness of working and waiting: it is "eternal task" only, demanding nothing but "eternal labor."[44] No help external to "labor" is either possible or necessary.

What "actuality," then, *is* "guaranteed" for "the ethical?" It may well seem that Cohen's philosophical "absorption" of the Jewish faith destroys every hope of an affirmative answer. For if man alone must do the work, then surely, to put it mildly, his record in the past provides little hope for the future, and no guarantee. A traditional Jewish believer might justifiably have said, "I must in my moral labor . . . be wholly independent of and unworried by the question of success";[45] for he believed that God and man each does his work. Such a statement, when appearing in the *Ethik des Reinen Willens,* may well seem to reflect a total and desperate divorce of ideality from the real world.

Yet it is precisely in response to this problem that Cohen arrives at his Idea of God. In my moral labor I *must* be independent of the question of success. I *can have* this independence only because of the Idea of God. The Idea of God, therefore, is by no means a religious Idea only, extraneous to ethics. It is indispensably part of Cohen's ethics itself and, indeed, its "basic principle of truth."

What is Cohen's Idea of God? Not the existing God of Judaism, for his philosophical ethics can accept no God who is the source, external to the moral will, of either given commandments or (pre-Messianic or Messianic) salvation. But, as Franz Rosenzweig has stressed, neither is He a "mere"— i.e., human—idea. Even a moral Idea is not a merely human idea, for it has power over the will. The Idea of God, moreover, is not a moral Idea only but rather the Ultimate Idea in which *what is* is linked with *what ought to be.* The Idea, therefore, has power over theory as well as practice, over human cognition as well as over the human will. The God of Judaism promises perfection on earth. Cohen's God-Idea guarantees "*self*-perfection . . . on earth."[46] The *existing* God of Judaism *acts*, both in commanding men to prepare the world for the Messianic Kingdom, and in Himself helping to bring that kingdom about. Cohen's God-Idea is a *necessary Thought*—indeed, the *ultimate* necessary Thought—which arises in the philosophical consciousness as, having been forced to separate what is and what ought to be, it is forced also to join together what it has set apart. For all one can tell from the *Ethik des reinen Willens,* Judaism has dissolved itself into a rational, philosophical ethics. But in so doing it has done nothing less than give that ethics a stamp which it could have received from no other source.

V

Franz Rosenzweig made a prediction concerning Hermann Cohen's great posthumous work, the *Religion der Vernunft aus den Quellen des Judentums.* He wrote that "it will still be alive when one day his [philosophical] system will have gone the way of all systems."[47] Fifty years after Cohen's death it looks as if both parts of Rosenzweig's prediction are justified. It was when, toward the end of his life and almost as an afterthought, he turned to Judaism in its own right, that Cohen became what Julius Guttmann has called the renewer of the philosophy of Judaism, and earned immortality.[48]

Certainly one half of Rosenzweig's prediction seems confirmed. Not only Cohen's system of ethical idealism, but all philosophical systems have come under severe criticism during the last fifty years—on the one hand, by Anglo-Saxon philosophical analysis, and, on the other hand, by Continental, existentialist protests. Moreover, Cohen's particular system—his idealism, his optimism, his progressivist interpretation of history—might have suffered collapse under the impact of recent history, even if it had survived during the recent history of philosophy. Great indeed is the gulf between the present age and the pre–World War I era. To be sure, present philosophers—and theologians too—would do well not to dismiss Cohen's ethical idealism too cavalierly, for many of their themes are but pale reflections of what is found in Cohen. Even so, only fragments of Cohen are acceptable. Taken as a whole, Cohen's system, it appears, has gone the way of all systems.

Still more obviously gone is any notion, offered on whatever grounds and coming from whatever source, that Judaism be dissolved into pure universalism. Cohen in any case never quite adopted that view,[49] and he explicitly turned away from it in the last phase of his thought which is yet to be considered. What concerns us presently is that his philosophical version of the Messianic faith would no longer be Jewishly acceptable even if philosophers could still accept it. After the Nazi Holocaust and the rise of the state of Israel—free but embattled and endangered—the Messianic faith is in any case gravely problematic, for even the most pious of Jews knows himself to be commanded to fight for the survival of Jewish particularity in the here and now, even as he waits and works for universalistic Messianic goals. Quite certain is that the Jew of today can put far less trust in Cohen's God-Idea than in the ancient God of Israel. What remains "guaranteed" by the God-Idea in a world in which Auschwitz is actual? Cohen asserts that "the perfectibility of development . . . can take place, must take place," and he cites as empirical support of this "must" that biological evolution has not stopped with the apes, nor historical development with savagery.[50] Yet Auschwitz dwarfs all savagery. For the Jewish philosophy of today to stay with the God-Idea would be to reduce it to a necessary thought *only*, divorced from history and therefore impotent. Such a divorce, however, would be contrary to Cohen's innermost intentions.

So much for one-half of Rosenzweig's prediction. What of the other half? This too seems confirmed, and this despite the fact that, to judge by the conflict among the interpreters of the *Religion der Vernunft*, it is still too soon to appraise the final significance of this masterpiece of Cohen's old age. Thus according to one group of interpreters (which includes Rosenzweig himself),[51] Cohen's work breaks through the circle of idealism, reaches out, beyond the Idea of God, to God, and thus initiates our own contemporary, postidealistic philosophy of Judaism. According to the other group,[52] however, it remains within the circle of idealism and merely extends its scope. What is not doubted by either group is that, whereas in Cohen's earlier thought aspects of Judaism are taken from their native context into another, in Cohen's last phase Judaism remains in its own context even as it is transformed into a "religion of reason." Moreover, the transformation may not be purely one-sided. A religion of reason is *illustrated* by "the sources of Judaism." At the same time, these "sources" have a living power which may well expand, or alter, the bounds to which normal "reason" is confined. It is, in any case, not in doubt that Judaism and philosophy are both alive in the *Religion der Vernunft*. And this fact alone would suffice to give Cohen's work a lasting significance in Jewish religious philosophy.

Concerning Cohen's earlier thought, Rosenzweig asks whether "he could ever have seriously believed that his distant image of God and man in a Messianic mankind exhausted everything that could happen between God and man."[53] Whether or not Cohen ever seriously believed this he was in any case philosophically compelled to assert it. And the question therefore arises as to the philosophical grounds which enabled him to abandon the earlier view in his last period, and thus to reestablish contact with Judaism in its own right. In the *Religion der Vernunft* we find not only Messianic redemption but also creation and revelation. We come upon not only moral action but also human prayer and divine forgiveness. These aspects of what in Judaism "happens between God and man," Cohen, a pious and knowledgeable Jew in his youth, had been forced to suspend, reinterpret or abandon during his Marburg period. How and in what sense was he able to restore them in the great work of his old age?

The *Religion der Vernunft* continues to insist on an "unshakable connection" between ethics and religion; it recognizes, however, a "limit" to ethics, at which limit it appears that religion is "*sui generis*."[54] Ethics is confined to the universal; religion, insofar as it differs from ethics, is concerned with the individual. More precisely, there is a cleavage between the universal which I ought to do and be, and the individual who I am; but whereas before the bar of ethics the meaning of individuality is exhausted by the universal goal to which it is directed, in the light of religion individuality achieves meaning and significance in its own right, i.e., for what it is, as well as for what it ought to be. Morality demands the recreation of actual men in the image of the idea of mankind. Sympathy loves actual men for what they are. The God of the prophets looks forward, to the Messianic future. The God of the psalmist looks downward, to forgive present men in their sinful misery. In short, what may be called a reality principle has appeared in Cohen's thought which was wholly absent in its earlier phase.

One can readily see why it might seem obvious that with these assertions Cohen breaks through the circle of idealism. A God-Idea may be the source of moral commandment, and perhaps guarantee, if not Messianic fulfillment, so at least our necessary belief in it. Surely none except an existing God can love the sinner, hear prayer and grant forgiveness. The case, however, is far from being so obvious. For one thing, Cohen grants that religion is *sui generis* but denies its independence from morality, and indeed for him to do otherwise would be to produce a crisis in his whole ethical idealism. For another thing, he is in the *Religion der Vernunft* still able to make statements such as the following: "How can one love an Idea? One must answer: how can one love anything except an Idea? Even in sensuous love one loves only the idealized person, only the Idea of the person."[55]

The settlement of the dispute between the Cohen interpreters depends on the meaning of one crucial concept which appears only in the last phase of Cohen's thought: that of a *God-man correlation*. Concerning this concept (which in the *Religion der Vernunft* appears in the most varied connections) one thing is clear: the separateness of man and God is affirmed in their very relation. This separateness, indeed, constitutes the "ultimate meaning"[56] of correlation. Pantheism dissolves man into God. Even a monotheism which were ethical only might do so in the infinite future, if not now. Correlation keeps God and man apart even as it relates them; thus it makes possible "the salvation of individuality [which] is the proper task of religion."[57] Whatever else it may mean, then, the concept of correlation grounds what has already been referred to as the new reality principle in the last phase of Cohen's thought.

But precisely *how* is this reality principle grounded and what is its significance? Is there an actual, correlative relation between man and God? Or is that relation a necessary philosophic thought? On weighing the evidence—which here cannot be reproduced—we must agree with those who deny that Cohen's *Religion der Vernunft* breaks the circle of idealism.[58] The Jewish worshiper may stand in a living relationship to the forgiving God. For the philosopher, the loving God, His acts of forgiveness, His correlation with man which preserves human individuality, are all necessary Ideas. "God, as member of the correlation, is not a personal Thou, but Idea, however much what fills . . . this methodically deduced concept in the religious life may assume personal features."[59]

If this is the correct interpretation of Cohen's *Religion der Vernunft*, it would certainly follow that the work is not, as Franz Rosenzweig thought, the first pioneering work in the development of a postidealistic philosophy of Judaism. Martin Buber, in that case, spoke in criticism of Cohen when he said:

> The love of man for God is not the love for the moral Ideal; it only includes the Ideal. He who loves God only as moral Ideal may easily despair of the guidance of the world, which appears to contradict in every hour all principles of his moral ideality. . . . He who loves God loves the Ideal, and loves more than it. Moreover, he knows himself to be loved, not by an Idea or Ideal but rather by Him who cannot be grasped by Ideality alone—who is absolute Person.[60]

Even so, however, Rosenzweig's prediction remains valid. The *Religion der Vernunft* remains alive even if what must be sought by a postidealistic philosophy of Judaism is not the God-Idea but, beyond it, the absolute Person. For a postidealistic philosophy of Judaism is one thing; a lapse into philosophical naiveté would be another. The circle of idealism must be broken; its existence can be neither denied nor ignored. The living God of Judaism does not reduce Himself to the Idea of God; except for the idea of God, He can neither withstand philosophical criticism nor, indeed, be comprehensible. The conclusions reached by Hermann Cohen's *Religion der Vernunft* are no longer alive in Jewish religious philosophy; the issues with which that work grapples will live on.

VI

This would hardly be the case if the work had been inspired by abstract philosophical thought alone. Perhaps the most remarkable fact about this remarkable Jewish thinker is that, rigorous though Hermann Cohen is as regards self-imposed intellectual discipline, a genuinely Jewish passion can be felt again and again underneath. It can be felt even in the writings of his Marburg period, which touch only marginally upon Judaism. In the *Religion der Vernunft* it is unmistakable. To be sure, even here philosophical thought contains and controls the religious life which is comprehended and interpreted. But perhaps the greatest moments of this great work occur when containment is strained and control is only barely possible. With great perception Martin Buber said:

> Hermann Cohen is a great example of the philosopher who is overwhelmed by faith. He objectified the results of having-been-overwhelmed philosophically, and incorporated them into his system of concepts. Nowhere in his writings does he give direct testimony. Nevertheless, the signs are unmistakable.[61]

Four

Martin Buber's Concept of Revelation

I

The core of both the Jewish and the Christian faiths is the belief that a God who is other than the world nevertheless enters into the world; that He enters into the world because He enters into the life of man. The Jewish and Christian God descends to meet man, and "a man does not pass, from the moment of supreme meeting, the same being as he entered into it."[1] Judaism and Christianity, or groups within either faith, may differ as to what, more specifically, revelation is; they may also differ as to when it has taken place, when it takes place, or when it will take place. But they agree that God *can* reveal Himself and that, in the entire history of man, He has done so at least once.

This core of religious belief persisted unimpaired until the Age of Enlightenment. But since that time it has become the object of ever more formidable criticism. There may be no conflict between modern thought and Biblical "monotheism," taken by itself, or between modern thought and Biblical "ethics," taken by itself. But there does seem to be a necessary conflict between modern thought and the Biblical belief in revelation. All claims to revelation, modern science and philosophy seem agreed, must be repudiated, as mere relics of superstitious ages. But Biblical "monotheism" is the monotheism of a self-revealing God, and Biblical "ethics" is an aspect of His revelation. Neither the monotheism nor the ethics can, without distortion, be taken by itself. The conflict between modern thought and the Biblical faith is therefore radical.

This fact did not become fully clear until the nineteenth century. Until that time, most modern thinkers were prepared to exempt spheres of reality from critical inquiry, provided they were protected by the walls of a sacred authority, and the "supernatural" was permitted to live behind such walls. But the nineteenth century—the age of critical history, Biblical criticism, and, last but not least, critical psychology—did away with all authorities, sacred or otherwise, and the moment this happened the modern assault on revelation exhibited itself as unqualified and radical.

The modern attack was directed not merely on a particular claim on behalf of an actual revelation, or even on all such claims. It was directed on the very *possibility* of revelation; and this was because it seemed radically incompatible not merely with this or that modern principle, but with the one principle basic to all modern thought, namely, the supreme principle of rational inquiry. This asserted that knowledge consisted in the discovery of uniformities, and that to hit upon the nonuniform was not to discover an exception to uniformity, but merely to become aware of one's ignorance. There were no lawless or causeless events; there were merely events whose laws or causes were not, or not yet, known.

It followed from this principle that there could be no revelations, that is, events not wholly due to natural laws or causes. There could only be a belief in revelations; and this was possible only because of partial or total ignorance of the laws or causes actually responsible for the events in question. To refute the belief in revelation, it was not necessary to discover the particular natural laws or causes of particular "revelations"; it was enough to know that all events must have such laws or causes: and to know *that* was to understand that revelation is in principle impossible.

Despite his rationalism, a medieval metaphysician such as Maimonides could allow miraculous interruptions of the order of nature, of which revelation was the most important instance.[2] A modern metaphysician could not allow such interruptions. To him, all miracles were only apparent miracles, and all revelations only apparent revelations. God, if admitted at all, was either a power beyond the universe or a force within it. The Biblical God—who is beyond the universe yet enters into it—was a mere myth of bygone ages.

The same conclusion was reached by those who, scorning metaphysical speculation, confined themselves to the analysis of human experience. A medieval empiricist such as Judah Hallevi[3] could argue for revelation by pointing to the authority of the six hundred thousand Israelites who had been present at Mount Sinai. A modern empiricist would reject this argument even if the dubious appeal to authority could be eliminated, that is, if he could project himself into the past so as to be personally present at Mount Sinai. To be sure, he might, in such a situation, hear not merely the thunder but also the voice of God. But his subsequent analysis would quickly eliminate the latter. He had heard the thunder because there had been thunder to be heard. But whatever the causes of his hearing of a voice of God, among them had not been an actual voice of God. For such a voice was not, on the one hand, a physical or psychical event, nor could it, on the other, interrupt the orderly sequence of such events. Hence the hearing of the voice of God had merely been an imagined hearing, mistaken for real hearing only by the ignorant.

How could the modern Jew or Christian meet this attack on revelation? He could, of course, simply refuse to meet it at all. But this could perhaps satisfy his heart but hardly his mind. Or he could seek shelter behind ancient authorities. But these no longer provided shelter. For a time it seemed that there was only one thing that could honestly be done, and that was to give in by "modernizing" the ancient faiths. A modernized faith was a faith without revelation. God became—as in Deism past and present—a reality external to the world unable to enter into human experience; or He became—as in religious idealism past and present[4]—a force immanent in human experience which could not exist, or could exist only incompletely, apart from human experience.[5] All these modernized versions of the ancient faiths had this in common: God could not reveal Himself, that is, be present to man. The God of religious idealism is at most present *in* man, never present *to* man; and the God of Deism cannot be present at all.

But since the middle of the nineteenth century, it has become gradually clear that retreat was not the only way in which to meet the modern attack on revelation. It was possible to counterattack. But this had to be done in rather a special way. One could not meet the attack on revelation by simply attacking, in turn, the principle on which the attack was based. To reject, or arbitrarily limit, the principle of modern rational inquiry was merely to fall prey, wittingly or unwittingly, to obscurantism. But it was possible that that principle, while unlimited in application, nevertheless applied only within a sphere which was itself limited, and that revelation fell outside that sphere.

This possibility first became obvious through the work of Immanuel Kant, who argued that the law- or cause-discovering kind of knowledge discloses only a phenomenal world. But Kant's argument neither sprang from a wish to defend revelation, nor did it issue, in Kant himself, in a defense of revelation. This latter task was undertaken by religious existentialism. If the law-or cause-discovering kind of knowledge is phenomenal, existentialism argues, it is because it presupposes the detachment of a knower who makes the world his object. So long as he perseveres in this standpoint he discovers laws upon laws or causes upon causes. But what he discovers in this way is, as a whole, not reality, but merely reality made into an object or objectified. Reality ceases to be an object if we cease to view it as an object; that is, if instead of viewing it in detachment we become engaged with it in personal commitment. In such a personal commitment there is knowing access to the transphenomenal, an access which consists not in the discovery of laws or causes, but in a direct encounter. And the most important fact that can be encountered is divine revelation.

This argument, first stated by Schelling and Kierkegaard in the mid-nineteenth century, has found its most profound spokesman in our time in Martin Buber. To examine his argument is the task of the present essay. Such an examination must necessarily subordinate all its efforts to answering a single question: is Buber's counter-attack on the modern attack on revelation successful? Does he make it possible at the same time to accept without compromise the modern principle of rational inquiry and yet to embrace the ancient faith in a self-revealing God?

II

This question cannot even be raised, let alone be answered, by a biographical account, that is, the kind of account which explains an author's teachings in terms of his personal experience. The more perceptive of the modern critics of revelation are quite prepared to admit that there is experience-of-revelation; but they deny that there is revelation. They grant that there are those who sincerely believe themselves in dialogue with God; but they assert that all such dialogues are but disguised monologues.[6] If Buber has a reply to this criticism, it cannot consist in his personal experience; and the interpreter who looks for such a reply cannot look for it in that experience. For the question is not whether, from the standpoint of religious experience, there appears to be revelation. The question is whether there is, or at least can be, revelation; that is, whether the religious standpoint which accepts the category of revelation is justified.

The faults of the biographical approach are not remedied by an emphasis on Buber's lifelong encounter with traditional sources, notably Hasidism and the Hebrew Bible. There is no doubt that Buber's historical studies are closely related to his own views, particularly as regards revelation. Indeed, his chief merit as a Bible interpreter may well be seen in his insistence that the Bible be understood in Biblical ("dialogue between God and man") rather than in modern ("religious experience," "evolution of ideas," and the like) categories. But by itself this insistence only means that Buber has understood the Biblical belief in revelation; it does not mean that he has justified his own acceptance of it.

This last point is nicely illustrated by the fact that Buber did not always accept the belief in revelation. In 1911 he wrote: "the spiritual process of Judaism is . . . the striving for the ever more perfect realization of three internally connected ideas: the idea of unity, the idea of action and the idea of the future; these ideas . . . are not abstract tendencies, but natural tendencies of folk character."[7] Had Buber retained the standpoint indicated in this passage he could without doubt have mustered, as a historian, the imagination necessary in order to understand the Biblical belief in revelation; but he would have at the same time asserted, as a philosopher, that what was to Biblical man a dialogue with God was in fact a form of human self-realization and nothing else; that is, a disguised monologue.

The conclusion, then, is clear. Our approach to Buber's work must be systematic, not biographic. Only a systematic account can answer the questions which must be answered if Buber's stature as a thinker who is modern and yet affirms revelation is to be fairly appraised. The questions are: Does

Martin Buber's Concept of Revelation

Buber offer a doctrine intended to meet the modern critique of revelation? And if so, does his doctrine in fact meet that critique?

III

The first of these two questions can be answered at once in the affirmative. Buber does offer a doctrine of revelation intended, among other things, to meet the modern critique of revelation. This is an extension of a wider doctrine which must first be considered briefly. We refer to the celebrated doctrine of the "*I*" and the "*Thou.*"

There are, Buber teaches, two types of relation I may establish with another, namely, an *I-It* and an *I-Thou* relation. I have an *I-It* relation when I use the other, or when I know the other in an attitude of objective detachment. These relations are one-sided, for the other is for me while I am not for the other. When I use or observe the other, my person remains unengaged. The other cannot *do* anything to me; that is, even if the other happens to be a person, I am not open to him as a person but treat him as a mere object.

The *I-It* relation is abstract. Users and objective observers, on the one hand, objects of use or observation, on the other, are interchangeable. In using an object, I never intend the unique object but merely a *kind* of object; and in observing it my inevitable aim is to bring it under general laws of which it is a mere instance. The unique individuality of the other does not enter into the *I-It* relation.

Nor does the unique individuality of the *I*. *Qua* user, I am only a *kind* of user; and the supreme condition of all objective observation is that anyone who would take my place would observe the same. In the *I-It* relation anyone else *could* take my place.

The *I-It* relation contrasts in every respect with the *I-Thou* relation. This relation is, above all, mutual. The other is for me, but I am also for the other. I do something to the other, but the other also does something to me. This happens in the relation of dialogue, which is a relation of address and response-to-address. The other addresses me and responds to my address; that is, even if the other happens to be a lifeless and speechless object, it is treated as one treats a person.

It would, to be sure, be gross anthropomorphizing to assert that the lifeless object *is* a person; that a tree or a stone can be an *I* to themselves and I a *Thou* to them. But it is not anthropomorphic to assert that I can be an *I* to myself, and the tree or stone a *Thou* to me. From the standpoint of one partner at least, the human partner, *I-Thou* relations are possible, not only with other human beings, but with anything whatever. This is not to say that such relations are easy, or possible to anyone, or possible at any time. It is merely to say that there are no a priori limitations to the possible partners I may have in an *I-Thou* relationship.

While the *I-It* relationship is necessarily abstract, the *I-Thou* relationship cannot be abstract. The partners communicate not this or that, but themselves; that is, they must be in the communication. Further—since the relation of dialogue is mutual—they must be in a state of openness to the other, that is, to *this* other at *this* time and in *this* place. Hence both the *I* and the *Thou* of every genuine dialogue are irreplaceable. Every dialogue is unique.

All this is possible only because the *I* is not a complete, self-sufficient substance. In the *I-Thou* relation I *become* an *I* by virtue of the relationship to a *Thou*. My whole being enters into the meeting, to emerge from it other than it was. And what is essential between an *I* and a *Thou*—such as love and friendship—is not in the mind of either the *I* or the *Thou*, or even in the minds of both; it is *between* an *I* and a *Thou*, who would both be essentially different if the relation did not exist. To be sure, there are relations in which there is nothing between the *I* and the other, and which do not alter the substance of the *I*; but these, far from being original relations with another, are merely the kind of derivative relations in which "reflexion" or "withdrawal"[8] has corrupted the immediacy of openness: in other words, *I-It* relations. Only from the standpoint of this corrupt state—into which we all perforce often fall—does the dialogue with a *Thou* appear as an unessential act on the part of a self-complete and self-sufficient *I*. In truth it is what constitutes both the *I* and the *Thou*, to the extent to which they are constituted at all. And in the actual dialogue this is known to both.[9]

It is not necessary, for our present purpose, to describe Buber's doctrine of the *I* and *Thou* in further detail. But it is necessary to ask: Is it a doctrine at all, that is, a body of metaphysical and epistemological assertions? Or is it a pure homily, that is, the kind of teaching intended solely for spiritual guidance?

This question is of crucial importance. It will be seen that Buber's teaching concerning revelation is an application of his teaching concerning the *I* and *Thou*. If the latter were a pure homily the same would necessarily be true of the former. But whatever the undoubted religious merits of a homily on revelation, it could only ignore, but not come to grips with, the modern critique of revelation. This latter, as we have seen, readily admits that there may be experience-of-revelation yet stoutly denies that there can be revelation. If this criticism is to be met rather than ignored, there is need, in addition and indeed logically prior to appeals which might make men spiritually receptive to revelation, for a doctrine which argues, against the modern critique, that the category of revelation in terms of which the religious standpoint understands itself is the category in terms of which it must be understood.

But Buber's teaching concerning the *I* and *Thou* is not a pure homily; it is a doctrine as well. Indeed, it is the latter rather than the former that distinguishes his work from that of many others. Literature abounds with poems which describe, and sermons which exalt, the wealth of interpersonal relationships. *Buber's distinctive teaching lies in his interpretation of the* I-Thou *relation, as such, and as contrasted with the* I-It *relation, as such.*

An illustration will serve to show, both that Buber's teaching is a doctrine, and what the doctrine is. Consider a scientific psychologist who also, it happens, has near-perfect *I-Thou* relations with his wife, his children and close friends. His professional business is to understand people as cases falling under laws; but his private life is such as to enable him to understand those close to him in living dialogue. But would such a person grant that both kinds of knowledge *are* knowledge? If his outlook were typical, he would assert that only the former kind of knowledge has any chance of getting at the truth about human nature, for it alone is objective; the latter kind of "knowledge" cannot be regarded as knowledge at all precisely because it is engaged; it is the sort of "biased" opinion which has a right to persist only because it is indispensable in life.

Now if Buber has a quarrel with this hypothetical psychologist, it is clearly neither with his psychology nor with his way of life. As for his psychology, it must be, like all science, a form of *I-It* knowledge. And as for his way of life, it is *ex hypothesi* such as to find Buber's complete approval. It follows that if Buber's teaching were a pure homily, there would be no quarrel at all. Yet a quarrel there certainly is. It concerns the epistemological status of *I-Thou* and *I-It* knowledge, and the metaphysical status of *Thou* and *It,* respectively. The hypothetical psychologist has one doctrine in this matter, and Buber can quarrel with it only because he too has a doctrine.

But Buber's doctrine is diametrically opposite. It asserts that *in the committed* I-Thou *relation there is knowing access to a reality which is inaccessible otherwise; that uncommitted "objective" knowledge which observes as an* It *what may also be encountered as a* Thou *is a lesser kind of knowledge, and that the most profound mistake in all philosophy is the epistemological reduction of* I-Thou *to* I-It *knowledge, and the metaphysical reduction of* Thou *to* It.

We must subsequently ask whether, and if so how, Buber defends this most basic of all his doctrines. For the moment it is enough to observe that, if adequately defended, it can be the basis for a counterattack on the modern attack on revelation. For, first, it implies complete acceptance of the modern principle of rational inquiry; secondly, it yet limits the sphere to which that principle applies; thirdly, it points beyond this sphere to quite another sphere in which it is at least not impossible that revelation could be found.

Buber accepts the modern principle of rational inquiry because he finds a legitimate place for *I-It* knowledge. His acceptance of the principle is complete because there is no attempt on his part to limit arbitrarily the range of *I-It* knowledge. Science has the world as its object, and this world—which includes the psychological world—displays itself to rational inquiry as a unity shattered by no irrational incursions of God. The doctrine of the

I and *Thou* is not at war either with specific conclusions of science or with the assumptions which underlie science as a whole.

It is at war, however, with all metaphysics which regard reality as an *It* or a system of *Its*, and with all epistemologies which reduce all knowledge to *I-It* knowledge. It is also at war, therefore, with the kind of philosophy which identifies reality as understood by science with reality as it ultimately is, and scientific with metaphysical knowledge. For the doctrine of the *I* and *Thou*, every *It*, including the *It* of science, is something less than the fullness of reality, whether an "objectification," "abstraction" or "logical construct"; and all *I-It* knowledge, including scientific knowledge, falls short of being metaphysical knowledge, that is, of grasping reality in its fullness. Rational inquiry ties *It* to *It* but remains itself tied to the world of *It*. Thus Buber limits the sphere to which the principle of rational inquiry applies.

This sphere is transcended not when the *I* comes upon an *It* supposedly escaping rational inquiry, but when the *I* abandons the detachment of the *I-It* relation for the engagement of the *I-Thou* relation. If the *Thou* escapes rational inquiry, it is not because the latter is rational but because it presupposes detachment.[10] And the shortcomings of rational inquiry are epistemological and metaphysical only because the engaged *I-Thou* dialogue is itself a form of knowledge; indeed, it is the form of knowledge in which the fullness of reality is encountered.

It follows, as we have said, that the doctrine of the *I* and *Thou* can be a basis for a counterattack on the modern attack on revelation. For while the system of laws or causes is never shattered from the standpoint of *I-It* detachment it is always shattered from the standpoint of *I-Thou* engagement. If the doctrine of the *I* and *Thou* is true, there is no need for special doctrinal provisions for the reconciliation of the category of revelation with the principle of rational inquiry.

But the doctrine of the *I* and *Thou* is no more than a mere basis for a modern doctrine of revelation. By itself, it justifies not the positive assertion of the possibility of revelation, but merely the bare empty denial of its impossibility; and it justifies even that only on the assumption that it is part of an *I-Thou* rather than of an *I-It* relation. To justify more positive assertions, it is necessary that the general doctrine of the *I* and *Thou* be extended into a doctrine of revelation. This latter must accomplish three tasks. It must show that religion is an *I-Thou* rather than an *I-It* relation; it must identify the criteria which distinguish it from all other *I-Thou* relations; and it must locate revelation within it.

IV

We may begin with Buber's critique of the widely held view that religion is feeling. For Buber, all genuine religion is an *I-Thou* relation with God, rather than merely subjective feeling. "Feelings are a mere accompaniment

Martin Buber's Concept of Revelation

to the metaphysical and metapsychical fact of the relation which is fulfilled not in the soul but *between* the *I* and *Thou*."[11]

A "religion" whose essence is feeling is either the mere solitary disport of the soul with itself, cut off from God; or, if not cut off from God, not a relation; or, if a relation, not immediate. But the first—subjective feeling by itself—is not religion but merely the pseudo-religion of a degenerate age.[12] The second—God found in and identified with religious feeling— is mysticism, and mysticism is only a grandiose illusion. The third—God inferred from religious feeling—is at once pseudoreligion and bad philosophy.

Buber's argument in support of these assertions is the doctrine of the *I* and *Thou*. In every *I-Thou* relation the *I* is open to a *Thou*, not absorbed with images of a *Thou*; the latter state is not original, but the mere product of the corruption of "withdrawal."[13] Absorption with God-images too is a mere corruption; and this corruption is by no means overcome by an attempt to proceed by inference from the God-image to God Himself. For the God-image is a mere part of the self, and the inferred God a mere *It*.[14] If there is genuine religion at all, it can only consist of the direct dialogical meeting of the human *I* with a divine *Thou*.

This is why mysticism, too, is a form of pseudoreligion. For it denies either the reality of all meeting, or else at least that the supreme moment is a moment of meeting.[15] In the supreme moment of mysticism the *I*, rather than meet a *Thou*, dissolves into the Ineffable. But "all real living is meeting."[16] Mysticism, far from being a way into reality, is on the contrary a flight from it.

If there is such a thing as genuine religion it involves, on the human side, the kind of committed openness which is ready to address God and to be addressed by Him. But it also involves, on the divine side, a God who at least *can* be the partner in such a dialogical relationship. To be sure, it is not necessary that God should always be available for partnership, and genuine religion may consist, for long periods of time, of the mere human address which listens in vain for a reply. But all such addressing and listening would be wholly vain if God could not, by His very nature, be addressed or listened to. If religion is to be—as it must be—*between* God and man, revelation must at least be possible. Thus, the "modernized" religions without revelation are not merely religions which Buber happens to disagree with; they are not genuine religions at all. *Merely by virtue of being an* I-Thou *relation, all genuine religion involves at least the possibility of revelation.*

Further, merely by virtue of being part of an *I-Thou* relation, revelation must have certain characteristics. Above all, it must be the address of a *Thou* who *is in* what He communicates. Consequently, revelation cannot be either a system of dogmas[17] or a system of laws.[18] For both would cut the communication off from Him who communicates, thus perverting the living *I-Thou* dialogue into the fixity of the *I-It*. It will be seen, to be sure, that revelation must translate itself into human statement, and that an essential part of the statement is commandment.[19] But a genuine translation must spring from, and reflect, the pregnancy of the event of divine presence; and the commandment must give Him who commands along with the commandment. A *system* of dogmas is not the reflection of His presence, but a statement made about Him in His absence; and to obey a *system* of laws—independent in its validity of the Giver and of the hour for which He gives it—is not to respond to revelation but on the contrary to flee from it.

All this is true because the Giver who is present in the given is not a timeless Presence. The God of dialogue, like any Thou of any dialogue, speaks to a unique partner in a unique situation, disclosing Himself according to the unique exigencies of each situation. "If we name the speaker of this speech God, then it is always the God of a moment, a moment God."[20] If He has a general name at all, it is "I shall be who I shall be,"[21] that is, He who cannot be comprehended as He may be in His timeless essence, but can only be encountered in each here and now, as He may show Himself in each here and now.

These above implications for revelation may be derived from Buber's assertion that all genuine religion is an *I-Thou* relationship. But we must now ask what distinguishes religion from every other *I-Thou* relation, the divine *Thou* from every other *Thou*, and revelation from every other address. Such a quest for distinguishing criteria is clearly necessary. For in their total absence the very words "religion," "divine" and "revelation" would be meaningless to those not—or not yet—participating in a human-divine dialogue; and Buber would have to persuade them to decide to participate in such a dialogue, in total blindness not only as to whether it exists but even as to what it means. In short, Buber's doctrine of the *I* and *Thou* would turn into a pure homily at the precise point at which an attempt is made to extend it into a doctrine of revelation. And as we have already seen, such a homily on revelation, whatever its religious merits, could not come to grips with the modern critique of revelation. Why, even if he granted that there are all sorts of *I-Thou* relationships, should anyone grant that among them is a divine-human relationship, if the very word "divine" is meaningless to all except those who stand in such a relationship?

But would that word be meaningful even to those who *do* stand in such a relationship? To be sure, Buber tells us that the self-revealing God must be a *moment*-God, that is, a God whose self-disclosure cannot be anticipated by means of universal criteria. But he also tells us that the moment-God is a *God*, and that "out of the moment-Gods there arises for us with a single identity the Lord of the voice, the One."[22] But if all criteria of identification were totally lacking, how could the moment-Gods merge into the One God? Indeed, how could the moment-Gods be, and be recognized to be, Gods at all?

It is clearly necessary, then, to seek criteria in terms of which *concepts* of

Martin Buber's Concept of Revelation

God, religion and revelations may be framed. But we must not seek the wrong kind of criterion and the wrong kind of concept. A concept of revelation which contained, even only implicitly, the whole content of revelation would be a contradiction in terms. For revelation is the reception of the wholly new, but the concept would deny that it is wholly new; revelation demands committed openness which the concept would make impossible. The kind of concept required is the same that may be given of a *Thou* as such, or of a human *Thou* as such. The former may be defined as the kind of other who can be in dialogue with me, and the latter, as the kind of other who can be in human dialogue with me, that is, the kind of dialogue carried on through words and gestures. Both definitions, far from denying the uniqueness of every *Thou* and of every address, explicitly contain this element.

God, Buber asserts, is the *Thou* "that by its nature cannot become an *It*."[23] All genuine religion, therefore, is an *I-Thou* relationship with the *Thou* that cannot become an *It*; and every revelation reveals the *Thou* that cannot become an *It*. Here we have Buber's criterion of distinction.

But it is one thing to state the criterion, another to understand it. How can revelation be tied to the moment of encounter, revealing only a God of the moment, and yet reveal a God who cannot be an *It* at *any* moment? How can the God of the moment at the same time be recognized as infinite[24] and eternal?[25] And yet if He is not so recognized, it now seems, He is not recognized as God at all. Does this not mean that expressions such as "moment God" and "divine *Thou*" *are nothing less than contradictions in terms?*

The answer to all these questions is this, that *in the moment of revelation no It retains its independence.*[26] In that moment, every *It* becomes either a symbol through which God speaks, or the partner to whom He speaks. But the former is not an independent *It* and the latter is not an *It* at all. In making transparent every *It*, in the moment of His presence, God discloses that no *It* can remain opaque to His presence; that there can be both an independent *It* and a present God, but not both at the same time. In revealing Himself as "I shall be who I shall be," God does not disclose when or how He will be present. But He does disclose that He will be present as an *I*, if present at all.

Thus if God is known as eternal and infinite, it is not by thought which rises above the encounter to speculate on His essence; it is known *in* the encounter. God is infinite, because in the moment of encounter there is no *It* which can limit Him; He is eternal, because it is known in the here and now that He cannot turn into an *It* in any here and now.

This, then, is the minimum content of all revelation. But why is the minimum content not also the maximum content? Why does the God who reveals Himself as God nevertheless speak differently in every situation? This is because, while in the presence of the divine *Thou* no independent

It remains, an independent human *I* remains; indeed, it must remain if the divine *Thou* is to be a *Thou* at all. But while the divine *Thou* is infinite and eternal the human *I* is finite and temporal. The divine *Thou* speaks *into* the situation to a human *I* who can respond only out of the situation. But what He says into each situation transcends all conceptual anticipation.

Can there be conceptual anticipation of the human response to the divine address? Not, to be sure, of the particular response appropriate to each particular situation. But just as every revelation reveals the divine *Thou* every human response must be *to* the divine *Thou*. And this lends it a characteristic which distinguishes this response from every other kind.

Any response to any *Thou* requires, ideally, total commitment. But committed *I-Thou* relations in general can, and always do, degenerate into uncommitted *I-It* relations. Commitment, therefore, admits of degrees; and perhaps total commitment is an ideal which may be approximated but not wholly attained. But all this is impossible in the case of the human response to revelation. For revelation reveals the divine *Thou* who cannot become an *It*. The kind of *I-Thou* relation which it initiates cannot, therefore, degenerate into an *I-It* relation; and commitment cannot here admit of degrees. This relation is the absolute relation,[27] that is, the relation which exists either absolutely or not at all.

We have given an account of the divine address and of the human response. We must now turn to their relation. The central question here is this: Is revelation independent of the response? Or does it not become revelation unless and until there is response? Buber would appear to lean at times toward both alternatives, but to end up rejecting both.

Revelation is an address to a *Thou*. It is not revelation unless it has its *Thou*. This implies that, if revelation is independent of human response, being-a-*Thou* is, in this case, not a matter of human response but a product of revelation. "He is the infinite *I* that *makes* every *It* His *Thou*."[28] "In order to speak to man, God must become a person; but in order to speak to him, He must *make him* too a person."[29] In addressing us God forces us to listen; and having been forced to listen we give our free response.

But this conclusion is difficult. For according to Buber, the essence of human response to revelation is the committed turning to God; and this committed turning is involved, not only in whatever we do subsequently to hearing, but in the hearing as well. For unless we listen in commitment we do not hear at all.

Must we conclude, then, that revelation is not revelation until we respond? That it is not, at any rate, an address to *us* until we decide to listen? This would appear to be implied in Buber's suggestion that God speaks at all times,[30] for revelation manifestly does *not* occur at all times. Our committed listening would translate, in that case, what is in itself only potential revelation into actuality.

But this alternative, too, is in the end rejected, if only because there are

Martin Buber's Concept of Revelation

times in which God is silent. To be sure, an eclipse of God may be due to our failure to listen to what there is to be heard; but it may also be due to a divine silence which persists no matter how devoutly we listen.[31]

Buber's final conclusion is that the relation between divine address and human response is an antimony which thought cannot resolve.[32] In speaking to *me* the Infinite *Thou* makes me His listening *I*; yet unless I make myself His listening *I* neither shall I be His *Thou* nor He mine:

> I know that "I am given over for disposal" and know at the same time that "It depends on myself.". . . . I am compelled to take both to myself, to be lived together, and in being lived they are one.[33]

This conclusion has important implications concerning the content of revelation. The philosophical task here is not the identification of a particular content, for this can be done only, primarily by the person who lives in the revealing situation, secondarily, by the historian who relives it in his mind. The task is to define the status of the content of revelation, namely, the extent to which it is divine and the extent to which it is human. But the attempt at definition ends in an antimony.

It was seen that the core of revelation is not the communication of content but the event of God's presence. Nevertheless, revelation must assume content. For it is an address which calls for a response; and the response called for is not some universal response, but the unique response appropriate to the situation. Speaking *into* the situation, "into my very life,"[34] revelation assumes the most concrete content there can be. But does revelation assume this content independently of our response or only by virtue of our response? Both alternatives are impossible.

Revelation is "hearable" content only in relation to committed listening. If it is to be nevertheless independent of our response, revelation must force us into committed listening. But this, we have already seen, is impossible. Hence there cannot be a divinely handed down content, passively received; all content is the result of committed appropriation, and thus "a statement which is human in its meaning and form."[35]

> I experience what God desires of me for this hour . . . not earlier than in this hour. But even then it is not given me to experience it except by answering before God for this hour as my hour.[36]

Is revelation, then, wholly without content apart from my answering? This too is impossible. Revelation would, in that case, not be an address at all, let alone an address to *me*. And the "statement which is human in its meaning and its form" would be, not a translation of revelation into human speech, but the product of self-sufficient human spontaneity. Yet it *is* a translation,[37] and the listener knows it to be a translation, that is, a human product "stimulated"[38] by God.

Once more Buber admits frankly the antimony at which he has arrived.

It is not man's own power that works here, nor is it God's pure effective passage, but it is a mixture of the divine and the human.[39]

In my answering I am given into the power of His grace, but I cannot measure Heaven's share in it.[40]

With this last point Buber's concept of revelation is complete. Whatever goes beyond it is concerned with the actuality of particular revelations, and this transcends the limits of the present essay.[41]

But if Buber's counterattack on the modern attack on revelation is to be wholly successful there is one task he must still accomplish. We have suggested that if Buber's doctrine of the *I* and *Thou* is true, and if it can be extended into a doctrine of revelation, the latter constitutes an effective answer to the modern critique of revelation. The question remains *whether* the former doctrine is true, and hence whether the latter is acceptable; or—to put it more modestly—whether the grounds on which both are advanced lend them an impressive claim to truth.

V

But in a search for such grounds one fundamental point must be borne in mind with the utmost clarity. Buber's doctrine—which asserts that in the committed *I-Thou* relation there is knowing access to a reality which escapes *I-It* knowledge—cannot itself be an instance of, or be based on, *I-It* knowledge. For the latter, which either ignores the *Thou* or else treats it as an *It*—can neither understand its own limitations as *I-It* knowledge, nor can it recognize *I-Thou* knowledge *as* knowledge.

Thus a psychologist who examined *I-Thou* relations would use *I-It* knowledge, not furnish a critique of it; and he would arrive, not at the doctrine of the *I* and *Thou*, but at laws of interhuman relationships. In his studies of religion, he would not be the committed partner in a dialogue with God, but only the detached observer of other people's dialogue with God. But for this detached standpoint there could not be an address of God, but only other people's *feeling*-of-being addressed-by-God; in short, "psychic phenomena." The investigation would be carried on within a system of categories which is merely "a temporary construction which is useful for psychological orientation."[42]

Must Buber's doctrine, then, be classified, without qualification, within *I-Thou* knowledge? This conclusion is inescapable if *I-Thou* and *I-It* knowledge constitute exhaustive alternatives, and this Buber in at least one essay[43] clearly implies. Conceivably there could be a third kind of knowledge which is unlike *I-It* knowledge in that it understands, and at least to that extent transcends, the limitations of *I-It* knowledge; but which is unlike *I-Thou* knowledge in that it is detached rather than committed. Such a knowledge would have to be classified as philosophical. But philosophy, Buber asserts in the essay referred to, is *I-It* knowledge pure and simple.[44]

But can the doctrine of the *I* and *Thou* really be classified, without qualification, within *I-Thou* knowledge? Let us begin our consideration of this question by turning once more to the hypothetical psychologist to whom we have already had recourse for illustrative purposes. We have argued above that Buber would find fault with neither his science nor his way of life, but rather with a third thing, namely, his interpretation, respectively, of *I-Thou* and *I-It* knowledge. But if this interpretation is to be classified, without qualification, within *I-Thou* knowledge, how can it be a third thing? Would it not follow that the psychologist, if in possession of the knowledge of but a single *Thou*, would *ipso facto* possess knowledge also of the true nature of *I-Thou* and *I-It* knowledge? Would Buber not be driven to the unpalatable conclusion of having to cast aspersions on the way of life lived by wrong-headed philosophers?

But perhaps this conclusion need not follow. For surely even if the doctrine of the *I* and *Thou* is to be classified wholly within *I-Thou* knowledge, a distinction must still be made between the immediate dialogical knowledge of a *Thou* and the knowledge of the *doctrine* of the *I* and *Thou*. The latter could not be identical with, but at most only be somehow implicit in the former. And it would be the philosopher's task to show how it is implicit, and to make the implicit explicit. It would follow that the hypothetical psychologist's mistake was, after all, not due to a lack of *I-Thou* relations, but merely to a failure to recognize their metaphysical and epistemological implications, or else to a tendency to forget them whenever he turned to his professional job.

Such a view may seem plausible enough in the case of interhuman *I-Thou* relations. After all, in the case of these even the most fanatical devotee of *I-It* knowledge must make two admissions: first, that there is an actual address by another, secondly, that this address is never *wholly* understood in terms of *I-It* knowledge. Of these two admissions, the first is primary; for unless it is made the question of understanding the address as address does not arise. In the case of these relations, therefore, it is not difficult to be persuaded that the doctrine that the *I-Thou* relation yields a unique knowledge of another should be implicit in the actual dialogical knowledge of the other. But it is not easy to be persuaded of this in the case of *I-Thou* relations in which the *Thou* is not human, whether it be a stone or a tree or God. For here one does not have to be a fanatical devotee of *I-It* knowledge in order to doubt that there is an actual—rather than merely an apparent—address by another; indeed, one should be lacking in intellectual responsibility if one did not doubt it, demanding an argument for the removal of the doubt. But the crucial difficulty is that, if the doctrine of the *I* and *Thou* is wholly derived from the dialogue with the *Thou*, such an argument must be in principle unavailable. The doctrine of the *I* and *Thou*, far from being able to argue that there is actual rather than merely apparent dialogue, would on the contrary wholly flow from the belief that there is the former rather than the latter. Buber could do nothing to argue that the category of revelation in terms of which the religious standpoint understands itself is the category in terms of which it must be understood; for his doctrine of revelation would, in the end, wholly spring from the religious standpoint, that is, from a dialogue with God whose actuality is accepted simply on faith.

Such a conclusion, we hasten to emphasize, would not be as irrational as it may at first sight appear. For Buber's body of doctrine, even if wholly derived from committed *I-Thou* knowledge, would still be a body of doctrine. It would contain a critique of *I-It* knowledge and an interpretation of the status of *I-Thou* knowledge; it would identify revelation as part of a kind of *I-Thou* knowledge and refute those who assert that revelation is impossible. It would, to be sure, in all its doctrinal assertions be unconvincing to those who stubbornly remain on the *I-It* standpoint; but it would at least show that the objections raised from the *I-It* standpoint have no force for those who adopt the *I-Thou* standpoint. It may be said that this is all that may be asked of a body of doctrine, particularly of a body of religious doctrine into which faith must presumably at some point enter.

But the fact would still remain—at least in the case of all but interhuman *I-Thou* relations—that Buber's entire thought would spring from, rather than be able to argue for, the reality of dialogue; that is, it would have to presuppose that there *is* a reality of dialogue. But is it possible for the modern-minded to grant this presupposition? An ancient prophet could take it for granted that the voice of God may be heard by the committed listener; a modern man can hardly take this for granted, though he may very well be led to accept it. But he will surely accept it only if he is offered some kind of argument, cogent to the *I-It* standpoint, which points to the *I-Thou* standpoint as being, in the case of divine-human as well as interhuman relationships, a standpoint of truth. But if the whole doctrine of the *I* and *Thou* derives from *I-Thou* knowledge such an argument cannot be given.

But perhaps Buber's doctrine does not derive wholly from *I-Thou* knowledge, after all. To the present writer at least it appears that while Buber characterizes philosophy as *I-It* knowledge,[45] the pure philosophizing which he himself does is a *critique* of *I-It* knowledge. It is pure philosophizing because it is detached rather than committed, but it nevertheless transcends the realm of *I-It* in that it recognizes its limitations and, in recognizing them, points beyond them to the realm of the *I* and *Thou*.

Consider the following very remarkable passage.

> The philosopher, if he were really to wish to turn his back on that God [i.e., the *It*-God of the philosophers], would be compelled to renounce the

Martin Buber's Concept of Revelation

attempt to include God in his system in any conceptual form. Instead of including God as one theme among others, that is, as the highest theme of
all, his philosophy both wholly and in part would be compelled to point toward God, without actually dealing with Him. This means that the philosopher would be compelled to recognize and admit the fact that his idea of
the Absolute was dissolving at the point where the Absolute *lives*; that it was
dissolving at the point where the Absolute is loved; because at that point the
Absolute is no longer the "Absolute" about which one may philosophize, but
God.[46]

How is philosophy to "point toward God without actually dealing with
Him?" If the division into *I-Thou* and *I-It* knowledge is exhaustive this must
be impossible. For the latter knows nothing of the *Thou*-God and hence
cannot point to Him, whereas the former not merely points to, but deals
with Him; moreover, being committed it is not philosophy. The passage
quoted clearly implies that the division into *I-Thou* and *I-It* knowledge is not
exhaustive; that philosophy, at least at its profoundest point, is not *I-It*
knowledge but the dialectic of *I-It* knowledge. As such it mediates between
I-It and *I-Thou* knowledge; for, being a detached critique of detached knowledge, it points beyond detached knowledge and thus beyond itself; and what
it points to is the commitment of the *I-Thou* standpoint. This is the kind of
philosophizing which Buber, at least on important occasions, would appear
to be doing. And it is, at least in the opinion of this writer, the only kind
of philosophizing which properly belongs, not only with Buber's doctrine
of the *I* and *Thou*, but with any kind of existential thought. Indeed, a study
of post-Kantian and more particularly post-Hegelian thought would show
that it is in connection with this kind of philosophizing that existential philosophy has emerged as a philosophy.[47]

But while there are many samples of such philosophizing to be found in
Buber's writings,[48] it must be said that they do not add up to a systematic
body of thought. Possibly this is because Buber has chosen, throughout his
life, to concentrate on the kind of thinking which flows out of the reality
of the dialogue, leaving it to others to supply the propadeutic, namely, the
thinking which argues for the reality of the dialogue. But it is possible that
Buber's ultimate stand is that philosophy is only *I-It* knowledge, after all.
This would mean that not only the critique of *I-It* knowledge but Buber's
doctrine as a whole would derive from *I-Thou* knowledge and nothing else.
It would also mean that it is not, strictly speaking, philosophical. Such detached criticizing of detached knowledge as Buber may be doing would
have to be regarded, in that case, as a mere series of lapses, due possibly
to Kantian or post-Kantian influence.

If this interpretation should be correct, Buber would emerge, in the ultimate analysis, not as a philosopher but as a Hebrew sage in modern garb.
He would be in modern garb because, taking note of the modern attack
on revelation, he develops a body of doctrine wholly capable of repulsing

that attack; but he would be a sage rather than a philosopher because the ultimate basis of his doctrine is an unargued commitment to the dialogue with the ancient God of Israel, a commitment which the reader is called upon to share. Buber's own commitment, and the commitment he asks of his reader, would simply rest on the ancient and irrefutable faith that God can speak even though He may be silent; that He can speak at least to those who listen to His voice with all their hearts.

Five

Martin Buber

Universal and Jewish Aspects of the I-Thou Philosophy

According to a presumably apocryphal story, a Christian theology student once wandered into a lecture on Martin Buber, became more and more engrossed as the lecture went on, and was overheard to remark on leaving that this man Buber was all right, except that he seemed to be pretty weak in his Christology. That this story, like so many apocryphal stories, has an element of truth in it was observed with particular astuteness by Milton Himmelfarb, in an introduction to a volume of collected essays called *The Condition of Jewish Belief.*[1] (Some forty-odd Jewish thinkers in America outline their Jewish beliefs in that book.) Himmelfarb rightly states "that Buber was the first Jewish religious thinker since Maimonides eight centuries earlier who was able to influence Christian theology." He also rightly compares this fact with Buber's relatively small influence on the American Jewish thinkers represented in the volume. His explanation of the last fact, however, seems somehow insufficient. While it is true that Buber's well-known opposition to *Halakhah*, the Jewish law, makes him, as Himmelfarb puts it, "unusable to the orthodox," surely it does not make him entirely unusable when Buber, though rejecting *law*, is very firmly committed to *mitzvah* or *commandment* and above all to the *Metzaveh*, or Him who commands.

Again, to quote Himmelfarb, "classical reformers can be made uncomfortable by Buber's talk about encounters between man and God"— but then reformers nowadays are hardly classical any more; moreover, unlike Kierkegaard's Christian existentialism (which opposes divine-human encounters to interhuman ones), Buber's existentialism shows its Jewishness when it makes divine-human encounters exclusive of interhuman ones quite impossible. When you add to this that Buber was a lifelong Zionist and that his dialogical philosophy is at most only one-third of his work, the other two-thirds of which is undisputably Jewish, namely, his Hasidic and Biblical writings,[2] then the failure of Jewish thinkers to recognize the essential Jewishness of Buber's work becomes a remarkable enigma.

One might cope with this enigma in a polemical way—by pointing out that the failure of Jewish thinkers to recognize the Jewishness of Buber's work is fully matched by failures among non-Jews. For example, Christian theology often pays due homage to Buber only in order forthwith to emasculate him of, or at least pay little attention to, his Jewishness. Philosophy on its part either ignores Buber altogether or ignores his Jewishness in a philosophical rather than a theological way. So one might explain the Jewish disregard for Buber in a polemical way by first seeing Buber through the eyes of these varying non-Jewish interpreters and then wondering whether Jewish thought has been so assimilated to genuine or spurious Christian theology, or else to non-Jewish philosophy, as for that reason to fail to confront Buber the Jew himself.

Such an approach would be in keeping with the spirit of the times. However, while properly militant, it would not get us beyond some rather obvious insights. But surely there must be something in Buber *himself* which is an enigma when people who are beyond doubt honest and intelligent (and I am referring to the philosophers on the one hand, to the Christian theologians on the other), habitually distort or misunderstand him, and it is the enigma in Buber himself to which I wish to address myself here.

It is often assumed that Buber's so-called I-Thou philosophy is a universal philosophy (and of course philosophy is always universal), which can for that reason be detached from the Jewish aspects of his thought. What I would like to do in a circumscribed and limited way here is to reconnect the universal or philosophical elements in Buber's thought with its particularistic or Jewish elements, at the same time showing that perhaps the first, far from being abstractable from the second, depend on and derive from them. Let me first limit my topic. I said before that Buber's work falls broadly into three parts—his dialogical philosophy, his Hasidic work, and his encounter with the Bible. Right from the outset I would like to exclude the Hasidic, partly because of limitations of space, partly because I must disqualify myself as an authority in this field (and in this case an authority is required since Buber's contribution to Hasidism is controversial), and finally and above all, because of a statement made by Buber himself.

Just a few years before his death, Buber was asked to prepare a German edition of those of his works which he considered to be of permanent value. He divided his selections into three volumes: Hasidic writings, philosophical writings, and Biblical writings. Having collected what he thought was of permanent value, he then wrote in his introduction: "When I apportion to these three volumes their respective contents, the fact gave me pause that the oldest piece of the first volume (devoted to philosophy) and the oldest piece of the third volume (devoted to Hasidism), were written before I was thirty. In contrast, the oldest piece of the second volume, devoted to the Bible, originated nearly two decades later. This fact disclosed to me quite inescapably something which to be sure I had known before but had not duly considered. *In order to serve the Bible I had to become mature.*"[3]

When I first read this statement by Buber about himself, I was immediately convinced of its profound truth. For if one follows Buber's writings chronologically, what above all assures one of their lasting value is the author's steady growth in seriousness, depth, and maturity. I myself had my only real encounter with him when he was nearly eighty, and the main question under discussion was something which then, when I was just forty, was beyond my comprehension: what does a philosopher do when he becomes old? Assuming that he is not senile, he learns the meaning of ultimate seriousness. Buber himself seemed almost obsessed with the idea whether other philosophers before him had not called everything they had ever thought once again into question. Kant was one example. And Kant, indeed, in his old age did write a work which he never published, and in which he did seem to doubt much that he had been certain of at the height of his career. And Schelling was another such example.

I resisted Buber's conclusion in both cases—but then, I was so much younger. One thing in any case was clear—that Buber went to his death, at least as close to it as I know, never ceasing to have an open mind in which everything was again and again called into question. And this includes, of course, the most monumental of all his notions—that there can be a mutual relationship between man and God. Now, if as I have said he became ever more serious, and if, according to his own self-examination, he had to mature for his work with the Bible, it is well for us to take this seriously. And if in any case it is true that when a great thinker gives you an enigma, instead of quickly criticizing him, you should try to understand him, then we are probably well advised to suspect that the clue to the Buber enigma will ultimately be found in his meeting with the Bible.

I am forced to confine myself to two books. One is the work with which Buber's career, so to speak, began. *I and Thou* may seem to be a purely philosophical and universal work, and this largely accounts for its wide appeal. But considered as such it raises many problems which may resolve themselves only in terms of Buber's lifelong commitment to the Bible (Hasidism may be an alternative, no less valid, approach). So I shall select as my second book what I consider to be perhaps Buber's greatest work on the Bible, *Moses*, written twenty years later.

Let me begin then with *I and Thou*, and with a preliminary summary, with apologies to those who may not require it. We shall get its enigmatic character soon enough.

Buber begins the work with the flat assertion of a twofold relationship which we have with reality. This, from the very outset, is a challenge. To be sure, many philosophers have asserted various kinds of dualism—body and mind, matter and spirit, nature and history, time and eternity, and so forth. Buber maintains not a dualism in reality but a dualism of relations—an I-It and an I-Thou relationship. The contents of these two relationships we shall consider in a moment. But to pause at the very beginning, the other dualisms mentioned before do not involve on the part of the "I" the adoption of two different standpoints. You become an observer of nature, you become an observer of history, or of matter and mind, or of body and soul, as the case may be: in contrast, when you have an I-It or I-Thou relationship, it is not only the "It" and the "Thou" that is different, the "I" is different as well. The I-It relationship may require the standpoint of detachment; the I-Thou relationship demands a commitment or involvement.

When we consider briefly these two relationships, we shall quickly see that the I-It relationship is more or less familiar, for the philosophers are more or less geared to it. It is the I-Thou relationship that is unfamiliar and requires closer scrutiny.

An I-It relationship, in the first place, is unilateral. When I view an object, when I analyze the parts of a piece of matter in a laboratory, when I develop a theory about the stars, the objects I am dealing with do not do anything to me. I do something to them, whether it is for practical use or pure theory. In relating myself in these two ways to these objects, I am "abstract" and the object is "abstract," by which Buber means that both the "It" and the "I" are replaceable. For example, when I look through a microscope, then I look indifferently at one amoeba or another amoeba, because what I look for as a scientist is the kind of amoeba and not the *individual* one. Also, first I look at it, then I ask my scientific colleague to look at it, and to the extent to which we manage scientific objectivity we observe the same. Indeed, universality in this case requires abstraction from involvement so that all "bias" should be excluded.

At present, this is all that needs to be said in this brief summary of the I-It relationship, except that you already see that if the I-It relationship were ultimate, then what Buber calls an I-Thou relationship would have no place. We are now concerned with its nature and its place. (Buber also calls it a "dialogical" relationship.) He likes the metaphors of "speaking" and "hearing," and when I say "metaphor" I mean that actual physical speech is not necessarily involved. One must be involved in the I-Thou relationship with one's *whole being*, and that, in a way, is addressing, being addressed, and responding.

The scientific observer or user of an object is in one position as observer or user, in another entirely when he enters into an I-Thou relationship, which he must do with his whole being. What is more—falling back on the metaphors of speaking, listening and responding—it must be a mutual relationship. I must be open to the other even as the other must be open to me. It is a dialogical relationship in which each in his or her uniqueness is open to the uniqueness of the other. An example here serves to show the inadequacy of language. It is a three-word sentence which a man would perhaps say only a few times genuinely in his entire life, and possibly once. "I love you." The words always seem to be the same for some reason or other, yet in each case the "I" is different, the "you" is different, and the "love" is different.

Suppose for the purpose of the argument you manage to fall in love more than once in your life, and you therefore the second time say "I love you" to someone else, and you do not mean that the first time it wasn't the real thing. Certainly the "you" is different now; but Buber would say that if it is real love, the "you" couldn't be different without the "love" also being different. And the "you" and the "love" could not be different without the "I" being different. If you do not become different from what you were in a genuine encounter such as this, then the "I love you" is not genuine. Hence Buber says from a genuine meeting one does not emerge the same as one was before.

This may seem simple or even naive to some, self-evident to others. Yet it gives rise to all sorts of deep questions, such as the strange mystery of language, which can be at once so completely universal that everybody always uses the same words, and yet so completely unique that its meaning is never the same. On this subject alone one could dwell at great length.

However, something else is of greater importance here. Buber tells us quite unequivocally that an I-Thou relationship does not consist of feeling. This may come as a surprise, not to say a shock, to many who are "turned on" or want to be so, including those who may look to Buber for help. Yet the fact is that Buber affirms that my feeling is mine, your feeling is yours, and that love is neither the one, nor the other, nor the sum of the two. Then what is love? Love is *between* us. And so central is this "between" that it reduces all feeling to a mere by-product of the relationship.

This assertion is of the most monumental significance, though not original with Buber—Kierkegaard made it before him. If the assertion is true, then it is possible to mistake for a genuine dialogue what is in fact only a "disguised monologue." I am in love not with you but only with what I have projected on to you. Well, if one mistake is always possible, how can I be sure that an I-Thou relation is *ever* actual? How can one ever be certain that a supposed dialogue is not a disguised monologue, since after all the monologue *is* disguised? You might go on with the disguised monologue for ten years, or—to anticipate—if it is with God, forever.

How can you ever be certain? Buber says there is no way other than *standing in* the relationship and enduring its risk.

This must suffice as a general summary of Buber's teaching. We must now give an explication, for despite the seeming clarity and evidence of Buber's teaching, it becomes rather complex upon closer scrutiny, as well as questionable when one considers its implications.

Buber maintains throughout the book that there are I-Thou relationships with nature, with other human beings, and climactically, with God. Let me deal very briefly with Buber's very puzzling assertion that there can be an I-Thou relationship not just with a cat or a horse, but even with a heap of hay, an assertion so puzzling that over thirty years afterward in a postscript Buber still had to come back to the cat. Perhaps it is best to sidestep this whole sphere except for one crucial point—the assertion that there can be at least in principle an I-Thou relationship even with nature. Buber needs this assertion, unless he is to give up his fundamental conviction that there are not two realities to which we stand in the relationship of an impartial observer, but rather that the basic dualism is two relations with *all* of reality. Only the latter permits the view that one of them, the I-Thou relation, is deeper and richer, and that ultimate reality becomes accessible to us only when it is confronted as a Thou and not when it is observed as an It. But more of this later on.

With this, we may proceed to the second type of I-Thou relationship, namely, with fellow human beings. Here we come to a far more reasonable form of the claim that Buber is making; some might say, to the *only* sphere in which it is reasonable. As with nature but (as we shall see) not as with God, no one doubts the existence of other human beings, or that in some sense there is a relationship with the other which expresses itself among other forms in speech. But unlike the case of nature, no one will contend that there is not in some way mutuality and a dialogue in interhuman existence. Most philosophers would admit, or can be induced to admit, that the relationship between man and man can be dialogical more or less in the sense in which Buber means it. What then is the argument? Empiricists would certainly say that there is a relationship between human beings. You can't deny it. What then *do* they deny? Its immediacy—to such an extent that the existence of other minds is for them a serious topic. How do you know that there are other beings like you? You see other people making faces. You hear them say "Ouch" when you would say "Ouch" but you don't feel their pain. Then how do you know they *are* feeling pain? A genuine problem. In other words, for an empiricist of a certain type, the fundamental and basic condition is human isolation, and relationship is a *derivative* fact which comes about only through inference.

Now while I would be the last to deny that the position known as solipsism can be dismissed, one can nevertheless show quite simply that attempts to refute it are rather silly. One of the things empiricists never do (and I think this is a sin of which many philosophers are guilty) is to consider the fact that human beings are born as babies. Extraordinary that philosophers should forget that! But the fact is that they do. In their theories of man and of human relations they act as though, like Athene, people jumped fully armed out of the head of Zeus. So you get some who ask, how does John Doe know that he is not alone in the world? Well, when he shouts "Ouch" because he has a toothache, he both feels his pain and shouts his "Ouch." But of the other fellow he just hears the "Ouch." So he goes through a complicated process of reasoning to conclude that it is most likely that the other is not a machine of some sort which shouts "Ouch," but rather that he shouts "Ouch" for the same reason that he himself would shout "Ouch," namely because he too feels a pain.

Now you just try to apply all this to a baby. Have you ever observed a baby when the mother has a sudden pain? He certainly can feel the mother's pain. Is this because of some reasoning on his part to the effect that the mother's screaming or groaning is likely to be due to pain? Of course not! The baby cannot yet reason, but can and does feel the feelings of another. Here the idealist tradition is much wiser than the empiricist. This recognizes that the baby cannot yet organize his experience. In the words of William James, everything is "booming, buzzing confusion." But this does not mean that even then he is alone in the world. The baby is born with a primal experience which is communal, and out of which gradually emerges the separation of self from other, so that it may be said that the newborn baby almost feels his mother's feelings, and that prior to this separation of self from other there exists a more primitive bond.

The idealistic school thus agrees with Buber that man is not primordially alone but rather with others. But it will maintain against Buber that the I-Thou relationship is *not immediate*. It is only when a tremendous development of mediation and interpretation has taken place that the I-Thou structure comes into being. So we must go further to look for companions of Buber, and we find them, of course, among fellow existentialists.

Like the idealists, the existentialists maintain that the self is open to another presence, that we are not primordially alone, so that solitude would be overcome only by inference. Like Buber, too, they maintain that the encounter with the other can be immediate. (This is lacking in idealism.) But, if you then go and compare Buber, say, with Jean-Paul Sartre, you find that the description given of the I-Thou relationship is not only different but diametrically opposite. In Buber's account of the I-Thou relationship, I become more totally myself *through* my relationship with the other, and the highest manifestation of this relationship is love. In Sartre (at least the early Sartre), in order for me to realize my freedom I must negate rather than confirm the other, so that a tragic sadomasochistic conflict arises between the two. If one then confronts Sartre with Buber (an interesting thing to do), one does not really doubt with whom one wants to side, one knows with whom one wants to side: with Buber, in his emphasis on the possibilities of human love. But in an age which has seen a Hitler (for whom, incidentally, I think Buber's philosophy leaves too little room, just as it fails to confront radical evil in general: that is one of its weaknesses),[4] then one has to give Sartre his due. The evil aspect of the interhuman involvement, destructiveness, is here fully recognized: yet, who would want to accept the early Sartre so totally that sadomasochistic relationships become the norm? (Sartre, in his later work, abandoned this position.)

The contrast between Sartre and Buber at any rate suffices to raise one question. What is the *justification* of Buber's side in the conflict? Is it just arbitrarily asserted? So we must once again go on and look for still more appropriate philosophical company—to a philosopher to whom he actually expresses a profound debt. Ludwig Feuerbach, long before Buber, asserted an interhuman I-Thou relationship culminating in love. So close is Buber to Feuerbach that some critics have actually denied any originality in Buber. This, however, is quite mistaken. Thus if one inquires into the *grounds* on which these two thinkers assert a similar or even the same position, one finds that they not only differ but are radically opposed. Feuerbach maintains that not until man realizes his freedom in a manner which so radically overcomes his dependence on God as to deny Him (to bring about the death of God, to use the contemporary phrase)—not until then is an I-Thou relationship between human beings a genuine possibility.

Buber is in such a sharp contrast to this that one must wonder whether what ultimately makes the interhuman I-Thou relationship possible is not an act of human freedom but rather a given mystery of mysteries—that, though finite, an "I" can go outside himself and relate himself to a "Thou." If we ask the final question of what the grounds of *this* mystery are, it is that the I-Thou relation among men points to an I-Thou relationship which is no longer between humans alone but between men and God. So we must take the step to the third type of I-Thou relationship, the climactic step to the relationship between a human "I" and a "Thou" that is divine.

Humanists will make much, perhaps too much, of the fact that a large part of *I and Thou* develops without God coming into the picture at all. Too much, because it is undeniable that the climax of the book is reached with the divine-human I-Thou relationship. Not only that, but the climax is intimated before, perhaps throughout, in a certain dialectic. If you take the *difference between* the "I" and "Thou" as seriously as their openness to each other, then the relationship shows itself as dialectical. The "I" is open to the "Thou" but cannot *force* him into a relation. The more you seek a "Thou," the less you may find that "Thou." The more you deliberately search for love, the less will it let itself be found. It must *come upon* you—here one resorts almost involuntarily to Biblical language—like Jacob when he "came upon the place," unexpectedly. Yet, if this happens and you are like a brick, *nothing* happens. The "Thou" may be a "Thou" but you are not *there* as an "I." So the "I" must *respond*, as Jacob did.

This dialectic between giving and taking, receiving and responding, gradually builds up in the book to find its climax in the human-divine I-Thou relationship.

When Buber takes that last step, let no one say he is not aware of what he is doing. The situation half a century ago when *I and Thou* was written, as regards doubt concerning God, was not as different from today as the young may believe. Indeed, doubt was far more radical, and few theologians would use the word "God" glibly. Buber himself was tempted to abandon the word altogether and chose otherwise only when he came to the conclusion that it is one of those "original" words for which there is no substitute. Nevertheless, he used the word with great hesitation, not to speak of the hesitation with which he took the step to the divine Thou. This is because he had to face secularism, that is, the thesis that the world is closed to the incursion of a divine "Thou" into the world of the human "I."

In order for this closedness to dissipate itself, it requires in Buber's thought the most radical of all turns conceivable. And in Buber's entire religious thought the most radical question is: "Is the world closed to the incursion of the Divine, or rather open?"—a question to which we shall have to return. At this point Buber maintains that it is only as one turns *radically* and becomes *wholly* open that the divine-human I-Thou relationship becomes a possibility.

At this point you want of course to raise immediately the skeptical question—what I call the question of subjectivist reductionism. I said before that some might say that the only plausible or reasonable case for an I-Thou relationship is the inter-human one. For when one sees the step taken where God is spoken of as "Thou," what is more reasonable than to object that this is anthropomorphism, and, more radically, a case of unconscious projection. Doubtless religious believers throughout the ages have been *subjectively* sincere when they considered themselves to address God and to be responded to by God. However this does not prevent Freud and many others from objecting to claims for its *objective* truth, that is, from exposing the experience as a fundamental illusion. Subjectivist reductionism withdraws the projection and exposes all such dialogues as in fact being "disguised monologues."

Buber maintains (and the grounds for his maintaining this remain to be seen) that subjectivist reductionism in all its forms is not a discovery of the objective truth, but rather a flight from God. As we may also put it, it is a form of existence and thought which does not take the Divine seriously enough to be able to distinguish it from the pseudodivine. Certainly there are many "dialogues" with God which are in fact only disguised monologues. (Buber himself has coined the phrase.) But to maintain that any and every such dialogue is *necessarily* a disguised monologue is not to *experience* but rather to *presuppose* that the world is closed to the incursion of God into it.

Now, the justification for this view of Buber's remains to be seen. Thus far, it seems to be a mere assertion. And it must be more than that in a world largely composed of subjectivist reductionists. Perhaps this issue is best approached obliquely, by juxtaposing one question with its opposite—a juxtaposition which may come as a considerable surprise. Might one say that if subjectivist reductionism (which disposes of a divine Presence) does not take God seriously enough, perhaps mysticism takes God too seriously? (Buber rejects mysticism.) Here, perhaps a short exposition is in order.

Mysticism can mean many different things. It is best to state briefly what Buber means by mysticism in this context. (I mention in passing that Buber started out as a mystic, and no thinker is ever as harsh on an error as on his own which he has surpassed.) Mysticism at this point means not an

I-Thou relationship in which the I remains human, and the Thou divine. It is an ecstatic conflux in which the human I dissolves into the divine ocean. I use the word "ocean" as a metaphor, suggesting that a drop of water falling into the ocean loses its identity to become one with the ocean. This is the mysticism which Buber criticizes—the human soul, touched by the divine Presence, in ecstasy transcends itself, loses its identity, and becomes one with the One.

Of such mysticism Buber says:

> "I" and "Thou" merge, and humanity which was just open over against Divinity now dissolves into it. . . . But what profit is any such divine joy to a life which is torn asunder? If that infinitely rich heavenly moment has nothing to do with my poor earthly moment, what is to me when I must still live on earth *and do so seriously?*[5]

This is the substance of Buber's opposition to mysticism.

Just as subjectivist reductionism is a flight from the divine Presence into a world rendered spuriously godless, so the dissolution of the self into God is a flight from earthly necessity, a flight from worldliness that is equally spurious, and both these flights are equally opposed by a reality—the I-Thou relationship between God and man.

Such a relationship is easily asserted. But anyone who for a moment considers what he is asserting must follow Buber in also asserting that such a relationship is paradoxical. While I am finite God is infinite, and the question thus arises (and I cite Schelling when I might also cite many others): "If God *were,* how could *I* be?" Schelling then proceeds to say that since I *must* be, God can only be an eternal process of self-realization, the infinite end of which is the merging of God and man. But the mystic maintains that God is, and God is infinite. How then can his Presence fail to overwhelm me? And this mystical dissolution of man and world is what I meant before when I said that perhaps the mystic takes God too seriously. But no more seriously than Buber.

Yet Buber says with unyielding stubbornness, God is the infinite—*yet* I am finite and *over against* Him. God is absolute *yet* He is personal. Then he adds: "To speak of an absolute person is the paradox of paradoxes."[6] A person is by definition relative in that he needs other persons. That is what *constitutes* a person—the relation to other persons. But God is absolute, that is, precisely *not* in need of other persons. And yet, unyieldingly and fearlessly, Buber asserts his paradox of paradoxes. Toward the end of the book he says that there is no choice but to remain with an antinomy. "I am given over for disposal"—that is one side of the antinomy. Vis-à-vis another man I am not given over for disposal, for he is as finite as I am. But vis-à-vis God—my very being dissolves into Him. This is one side, and if it were the whole truth mysticism would be the answer in that the I-Thou relationship would vanish. But there *is* another side: "It depends on me." How then can

Aspects of the I-Thou Philosophy

you hold this antinomy together? Buber says that "I must take both upon myself to be lived together, and in being lived, they become one."[7] Buber's sticks to the *living* of both, and to their *unity* in life to the very end of the book, the last sentence of which is as follows: "That event whose worldly side is turning [in other words, something *I* do] has at its divine side what is called redemption [in other words something done by God]."[8]

So much for the exposition and *I and Thou*. And now I come to the crucial question: Is this a philosophical work? To some extent it surely is, and therefore also a purely universal work, and doubtless all the Christian and philosophical interest in the book that overlooks its essential Jewishness finds its inspiration in those elements.

However, a philosophical work requires justification for its central assertions. *On what grounds* does Buber simply say no to the reductionist dissipation of the divine Thou into a purely atheistic human world? *On what grounds* does he reject as simply false the mystical conflux? Toward both sides Buber seems equally arbitrary. Of course, as we said in the beginning, many people today follow Buber, but I doubt that many of them take seriously the pivotal role, for the whole book, of the divine-human I-Thou relationship. But these might just as soon stay with Feuerbach, or for that matter go on from Feuerbach to Marx. However, the divine-human I-Thou relation is the climax as well as the animating principle of Buber's *entire* book. So much for humanism. What about mysticism? On what grounds does Buber reject the mystical possibility when he says it is escapism? I have quoted the crucial passage, and I paraphrase it again, because of the current widespread interest in mysticism. Buber asks us what is the use of the mystical divine joy to a life which is torn asunder, what is it to me when I must still live on earth and *do so seriously*? Here is the key commitment— that with the mystic the truth of the divine, infinitely rich, heavenly reality is such as to dissolve any *living on earth* into mere appearance, dust and ashes which are *not serious*.

So it emerges at this point that Buber has a commitment which at the same time appears as arbitrary. This must find an anchor if it is to be saved from arbitrariness. Here Buber's thought displays a feature which in my view is characteristic of every form of existentialism. The term "existentialism" has become so vague today as to be virtually meaningless. Yet certain features remain. One is that every existentialist structure of philosophical thought must ultimately have roots in existence itself. Heidegger's *Being and Time* develops a structure of existence which is in some ways very different from Buber's I-Thou relationship. What the two share, in an otherwise very different situation, is the philosophical necessity for roots in an existential decision. Buber never wrote a systematic work. He says somewhere that he philosophizes no more than is necessary, and *I and Thou* is perhaps the greatest example of his fragmentary philosophizing. Even so it cannot dispense with the need for existential roots. In Heidegger's case, we have an authentic openness of *Dasein* as being-toward-death. *In Buber's case it is a Jewish encounter with the Bible.*

I said above that now as before I must confine myself to one book, namely, *Moses.* A further restriction is necessary, indeed to just one strategically chosen example. And the most strategic example for our purpose is not where the divine-Jewish relation starts, with Moses at the burning bush. It is not where the relation finds a unique climax, at Sinai. Its crucial characteristics are best discovered where the covenant is established. The convenantal relationship, like the I-Thou relationship, is undisputably mutual, and as Buber develops it in his Biblical exegesis, it makes its case against the mystics, on the one hand, and the reductionists, on the other. *God is God, and man is man; a veritable gulf separates the two: and yet they are* immediately *related.* This, one might say, is Buber's Jewish root commitment. It is the basic religious reality he finds in the Jewish Bible. As such, it is the ultimate foundation of his dialogical philosophy.

The covenantal reality is described in the Bible in a passage which I may perhaps quote from the Bible itself.

> You have seen what I did unto the Egyptians, and how I bore you on eagles' wings and brought you unto Myself. Now, therefore, if you will hearken unto My voice and keep My covenant, then you shall be Mine own treasure from among all peoples, for all the earth is Mine; and you shall be unto Me a kingdom of priests and a holy nation. (Exod. 19: 4–6)

After having commented that this refers not to revelation (which has already begun) but to the fact that the hour of the covenant has come, Buber then observes first of all that this covenant is "theologico-political." It must be *political* because the people is *completely human.* (It is not mystically dissolved into Divinity.) It is *theological* because the people is not alone in its human solitariness. It stands in the immediate presence of God, the King.

Buber then concentrates (this is essential) on the image of the eagles' wings. This image, he states, is election, deliverance, and education all in one. This is one of the most profound sentences in the entire book. (It is also one of the most compelling things ever said about a covenant which is not between God and unearthly souls, but between Him and a flesh-and-blood people.) Without *deliverance* the people would be dead, and even God cannot have a covenant with a dead people. Without *election* the human partner would be an abstraction such as mankind-in-general but no one in particular. And without *education* everything would remain the doing of God, and nothing would be the doing of man. Mutuality—the covenant—would vanish.

Out of this simple image we could draw the whole convenantal relationship, and what is more, the conclusion that in this mutuality the divine *infinity* cannot be dispensed with. Therefore, Buber goes on to stress that the assurance that Israel will be "a peculiar treasure among all the nations" is immediately explained here by the words "for the whole earth is Mine."

> It is impossible to express more clearly and unequivocally that the liberation from Egypt does not secure the people of Israel any monopoly over their God. . . . The expression "peculiar treasure" is directly imperilled by an atmosphere of restriction unless it is accompanied by such an explanation. . . . The danger of particularistic misunderstanding is so obvious that in the first passage a warning is issued against ascribing the choice made by God to their own importance.[9]

Here I suggest we have the existential root of Buber's I-Thou philosophy whose counterpart in Heidegger's *Being and Time* is being-toward-death. You may now ask why I single out this particular passage. Buber himself points out that certain psalms are more universalistic as regards covenants with all the nations. He answers, however, that such universalism in the Psalms is eschatological, and that to make it present here and now would be to pay the price of loss of reality. Thus the covenant does not exist without the *particularity* of the covenanted people. At the same time, this particularity is unintelligible without the universality of the God subsequently glorified as "the liberator of the nations."[10]

Otherwise put, precisely because this relation is theological and political at once, it must be, pre-eschatologically, a mutuality between a God who is infinite and universal, and a people that is particular: that makes up the essence and the life of this covenant. We have asked: on what basis does Buber assert this divine-human I-Thou relationship, on the one hand, against subjectivist-reductionism, and, on the other hand, against the mystical union? We answer now: on the basis of his encounter with the scriptural testimony. (This is at least a partial answer.)

This leaves us now with one final question: what is the nature of Buber's encounter with the Bible? After all, many among us have studied the Biblical faith without sharing it, and all of us know that this is possible. One may study the Bible from the standpoint of a dialectical (Marxist or other) superiority which has "overcome" the Biblical God, or as a simple reductionist, or as a detached scholar who suspends judgment. Since Buber lays claim to historical scholarship in his books on the Bible, he must share at least in part the standpoint of detachment. Hence if we ask the question, what does Buber *himself* believe, why does he not *totally* and *throughout* suspend his judgment, we shall not be surprised to hear him tell us that there can be a reductionist kind of scholarship too. It is true that the scholar, qua scholar, has no access to the Biblical Presence of God. He does have access, however, to the Biblical *experience* of the Presence of God. This Biblical experience, whenever it occurs, shows itself as shot through with radical surprise. What, then, in Buber's view, is the historical fact of the scholar? It would have to be, for anyone, the Biblical experience. In Buber's view, it includes the radical surprise as well. Biblical man never experienced himself seriously as addressed by God, except when the experience filled him with radical surprise.

Now as historical scholars, we may not be radically surprised. But we must at least sympathetically reenact the radical surprise of past ages if we are to do justice to the facts, and it is this that Buber refers to when he says that there is no other scientific historical understanding except the rational one, but that one must begin, by letting the "restricted and restricting" ratio be overcome by a "higher, more comprehensive one."[11] The "restrictive" ratio would refuse to recognize that ancient man may have experienced a Presence which we do not have. The larger ratio keeps all possibilities open.

This view of scholarship implies two points for Buber's own works on the Bible. The positive point is that they aim at an extraordinary openness to the Biblical faith. The negative point is that this openness does not by itself justify Buber's own commitment to dialogical realities—at least not to the climactic possibility and actuality of a divine-human dialogue.

Buber therefore requires as a last step the step from historical understanding to faith. At the threshold is the question: is this quest open or closed to the incursion of the Divine? Buber's last word is a promise that speaks to him from the Bible, namely, that he who engages the Bible may find that he has to struggle with it or oppose it, but that so long as the struggle with this Book is not ended another struggle also is not ended—the struggle between man and God. This book, he says in an essay on the Bible,

has confronted generation after generation. Each generation must struggle with the Bible in its turn and come to terms with it. The generations are by no means always ready to listen to what the book has to say, and to obey it. They are often vexed and defiant. Nevertheless, the preoccupation with this book is part of their life. . . . Yet, even if we were able to approach this whole book with our whole selves, would we not still lack the indispensable prerequisite for its true reception? . . . Can we do more than believe that people once did believe as this book reports and claims?[12]

Buber answers his own question as follows:

The man of today has no access to security in faith, nor can this security be made accessible to him. . . . However, he is not denied the possibility of holding himself open to faith. If he is really serious he, too, can open himself to this book, and let its rays strike him where they will.[13]

Six

The Systematic Role of the Matrix (Existence) and Apex (Yom Kippur) of Jewish Religious Life in Rosenzweig's *Star of Redemption*

I

In his essay "The New Thinking"[1] Franz Rosenzweig expresses his willingness to let his *Star of Redemption*[2] be characterized as a case of "absolute empiricism."[3] Here I shall explore the nature of this empiricism, the search for the "verification" or "confirmation" (*Bewährung*)[4] by virtue of which it does not remain a mere plan but is actually carried out; but I will confine myself to its crucial Jewish aspects, even though a complete account would include the structure of the Jewish and the Christian reality, both taken as a whole albeit viewed in Jewish perspective. This self-confinement on my part is not due to limitations of space alone. The two crucial aspects of the Jewish verification or confirmation of the *Star* are the matrix of the Jewish religious life (Jewish existence) and its apex (Yom Kippur). My chief task will be to identify the role of these two aspects in the "absolute empiricism" of the *Star*. But I shall also ask whether that role could be today what it still could be when Rosenzweig wrote his work. Since the essay is published in post-Holocaust Germany a century after Rosenzweig's birth, I consider it impossible—as well as un-Rosenzweigian—to confine myself wholly to the first question, thus suggesting that the second can be suspended, postponed, or even ignored altogether.

II

I begin with some necessary preliminaries. Virtually from its first page the *Star* introduces itself as an activity called "new thinking." (Also, this is the title of the essay already cited, published by Rosenzweig four years after the *Star* came out, for the sake of clarifying the work's purpose.) The new thinking rejects the "old" philosophical thinking. Of this latter Rosenzweig regularly asserts that it reduces reality to something supposedly more ulti-

89

mate and more real. That such reductions presuppose a rise of thought above existence, Rosenzweig does not state regularly but unmistakably implies when he asserts that the history of the "old" philosophical thinking, having begun in "Ionia," ends in "Jena," i.e., with Hegel. If no rise of thought above existence were implied, the old thinking, first, would be nonsense, and second, could go on forever. As will be seen, however, the "old" philosophical thinking, far from being considered nonsense, is presupposed by Rosenzweig's own "new thinking"; and it does not end in "Jena" not because there were no "old" philosophers succeeding Hegel, but rather because with Hegel it is complete: whatever the rise of thought above existence could accomplish has been accomplished.

The "new" thinking also rejects the "old" one in theology, the latter being "fanatical" inasmuch as it accepts revelation on authority. (In the "old" Jewish theology the Torah is accepted as divinely revealed on the authority of the 600,000 Israelites that supposedly witnessed the Sinaitic event; and that these actually were present at Sinai, and did witness the event, is accepted on the authority of a chain of reliable witnesses, a chain supposedly unbroken from Moses to the present day.) Having passed through modern criticism, modern theology must be "unfanatical":[5] its central concern remains revelation, but it cannot accept revelation on authority. Hence we need a fundamental shift from the authority of the Torah to the testimony (*Zeugnis*) to the Torah by the Jewish people; and, as will be seen, the *Star*'s "absolute empiricism" is bound up with that shift.[6]

Rosenzweig advises the reader to follow a "Napoleonic strategy" in reading the *Star*, i.e., to leave "unconquered fortresses" behind, since after "victory" these will "surrender" without a "fight".[7] This strategy is most suitable for the present purpose. The "absolute empiricism" of the *Star* will disclose itself only toward the end of the work. Hence we shall rush through its earlier parts with utmost speed, stopping only to understand what understand we must.

III

What are we to make of the three "elements" of Part One of the *Star*— God, World, Man? Are they metaphysical entities? But then they would be products of a species of "old" thinking, and arbitrary ones to boot! Are they, then, subjective-human conceits? But then the *Star* would never reach what it is centrally seeking, i.e., revelation as the presence of God to Man in the World; revelation, that is, as an objective reality, not as a figment of the human mind. The three elements of Part One, so Rosenzweig tells us, are "Noughts," or rather "Not-Yets," and he goes on as follows:

If a real Nought corresponds to the Nought of our knowledge . . . , then they are mysterious for us, beyond any reality that will ever be visible for us, occult powers that are at work inside God, World and Man—before God, World and Man are revealed. (*Star*, 88)

But how do we know that "real" Noughts do "correspond" to our "knowledge" when they are "mysterious" for us, i.e., how do we know that the "Noughts" of our "knowledge" are not merely figments of the human mind? This question calls for a Schelling-type negative philosophy, and this, indeed, is the type of philosophy Rosenzweig sketches in "The New Thinking" without ever elaborating it. This latter would show that the "new thinking," arising as it does *post Hegel mortuum*, presupposes not only the falsehood but also the truth of the old one "from Ionia to Jena." Its falsehood: this is the rise of thought above existence, whereas thought in fact, as a human activity, is limited both by death and by the fear of it; also it is the consequent reduction of reality to realms purportedly more ultimate and more real. Its truth: this is the exploration of all possibilities of reduction, i.e.: reduction to the World (ancient philosophy), to God (medieval philosophy), and to the Self (modern philosophy).[8] But it is because Hegel's philosophy is not merely a modern alternative to the ancient and medieval ones but rather incorporates all three that it contains the *complete* Truth of the "old" philosophical thinking. And only then can and must the "new" thinking come upon the scene and expose the falsehood of the old one.[9] This task Part One of the *Star* accomplishes by, as it were, tearing apart God, World, and Man which were united in Hegel's philosophy;[10] and through this act it makes the three to be inaccessible "Noughts" even as, by the same act, it is itself plunged back into human finitude.

IV

Napoleonically we will rush on—but where to? If God, World, Man, inaccessible in themselves, are to become accessible through revelation, the possibility arises of revelation coming on the scene as that which, by some Anglo-Saxon empiricists, is claimed to be a self-authenticating experience. Among empirical "data" some are said to be "God-data," disclosed in experiences that those having them can refuse to believe just as little as they can doubt sounds, colors, smells.[11] However, God-data are as firmly rejected by Rosenzweig as they were, before him, rejected by others whom he considers fellow–"new thinkers," e. g., Schelling and Kierkegaard: the claim to self-authenticating (i.e. purportedly infallible) religious experiences (1) is an open invitation to arbitrariness and entails the destruction of the distinction between the sane and the insane, between true prophets and false ones; (2) does away with the distinction—which is all-important not only for Rosenzweig but for all thinkers one could broadly specify as existentialists—between experience on the one hand and commitment or faith on the other hand, the latter (unlike the former) being shot through with risk;

(3) would not lead to the *Star*'s "absolute empiricism" but rather to an empiricism of the plain and simple type. Part One and even Part Two of the formidable structure of the *Star* would vanish entirely, and Part Three would have to be quite different from what it is.

The "fanaticism" of the "old" theological thinking has already been rejected. Now self-authenticating religious experiences are also rejected. With regard to the *Star*'s crucial concern with revelation, this double rejection entails a logical circle. Revelation can *be* revelation—the *actual* incursion of the divine Other into the World for Man, rather then the mere subjective human feeling of such an incursion—only if the three "Noughts" of Part One of the *Star* are "real" Noughts rather than mere subjective conceits; yet they can be *known* to be real only in and through revelation—which is not self-authenticating!

The *Star* recognizes this circle, and seeks to cope with its seeming—or possibly actual—viciousness by means of a series of verifications or confirmations (*Bewährungen* of *Wahrheit*) which increasingly become both concrete and comprehensive. One is therefore tempted to rush Napoleonically straight to the final verification, i.e., the celebrated Jewish-Christian double covenant. This, however, would lead to a theological thinking no less "fanatical" in its new way than the old theological thinking was in its old way. A Jewish (or possibly a shared Jewish-Christian) faith-commitment would affirm itself *against* all rivals, without relying on anything more universal or objective than its willingness to bear witness—if necessary, to be sure, unto death. But although such a bearing-witness does play a role in Rosenzweig's "absolute empiricism," he is far from simply ignoring Spinoza's famous letter to Burgh,[12] in which the former states that neither the number nor the sincerity of the martyrs of a faith is proof of that faith's truth. We must, then, move on Napoleonically, but not so speedily as to rush into defeat.

V

To move with the necessary caution is to move to Part Two, or, more precisely, to its second book, the concern of which is revelation. Rosenzweig calls this the *Herzbuch*,[13] i.e., the core on which the construction of the *Star* as a "philosophical system"[14] depends. This is so because its concern is neither the Jewish nor the Christian revelation, nor a possible togetherness of the two. Its concern is with revelation-as-such-and-in-general.

But is there such a thing as revelation-as-such-and-in-general? Is this not an empty abstraction, since all revelation is particular and concrete? Perhaps the most striking move in the whole work, considered as a "philosophical system," is made by placing into its center the *Song of Songs*' "strong as death is love."[15] Love and death are the two experiences that are both universally human yet irreducibly individual and totally concrete: not universally human, however, is the equality of the two. Presumably for the vast majority of mankind death is stronger than love, a form of existence that is tragic and pagan. For a minority love is stronger than death, a form of existence in which death and the self are swallowed up in a mystical oneness with "the One." Beside these two, only sporadically a form of existence appears for which death is as strong as love, and love as strong as death: here alone the self remains itself, i.e., confined to its finitude by death, while yet—love being no less strong than death—being open for dialogue with the other (as well as "*the* Other") in his (and His) otherness. Wherever this form of existence is real, there occurs an "ever-renewed rebirth of the soul."[16] It is in this rebirth that tragic paganism and mystic pantheism are both rejected, the one as having once been real but now overcome, the other as being a spurious flight from reality. And as this dual rejection occurs, revelation—the incursion of the Other into the world of finite self-hood—is verified or confirmed (*bewährt*).

But since "strong as death is love" is only sporadically real, embodied in existence only *beside* other forms of existence, confirmed is merely the concept of revelation; and unless revelation is to remain a concept merely *asserted against* others, it stands *itself* in need of verification or confirmation, and this latter can only occur *in history*. It is with that *Bewärung* that Rosenzweig's "absolute empiricism" will at length disclose its nature.

VI

Rosenzweig writes:

> There is only one community in which . . . a linked sequence of everlasting life goes from grandfather to grandson, only one which cannot utter the "we" of its unity without hearing deep within a voice that adds: "we are eternal". It must be a blood-community, because only blood gives present warrant to the hope for the future. . . . All eternity not based on blood must be based on the will and on hope. Only a community based on common blood feels the warrant of eternity warm in its veins even now. (*Star*, 298 ff.)

This is the matrix of the Jewish religious life, i.e., Jewish existence. On grounds of passages such as this one, Rosenzweig has sometimes been accused of racism. If this were correct, he would have any blood community "feel the warrant of eternity warm in its veins even now," which of course is not the case.

Rosenzweig's meaning is best grasped by way of contrasting Christian confirmation and Jewish Bar Mitzvah. Although Christian parents have their child baptized, the child becomes truly a Christian only with confirmation, and whether or not confirmation takes place depends on the child's own faith and/or will. For the believing parents, therefore, eternity is based only on hope. And since conceivably a time might come in which *all* children of *all* Christian parents reject the faith of their parents, the "rays" which are Christianity depend for their link with eternity on the "fire" which is Judaism. For if the Jewish community "feels the warrant of eternity warm in its veins even now," it is because a Jewish boy becomes Bar Mitzvah at thirteen years of age, regardless of his will and regardless of his faith or lack thereof. The Christian faith-community is constituted by testimony (*Zeugnis*), whereas in the Jewish faith-community, *Zeugnis* comes after *Erzeugnis* (product, i.e., Jewish birth).[17] Hence even though no Jewish individual knows whether he/she will have children's children, for the Jewish community as a whole, though it may decrease in number, the warrant of eternity is built into its faith even now.

It is built, however, *into its faith.* Existence is only the matrix of the Jewish religious life; its apex is Yom Kippur, and here the eternity of which existence is only the warrant, is *actually experienced* in the very midst of time. Rosenzweig writes:

> Death meant to mow down all life lest it live on to eternal life. He had presumed that no end could be reached except by dying. But the eternal people is held up to him as a triumphant proof that the end can be experienced also by living. With that, the scythe of the grim reaper breaks. (*Star,* 393)

In Part Three of the *Star* Rosenzweig makes an effort to establish parallels between Jewish and Christian festivals. No such effort is made by him in the case of Yom Kippur. There is no Christian counterpart for the holiest of Jewish days, and according to Rosenzweig there can be none. For while Jew and Christian are equally concerned with eternity, it is the Jew, and he alone, who anticipates the eternity that is sought by Christian and Jew alike, and he does so in the Yom Kippur experience. And since eternity is the destiny of all mankind (to be brought *by* Christianity *to* mankind), on Yom Kippur, the Jew, so to speak holds the fort for all humanity. More precisely, the Jew holds that fort with the whole of his religious life, and the Yom Kippur experience is both its highest expression and the disclosure of its significance. Jewish life is lived between its matrix—the "eternal people" for which *Erzeugnis* precedes *Zeugnis*—and its apex—a *Zeugnis* to eternity in the midst of time.

With this conclusion, Rosenzweig's "absolute empiricism" has at length disclosed itself. *The Three "Not Yets" of Part One of the Star, so to speak have become "Yets" in the Jewish experience of eternity.* That God is God, World is World, Man is Man, is verified or confirmed in the Jewish religious life which is stretched between the "we are eternal" that is its matrix and the "breaking" of the "scythe of the grim reaper" in which the ultimate destiny of God, World and Man is anticipated in experience.

VII

But does the Jewish hearing of the voice that says "we are eternal" guarantee that the Jewish people is *in fact* eternal? Rosenzweig does not inconsistently lapse into a premodern theology that would derive such a guarantee from a divine promise accepted "fanatically" on authority. His "unfanatical" theology is, and remains, based not on the authority of the Torah but on *the Jewish commitment* to the Torah. Therefore his "warrant" of eternal existence does not rest on anything else than a holy remnant, however small, and, in spite of pogroms (which have caused the death of some Jews) and apostasies (which have caused the falling away of others), that some Jews would always exist was at Rosenzweig's time still a reasonable assumption. Indeed, the Purim experience, celebrating as it does the failure of Haman, who sought to kill all Jews, made the possible success of a future Haman religiously all-but-unthinkable.

It is no longer unthinkable. Where Haman failed, Hitler succeeded; and only by way of relapsing into a premodern "fanatical" theology could his failure to achieve total success be ascribed to divine Providence. The voice that speaks "we are eternal" has been fractured, and what Rosenzweig, resurrecting a Biblical theme, could still view as a holy remnant has become an accidental remnant.

As fractured as the matrix of Rosenzweig's religious Jewish life is its apex. If on Yom Kippur a Jew experiences eternity in the midst of time, this happens, in any case for Rosenzweig, because on this day he is out of time altogether. This experience was possible in every previous world: not in the world of Auschwitz ruled by Dr. Mengele. A Yom Kippur prayer has it that on that day the judgment will be sealed as to who, in the year to come, shall live and who shall die. Fond of conducting his "selections" on Jewish festivals, Dr. Mengele was wont to boast that it was he and not God who decided which Jew was to live and which was to die. In Auschwitz a Jew could not be out of time. For Rosenzweig, the "eternal people" can *be* eternal, and anticipate in experience the eternity that is the destiny of all humanity, only because this people exist outside history, and so to exist is its world-historical role. But in Auschwitz this people could not be outside history but rather was its singled-out victim.

In response to being thus forced *into* history, it has become a Jewish religious necessity to return into history, i.e., to restore a Jewish state. That this momentous act has altered the nature of Yom Kippur was glaringly revealed on the first day of the Yom Kippur War, when some Jews had to fight in order that others could pray. A Rosenzweig today would doubtless also hold the reverse to be true, i.e., that some Jews had to pray in order that the fight of the others might be just and meaningful. This fact alone would suffice to demand of a Rosenzweig today a new *Star of Redemption*, which would chiefly differ from the old one by rendering the theological work into a theo-political one. It would be reckless to speculate about how the structure of such a new *Star* would differ from that of the old one in virtue of the radically altered *Bewährung* of its *Wahrheit*. One speculation, however, seems to be safe enough: the *Lehrhaus* Rosenzweig would found today, after having completed his revised *Star*, would not be located in Frankfurt but in Jerusalem.

Seven

Leo Strauss and Modern Judaism

This is an unusual and indeed a first occasion for me.[1] Never before have I given a lecture on Leo Strauss. I spoke publicly about him only briefly, at a memorial occasion in Toronto after his death, when a few of us spoke who felt that we had been touched by the thought of Leo Strauss. I also should say from the beginning, I seem to hear the voice of Leo Strauss himself, that I really have no great competence, and I'm quite sure there are many in this room who could give this lecture better than I can. Moreover, if controversy arises—and I understand there is such a thing as controversy on the subject of Strauss's thought—I'm not quite sure whether I'll be able to hold my own.

So, then, why have I been asked? As has been mentioned, I dedicated my last book to the memory of Leo Strauss.[2] But why did I do that? One does not do such a thing lightly. I think if one dedicates a book at all, there should be some thought behind it. I could quote Allan Bloom, who has written, "[T]hose who have lived with his books over a period of many years have been changed, as were Glaucon and Adeimantus, by the night they spent with Socrates." I take it this is not a controversial statement. In my case this has been true, though not with his books but with certain crucial encounters. I would not be immodest enough to mention my own affairs were it not for the fact that I think that Judaism—or at least Jewish faith and destiny in our time—has been at stake in these encounters.

I'll begin with the year 1935, when I went to the Hochschule für die Wissenschaft des Judentums in Berlin for a simple reason which would have found Strauss's total approval: to discover the truth. It sounds very naive, and maybe it is. The truth that I was looking for was the truth of Judaism, because the one thing I had been convinced of was that there was a truth of Judaism to be discovered in the terrible times that were at hand. Berlin of that day was the most absurd and the most appropriate place for the study of Judaism: The most absurd for the obvious reason that we all should have sought refuge as quickly as possible from the dangers which we underestimated; the most appropriate because rarely before or since has there been a place or set of circumstances calculated to make a young Jew take the study of Judaism so seriously. The name of the institution, Hochschule für die Wissenschaft des Judentums, roughly translated means "Higher Academy for the Science of Judaism." It's a bad translation, for "Wissenschaft"

Jewish Philosophers

and "science" are not quite the same. And the story which I will briefly rehearse might be set over a hundred years earlier when a group of young Jewish intellectuals formed an organization with the bold purpose of saving the future of Judaism. Among the famous were Eduard Gans, subsequently one of the most significant Hegelians; Heinrich Heine, the poet (surely the greatest of them); and Leopold Zunz. Their first principle was that, since they believed that the future survival of Jews and Judaism was necessary, it must also be possible. The minimum condition of survival was that conversion to Christianity for opportunistic reasons was to be ruled out. Shortly after, Gans became converted in order to be able to secure a professorship at Berlin. Heine became a convert, as he himself called it, as an "admission ticket to European civilization," and never got over the trauma. The man who remained, Leopold Zunz, became the founder of the scholarly study of Judaism. Now I had come to Berlin in search of truth. What I got instead was the scholarly study of Judaism. What it meant to Zunz was never quite clear, but Moritz Steinschneider, a colleague of Zunz who was even more scholarly than Zunz himself, said it bluntly: "Judaism is dead, scholarship means giving it a decent burial."

I don't think you can search for the truth of Judaism without the help of Jewish philosophy or, for that matter, general philosophy. But what we were given was the scholarly study of past philosophy, which meant that many questions were raised of what, for example, Maimonides had said or meant. Whether what Maimonides had said was true was considered an unscholarly question. It was at that point in my career that my first encounter with Strauss took place, when I read the one and only book of his which to this day (disgracefully, I think) has not been translated into English: *Philosophie und Gesetz.*[3] It hasn't been published yet, so I feel free to give a few quotations. I read this book as a very young student and was immediately gripped by it. This is what he says at the very beginning: "If the belief in the creation of the world, the reality of Biblical miracles, the valid law based on revelation at Sinai, is the foundation of Judaism, then one must say that modern Enlightenment has undermined its foundation." There seemed to be a man who uttered a radical challenge, a challenge which a scholarship simply confined to the sayings of men in the past didn't face. Since it is clear from the very beginning of the book that Strauss does not take this simply lying down, one could not but go on and read from there. A few pages later Strauss asks this question: "Should one say that world history is the world judgment or, more precisely, just the last three hundred years?" The allusion is to Schiller, who made that statement, and more especially to Hegel, who endorsed it. Does that mean that since the Enlightenment is more recent than Maimonides, it has won? For no reason other than that it is more recent? Then he raised the question which immediately fascinated me: maybe one must pick up those dusty old books and read them? And maybe one should not prejudge the question, "Who, in this struggle between what he calls Jewish orthodoxy and modern Enlightenment, is right?" There was no question that here there was a search for truth.

Strauss goes on to close the chapter by saying, "Since it is clear that on the one hand there seems to be a conflict between modern Enlightenment and a philosophy based on revelation, while on the other hand certainly enlightenment of some sort is a modern necessity, one ought to ask whether modern Enlightenment is the only enlightenment that is possible." Now these are trenchant words. Some of the cognoscenti, the experts on Strauss (of whom I am not one), say this belongs to the early period of Strauss. This should not mean that the early period is superseded or insignificant because I see these words reverberating to the very last words of Strauss so far as I am familiar with them. Perhaps there is such a thing as an enlightenment which is fully as rational as modern enlightenment claims to be, but which does not turn against the traditional verities? In this case, the issue that interested me, that concerned me above all, was revelation. Strauss goes on, just a little, into what revelation might mean. "Revelation is looked for only if man needs it," he says, "that is to say, if his own reason is not satisfactory for all questions." There are overtones here to a debt Strauss himself owed, that began with his saying that one does not dedicate a book lightly. Certainly that was not Strauss's practice. He had dedicated his first book to the memory of Franz Rosenzweig, the great renewer of the quest for revelation in Judaism.

Now, under the impact of just that small volume, I decided to change my course of studies. That is why I quoted Bloom, and I think that statement, at least, is uncontroversial. I'm sure many people who never met Strauss in person simply were gripped by a book of his, and it did change their lives. In my own philosophical search, the names that were then around were obviously Kierkegaard, Heidegger, and not quite so obviously the late Schelling, who has been a great concern of mine all my life.

But that presupposed that the ancients or, in this case, the premoderns were not to be taken seriously in their own right. I then decided that I could not possibly deal with the question of Kierkegaard and others adequately unless I had considered the alternative first. So, purely under the influence of Strauss's book, I decided to do my Ph.D. thesis on medieval philosophy. I was blessed by the winds of fortune to be driven to Toronto, where there was an institute that I think, in the Germany of the Weimar Republic or what followed, was not conceivable: the Institute of Medieval Studies, where Thomism was taught as the simple truth. If you asked, "Well, what about the modern philosophy that came since?" the answer is really quite simple: "It's a mistake." Jacques Maritain, one of my teachers, put it most bluntly, in a way with admirable boldness (or, if you wish to put the same thing in Hebrew, admirable *chutzpah*). He wrote a book in which he advocated intellectual intuition, which, of course, Kant rejects (and Kant is not a philosopher to be taken lightly). But Maritain said (I forget whether verbally or in one of his writings), "Intellectual intuition means you see—there are philosophers who see and those who don't see." That was the end of the subject; Kant was a philosopher who didn't see.

It wasn't the end of the subject for me. And I must say, when I now think of my teachers, it was very refreshing then (coming as I did from what you might call decadent central Europe) to see and to hear the *philosophia perennis*. There were Gilson, Maritain, and other less-well-known names that meant a great deal to me. And then there was Leo Strauss. The influence of Gilson and Maritain is long past. There was one fundamental difference between them and Leo Strauss. For Leo Strauss, to get back to the premoderns—whether it was the Greeks or the Jews, whether it was Athens or Jerusalem—required an extraordinarily difficult act of recovery. They were not automatically contemporaries. I recall that I once attended a meeting at the American Philosophical Association where there were two significant philosophers whom I knew, but who didn't know each other: one was Leo Strauss, the other was Paul Weiss. I introduced them to each other, and afterward each told me what he thought of the other. Paul Weiss thought Leo Strauss was perverse, and Leo Strauss thought that Paul Weiss was naive. And I think that sort of sums up the situation. You just don't reopen the questions of Plato and Aristotle in an historical vacuum. If you want to ask, "What is it that made the difference between Weiss and Strauss?" you could simply point to one figure: Martin Heidegger. There is history, and there is a threat that history is destructive of eternal verities, or, to put it otherwise, "the threat of historicism and how to overcome it." That, or something similar—*Die Überwindung des Historismus*—was the title of a book by Ernst Troeltsch. I read the book, but it did not fulfill the promise of its title.

Well, as I say, I was at Toronto and decided to take a daring step for a young man—namely, to seek out Strauss in person. He was still living in New York, and he welcomed me with open arms. I was afraid of stealing his time, but he didn't seem to consider me a thief of his time. We must have spent four or five hours talking, and I thought, could it really be that this man is as lonely, intellectually, as I? In any case, he was very kind to me, and whenever I got sort of depressed—philosophically depressed, that is to say—I would take a train or a plane to New York and spend a few hours with him.

I found that some of these meetings had a great shock value. I was writing the only paper on Maimonides I ever published—of course largely under Strauss's influence—and as I discussed it with him, I learned a few lessons about what it means to read a text carefully. If indeed, Heidegger notwithstanding, it is to be possible to span that gap from the "now" to the ancient text, then the first condition is that the text is to be taken with the greatest seriousness. I forget what the issue was, but I asserted something

Leo Strauss and Modern Judaism

about the *Guide of the Perplexed* which appears in the second book, and Strauss said, "Have you noticed that he comes back to the subject in the third book?" Well, I hadn't noticed it. I was too young and innocent and ignorant. He not only made me notice it, but he showed that there must be great significance if Maimonides returns in the third book to the subject already dealt with in the second. Maybe what is in the second book is only exoteric and meant for the people who don't read any further. I think that, for those who were fortunate enough actually to study with Strauss, one of the greatest lessons must have been to learn how to treat a text carefully, to read it in its own right. To some extent this must have been his Jewish heritage, because it is a Jewish tradition that the text must be read carefully—primarily, of course, the Bible. And in the *Sayings of the Fathers* it is said, "Turn it and turn it, everything is in it." Then it applies derivatively to the Talmud, and then it applies derivatively to the commentaries on the Talmud. Heinrich Heine, who was able to mock things sacred and get away with it, told of a Christian-Jewish disputation which is foredoomed from the start because each quotes his own authorities. Finally, the rabbi quotes an obscure Talmudic commentary, and the Christian says, "The *Tausvos-Yontef* can go to the Devil!" The rabbi goes crazy because for him this commentary is God Himself. I think the tradition mockingly alluded to here must have had a share in the development of Strauss's thought.

Of course, Strauss has his own philosophical concern with the text. If, indeed, there is a gulf between the here and the then, one must read the text with the greatest closeness in order to bridge that gulf. I won't go into doctrines of Strauss's which are well known, of the esoteric and the exoteric, but what I am limiting myself to goes on in all of his writing. The text does not disclose its secrets easily, and then perhaps a derivative thing should be that the writer about the text should not disclose *his* secrets easily, and I think the fact that there is controversy surrounding Strauss has something to do with it. Of course Strauss is a most extraordinary subtle writer, and one reads him and reads him and finds more in him all the time.

In my meetings with him, it soon became clear that for him there are two alternatives, and I think all his life he must have struggled with them. They go by the names "Athens" and "Jerusalem." He spoke very lovingly of the *Yevanim*, the Hebrew word for Greeks, and, of course automatically, he spoke lovingly of the Jewish tradition with which he wrestled all of his life. Incidentally, near our home in Jerusalem is a square dedicated to the "sages of Greece." Strauss would have loved that.

The fundamental point about Jewish tradition, which came out again and again in further meetings I had with him, was that Torah is either the Word of God or else it has no essential significance. If the whole tradition was mistaken on this fundamental point, and if Torah is just a part of culture (and maybe a minor part), to treat it as mere culture would revolutionize the whole past. But perhaps the tradition was right? This was the obvious question, but there was also an underlying question: How does one know that to get back to either the Greeks or the Jews, Athens or Jerusalem, is possible? It must be possible because it is necessary! And why is it necessary? Because the shadow of Nazism hung over us all.

I don't know of any place where Strauss discusses Nazism in great detail, and, particularly when it came to evil, he exercised great self-restraint. I think his restraint on this subject could be best contrasted with the lack of restraint of his contemporary, Hannah Arendt, who wrote about it at length, sometimes well, sometimes not so well. Strauss exercised the greatest restraint, and I think here perhaps is one point where I would dissent with him. But the underlying theme that the possibility and actuality of Nazism was a sign of corruption in modern civilization was surely an essential element in this search for a possibility of a return to the ancients which must be necessary.

After this, I lost touch with Strauss. There was an external reason: he moved to Chicago, and I didn't get to Chicago as often as New York. There was also another reason: for me, the medievals became less and less relevant because of one figure, and I think this is the figure one has to choose as an alternative to Plato. That figure is Hegel. I think the essential difference between Hegel and Plato, both of whom are concerned with eternal verities, is that for Hegel history falls inside the realm of verities, and this is made possible by Christianity. I found it necessary to become more and more involved with Hegel, and I think, by the same token, more and more remote, during this period, from Strauss. Strauss spoke to me about Hegel from time to time, and he had only noble things to say about him. In his terms, "Man muss seine Rechtschaffenheit bewundern (His rectitude is admirable)," which is, I think, an excellent judgment because most people don't recognize it in Hegel—Hegel uses big words, and people who use big words generally don't have philosophical rectitude. Of course there is a whole German tradition, and I've had a lifelong doubt as to whether Heidegger is really to be included among the greatest of philosophers: he often does use big words without one being able to see the necessity. The more one studies Hegel, the more one sees that he uses those big words as little as possible, and only when they are necessary. So this rectitude in Hegel, Strauss recognized. He just chose the alternative way, and this difference between us led us very far apart.

Nevertheless, we remained in contact. When I wrote to him and sent him my first attempt (a small attempt) to deal with historicism, in *Metaphysics and Historicity*, he wrote to me (a sign of Strauss's own rectitude) that my attempt, in retrospect naive, to refute Heidegger was inadequate. I tried to refute Heidegger by accusing him of self-contradiction, which is a sort of sophomoric philosophical activity. And Strauss pointed out, knowing Heidegger to be, for better or worse, the greatest philosopher then in opposition, that this was inadequate. I accepted his criticism for the validity it had, and I must say I'm sorry he was no longer alive when my last attempt to cope with Heidegger appeared. I've wondered whether he would have considered that one sophomoric, too. I don't know—I hope not—but that is what happened at the time. Recently, when I reread his *Jerusalem and Athens*, I still noticed that, whereas he had moved to the *Yevanim*, to the Greeks, he had left open the option of Jerusalem and revelation. But I must say I now found myself necessarily compelled to dissent on two points in his account. This may explain our moving apart.

I spoke before of restraint vis-à-vis Nazism in Strauss. I think there is a restraint in him vis-à-vis evil altogether. This is what Strauss wrote about the serpent in his account of Genesis: "It is reasonable to assume that the serpent acted as it did because it was cunning; that is, possessed a low kind of wisdom, a congenital malice. Everything that God has created would not be very good if it did not include something congenitally bent on mischief."[4] Now of course it depends on what one has in mind when reading this passage in Genesis, but I find myself dissenting from this view. Perhaps one thing that Plato and Hegel have in common is not to take evil sufficiently seriously, though for different reasons.

Now I would not be honest if I did not push this doubt to its full conclusion. In a great essay, Strauss writes:

> It is safer to try to understand the low in the light of the high than the high in the light of the low. In doing the latter, one necessarily distorts the high, whereas in doing the former one does not deprive the low of the freedom to reveal itself fully for what it is.[5]

This is clearly Platonic: You understand the perverse state of the tripartite "soul" in terms of its healthy state. Perversity and chaos come in many forms, and you recognize them for what they are. It seems to me that there are limitations here. The limitation is that there is one low that cannot be understood, or does not fully reveal itself, if looked at from the standpoint of the high. That low is Nazism and especially the Holocaust. I think Plato—and maybe I should say both Athens and Jerusalem—is not adequate when it comes to confronting the diabolical evil that is the Holocaust.

I used to read during the evening of the Passover Seder a statement which the Orthodox Rabbinate in New York distributed. It was a great accomplishment to take note of the Holocaust at all in the ritual. This is what it says after alluding very, very vaguely to the Nazi crimes: "We refrain from dwelling on the deeds of the wicked ones, lest we defame the image of God in which man was created." I no longer find this satisfactory, just as I find Strauss's statement no longer satisfactory, because, in the first place, *we* don't defame the image of man, *they* defamed it. It's a very different thing. In the second place, the defamation has consequences, and what is necessary is to take note of them and to confront them. I think, in determining to confront them, I could take a cue from Strauss himself, from the very early work which I alluded to initially, where he raises the question of the conflict between traditional Judaism and the Enlightenment. There he asks, "Shall we go back to premodern naivity?" That's not possible. What we have to do is *radicalize* Enlightenment reflection, and overcome it. I would say that if the turn to history is, after all, inevitable, and Heidegger and all he stands for in this matter has to be coped with, then I think that what has to be done is to confront Heidegger with the Holocaust. I think this would be an attempt to confront the evil and to cope with it. I fully agree with Strauss that the high has to be understood in its own terms; that if it is understood in terms of the low, it is necessarily distorted. But if *all* the low is indiscriminately viewed in the light of the high, Auschwitz becomes just one "tyranny" among others. It will be remembered in Plato's *Republic*, the ultimate political perversion is tyranny. But Plato did not and could not conceive of the Holocaust because it had not yet happened.

Let me end up by making just two points on Strauss's last posthumous book. I think all the Straussian experts are somewhat puzzled by the title: *Studies in Platonic Political Philosophy*. It does not say "and other essays," so that must be intended—and it was Strauss's own title. Not only the essays, but also their order was requested by Strauss. The last of the essays, in a book on Platonic philosophy, is on Hermann Cohen. Hermann Cohen was a Jewish philosopher; in fact, he was Strauss's teacher. I think it proves that Strauss never gave up on Jerusalem any more than on Athens.

This is my first point. The second is that the end of the Cohen essay seems unsatisfactory. This illustrates his excessive restraint in dealing with radical evil, which is characteristic of the Platonic tradition. In the case of Hermann Cohen, he saw things both too brightly and too darkly. Strauss ends the essay on him—and this is the end of the book—by saying, "It was a blessing that Hermann Cohen lived and taught." On this I think we can fully agree. Then he makes two statements connected with this: "Even though Hermann Cohen didn't know it [he died in 1917], this teaching on the nobility of martyrdom gave strength to the Jews in the sufferings that were to come." Unfortunately, this is much too positive an appraisal. Cohen calls martyrdom meaningful and implies that it is always possible and always meaningful, but the Holocaust robbed most of its victims of the very possibility of martyrdom. Martyrdom involves a free choice. The Jews of the Holocaust were not willing martyrs but unwilling victims. In this respect, then, Strauss's view is not grim enough; in another respect, it is too grim. He continues, "Hermann Cohen gave no comfort and no guidance to the Jews of the Soviet Union, because no philosophy can give them any guidance." Why? Because here is a tyranny that robs Jews of the knowledge of Judaism.

My wife and I visited the Soviet Union in 1977. Our purpose was precisely to defy that Soviet policy. If Jews who want to know about Judaism are deprived of that possibility, then it is necessary for us to visit them and give them that knowledge. So that was our purpose. I made my first phone call, trembling with fear of not reaching anybody, but I reached someone right away. We rushed right over, and he said his group was meeting in an hour, so we had to settle what we would talk about. I asked him, "What do you want me to talk about?" He said, "Jewish philosophy." I asked him, "What do you mean by Jewish philosophy?" He gave a magnificent answer: "We all know that it is our duty to survive as Jews. Jewish philosophy will tell us why." Here, then, Strauss was too pessimistic. He did not reckon with Jews who, though robbed of the knowledge of Judaism, defy their oppressors in heroic fidelity to a heritage they do not know. In trying to recover it, some will find a great blessing in Strauss. Strauss said about Hermann Cohen that it was a blessing that he lived and taught. To paraphrase this: It was a great blessing for the future of Jewish philosophy that Leo Strauss lived and taught.

Eight

Pinchas Peli as a
Jewish Philosopher

I

I remember one of my most promising students, many years ago in Toronto. He became interested in Jewish philosophy already in high school.
Going on with the subject at university, he studied in Toronto and Jerusalem, at length ending up at Columbia University. One day he telephoned
me from New York, in a confusion bordering on despair: his Ph.D. supervisor had suggested that he find a medieval treatise obscure and trivial
enough never to have engaged anyone's interest, prepare a critical edition
of the text, and that, together with an introduction and scholarly notes,
would be his thesis. Today, this former student of mine has long turned
away from—even against—things Jewish: yet he might have become a major Jewish philosopher had Abraham Heschel been his supervisor. Or
Pinchas Peli.

Heschel and Peli: some years back Pinchas told me how Heschel once
telephoned him late one Motza'e Shabbat, in mock excitement about news
that could not wait till the next day. A breakthrough in Biblical scholarship: someone had suggested a new meaning for a hapax legomenon! It was
either this, or something else equally world-shaking.

Peli's thought and my own: once we shared a taxi to Jerusalem, back
from a Tel Aviv conference, the subject of which had been responses to the
Holocaust. A paper given at the conference had listed "options" or "models"
of responses to catastrophe available within the Hasidic tradition, together
with examples of how many Hasidim among the victims had had recourse
to these during the Holocaust. The paper, we agreed, had displayed admirable scholarship, but something had been lacking: the anguish, the hope
against hope, the desperate wish to remain faithful even when "hope was
the last to die." (The title of a survivor's memoir.) We agreed, too, on the
epistemological import of this lack: precisely to the extent to which the
paper was self-imprisoned by the ideal of Wissenschaft—"scientific," even
clinical, detachment—it had failed to convey the objective truth. To put it
somewhat paradoxically, the paper had not been objective enough because
it had not been subjective enough.

Peli the person and my family: more than anyone else, Pinchas has been

Pinchas Peli as a Jewish Philosopher

the *Shaliach* of my family, during our many visits prior to our Aliya in 1983. He and his wife Pnina took us to many places, of which the most significant, perhaps, was Kibbutz Yad Mordecai. We first ascended what, in the War of Independence, had been the hill of the defenders against, by the standards of the time, overwhelming Egyptian forces. What a miserable little hill! No less little had been the number of both the defenders and their guns, the latter themselves little in quality, all this recalling—as does, of course, the very name of the kibbutz—the Warsaw Ghetto Uprising and its hopelessness. We asked ourselves at the kibbutz—just as one must ask again and again when thinking of the Ghetto Uprising—just how they managed to hold out day after day, night after night, with few arms, little food, drink and sleep and—this above all!—to all evidence without hope.

We asked that question on that little hill—and found it answered when we ascended the other kibbutz hill: there, justly larger than life, is the statue of Mordecai Anielewicz, the leader who died in the Warsaw Ghetto Uprising. Behind the statue is the water tower the Egyptians smashed in the War of Independence, a mute symbol that murderous Jew-hatred is not yet dead, for in the desert, without water there is no life. But these—the smashed water tower and the hatred—are behind the statue: in front are things that the real Anielewicz could only dream of: grass, butterflies, cows, freedom, Israel.

I have begun with these four anecdotes because, quite by themselves, they show why I consider Pinchas Peli an authentic Jewish philosopher. Just as a scholar does not become authentic through the multiplicity of his footnotes, so a philosopher, hence a Jewish philosopher, is not made authentic by the subtlety and sophistication of his arguments. Generally, I would define a Jewish philosopher (as distinct from a Jewish thinker) as one—this in modern times was the case, for example, with Hermann Cohen, Franz Rosenzweig, and, to a lesser degree, Martin Buber—who exposes his Jewish commitments to general philosophy, and the latter to his Jewish commitments. That I view Peli as an exception may be gathered from his above-cited judgment on that paper on Hasidism, which was as if he had been deeply engaged with some of the greatest modern philosophers, among them Hegel, Kierkegaard, Heidegger, and even Immanuel Kant.[1]

What makes a Jewish thinker into a philosopher *today*? This too is evident from the four anecdotes. There has to be, of course, consistency, but with Peli another criterion too must be satisfied—what Eberhard Bethge, Dietrich Bonhoeffer's biographer, has called a "reality-relatedness" that Bonhoeffer himself acquired only painfully, when he joined a plot against Hitler, an act which cost him his life. Surely nothing so powerfully makes a philosopher *Jewish* as "Torah": but can he be either Jewish or a philosopher today if, in the name of Torah but unexposed to the reality of the Holocaust, he views all Jewish suffering as punishment for Jewish sins? Or if—this too in the name of Torah but unexposed to that other new reality, the Jewish state—he demands obedience to *mitzvot* that, if obeyed by the state, would threaten its very survival? Peli's thought, in contrast to Jewish thinkers of this kind, is self-exposed to the two new realities, the Holocaust and the Jewish state, but this without ever letting go of "Torah" as having, for him, a continued reality of its own. Reality-relatedness, I would argue, requires of Jewish philosophy today *three* self-exposures, and the special genius of Peli's philosophy is its endurance of the tension between them as, to be sure, it struggles for consistency, but never at the price of infidelity to the realities. His thought is, as it were, a triangle that would collapse if any of the angles were viewed as though they did not exist.

II

In this threefold fidelity Peli's thought bewares lest it be not objective enough because it is not subjective enough. This doctrine, already cited and seemingly "irrationalist," was supported by no less "rationalist" a philosopher than Hegel when he wrote: "it is only in inspired terms that the Divine can be rightly spoken of."[2] If he was alive today, Hegel would have to add that it is only in horrified terms that the Holocaust can be rightly spoken of. With Peli's triangle, we must therefore first turn to the Holocaust, since the possibility cannot be ruled out that its horror destroys the "inspired" terms evoked for Jewish readers by Torah at all times and, in our time, also by the state of Israel.

In 1983 Peli considered this dread possibility, hence the Holocaust itself, in an article in the *Jerusalem Post*. His choice of this medium, in preference to a learned journal, was itself significant in that it implied that *amcha*—ordinary Jewish folk—is not excluded from deep, even philosophical, Jewish thought, while on their part philosophers and theologians, if divorced from *amcha*, may go astray. Theodicy—philosophical or theological systems showing that in God's world evil makes sense, is for the best, is not evil at all—Peli writes in his "Where Was God during the Holocaust?" is often "arrogance that sometimes borders on sanctimonious cruelty."[3]

The two-part *Post* article cites, but quickly disposes of, past "models" of Jewish religious responses to evil, not only because of what they are but also because they are characteristically presented as "options" between which to choose, as if Peli's title question were for theoretical classroom debate rather then a life-and-death one, at one time for individual Jewish lives then and there and, here and now, for collective Jewish life as a whole—its quality, its meaning, its very survival in its Jewishness. If "options" were the right way of describing possible responses, the most radical ones would be most appropriate. But of these, one—the "death" of God, at Auschwitz as much as anywhere else—is outside the parameters of Judaism. As for the other—Buber's "eclipse" of God—for a Jew who seeks "Torah Today," any such answer only gives rise to the further question of how a God, in "eclipse" precisely when His presence was needed most, can ever be a meaningful Presence again. Hardly a classroom "option," when the destiny of all future Jewish life—Jewish *religious* life—is at stake with it!

Peli deals lightly with past options, not only because they *are* options but also because they are *past*. Writing in the 1950s, Buber had already considered the Holocaust a *novum* for Judaism.[4] Writing over three decades later, Peli more fully confronts the Holocaust as a catastrophe for Judaism that is without precedent. Hence, although he harks back to the pre-Holocaust Rabbi Levi Yitzhak of Berdiczev, he finds that, as a "model," the Berdiczever breaks down at the crucial point. In a well-known and much-cited prayer, this Hasidic rabbi—to this layman in Hasidic matters, the greatest of them all—asks the Master of the Universe to let him know, not why he suffers—a mystery he could not understand—but only that he suffers for His sake. This was prior to the Holocaust. The post-Holocaust Pinchas Peli finds it necessary to amend: "I do not want to know why I suffer . . . but only if You know that I suffer."[5] Why this emendation? Why its necessity?

The answer is simple: the children. That the children—not only adults who, being adults, are capable of rising or at least aspiring to martyrdom— might suffer for God's sake Peli finds unacceptable. Yet if the Holocaust is a catastrophe qualitatively *other* than others and, as such, *without precedent*, it is most eminently by dint of the unheard-of Nazi conjunction of crime *and birth*. Children have suffered before the Holocaust and since. But only in the Holocaust, and for Jews alone, the "crime" deserving torture and death, punished with torture and death, was not belief or unbelief, actions or non-actions, but rather *birth*: children, if they were Jewish, were "criminals" from the moment of birth, nay, while still in the womb.

The Holocaust, for Peli, is without precedent: is it thoughtlessly, inconsistently, then, that elsewhere he affirms *one huge* precedent? "Midway between Adam and Abraham, *after the holocaust of the deluge,* the world which God has created gets another chance. A new page is opened . . . " (italics added).[6] There is no inconsistency, for while the Holocaust is in history, the Biblical flood is *prehistorical*, history beginning in earnest only as the Noachidic "new page" is opened. Still less than inconsistency is there thoughtlessness but, on the contrary, a new, post-Holocaust thoughtfulness. Why, for Peli, is the Biblical flood a "holocaust"? Because here, too, *all* are destroyed—all, that is, including the children. "Never again will I curse the ground because of man . . . and never again will I destroy all living creatures, as I have done" (Gen.8: 21). With the opening of this, the Noachidic page, "there is a smile again on the face of God," a first indication for us here that for Peli the "inspiration" of "Torah" is not destroyed for us by the Holocaust horror—but an indication also that for *our* today *Torah Today* reveals a horror of its own. A smile may be again on the face of God as history begins in earnest. However, as for the drowning of the pre-Noachidic children, nothing is explained, nothing justified, with the result that—for post-Holocaust Jews reading their Torah—all history rests on the ground of a prehistoric horror.

III

In his *Torah Today*, Peli thus harks back to prehistory. In the same work— but also frequently elsewhere—he veritably plunges *into* history when he turns to the "reality" of Israel. The Jewish state is *itself* a plunge into history and—if history is intrinsically precarious—*this* plunge, and the history set in train by it, are uniquely precarious. After nearly two millennia of Jewish statelessness, this would in any case be true for Judaism. In the prevailing historical circumstances, it is also for Jewish existence. Other contemporary states may face this or that threat: only the Jewish state's very existence has been threatened since the day of its birth. And what Jewish existence there would be in case, God forbid, this state were destroyed? This dread, un-asked question lies beneath all serious Jewish existence today.

Peli's "reality-relatedness" to Israel—sensitivity to precariousness—is seen most succinctly in two essays read together, but with an awareness of the event that separates them. *Israel: The Religious Dimension* was published in 1969, *The Future of Israel* in 1974, and between the two dates lies the shock of the 1973 Yom Kippur War.[7] "There is no instant solution to to the problem of religion in Israel."—thus Peli disposes of such "instant solutions" as, at one end, a "democratic" Western-style separation of "state" and "church" and, at the other, a "Jewish"-because-halachic state: these, and many other proposals, fail to confront the deepest dimension of the Israeli "reality," the sharing of one Jewish destiny in a single state by "religious" and "nonreligious" Jews alike.

Thus, in 1969 the future of Israeli Judaism—and, for Peli, with it of Ju-daism as a whole—is open, hopeful to be sure, but in any case uncertain. In 1974, he faces up to a still deeper, more existential uncertainty: the threat to Israel's very survival and—for him—to Jewish survival as a whole. De-pressed by the 1973 war, he expressed his feelings in an address to Diaspora leaders, and went on as follows:

> Though it is not easy for me to say this, it was you, my friends, who contrib-uted . . . to that depression by your conspicuous absence. Weeks went by be-fore we saw American Jews (excluding a small group of volunteers) who came to us after the Yom Kippur blow.

What with Israel, and with it all things Jewish, plunged into history's precariousness, how is it that Peli, nevertheless, finds a firm yet "reality-related" ground on which to stand? In 1969 he writes:

> By its very existence, Israel is a religious act. . . . The people who give their lives to build Israel, to defend it are—whether they themselves are conscious of it at the moment or not—priests, doing divine service in the Holy Temple of the God of Israel.

Pinchas Peli as a Jewish Philosopher

Even in 1969, putting it mildly, such a view was not universally accepted; today—again putting it mildly—in many places purportedly devoted to free speech it would not be allowed expression. Yet what Peli affirmed in 1969 he confirmed—with hammer-blows, as it were—in 1974; and, had he still been alive when the scud missiles fell on Tel Aviv and Haifa, he would doubtless have hit even harder:

> Israel was established in the Warsaw Ghetto. . . . The only drive for "normali-zation" which remained valid was that which long ago was crystalized in the words of the Psalmist: "Do not give me death. I wish to live." . . . And if we have to die, we are going to die in battle, not in crematoria.

A near-desperate, but well-warranted defiance! How does hope, neverthe-less, survive? Only if its "religious" dimension is bolstered by a "secularist" determination: "We try to transpose Jewish fate into Jewish destiny, and to shape our future with our own hands." This determination concerns by no means Israel only, for "without Israel Jewish life would have lost its meaning and dignity."

Thus "reality-relatedness" requires Peli to utter some radically un-Bibli-cal—some would say, impious—sentiments. Yet these come from the author of *Torah Today*, a work inspiring Jews all over the world because it shows that the Torah is as "reality-related" today as it ever was in days of yore.

IV

Of this some crucial examples must here suffice. *What of the Land?* Com-menting on Genesis 26, Peli writes:

> Isaac knew well enough that not one peace treaty, not even many of them, would make him fulfill God's command to "dwell in the Land." This would come only through persistent hard work of digging more and more wells of living water.[8]

Who is a Jew? Having in mind Jacob's blessing of his grandchildren—in-stead of Joseph, his two sons Ephraim and Menashe—Peli replies: "Not one who can boast about his Jewish grandparents . . . but one who can speak with confidence about his Jewish grandchildren."[9]

The first comment reads like today's newspaper in Israel, the second like today's Jewish newspaper anywhere.

What of Pharao's slavery?

> This is all Pharao has to say to them: "You will not be given any straw; but you must produce your full quota of bricks" (Exodus 5:17–18).[10]

Hitler's concentration camp—if not his extermination policy—has an Egyptian precedent! The writer Jean Améry has shown that the concentra-tion camp was ruled by a "logic of destruction": the inmates must keep clean but are given neither soap nor water; severe punishment is meted out for buttons missing on jackets, but neither buttons nor thread nor needles are supplied. Where did Hitler get the idea? Perhaps on reading the Old Testament (which he hated) from the Pharao (whom he loved).

The "language" of faith? Ever since the Salvation at the Sea and the Song that celebrates it "Song and praise has remained . . . the most genuine [Jewish] language of faith."[11] More than anyone else, Pinchas Peli has been our *Shaliach*: we first met him when we heard him sing.

Just how crucial in the "language" of song is the dimension of song? King Hezekiah was meant to become the Messiah. Yet, although he experienced the salvation from the hand of Sanherib, he was unable to sing, and such a one cannot be the Messiah. Indeed, Hezekiah "could not secure that even his son would follow in his footsteps. King Menashe, the son of Hezekiah, is known as the most wicked among Biblical kings."[12]

What of gentiles? Now as then, the Jewish people has enemies: but now as then, not true is that "the whole world is against" them.[13] Amalek there has been and is. Amalek, however, is not the gentile world as a whole.

> Not only did [Jethro] rejoice with Israel during one of its best hours, but he was also, as the Talmud points out, the first to offer a formal blessing in praise of the Lord. "And Jethro said: Praised be the Lord who hath delivered you out of the hand of the Egyptians and of Pharao." Many pious Jews today who frequently use the phrase *baruch hashem* (Praised be the Lord) in their daily speech are probably unaware that it was the non-Jew Jethro who coined the expression.[14]

V

A philosopher but also a poet, Peli wears his philosophical mantle lightly. One passage, concerning "Two Sanctuaries," suffices to show that wear it he does.

> Moses prefaces his words regarding the sanctuary with a reminder about the Sabbath [in Exodus 25]. There are, he tells them, two sanctuaries, one in space, another in time. The sacredness of the spatial and visible sanctuary ranks second when compared to the temporal and invisible sacredness of the Sabbath.
>   All work done toward building the tabernacle must cease with the onset of the Sabbath. Time was made holy by God Himself (Genesis 2: 3), while space may be sanctified by man. The holiness of the Sabbath thus surpasses the holiness of the sanctuary.[15]

Holiness of time in Franz Rosenzweig and Abraham Heschel; holiness of space in Martin Buber: Peli knows all their teaching but finds the apt relation of time and space for "today" in the Torah itself. The holiness of Sabbath time supersedes that of the Temple space, which is why Jewish faith could survive during the millennia of dispersion. But the return to the Land is a reminder that space can have a holiness of its own. This, however, would degenerate into idolatry if it became the worship of dust and stones, for whereas time was made holy by God, only man can bestow holiness on space—by his dedication, his integrity, his work.

PART II

The Holocaust and Philosophy

Introduction to Part II

If Jewish philosophy is an historical phenomenon, real encounters between the Jewish heritage and philosophical thinking, then Jewish philosophy *today* is not what it was yesterday. Fackenheim makes this point again and again in a graphic way: thinkers like Rosenzweig, if true to their principles, would today—after Auschwitz and in the age of a new Jerusalem—revise their conclusions. A Rosenzweig of today would rewrite the *Star* as a "theo-political" work and "the *Lehrhaus* Rosenzweig would found today, after having completed his revised *Star*, would not be located in Frankfurt but in Jerusalem."[1]

In this collection, the first seven chapters dealt with the Jewish philosophy of yesterday. In the eighth, a tribute to his deceased friend Pinchas Peli, Fackenheim made a double shift.[2] First, he acknowledged that the Jewish philosopher of today need not be a philosopher in the traditional sense, for Peli surely was not that. He was a theologian, a teacher, a pious Jew, but not a philosopher. Second, Fackenheim focused on the historical desiderata of any genuine contemporary Jewish philosophy—the Holocaust and the state of Israel. To be authentic, Jewish philosophy must confront these realities; it must expose itself to them, examine them, interrogate them, and rethink its commitments as a result. So it is that in part II we turn to four essays that do just this with regard to the Holocaust.

What is the Holocaust? What happened in those years? What was the crime? Who were the criminals? Who were the victims, who the bystanders? And what was the evil? Why did they do it? For more than twenty-five years Fackenheim has pondered these questions and others like them.[3] The first chapter in this part summarizes his encounter with this dark event. It is a survey, written as a single presentation of the Holocaust for a dictionary of contemporary Jewish thought. Here Fackenheim asks deep questions and gives summary answers: Why is the event unique and unprecedented? How did the Nazis carry out the exterminations? Why did they do it? He then explores the challenges faced by historians and philosophers, challenges about explanation and understanding, about human nature and the human condition, about new ways of dying, new ways of living, and about the very notion of a "rupture," a "caesura," in human history. Finally, Fackenheim notes the challenges that Auschwitz poses for theology, Christian and Jewish, and the changes it mandates for an authentic contemporary Jewish life—a new piety, moral, political, and religious all at once. Such a piety, he claims, is no mere whim. It is a duty, a necessity, and one that is as significant as it is demanding.

Readers of Fackenheim's works from 1967 to the present will recognize how much this chapter draws on his thinking in works from *God's Presence in History* to *To Mend the World*. What the essay does so well is identify the specific issues that a genuine post-Holocaust Jewish philosophy, as philosophy, must address. The first of these issues concerns the event and its uniqueness or, as he points out, its unprecedented place in history. A second issue involves the questions of why they did it and what this tells us about the evil and its uniqueness. These are the subjects of the remaining three essays in this section.

"The Holocaust and Philosophy" was originally delivered at the Eastern Division Meetings of the American Philosophical Association on December 30, 1985, in Washington. The event was a significant one, the first discussion of the Holocaust at a major philosophical conference. The response to Fackenheim's essay was given by Berel Lang of the State University of New York in Albany, whose later work, *Act and Idea in the Nazi Genocide*, is certainly one of the most important philosophical responses to the Holocaust that we have. The context, then, was a philosophical one, and it required of Fackenheim something unusual for him in these years after 1967, to clarify to philosophers why and how the events of 1933 to 1945 should be as traumatic for the philosophical world as, he had argued, they should be for Jews, Christians, Germans, and others. At that moment, the philosopher in Fackenheim was called upon to emerge in a special way, to justify the philosophical significance of an event that he had often called not parochial but "world historical" and "epoch-making."

What makes the Holocaust distinctive, ultimately, is its evil, a new horror of the whole that supersedes the particular evils of the parts. "Auschwitz"—a universe, a planet—"was a kingdom not of this world" (chapter 10). Fackenheim sketches several issues of philosophical significance, from the event's uniqueness to the radical character of its evil, drawing closer and closer to a central philosophical question that Auschwitz places in jeopardy. "Pursuing his own age-old goal, the Socratic quest, 'What is Man?', the philosopher, now as then, is filled with wonder. But the ancient wonder is now mingled with a new horror" (chapter 10). Fackenheim calls to mind the Socratic legacy and the Aristotelian notion that philosophy begins in wonder. In a short essay "A Plea for the Dead," Elie Wiesel had alluded to Plato when he said "Not only man died at Auschwitz but also the idea of man." The death camps, Hannah Arendt had claimed in *The Origins of Totalitarianism*, were laboratories for experimenting on the very idea of human nature. Fackenheim returns to this theme, and in a short discussion of the *Muselmänner*, the living dead at Auschwitz, he suggests that the challenge extends beyond a Socratic or even a Platonic model to a Heideggerian one. For Heidegger, the "freedom to die one's own death" is a fundamental feature of human existence, but in Auschwitz, this freedom was systematically destroyed. The *Muselmänner*, the drowned, are mute refutations of human finitude as Heidegger conceives it.

Fackenheim's reflections in chapter 11 on Claude Lanzmann's extraordinary film *Shoah* turn from the victims and the bystanders finally to the agents. How horrible is man? he asks; this is the old philosophical question. As in the central chapter of *To Mend the World* and in the preceding chapter of this collection, Fackenheim begins with the so-called banality of the mere "philistines" who acted, as directed, on orders simply to do their jobs and secure their pensions. Then, one by one, higher and higher on the ladder of authority and command, agents appear and are examined, only to find the evil slipping away in the midst of rationalization, obfuscation, and fanaticism. Then, finally, comes the realization: "the philosopher who contemplates what historians, biographers and others have done with the evil of the Holocaust discovers that *wherever these scholars are looking, the evil is somewhere else.* But of course it *isn't* anywhere else but rather in the Holocaust whole, of which every one of the perpetrators was part. . . . It is that whole-of-horror—'Planet Auschwitz,' one survivor calls it—that the philosopher must contemplate" (chapter 11).

A central component of these philosophical reflections on the evil and its uniqueness involves dealing with the question "why did they do it?" In the final chapter in this part, Fackenheim focuses on this question and the role played in Nazi action by the notion of *Weltanschauung*. The big questions, Fackenheim claims, are why the Nazis decided to exterminate the Jews, why they acted on this decision, and "why this action *remained sacrosanct* even when at length it became contrary to their most elementary interest" (chapter 12). He argues that various conceptions of historical explanation prove impotent before these questions. In the end the only notion that satisfies the evidence is *Weltanschauung*; the Nazis had a cosmic, internally coherent view to which they were unqualifiedly committed, a view that was understood as a *Weltanschauung*, with all the comprehensiveness, finality, awesomeness, and effectiveness that the term had come to connote. To call something a *Weltanschauung*, Fackenheim argues, was to ascribe to it a rare potency; it was to locate oneself in a place of power and cosmic order, a saving order. To explain why they did it, then, is to transcend the limits of human agency into another domain, not to absolve the perpretrators of responsibility but to understand the nature of it and the special inheritance of contemporary German thinkers.

Nine

Holocaust

Holocaust is the term currently most widely employed for the persecution of the Jewish people by Nazi Germany from 1933 to 1945, first in Germany itself and subsequently in Nazi-occupied Europe, culminating in "extermination" camps and resulting in the murder of nearly six million Jews. However, the Hebrew term *Shoah* (total destruction) would be more fitting, since *Holocaust* also connotes "burnt sacrifice." It is true that, like ancient Moloch worshipers, German Nazis and their non-German henchmen at Auschwitz threw children into the flames alive. These were not, however, their own children, thrown in acts of sacrifice, but those of Jews, thrown in acts of murder.

Is the Holocaust unique? The concept *unprecedented* is preferable, as it refers to the same facts but avoids not only well-known difficulties about the concept of *uniqueness* but also the temptation of taking the event out of history and thus mystifying it.[1] To be sure, Auschwitz was "like another planet," in the words of "Katzetnik 135683," the pen name of the novelist Yechiel Dinur, that is, a world of its own, with laws, modes of behavior, and even a language of its own. Even so, as *unprecedented*, rather than *unique*, it is placed firmly into history. Historians are obliged, so far as possible, to search for precedents; and thoughtful people, by no means historians only, are obliged to ask if the Holocaust itself may become a precedent for future processes, whether as yet only possible or already actual. Manés Sperber, for example, has written: "Encouraged by the way Hitler had practiced genocide without encountering resistance, the Arabs [in 1948] surged in upon the nascent Israeli nation to exterminate it and make themselves its immediate heirs."[2]

The most obvious recent precedent of the Holocaust is the Turkish genocide of the Armenians in World War I. Like the Nazi genocide of the Jews in World War II, this was an attempt to destroy a whole people, carried out under the cover of a war with maximum secrecy, and with the victims being deported to isolated places prior to their murder, all of which provoked few countermeasures or even verbal protests on the part of the civilized world. Doubtless the Nazis both learned from, and were encouraged by, the Armenian precedent.

But unlike the Armenian genocide, the Holocaust was intended, planned, and executed as the "final solution" of a "problem." Thus, whereas, for

The Holocaust and Philosophy

example, the roundup of Armenians in Istanbul, the very heart of the Turkish empire, was discontinued after a while, Nazi Germany, had it won the war or even managed to prolong it, would have succeeded in murdering every Jew. North American Indians have survived in reservations; Jewish reservations in a victorious Nazi empire are inconceivable. Thus the Holocaust may be said to belong, with other catastrophes, to the species *genocide*. Within the species, defined as intended, planned, and largely executed extermination, it is without precedent and, thus far at least, without sequel. It is—here the term really must be employed—unique.

Equally unique are the means without which this project could not have been planned or carried out. These include: a scholastically precise definition of the victims; juridical procedures, enlisting the finest minds of the legal profession, aimed at the total elimination of the victims' rights; a technical apparatus, including murder trains and gas chambers, and, most importantly, a veritable army not only of actual murderers but also of witting and unwitting accomplices—clerks, lawyers, journalists, bank managers, army officers, railway conductors, entrepreneurs, and an endless list of others.

All these means and accomplices were required for the *how* of the "Final Solution." Its *why* required an army of historians, philosophers, and theologians. The historians rewrote history. The philosophers refuted the idea that mankind is human before it is Aryan or non-Aryan. And the theologians were divided into Christians who made Jesus into an Aryan and neopagans who rejected Christianity itself as non-Aryan. (Their differences were slight compared to their shared commitments.) Such were the shock troops of this army. Equally necessary, however, were its remaining troops: historians, philosophers, and theologians who knew differently but betrayed their calling by holding their peace.

What was the *why* of the Holocaust? Even the shock troops never quite faced it, although they had no reason or excuse for not doing so. As early as 1936 Julius Streicher was on record to the effect that "who fights the Jew fights the devil" and "who masters the devil conquers heaven."[3] Streicher was only expressing more succinctly Hitler's assertion in *Mein Kampf* that "if the Jew will be victorious" in his cosmic struggle with mankind, his "crown" will be the "funeral wreath of humanity, and this planet will, as it did millions of years ago, move through the ether devoid of human beings."[4]

Planet Auschwitz was as good as Streicher's word. When the Third Reich was at the height of its power, the conquest of heaven seemed to lie in the apotheosis of the master race; even then, however, the mastery of the Jewish devil was a necessary condition of the conquest. When the Third Reich collapsed and the apocalypse was at hand, Planet Auschwitz continued to operate until the end, and Hitler's last will and testament made the fight against the Jewish people mandatory for future generations. The mastery of the Jewish devil, it seems, had become the sufficient condition for the "conquest of heaven," if indeed not identical with it.

To be sure, this advent of salvation in the Auschwitz gas chambers was but for relatively few eyes to see. What could be heard by all, however, was the promise of it years earlier, when the streets of Germany resounded to the storm troopers' hymn: "When Jewish blood spurts from our knives, our well-being will redouble."

Never before in history had a state attempted to make a whole country—indeed, as in this case, a whole continent—*rein* (free) of every member of a whole people, man, woman, and child. Never have attempts resembling the Holocaust been pursued with methods so thorough and with such unswerving goal-directedness. It is difficult to imagine and impossible to believe that, this having happened, world history can ever be the same. The Holocaust is not only an unprecedented event. It is also of an unfathomable magnitude. It is world historical.

As a world-historical event, the Holocaust poses new problems for philosophical thought. To begin with reflections on historiography, if, by near-common philosophical consent, to explain an event historically is to show how it was possible, then, to the philosopher, the Holocaust historian emerges sooner or later as asserting the possibility of the Holocaust solely because it was actual. He thus exposes the historian's explanation as being, in fact, circular. This impasse, to be sure, is often evaded, most obviously when, as in many histories of World War II, the Holocaust is relegated to a few footnotes. An impasse is even explicitly denied when, as in Marxist ideological history, Nazism-equals-fascism-equals-the-last-stage-of-capitalism, or when, as in liberalistic ideological history, the Holocaust is flattened out into man's-inhumanity-to-man-especially-in-wartime. (Arnold Toynbee, for example, considered that "what the Nazis did was nothing peculiar.")[5] The philosopher, however, must penetrate beyond these evasions and ideological distortions. And when such a philosopher finds a solid historian who states, correctly enough, that "the extermination grew out of the biologistic insanity of Nazi ideology, and for that reason is completely unlike the terrors of revolutions and wars of the past,"[6] he must ponder whether "biologistic insanity" has explanatory force or is rather a metaphor whose chief significance is that explanation has come to an end. As he ponders this, he may well be led to wonder "whether even in a thousand years people will understand Hitler, Auschwitz, Maidanek, and Treblinka better than we do now. . . . Posterity may understand it even less than we do."[7]

Such questions turn philosophical thought from methodological to substantive issues, and above all to the subject of man. Premodern philosophy was prepared to posit a permanent human nature that was unaffected by historical change. More deeply immersed in the varieties and vicissitudes of history, modern philosophy generally has perceived, in abstraction from historical change, only a human condition, which was considered permanent only insofar as beyond it was the humanly impossible. At Auschwitz, however, "more was real than is possible,"[8] and the impossible was done by some and suffered by others. Thus, prior to the Holocaust, the human condition, while including the necessity of dying, was seen as also including at least one inalienable freedom—that of each individual's dying his own death.[9] "With the administrative murder of millions" in the death camps, however, "death has become something that was never to be feared in this way before. . . . The individual is robbed of the last and poorest that until then still remained his own. In the camps it was no longer the individual that died; he was made into a specimen."[10]

As well as a new way of dying, the Auschwitz administrators also manufactured a new way of living. Prior to the Holocaust no aspect of the human condition could make so strong a claim to permanency as the distinction between life and death, between still-being-here and being-no-more. The Holocaust, however, produced the *Muselmann* (Muslim; pl., *Muselmänner*)— camp slang for a prisoner near death, the skin-and-bone walking corpse, or living dead, the vast "anonymous mass, continuously renewed and always identical, of non-men who march and labor in silence, the divine spark dead within them, already too empty really to suffer. One hesitates to call them living. One hesitates to call their death death."[11] The *Muselmann* may be called the most truly original contribution of the Third Reich to civilization.

From these new ways of being human—those of the victims—philosophical thought is turned to another new way of being human, that of the victimizers. Philosophy has all along been acquainted with the quasi-evil of sadism (a mere sickness), the semievil of moral weakness, the superficial evil of ignorance, and even—hardest to understand and, therefore often ignored or denied—the radical or demonic evil that is done and celebrated for its own sake. Prior to the Holocaust, however, it was unacquainted with the "banality of evil"[12] practiced by numberless individuals who, having been ordinary or even respected citizens, committed at Auschwitz crimes on a scale previously unimaginable, only to become, in the Holocaust's aftermath, ordinary and respectable once more—without showing signs of any moral anguish.

The evil is banal by dint not of the nature of the crimes but of the people who committed them: these, it is said, were made to do what they did by the system. This, however, is only half a philosophical thought, for who made the system—conceived, planned, created, perpetuated, and escalated it—if not such as Himmler and Eichmann, Stangl and Hoess, to say nothing of the unknown-soldier-become-S.S.-murderer? Already having difficulty with radical or demonic evil, philosophical thought is driven by the "banal" evil of the Holocaust from the operators to the system, and from the system back to the operators. In this circular movement, to be sure, banal evil, except for ceasing to be banal, does not become intelligible. Yet the effort to understand is not without result, for from it the Holocaust emerges as a world or, rather, as the antiworld par excellence. The human condition does not dwell in a vacuum. It "always-already-is" within a world, that is, within a structured whole that exists at all because it is geared to life and that is structured because it is governed by laws of life. Innocent so long as they obey the law, the inhabitants of a world have a right to life, and forfeit it, if at all, only by an act of will—the breach of the law. The Holocaust anti-world, while structured, is governed by a law of death. For some—Jews—existence itself was a capital crime (a hitherto unheard-of proposition) and the sole raison d'être of the others was to mete out their punishment. In this world, the degradation, torture, and eventual murder of some human beings at the hands of others was not a by-product of, or means to, some higher, more ultimate purpose. They were its whole essence.

Modern philosophers, we have said previously, were able to conceive of a human condition because not all things were considered humanly possible. Even so, some of their number, possibly with modern history in mind, have not hesitated to ascribe to man a "perfectibility" that is infinite. Auschwitz exacts a new concession from future philosophy: whether or not man is infinitely perfectible, he is in any case infinitely depravable. The Holocaust is not only a world-historical event. It is also a "watershed,"[13] or "caesura,"[14] or "rupture"[15] in man's history on earth.

Is the Holocaust a rupture in the sight of theology? This question requires a separate inquiry. Theology, to be sure, at least if it is Jewish or Christian, is bound up with history. But it can be, and has been, argued that this is a *Heilgeschichte* immune to all merely secular historical events. Thus, for Franz Rosenzweig nothing crucial could happen for Jews between Sinai and the Messianic days. And for Karl Barth it was "always Good Friday *after* Easter," the implication being that the crucial saving event of Christianity has already occurred and is unassailable ever after.

Is the Holocaust a rupture for Christianity? German Christians, and possibly Christians as a whole, "can no longer speak evangelically to Jews."[16] They cannot "get behind" Auschwitz; they can get "beyond it" if at all only "in company with the victims," and this latter only if they identify with the state of Israel as being a Jewish "house against death" and the "last Jewish refuge."[17] Christians must relate "positively" to Jews, not "despite" Jewish nonacceptance of the Christ but "because" of it.[18] Even to go only this far and no further with their theologians (it seems fitting here to cite only German theologians) is for Christians to recognize a post-Holocaust rupture in their faith, for the step demanded—renunciation of Christian missions to the Jews, as such and in principle—is, within Christian history, unprecedented. (Of the Christian theologians who find it necessary to go much further, A. Roy Eckardt is, perhaps, the most theologically oriented.) To refuse even this one step, that is, for Christians to stay with the idea of mission to the Jews in principle, even if suspending it altogether in practice, is either to ignore the Holocaust, or else sooner or later to reach some such view as that mission to the Jews "is the sole possibility of a genuine and

The Holocaust and Philosophy

meaningful restitution (*Wiedergutmachung*) on the part of German Christendom."[19] Can Christians view such a stance as other than a theological obscenity? The Jewish stance toward Christian missionizing attempts directed at them, in any case, cannot be what it once was. Prior to the Holocaust, Jews could respect such attempts, although of course considering them misguided. After the Holocaust, they can only view them as trying in one way what Hitler undertook in another.

It would seem, then, that for Christians Good Friday can no longer be always *after* Easter. As for Jews, was the Holocaust a crucial event, occurring though it did between Sinai and the Messianic days? Franz Rosenzweig's Jewish truth, it emerges in our time, was a truth not of Judaism but of *Galut* (exile) Judaism only, albeit its most profound modern statement. *Galut* Judaism, however, has ceased to be tenable.

Galut Judaism may be characterized as follows:

1. A Jew can appease or bribe, hide or flee from an enemy and, having succeeded, can thank God for having been saved.
2. When in *extremis* such salvation is impossible, when death can be averted only through apostasy, he can still choose death, thus becoming a martyr; and then he is secure in the knowledge that, while no Jew should seek death, *kiddush ha-Shem* (sanctifying God's name by dying for it) is the highest stage of which he can be worthy.[20]
3. Exile, though painful, is bearable, for it is meaningful, whether its meaning consists in punishment for Jewish sins, vicarious suffering for the sins of others, or whether it is simply inscrutable, a meaning known only to God.
4. *Galut* will not last forever. If not he himself or even his children's children, at any rate some Jews' distant offspring will live to see the Messianic end.

These are the chief conditions and commitments of *Galut* Judaism. Existing in the conditions and armed by the commitments, a Jew in past centuries was able to survive the poverty of the eastern European ghetto; the slander, ideologically embellished and embroidered, of anti-Semitism in modern Germany and France; the medieval expulsions; the Roman Emperor Hadrian's attempt once and for all to extirpate the Jewish faith; and, of course, the fateful destruction of the Jerusalem Temple in 70 C.E., to which *Galut* Judaism was the normative and epoch-making response. All these *Galut* Judaism was able to survive. The Holocaust, however, already shown by us to be unprecedented simply as an historical event, is unprecedented also as a threat to the Jewish faith, and *Galut* Judaism is unable to meet it.

1. The Holocaust was not a gigantic pogrom from which one could hide until the visitation of the drunken Cossacks had passed. This enemy was

coldly sober, systematic rather than haphazard; except for the lucky few, there was no hiding.

2. The Holocaust was not a vast expulsion, causing to arise the necessity, but also the possibility, of once again resorting to wandering, with the Torah as "portable fatherland."[21] Even when the Third Reich was still satisfied with expelling Jews there was, except for the fortunate or prescient, no place to go; and when the Reich became dissatisfied with mere expulsions, a place of refuge, had such been available, would have been beyond reach.

3. The Holocaust was not an assault calling for bribing or appeasing the enemy. This enemy was an "idealist" who could not be bribed, and he remained unappeasable until the last Jew's death.

4. The Holocaust was not a challenge to Jewish martyrdom but, on the contrary, an attempt to destroy martyrdom forever. Hadrian had decreed death for the crime of practicing Judaism and thereby inspired the martyrdom of such as Rabbi Akiva, which in turn inspired countless Jewish generations. Hitler, like Hadrian, sought to destroy Jews but, unlike Hadrian, was too cunning to repeat the ancient emperor's folly. He decreed death for Jews, not for doing or even believing, but rather for being—for the crime of possessing Jewish ancestors. Thus, Jewish martyrdom was made irrelevant. Moreover, no effort was spared to make martyrdom impossible as well, and the supreme effort in this direction was the manufacture of *Muselmänner*. A martyr chooses to die; as regards the *Muselmänner*, "one hesitates to call them living; one hesitates to call their death death."

It cannot be stressed enough that, despite these unprecedented, superhuman efforts to murder Jewish martyrdom, countless nameless Akivas managed to sanctify God's name by choosing how to die, even though robbed of the choice of whether to die; their memory must have a special sacredness to God and man. Such memory is abused, however, if it is used to blot out, minimize, or even divert attention from the death of the children as yet unable to choose and the death of the *Muselmänner* who could choose no more.

That these four *nova* have made *Galut* Judaism untenable has found admirable expression in an ancient midrash that was originally intended to expound the then-new form of Judaism. In this midrash God, at the beginning of the great exile initiated by the destruction of the Temple in 70 C.E., exacts three oaths, one from the gentiles and two from the Jews. The gentiles are made to swear not to persecute the Jews, now stateless and helpless, excessively. The Jews are made to swear not to resist their persecutors, and not to "climb the wall," that is, prematurely to return to Jerusalem.

But what, one must ask, if not Auschwitz, is "excessive persecution"? In response, some have said that the Jews broke their oath by climbing the wall, that is, by committing the sin of Zionism, and that in consequence God at Auschwitz released the gentiles from obligation. Any such attempt to save *Galut* Judaism, however, reflects mere desperation, for it lapses into two blasphemies: toward the innocent children and the guiltless *Muselmänner*, and toward a God who is pictured as deliberately, callously, consigning them to their fate. There remains, therefore, only a bold and forthright taking leave from *Galut* Judaism. It was the gentiles at Auschwitz who broke their oath, and the Jews in consequence are now released from theirs.

A "post-*Galut* Judaism" Judaism is, unmistakably, in the making in our time. Its most obvious aspects are that "resisting" the persecutors and "climbing the wall" have become not only rights but also ineluctable duties. After the Holocaust, Jews owe anti-Semites, as well as, of course, their own children, the duty of not encouraging murderous instincts by their own powerlessness. And after the absolute homelessness of the twelve Nazi years that were equal to a thousand, they owe the whole world, as well as, of course, their own children, the duty to say no to Jewish wandering, to return home, to rebuild a Jewish state.

These aspects of the Judaism in the making are moral and political. Their inner source is spiritual and religious. In the Warsaw Ghetto Rabbi Isaac Nissenbaum, a famous and respected orthodox rabbi, made the statement —much quoted by Jews of all persuasions in their desperate efforts to defend, preserve, and hallow Jewish life against an enemy sworn to destroy it all—that this was a time not for *kiddush ha-Shem* (martyrdom) but rather for *kiddush ha-hayyim* (the sanctification of life). It is a time for *kiddush ha-hayyim* still. The Jewish people have passed through the Nazi antiworld of death; thereafter, by any standard, religious or secular, Jewish life ranks higher than Jewish death, even if it is for the sake of the divine name. The Jewish people have experienced exile in a form more horrendous than ever dreamt of by the apocalyptic imagination; thereafter, to have ended exile bespeaks a fidelity and a will to live that, taken together, give a new dimension to piety. The product of this fidelity—the Jewish state—is fragile still, and embattled wherever the world is hostile or does not understand. Yet Jews both religious and secular know in their hearts that Israel—the renewed people, the reborn language, the replanted land, the rebuilt city, the state itself—is a new and unique celebration of life. There are many reasons why Israel has become the center of the Jewish people in our time; not least is that it is indispensable to a future Judaism. If a Jewish state had not arisen in the wake of the Holocaust, it would be a religious necessity— although, one fears, a political near-impossibility—to create it now.

Ten

The Holocaust and Philosophy

Philosophers have all but ignored the Holocaust. Why?

First, attuned to universals, they have little use for particulars, and less for the unique. The Holocaust thus becomes at most one case of genocide among others. *However*, philosophers *have* attended to the *momentously* unique. Hegel and Marx have treated the French Revolution, not revolutions-in-general.

Second, philosophers seldom consider things Jewish. As regards Judaism, the term *Judeo-Christian* rarely signifies more than token recognition. As regards Jews, they are one "ethnic" or "religious" group among others, just as antisemitism is reduced to a "prejudice." Rare is a work such as Jean-Paul Sartre's *Antisemite and Jew*,[1] and even it treats "anti-Semite" more adequately than "Jew." *However*, the Third *Reich*, not merely its Holocaust component, was "the only German regime—the only regime ever anywhere—which had no other clear principle than murderous hatred of Jews, for 'Aryan' had no clear meaning other than 'non-Jewish.' "[2] (The Japanese were honorary "Aryans," and the "Semitic" Mufti of Jerusalem was a welcome guest in Nazi Berlin.)

Third, the French Revolution, though momentous, is a positive event. The Holocaust is devastatingly negative. Qua humans, philosophers are tempted to flee from it into some such platitude as "man's-inhumanity-to-man-especially-in-wartime." (Arnold Toynbee: "What the Nazis did is not peculiar.")[3] Qua philosophers, having always had problems with evil, they have a new problem now. *However*, philosophers must confront *aporiae*, not evade or ignore them.

This essay treats the Holocaust as unique; as anti-Jewish not accidentally but essentially; and as a *novum* in the history of evil.

The Uniqueness of the Holocaust

The World War II Jewish genocide resembles most closely the World War I Armenian genocide. Both were (1) attempts to murder a whole people; (2) carried out under cover of war; (3) with maximum secrecy; (4) after the deportation of the victims, with deliberate cruelty, to remote places; (5) all this provoking few countermeasures or even verbal protests on the

129

part of the civilized world. Doubtless the Nazis both learned from and were encouraged by the Armenian precedent.

These are striking similarities. As striking, however, are the differences. The Armenian deportations from Istanbul were stopped after some time, whether because of political problems or the logistical difficulties posed by so large a city. "Combed" for Jews were Berlin, Vienna, Amsterdam, Warsaw. In this, greater Teutonic efficiency was secondary; primary was a *Weltanschauung*. Indian reservations exist in America. Jewish reservations in a victorious Nazi empire are inconceivable: already planned instead were museums for an "extinct race." For, unlike the Turks, the Nazis sought a "*final* solution" of a "problem"—final only if, minimally, Europe and, maximally, the world would be *judenrein*. In German this word has no counterpart such as *polenrein, russenrein, slavenrein*. In other languages it does not exist at all; for whereas Jordan and Saudi Arabia are in fact without Jews, missing is the *Weltanschauung*. The Holocaust, then, is but one case of the class "genocide." As a case of the class: "intended, planned, and largely successful *extermination*," it is without precedent and, thus far at least, without sequel. It is unique.

Equally unique are the means necessary to this end. These included (1) a scholastically precise definition of the victims; (2) juridical procedures procuring their rightlessness; (3) a technical apparatus culminating in murder trains and gas chambers; and (4), most importantly, a veritable army of murderers and also direct and indirect accomplices: clerks, newspapermen, lawyers, bank managers, doctors, soldiers, railwaymen, entrepreneurs, and an endless list of others.

The relation between direct and indirect accomplices is as important as the distinction. The German historian Karl Dietrich Bracher[4] understands Nazi Germany as a dual system. Its inner part was the "S.S. state"; its outer, the traditional establishment—civil service, army, schools, universities, churches. This latter system was allowed separate existence to the end, but was also increasingly penetrated, manipulated, perverted. *And since it resisted the process only sporadically and never radically, it enabled the S.S. state to do what it could never have done simply on its own.* Had the railwaymen engaged in strikes or sabotage or simply vanished there would have been no Auschwitz. Had the German army acted likewise there would have been neither Auschwitz nor World War II. U.S. President Ronald Reagan should not have gone to Bitburg even if no S.S. men had been buried there.

Such was the army required for the "how" of the Holocaust. Its "why" required an army of historians, philosophers, theologians. The historians rewrote history. The philosophers demonstrated that mankind is "Aryan" or "non-Aryan" before it is human. The theologians were divided into Christians who made Jesus into an "Aryan" and neo-pagans who rejected Christianity itself as "non-Aryan"; their differences were slight compared to their shared commitments.

The Holocaust and Philosophy

These were direct accomplices. But here too there was need for indirect accomplices as well. Without the prestige of philosophers like Martin Heidegger and theologians like Emanuel Hirsch, could the *National-Sozialistische Weltanschauung* have gained its power and respectability? Could it have won out at all? The Scottish-Catholic historian Malcolm Hay asks why what happened in Germany did not happen in France forty years earlier, during the Dreyfus affair. He replies that in France there were fifty righteous men.[5]

What *was* the "why" of the Holocaust? Astoundingly, significantly, even the archpractitioners rarely faced it. "Archpractitioner" indisputably fits Treblinka Kommandant Franz Stangl. (Treblinka had the fewest survivors.) In a postwar interview Stangl was asked: "What did you think at the time was the reason for the extermination of the Jews?" Stangl replied—as if Jews had not long been robbed naked!—"they wanted their money."[6] Did Stangl *really* not know? Yet, though Treblinka itself was secret, its *raison d'être* had always been public. In the Nazi *Weltanschauung* Jews were vermin, and one does not execute vermin, murder it, spare its young or its old: one exterminates vermin—coldly, systematically, without feeling or a second thought. Is "vermin" (or "virus" or "parasite") a "mere metaphor"? In a 1942 "table-talk," right after the Wannsee conference that finalized the "Final Solution," Hitler said:

> The discovery of the Jewish virus is one of the greatest revolutions . . . in
> the world. The struggle we are waging is of the same kind as that of Pasteur
> and Koch in the last century. How many diseases can be traced back to the
> Jewish virus! We shall regain our health only when we exterminate the Jews.[7]

For racism, "inferior races" are still human; even for Nazi racism there are merely too many Slavs. For Nazi anti-Semitism Jews are not human; they must not exist at all.

Stangl failed with his interviewer's first question. He failed with her second as well. "If they were going to kill them anyway," he was asked, "what was the point of all the humiliation, why all the cruelty?" He replied: "To condition those who actually had to carry out the policies. To make it possible for them to do what they did." The interviewer had doubted Stangl's first answer, but accepted his second as both honest and true. Honest it may have been; true it was not. The "cruelty" included horrendous medical non-experiments on women, children, babies. The "humiliation" included making pious Jews spit on Torah scrolls and, when they ran out of spittle, supplying them with more by spitting into their mouths. Was all this easier on the operators than pulling triggers and pushing buttons? *Treblinka—the Holocaust—had* two *ultimate purposes: extermination* and also *maximum prior humiliation and torture.* This too—can Stangl have been unaware of it?—had been part of the public *Weltanschauung* all along. In 1936 Julius Streicher declared that "who fights the Jew fights the devil" and that "who masters the devil conquers heaven." And this basest, most pornographic Nazi only echoed what the most authoritative (and equally pornographic) Nazi had written many years earlier: "With satanic joy in his face, the black-haired Jewish youth lurks in wait for the unsuspecting girl whom he defiles with his blood. . . . By defending myself against the Jew, I am fighting for the work of the Lord."[8] To "punish" the "Jewish devil" through humiliation and torture, then, was part of "Aryan" salvation. Perhaps it was all of it.

"Jewish devil" and Jewish "vermin" (or "bacillus," "parasite," "virus") existed side by side in the Nazi theory. For example, this Hitler passage of 1923 cited by Joachim C. Fest: "The Jews are undoubtedly a race, but they are not human. They cannot be human in the sense of being in the image of God, the Eternal. The Jews are the image of the devil. Jewry means the racial tuberculosis of the nations." Side by side in the theory, "devil" and "vermin" were synthesized in the Auschwitz *praxis*, and this was a *novum* without precedent in the realm of either the real or the possible. Even in the worst state, punishment is meted out for a *doing*—a fact explaining Hegel's statement, defensible once but no more, that any state is better than none. And, even in the hell of poetic and theological imagination, the innocent cannot be touched. The Auschwitz *praxis* was based on a new principle: *for one portion of mankind,* existence itself *is a crime, punishable by humiliation, torture, and death.* And the new world produced by this *praxis* included two kinds of inhabitants, those who were given the "punishment" and those who administered it.

Few have yet grasped the newness of that new world. Survivors have grasped it all along. Hence they refer to *all* the "punished" victims as *k'doshim* ("holy ones"); for even criminals among them were innocent of the "crime" for which they were "punished." Hence, too, they refer to the new world created by the victimizers as a "universe" other than ours, or a "planet" other than the one we inhabit. What historians and philosophers must face is that Auschwitz was a kingdom not of this world.

The Holocaust and the Historian

But the Holocaust took place *in* our world. The historian must explain it, and the philosopher must reflect on the historian's work.

Raul Hilberg[9] has studied closely the "how" of the Holocaust. In answer to the "why" he has said: "They did it because they wanted to do it."[10] This stresses admirably the respective roles of Nazi *Weltanschauung* and Nazi decision-making. But how accept *such* a *Weltanschauung?* How make decisions *such as these?* As if in answer to these further questions, Bracher has written: "The extermination [of the Jews] grew out of the biologistic insanity of Nazi ideology, and for that reason is completely unlike the terrors of revolutions and wars of the past." Again further questions arise. What or who was insane, the ideology or those creating, believing, implementing it? If the latter, who? Just the one? Or the one and the direct accomplices?

Or the indirect accomplices as well? And, climactically, is "insanity" *itself* an explanation, or merely a way of saying that attempts to explain have come to an end?

Historians will resist this conclusion. Has not the "Jewish devil" a long tradition, harking back to the New Testament? (See especially John 8:44.) As for the "Jewish vermin" (or "virus" or "parasite"), Hitler got it from anti-Semitic trash harking back decades. Doubtless without these factors the Holocaust would have been *im*possible, a fact in itself sufficient to mark off the event from other genocides. *But do these (and other) factors suffice to make the Holocaust* possible? *To explain an event is to show how it was possible; but the mind accepts the* possibility *of the Holocaust, in the last analysis, only because it* was *actual.* Explanation, in short—so it seems—moves in circles.

In his unremitting search for explanations the historian must respond to this challenge by focusing ever more sharply on what is unique in the Holocaust. The philosopher must ponder Hans Jonas's paradoxical Holocaust-dictum: "Much more is real than is possible." Minimally, what became real at Auschwitz was *always* possible, but is now *known* to be so. Maximally, Auschwitz *has made possible* what previously was *im*possible; for *it is a precedent.* In either case, philosophers must face a *novum* within a question as old as Socrates: what does it mean to be human?

The *Muselmann*

Allan Bullock stresses that Hitler's originality lay not in ideas but in "the terrifying literal way in which he . . . translate[d] fantasy into reality, and his unequalled grasp of the means by which to do this."[11] One original product of this "translation" was the so-called *Muselmann*. If in the Gulag the dissident suffers torture-through-psychiatry, on the theory that in the workers' paradise such as he must be mad, then the Auschwitz *praxis* reduces the "non-Aryan" to a walking corpse covered with his own filth, on the theory that he must reveal himself as the disgusting creature that he has been, if disguisedly, since birth. To be sure, the *Muselmänner* included countless "Aryans" also. But, just as "the Nazis were racists because they were anti-Semites" is truer than the reverse, so it is truer that non-Jewish *Muselmänner* were Jews-by-association than that Jewish *Muselmänner* were a sub-species of "enemies of the *Reich*."

The process was focused on Jews in particular. Its implications, however, concern the whole human condition, and, therefore, philosophers. Among these, few would deny that to die one's own death is part of one's freedom; in Martin Heidegger's *Being and Time* this freedom is foundational. Yet, of the Auschwitz *Muselmann*, Primo Levi[12] writes:

> Their life is short, but their number is endless; they, the Muselmänner, the drowned, form the backbone of the camp, an anonymous mass, continually

renewed and always identical, of non-men who march and labor in silence, the divine spark dead within them, already too empty really to suffer. *One hesitates to call them living; one hesitates to call their death death.*

To die one's own death has always been a freedom subject to loss by accident. On Planet Auschwitz, however, the loss of it was made essential, and its survival accidental. Hence Theodor Adorno[13] writes:

> With the administrative murder of millions death has become something that never before was to be feared in this way. Death no longer enters into the experienced life of the individual, as somehow harmonizing with its course. It was no longer the individual that died in the camps, but the specimen. *This must affect also the dying of those who escaped the procedure.*

Philosophers are faced with a new *aporia*. It arises from the necessity to listen to the silence of the *Muselmann*.

"Banal" Evil and Planet Auschwitz

From one new way of being human—that of the victims—we turn to the other, that of the victimizers. Since Socrates, philosophers have known of evil as ignorance; but the Auschwitz operators included Ph.D.s. Since Kant philosophers have known of evil as weakness, as yielding to inclination; but Eichmann in Jerusalem invoked, not entirely incorrectly, the categorical imperative.[14] From psychiatry philosophy learns of evil as sickness; but the "SD intellectuals" who so efficiently engineered the "Final Solution" abominated Streicher-type sadists, "wanted to be regarded as decent," and had as "their sole object . . . to solve the so-called Jewish problem in a cold, rational manner."[15] Philosophy has even had a glimpse of what the theologians call "radical" or "demonical" evil—the diabolical grandeur that says to evil "be thou my good!" However, just as people the world over experienced human shock when they watched newsreels of the big Nazis at the Nuremberg trials, so Hannah Arendt—a belated owl of Minerva—experienced philosophical shock when, more than a dozen years later, she observed Eichmann at his Jerusalem trial. *Of grandeur, there was in them all not a trace.* The characteristic Nazi criminal was rather a dime-a-dozen individual, who, having once been an ordinary, nay, respected citizen, committed at Auschwitz crimes of a kind and on a scale hitherto unimaginable, only to become, when it was over, an ordinary citizen again, without signs of suffering sleepless nights. Eichmann was only one such person. Others are still being discovered in nice suburbs, and their neighbors testify how they took care of their gardens and were kind to their dogs. Himmler himself, had he escaped detection and the need for suicide, might well have returned to his chicken farm. The philosopher in Arendt looked for some depth in such as these, and found none.[16] It was "banal" people who committed what may justly be called the greatest crime in history; and it was the system that made them do what they did.

The concept "banal evil," however, is only half a philosophical thought. Who created and maintained the system, if not such as Himmler and Eichmann, Stangl, and the unknown soldier who was an S.S. murderer? In reply, many would doubtless point to one not yet mentioned by us among the banal ones. And, it is true, Adolf Hitler *did* have an "unequaled grasp of the means" by which to "translate fantasy into reality." To go further, the whole Nazi *Reich*, and hence Planet Auschwitz, would doubtless have disintegrated had some saintly hero succeeded in assassinating just this one individual. Even so, it is impossible to trace the monstrous evil perpetrated by all the banal ones to some monstrous greatness in the *Fuehrer* of them all. For if it is a "superstition . . . that a man who greatly affected the destiny of nations must himself be great,"[17] then Hitler is the clearest illustration of this truth. His ideas, though blown up into a pretentious *Weltanschauung*, are trite; so, for all the posturing intended to disguise the fact, is the man. Other than a low cunning, his one distinguishing mark is a devouring passion, and even that is mostly fed by a need, as petty as it is limitless, to show them—whom?—that the nobody is somebody. Were even the beliefs of this "true believer" truly held? Did he ever dare to examine them? Certainly— all his biographers are struck by the fact—he never *re*-examined them. As likely, they too were part of a Wagner-style posturing, right up to his theatrical death.

Such historical considerations aside, we must face a philosophical problem. If we accept and philosophically radicalize Eichmann's plea to have been a mere "cog in the wheel," we end up attributing to the few—even to just one?—a power to mesmerize, manipulate, dominate, terrorize that is *beyond* all humanity and, to the many, a mesmerizability, manipulability, and craven cowardice that is *beneath* all humanity. Yet, whereas Auschwitz *was* a kingdom not of this world, its creators and operators were neither super- nor subhuman but rather—a terrifying thought!—human like ourselves. Hence, in however varying degrees, the mesmerized and manipulated *allowed themselves* to be so treated, and the dominated and terrorized *gave in* to craven cowardice. Not only Eichmann but *everyone* was more than a cog in the wheel. The operators of the Auschwitz system were *all* its unbanal creators even as they were its banal creatures.

A moment of truth relevant to this occurred during the 1964 Auschwitz trial held in Frankfurt, Germany. A survivor had testified that, thanks to a certain S.S. officer Flacke, one Auschwitz subcamp had been an "island of peace." The judge sat up, electrified: "Do you wish to say that everyone could decide for himself to be either good or evil at Auschwitz?" he asked. "That is exactly what I wish to say," the witness replied.

Then why were such as S.S. officer Flacke exceptions so rare as barely to touch and not at all to shake the smooth functioning of the machinery of humiliation, torture, and murder? And how could those who were the rule, banal ones all, place into our world a "kingdom" evil without precedent, far removed from banality and fated to haunt mankind forever? We cannot answer the first question. Gripped by the *aporia* of the second, the philosopher is unlikely to do better than fall back on a familiar dictum: Auschwitz—like the Reich as a whole, especially as revealed in the endless, empty *Sieg Heils* of the Nuremberg *Parteitage*[18]—was a whole that was more than the sum of its parts.

Philosophers have applied this dictum without hesitation to animal organisms. To human realities—a society. a state, a civilization, a "world"—they have applied it with hesitation, and only if the whole enhanced the humanity of all beyond what would be possible for the parts, separately or jointly, alone. It is in contrast to this that the *novum* of the Holocaust-whole is revealed in all its stark horror. It did not enhance the humanity of its inhabitants. On the contrary, it was singlemindedly geared to the destruction of the humanity (as well as the lives) of the victims; and in pursuing this goal, the victimizers destroyed their own humanity, even as they yielded to its being destroyed. Pursuing his own age-old goal, the Socratic quest, "What is Man?", the philosopher, now as then, is filled with wonder. But the ancient wonder is now mingled with a new horror.

Eleven

Philosophical Reflections on Claude Lanzmann's *Shoah*

The American columnist George Will has written that [the film] *Shoah* proves that the unspeakable is not, after all, inexpressible. I fully concur. Possibly this is the greatest film of all time, on possibly the most horrible subject of all time. It is a privilege for me to share this platform with [the maker of this film,] Claude Lanzmann. I find the privilege particularly great because I am a philosopher. As such I do not hesitate to say that the film should be required viewing for all future philosophers, for without seeing it they will be unable to do what since Socrates philosophers have tried to do: to put it in Socrates' own words, to ponder whether Man is a more horrible monster than "tryphon"—one gathers the most horrible mythical beast he could think of—or perhaps, after all, a being of a gentler sort.

I will begin with three scenes from the film itself—a witness, some bystanders, and a criminal, the criminals being what all efforts to confront the Holocaust must ultimately focus on. That, however, is precisely what we all wish to avoid. Of this we find ample proof all around us. Why didn't they fight? Why didn't the good people do more? Can't the banality of the criminals be granted and forgotten? And this above all: instead of nursing old grudges, shouldn't we turn to the problems of our own time? All this in the end reflects an all-too-understandable —but also ultimately cowardly— desire to divert attention from the criminals.

I begin with the witness. Filip Mueller had the most horrendous job at Auschwitz: he was in the *Sonderkommando*. His task was to pull the bodies from the gas chambers—dirt, feces, vermin, and all—and dump them into the pits to be burned. Having done this day in and day out, he at length sees a group of his fellow Jewish Czech countrymen pushed into the "undressing room." Most victims had no idea of what was in store for them. These victims know. They refuse to undress. They are defiant. They get pushed into the gas chambers and, defiant to the end, they begin to sing!

They sing the Czech national anthem and the ha-Tikva. Then Mueller goes on, "That moved me terribly. That was happening to my countrymen, and I realized that my life had become meaningless. Why go on living? What for? So I went into the gas chambers with them. Suddenly someone recognized me, came to me. He looked at me and said, right there in the gas chamber . . . " Lanzmann interrupts: "You were *inside* the gas chamber?" "Yes," Mueller goes on. " 'So you want to die,' the man said to me. 'But that's senseless. You must get out of here alive. You must bear witness' . . . "

This is the first scene from *Shoah* I wish to reflect on——and who, having viewed this scene, can ever forget it?

I turn next to the second scene, a few bystanders: Polish peasants gathered in a square. One of them relates to the others how he heard for sure that a rabbi asked permission from an S. S. officer to speak to his people; and how, having received permission, he gave them a sermon. "Just about 2,000 years ago," the rabbi is supposed to have said to his flock, "our forefathers condemned the innocent Christ to death, crying out, 'let his blood be on our heads and the heads of our children.' So perhaps now the time has come for us to be punished. So let us not resist but accept the punishment." Lanzmann interrupts: "So the person reporting this to you thinks that the Jews expiated the death of Christ?" "Well, he doesn't think so," the Pole responds, "or even that Christ sought revenge. The rabbi said it. It was God's will, that's all." Lanzmann: "What did she say?" (This about a woman referred to earlier.) "So Pilate washed his hands and said: 'Christ is innocent' and he sent Barrabas. But the Jews cried out: 'Let his blood be on our heads!' That's all. Now you know." Who, having watched that bit in *Shoah*, can ever forget it?

Now I come to the third scene, the criminal. As I have already stressed, I put him last because he is most impossible to forget—and hardest to remember. We want to push him away. We want to forget the criminal, or mix him up with other criminals or, better still, mix him up with other evils such as cancer or hurricanes, or best of all, tell ourselves that we must forgive him for he knows not what he does or—a modern version of the same thing—that he is banal. The criminal I focus on is *Unterscharfuehrer* Franz Suchomel of Treblinka. He reports how, naturally, the men and women were pushed from the trains straight to the funnel leading to the gas chambers. How, naturally, the men were pushed in fast, before they could know what was happening, for they might resist if they suspected. How, naturally, the women had to wait, for there was not enough room in the gas chambers for the women together with the men. They had to undress—naturally! And this was in winter as well as summer, and because of the crowded gas chambers the naked women sometimes had to wait for a long time. Lanzmann interjects: "Winter in Treblinka can be very cold." Suchomel: "Well, in winter, in December, anyway after Christmas. But even before Christmas it was cold as hell. Between fifteen and minus four. I know: at first it was cold as hell for us too. We didn't have suitable uniforms."

This is the last scene for me to comment on, and paraphrasing Kant, I say that all philosophers should be solemnly dispensed of their various duties, until they have answered, or at least asked, how these three scenes were possible. And I cannot imagine but that, having asked that question, their philosophical quest would be changed ever after: the ancient Socratic quest of whether Man is a more horrendous monster even than tryphon or, after all, a being of a gentler sort.

How must it change? Let me begin with Simone de Beauvoir, who, after seeing *Shoah*, wrote as follows: "After the war, we read masses of accounts of the ghettos and the extermination camps, and we were devastated. But when today we see Claude Lanzmann's film, we realize that we have understood nothing."

That's how a philosopher must begin: he has understood nothing! Beauvoir was a philosopher who did see the film. Let me tell you about philosophers writing before there was this film, and who yet thought that they had understood everything. First there is England. That is a nice country—so nice, in fact, that its philosophers have a hard time to acknowledge genuine evil, to say nothing of the Holocaust. J. M. Hare is a distinguished Oxford philosopher whose field is ethics. He is also decent enough to devote nearly half of a book to the Nazi murder of Jews. So he builds up an argument. He fancies himself arguing with a Nazi philosopher, pushing the latter at length to the point where he must answer whether, if it were discovered that he himself were "non-Aryan," he would voluntarily go to Auschwitz. If not, he is inconsistent. If yes, there is nothing more to say, but then, Hare comforts himself, Nazis so idealistic surely would be few. Well, they weren't few, philosophical argument or no philosophical argument! Nor were they bothered much by inconsistencies, such as how Jews could all be both communists and capitalists. Being such a nice man in a nice place such as Oxford, Hare hasn't even understood the first thing—that his putative Nazi philosopher would consider argument *itself* as "non-Aryan," and that he, Hare, if he had ever actually started such an argument, would have been lucky to get away unbeaten and unbruised—indeed, alive.

Let me next turn to a country that is not so nice. In fact, it is Germany, the country that perpetrated the Holocaust. Its most distinguished philosopher at the time was Martin Heidegger. Heidegger is now being increasingly recognized in America and even in Israel, so perhaps he is the most distinguished philosopher of the entire century. Heidegger became a Nazi in 1933, and I for one do not make too much of this, for in 1933 lots of philosophers got carried away, though one must mention that others, such as Karl Jaspers, didn't. There were many people then who said, "except for what he says about the Jews, Hitler is all right." Quite a few people say the same sort of thing today in America about such as Louis Farrakhan, and since we now know what this can lead to it is perhaps less excusable now than it was then. So I don't hold too much against Heidegger for what he did in 1933. What must be held against him is what he did —or rather, failed to do—in the two decades after the war. By his own claim he became

The Holocaust and Philosophy

an anti-Nazi early in the Nazi regime, yet the furthest his anti-Nazism ever got was an attack on *Fuehrers*. In the plural! One gathers that these included, along with Hitler, also Stalin, Mussolini, Franco, and—who knows?—maybe Roosevelt as well. After all, Heidegger invoked his philosophical wisdom to describe communist Russia and democratic America as "metaphysically" the same "technological frenzy," and in his anti-Nazi phase he viewed Nazi Germany as yet another form of it. To Heidegger, all *Fuehrers* and their deeds were only derivative results of something called "the loss of Being." That's as far as the most distinguished German philosopher—perhaps the most distinguished philosopher of the century—ever came vis-à-vis the Holocaust. (A weird conceit comes to my mind: I fancy Heidegger seeing *Shoah*. What would be the result? I cannot imagine. My mind boggles.)

Let me suggest what I think a German philosopher should have reflected on ever since 1945, when all was revealed. Except in the anti-Semitic mind, there never was such a thing as a "Jewish problem." There now is, however, a German problem. In every normal state, a person is innocent until proven guilty, and I say "normal" rather than "decent" because I wish to include states whose laws are not very decent—yet a person is innocent so long as he abides by these laws. Nazi Germany was the only state ever, in which everyone was suspect of "non-Aryan guilt" until he had proved his "Aryan innocence." Perhaps he didn't have to prove it. Perhaps he didn't even have to be prepared to prove it. Even so, he survived—if survive he did—on the *presumption* of "Aryan innocence." And the consequence today is an unprecedented German problem: except only for those who either fled Nazi Germany or else fought against it, all Germans alive today, by either themselves surviving on the presumption of Aryan innocence, or else by being the children of such survivors, are implicated in the death of those who did not survive, on account of their "non-Aryan guilt": survival on the presumption of "Aryan" innocence implies abandonment of those laden with "non-Aryan" guilt. Spiderlike, the Nazi Reich sought to implicate in its own crime all but the most heroic and saintly; and this scheme could have been thwarted only if millions had actually been heroes or saints, defying the Nuremberg laws with the cry, "We are all Jews." This, however, did not happen.

How are philosophers to cope with this German problem? Right after the war Karl Jaspers wrote about German guilt and said what needed saying, that there is no such thing as collective guilt: the new generation, therefore, is innocent. But then he went on to speak of "collective shame," and this does not get to the crux. And though one gets closer, the crux is not reached either by ascribing to Germans today, not guilt for the past, but responsibility for the future. Once, in the time of German greatness, a great German philosopher, F. W. J. Schelling, wrote of "innocent guilt" with regard to Oedipus, that he was implicated in a guilt of which he yet was innocent. When will the philosopher arise—he can only be German—who will address himself to a tragedy acted out on no mere stage but on the darkest

Claude Lanzmann's *Shoah*

page of German history? Heidegger was not that philosopher; nor, so far as I know, has another arisen. May one hope that, inspired perhaps by *Shoah*, such a philosopher may yet arise? At their best, Germans have always looked to philosophy in search of guidance. The tragedy of Oedipus, Aristotle tells us, is resolved for those who watch it on the stage by the emotions of terror and pity. But something quite other is needed than these or any other mere emotions by a tragedy that unfolded, and continues to unfold, on no mere stage, for spectators to watch, but on a bloody page in the book of history that those who come after cannot tear out and throw away.

The German problem, however, is not ours. The liberal democracies come much closer. Have Western philosophers confronted the Holocaust? If thus far just barely, it is largely because of what may be called the liberal mentality which, generally a virtue, is unhelpful here. The liberal likes to universalize. Also, he does not like the "dead" past but wants the "relevant" present. And the result is that when the Holocaust is mentioned the liberal-minded philosopher turns to some other catastrophe with great speed—in view of what is at stake, one must say with indecent speed, although of course the indecency is not conscious or deliberate. This kind of philosopher has yet to grasp the fact that one does not raise the significance of either Hiroshima or Auschwitz by linking the two: one rather diminishes both. Nor does one help either the cause of truth or that of human survival on earth by proposing a change of terminology, calling each H-bomb "an instant portable Auschwitz." (Thus Arthur Waskow in the premiere issue of *Tikkun*, an American Jewish magazine.) Once such a flattening out occurs, one does not have too far to travel to compare the Jews of the Warsaw Ghetto to the PLO encircled by the Israelis in Beirut. Of course, there are a few differences, such as that the PLO did much to arouse Israeli hostility whereas for Jews existence itself was enough to deserve murder at Nazi hands. And then there is the fact that the whole world came to the rescue of the PLO whereas no one rescued the Warsaw Ghetto Jews. But we have all observed just how small these differences have been in the liberal Western press. And if a philosopher has himself flattened out the scandalous particularity of the Holocaust, and this in the spirit of liberal ideals, his protests, if made at all, are powerless.

How ought a philosopher confront the Holocaust? With this question in mind, let me now turn to the three scenes from *Shoah* with which I began. Filip Mueller: I have often wondered why a victim forced into the *Sonder-kommando* did not commit suicide. Day by day, he was forced to do the most horrendous job imaginable—most horrendous, that is, except that performed by the Nazi murderers, and they don't seem to have found it horrendous. Day by day, moreover, he lived with the certainty that he was destined for murder as well, since the Nazis would not let witnesses to their crimes survive. Why not suicide, then? Opportunities existed, and many took advantage of them. Why did life lose its meaning for Filip Mueller only when he heard his compatriots sing the Czech national anthem and the ha-Tikva, and not before? It seems that he was the only person ever to be actually in a gas chamber and come out alive.

We know this much, at any rate, why he did come out alive: he tells us in the film. He let himself be pushed out of the gas chamber in order to be a witness. It was his duty to be a witness. And from his testimony arises the duty for us to listen. Who is this "us"? *Everybody*! Everybody includes philosophers. Let Jewish philosophers not flee from this testimony into cheap theologies, to the effect that the Holocaust poses no problems of "theodicy" not known before. Let general philosophers not flee into cheap anthropologies, to the effect that if there is evil in human nature, we already knew it, *all* of it, before. Let all this be silenced by the testimony of Filip Mueller.

Let me turn next to the scene in *Shoah* about the Polish bystanders. No rabbi in all history ever preached a sermon about Jewish guilt for the death of Jesus, thus accepting as true the slander recorded in the Christian Scriptures. No rabbi, we may be sure, ever preached any such sermon during the Holocaust. The sermon that mythical rabbi is supposed to have preached is about the most horrible passage in the Christian Scriptures, and the most horrible part of that is about the children. That passage, and a tradition that derived from this and similar passages, did not, of course, produce the Holocaust. But no one seeing that scene in *Shoah* can be left in doubt that, had there been no two-thousand-year-old slander of Jews as a deicide people, the Holocaust could not have happened.

A Jewish philosopher comes away from that scene in *Shoah* with a heavy responsibility. Like, it seems, everyone else, he nowadays is in "dialogue" with Christians: let him not be soft in this dialogue, that is, dwell only on the great things Jews and Christians share, the One God, the prophetic ethics, and so on. Let him not sweep under the carpet that bit about the Jews calling a curse upon their own heads and those of their children! For if he does, and if, God forbid, there is another Holocaust a thousand years hence, there will again be those who say, "but after all the Jews did kill Christ!" And it won't have to be Poles next time, nor will it have to be Christians. Indeed, they could be atheists, saying "there never was a Christ, but the Jews killed him."

What about Christian philosophers watching this scene from *Shoah*? On them, of course, rests the main responsibility. For my part, when I saw this scene I was happy not to be a Christian, nor would I know what to do if I were. So I can't tell Christian philosophers what to do, but only let them find out for themselves. I do know, however, how I would feel if I saw that bit of *Shoah* and were a Christian. I would feel like tearing up the New Testament.

I now come to the last and hardest of all, the criminal. We must all plead guilty to this, averting attention from him and in so doing inevitably diverting misplaced attention to others. Moreover, to do this is all too human, for who wants to belong to the same species as *Unterscharfuehrer* Suchomel? Not to dwell on him may even seem admirable, for aren't we supposed to look for the beam in our own eye before looking for the mote in the eyes of others? Such must have been Hannah Arendt's view when she wrote that for a Jew the darkest page in the whole dark chapter was the behavior not of the criminals (whom she considered banal) but of the *Judenrate* who were their tools. Paying insufficient attention to the criminals, she failed to notice, or at any rate to stress, that the system of the criminals, far from banal, was set up so as to use equally Jewish virtue and Jewish vice, Jewish courage and Jewish cowardice. No, if the bit about the beam and the mote ever was inapplicable, it was so in the case of *Unterscharfuehrer* Suchomel, and there is nothing admirable in diverting attention from such as him. As for his being part of the same species as the rest of us—alas, that's what he is!

But how *can* he be? Perhaps we still can understand those who, then and there, "only followed orders," even orders such as these. But how can we understand one who, thirty years or so later, "objectively" reports it all, including how women, stripped naked, had to wait in snow and ice for hours on end to be murdered—and then adds gratutiously that such as he, having inadequate uniforms, were cold as well? No qualms. No pity but only self-pity. And of remorse not a trace. Our tradition teaches that sins can be forgiven—if there is remorse and repentance. But of the utterly wicked the Talmud says that they do not repent even at the gates of hell.

Franz Suchomel reminds one of another Franz, Suchomel's superior, Treblinka *Kommandant* Franz Stangl. Lanzmann could not interview him, for he had died in prison. But Stangl was interviewed by someone else, Gitta Sereny, whose *Into That Darkness* (London, 1974) reports on these interviews, lasting no less than six weeks. "Why were they murdering the Jews?" she asked Stangl, and Stangl replied that they wanted their money. As if the Jews had not long been stripped naked! Stangl quite readily volunteered to be interviewed, for hours on end: and then he, the one who had been actually in charge of Treblinka, gave an answer he cannot possibly have believed. Then Sereny proceeded to ask what the point was of all the humiliation and torture of the victims if they were to be murdered anyway. Stangl replied that the purpose was to condition the future murderers to becoming murderers, and this seemed plausible even to Sereny.

Yet if one thinks about it—and philosophers are supposed to think—Stangl's answer cannot possibly be true. What was easier on the gentle consciences of such as Suchomel, to press the button of a machine gun or a gas chamber, or to resort, day by day, to the infinitely varied way in which the victims were humiliated and tortured? Are we to say that Suchomel did what he did without thinking about it, that he only followed orders? Are we to go higher in the ladder of command, and say the same thing about Stangl? Are we perhaps to go up higher and higher, until we get to the highest? That this one, however, could not have been interviewed by either Lanzmann or Sereny we learn from the time in 1923 when, so to speak, he was interviewed, in a trial for treason, and managed to make monkeys of his German judges. I am referring, of course, to Hitler. And from Hitler we do get the answers that Stangl, either a liar, refused to give, or else, a banal cog in the wheel after all, was unable to give. Hitler had this to say: "The Jews are undoubtedly a race, but they are not human. They are created in the image not of God but the devil. They are the racial tuberculosis of the nations."

So that's it! Because Jews are devils they must be humiliated and tortured. And because they are vermin—or the racial tuberculosis of the nations—they must be "exterminated." (After all, one does not let baby vermin survive.) I wonder why philosophers have paid no attention to this doctrine. Are they not supposed to notice the unusual, the absurd? And what could be both more unusual and absurd than that one group of humans is considered a race, to be sure, yet not a lower-but-still-human race but not human at all? Does a philosopher do justice to that view by flattening it out into racism-in-general? And what of the mixture of devils and vermin? Can the Jews be both? Yet at Treblinka and Auschwitz they were treated as if they were both.

We have no philosophers contemplating this view but plenty of biographies about the man who held it and put it into practice. We may ignore biographies that say either that there was no Holocaust or that Hitler did not order it or know about it: they are Nazi or neo-Nazi. But what of those who, like Joachim Fest, admit that Hitler knew about it, ordered it, but kept the order "abstract," didn't want to hear "the details," possibly because he couldn't stand them? Quite possibly Fest is right, for there is the well-known story about Himmler, arch-criminal second only to Hitler, who got sick in the stomach on the one occasion that he did more than merely hear the details, but went actually to watch them. Shall we say, then, that Hitler and Himmler, to be sure, ordered their *Weltanschauung* about Jews to be put into practice, but shrank from the details because they were not such bad fellows after all? Was only the *Weltanschauung* wicked? But that by itself, the biographer Allan Bullock tells us, was not original with Hitler or Himmler but had been platitudinous coffeehouse talk in European capitals for decades.

So a philosopher watches *Shoah*, and this without the slightest doubt that it displays an evil without precedent. But where, following the historians and biographers, is he to locate the evil? He looks at the lowest, such as Franz Suchomel, who does not think much—or at all—about the difference between naked women about to be murdered and shivering with cold, and himself who is "also" cold. So he goes higher in his search for the evil, and comes upon such as *Kommandant* Stangl, who, also does not seem to think much about the system of crimes he has himself ordered, and presumably frequently watched. So the philosopher must go higher still in the order of command—only to find in the end, on the one hand, a stale *Weltanschauung* long around, as ridiculous as it is banal, and, on the other, this *Weltanschauung* put into practice by perhaps just one "fanatical" individual who yet, except for this "obsession," was a little man, not a bad fellow really, and in any case no superhuman devil. In short, the philosopher who contemplates what historians, biographers, and others have done with the evil of the Holocaust discovers that *wherever these scholars are looking, the evil is somewhere else.* But of course it *isn't* anywhere else but rather in the Holocaust whole, of which every one of the perpetrators was part. And this is precisely what survivors have been trying to tell us all along. It is that whole-of-horror—"Planet Auschwitz," one survivor calls it—that the philosopher must contemplate, if he wishes to pursue Socrates' ancient quest in terms fitting our time.

But has planet Auschwitz not been destroyed? Does it present a task for philosophers still? The task has hardly begun!

I started out with the columnist George Will, and I will close with him. He refers to Lanzmann's *Shoah* as an act of continuing resistance. *Continuing?* he then asks, and answers in the affirmative. The Nazis meant to "exterminate" not only Europe's Jews but also all traces that they ever lived, as well as all evidence of what they, the Nazis, had done to erase both. To this end they exhumed bodies of Jews they had murdered, ground their bones to dust and threw the dust into rivers. When Margaret Thatcher visited Yad Vashem she realized that, had the war lasted but one year longer, European Jews, their bodies, their synagogues, prayer books, Torah scrolls would all have been *spurlos verschwunden*—vanished without a trace; except for museums already planned for an "extinct race," one would not have known that there had ever been Jews in Europe; and those who still knew would not have known what had happened to them.

Shoah is a continuing act of resistance, then, since the struggle against forgetting is lost unless remembrance is a continuing act. For philosophers, this resistance has yet to begin in earnest. The man who demands it above all others is Filip Mueller, the only person who ever was in a gas chamber and came out alive in order to testify. One must hope that never again will mankind require a witness like him. Yet we who live after the Holocaust do require him. In choosing to survive, in witnessing to us, Mueller has performed a holy task; and so has Claude Lanzmann by creating *Shoah*, a mighty weapon needed by us all as we struggle against the sin of forgetting—against doing, however unwittingly, Hitler's work.

Twelve

Holocaust and *Weltanschauung*
Philosophical Reflections
on Why They Did It

Corruptio optimi pessima est

The Unanswered Question

I once asked Raul Hilberg the following question: "Raul, you have thought as long and hard as anyone about how they did it. Now tell me, why did they do it?" Hilberg heaved a sigh and replied: "They did it because they wanted to do it."

I reported this incident at the 1985 meeting of the Eastern Division of the American Philosophical Association.[1] In the ensuing discussion someone substituted "They did it because they *decided* to do it." This emendation, I believe, is acceptable to Hilberg, who is given neither to absolving people of responsibility for their decisions nor to overlooking the fact that one does not do everything one wants to do.

Both answers, however, give rise to the further question of why they should have wanted—let alone decided!—to perpetrate a crime as unprecedented as it was "irrational." That Hilberg is aware of this further question his sigh would suffice to prove. But there is more. He has explained again and again that in his lifelong struggle with the Holocaust he has limited himself to "small" questions, for fear of giving too small an answer to the "big" question.

Claude Lanzmann's *Shoah* has followed the same course. Not once in his masterful film does he ask either a victim or bystander and least of all a criminal why they did it: had he asked this question, he would surely have got too small an answer. Answers which are too small have invariably been given and received by those who have failed to be supremely wary in getting anywhere close to the "big" question.[2]

I shall confine my present attention entirely to that question. I must therefore state what I take it to be. It is not why the Nazis practiced brutality on a scale hitherto unknown; built a vast system of concentration camps; preached and practiced an extreme form of racism; fanned the most radical conceivable anti-Semitism; put it into practice through laws that disenfranchised Jews, undoing a century of emancipation; staged the worst pogrom in a history not lacking in pogroms; or even why at length they resorted to genocide of the Jewish people. To these (and other) questions historians may find answers, citing historical parallels. For me the "big" question is why they decided quite literally to *exterminate* the Jews, i.e., murder *every available* Jew; why they *acted* on this decision, not letting even the old die in bed; and—this surely most startling but also most revelatory!—why this action *remained sacrosanct* even when at length it became contrary to their most elementary interest, i.e., when their own Reich was in its death throes. For me, that it was and remained sacrosanct will always remain a searing fact because of Bertchen Bacher. A spinster, my grandmother's best friend, and already old and frail, she was the most inoffensive of persons. Yet they would not let even her die in peace.

Among those who count, only a few such as Himmler—*der treue Heinrich*—gave up, betraying their Führer as well as their own *Treue*. Not most of the others. Eichmann diverted trains from the crumbling Eastern front so as to send more Jews to their death. The S.S. did not flee when the Russians approached Auschwitz; rather, at risk to themselves, they force-marched their victims westward, making sure that they perished by the thousands from exhaustion or shooting on the way.

As for the Führer himself, this is how he acted in the end. Trapped in his Berlin bunker, he had already expressed satisfaction at what he thought —perhaps hoped!—would be the annihilation of his own German *Volk*: the Russians would win, nay, being the stronger after all, would *deserve* to win, for such were the laws of social-Darwinist justice. Yet now, when it was time for suicide, he composed a "political testament" that did not view Jews by these same standards. To be sure, they were strong, nay, stronger than the Russians and indeed near-omnipotent. Yet they were not the master race that deserved to rule mankind, but rather its "poisoners." It was they—not the Führer himself—who had caused this most terrible of wars, just as they had caused every previous one. And Hitler's last words to his *Volk*—for this purpose, it seems, it must survive, after all—were an appeal to "practice merciless resistance to the world-poisoners of all nations, *das internationale Judentum.*"[3]

The "Big" Question and the Nature of Historical Explanation

It is not a philosopher's task to answer questions that baffle historians. His task is to reflect on the nature of historical explanations; and, attending to the "big" Holocaust question while engaged in this task, I shall here direct the historian's attention to a dimension of the question that has been insufficiently explored, if and when explored at all. Two theories of historical explanation have commanded philosophical assent in recent decades. Let both be tested with Hilberg's "big" question in mind.

The Covering Law Theory and the Holocaust

The first theory may be called positivist, since it asserts that explanation in the sciences is all of one kind and that therefore explanation in history does not differ in principle from, say, explanation in physics.[4] To be sure, physics aims at universal laws, through which the physicist both predicts the future and explains the past, whereas the historian explains nothing more than past particulars and is, moreover, rarely helped by success in this effort in predicting the future. This difference, however, is not one of principle but merely of situation and degree. Of situation: unlike the physicist, the historian cannot make—much less repeat—experiments by which to test his hypotheses. Of degree: human affairs are too complex to yield laws of human behavior as precise as those of physics. Taken together, these two differences suffice to explain why a professional historian, say, of post–World War I Europe was but little better qualified to predict the course of the Nazi movement than the amateur historian Winston Churchill. (In fact, of course, the qualifications of the whole lot, taken together, were much worse.) They also suffice to explain why historical explanations rarely take the precise form "*x* caused *y*," and mostly the vaguer form "*x* led to *y*" or "sooner or later was bound to lead to *y*." Yet, consciously or not, in explaining past particulars the historian implies general laws of human behavior; and if he does not, he explains nothing. He may then still be engaged in separating fact from fiction, and thus also scholarship from journalism, novel writing and other unscholarly activities. However, in venturing beyond establishing to explaining the past, his activity is, in that case, to paraphrase Aristotle, less scientific even than poetry.

This so-called covering law theory of historical explanation rests on the dogma of the unity of the sciences. Its plausibility to historians, however, derives far more from examples adduced in support. Hence in testing the theory by the "big," baffling question about the Holocaust, we shall shed light not only on that question itself but also on the whole theory—and, as will be seen, its limits.

It is not difficult to find lawlike generalizations implied in accounts not only of Nazism but also of the Holocaust. "Economic distress tends to cause social upheaval"; "defeat in war may lead to nationalist extremism fueled by resentment": no account of Nazism seems able to dispense with these generalizations, dubious though they are. (They *are* dubious: like Germany, America suffered the Great Depression; yet it produced not Hitler but Roosevelt.) Add to these two "laws" yet a third, and no account of the Holocaust seems able to dispense with all three, thus conjoined: "given a centuries-old calumny of one identifiable group, that group is apt to serve as scapegoat in times of economic distress, especially when this latter is compounded by national humiliation and resentment."

These lawlike generalizations explain much about the Holocaust: they come nowhere close, however, to the "big" question. The Jews-as-scapegoats "law" may have some plausibility so long as one deals with the early Nazi period, when Jewish-blood-spurting-from-knives was a song bellowed from the housetops; all plausibility is lost when public incitement was turned into top-secret action. And plausibility becomes sheer absurdity when at length the "big" question comes into view. Jewish scapegoating by the Nazis was presumably meant as a means, first, to bringing Nazism to power and, then, to preserving and strengthening it. Yet *in extremis* the relation became reversed: such power of the Nazi Reich as remained became a means to the murder of more, and still more, Jews.

When confronting this extremity the positivist theorist may protest that nobody can ever explain everything; that, for example, he himself could not so much as describe, let alone explain, every trivial thing that had occurred in the single classroom hour he has just spent expounding his theory—the itches, scratches, yawns of his students, the little noises from outside, and so forth. In this, however, he ignores that "why they did it" is not a trivial thing. Of all questions raised by the Holocaust, it is the most important.

Forced, after all, to confront the "big" question, the positivist may call for the historian's heaping laws upon laws, bringing his general laws ever closer to the Holocaust's particularity, with a view to capturing at length the scan-dalous "why" of it. "Given sufficient time, radical anti-Semites sooner or later believe their own propaganda." "Given sufficient stress, they continue to believe in Jewish power even when events—events like the Holocaust—demonstrate Jewish lack of power." "Given sufficient time *and* stress, they become so fanatical in their beliefs as to die for them rather than question them." Grant these or similar "laws," and you reach not only the *infima species* "events *like* the Holocaust" but the Holocaust itself, its "why" included.

What has in fact been reached, however, is the *reductio ad absurdum* of the theory. By the time the compounding of laws has reached that great, baffling "why", the historian, like the old-fashioned metaphysician with his old-fashioned God, is left with a class with but a single member. To make matters worse, the crucial characteristic of that single member is insanity. This, to be sure, is no little matter. Terms such as "insanity" and "paranoia" keep creeping into historical accounts of the Holocaust, all-but-unfailingly so as they approach the "big" question.[5] This fact ought to provoke thought. It does not provoke our thought here, however, for what matters presently is only this, that "insanity", "paranoia" and similar "explanations" are all answers too "small" to the "big" question.

The Covering Law Theory Modified

The covering law theory of historical explanation has now been widely abandoned. Its model, "given *a, b* is probable if not necessary," has yielded to the less doctrinaire and more sober "given *a, b* is possible."[6] With this there is no need to quarrel. Much has been said, and much more needs to be explored, about the circumstances that made the Holocaust possible. The "big" question, however, is not how it was possible but why it became actual; not how they could decide to do it, but why they made the decision.

The "Idealist" Theory of R. G. Collingwood

We must therefore attend to the second prevalent theory of historical explanation, "idealist" in that it stakes all on human decisions and their "why." Only nature, asserts R. G. Collingwood, its most distinguished exponent of recent decades, consists of "events." History consists of "actions"; and these, unlike events, have an "inside" as well as an "outside", the latter being the action itself, the former, the "why" of it in the mind of the agent. Give the reason (or reasons) why an agent did what he did, and you have explained the action. To look for behavioral laws beyond these reasons is a doctrinaire mistake.[7]

Like its positivist rival, this theory depends for its plausibility less on abstract doctrines than on examples cited in support. Collingwood's own favorite example is Caesar crossing the Rubicon. Few actions of great moment have ever been based so clearly, on the one hand, on one man's decision who, on the other, was so obviously rational. Bismarck may have been as rational as Caesar; yet the actions that led to the founding of his German Reich were not his alone, nor his in conjunction with those of other individuals equally rational; they were also—far more—all those countless ones motivated by a yearning for national unity, a yearning explosive ever since Napoleon at Jena dealt the death blow to the Holy Roman Empire of German Nation. However, "actions" such as these—they are those of a "movement"—are group-actions rather than individual ones; and while their "inside" may be ideas, they can hardly be called rational.

Never in all history was a movement as clearly the work of a single individual as was National Socialism. That a decision as crucial as the Holocaust stemmed from a *Führerbefehl* was therefore evident to people both honest and level-headed long before it was demonstrated.[8] Its "why" may therefore seem to fit well into Collingwood's model, since, after all, individual "actions" are less problematic for it than collective ones. Yet despite the *Führerbefehl* institution the "big" question is not about Hitler alone. Himmler may have complained that his particular Hitler order was hard; in the end he was even *treulos* enough to disobey it: yet while obey he did, he approved of it.[9] In Jerusalem Eichmann protested that he had been a mere cog in the wheel; he contradicted his own protest when he cited Kant's categorical imperative.[10] And simple common sense is very nearly enough to demonstrate that the death marches, occurring as they did in the last, chaotic days of the Reich, were ordered not by Hitler but by "decent"[11] subordinates.

To be sure, among the torturers and murderers were robots who obeyed orders blindly, as well as sadists who enjoyed obeying them. The "big" Holocaust question, however, involves not such as these, but only the "idealists" —Himmler until he became *treulos*; Eichmann, the S.S. murderers and countless others to the very end—who, to cite an obscure Nazi philosopher's novel version of Kant's categorical imperative, asked themselves while doing what they did whether the Führer, if he knew, would approve; who acted on the presumed Führer's will as though it were their own.[12]

The "why" of the Holocaust, then, is not a case like Caesar's crossing of the Rubicon, after all. This is true of the "action" itself, for it was collective rather than individual. It is true also of its "inside," for this was not "rational."

What was the "inside" of the "actions" of these many quasi-Hitlers, as well as of the one and only—and irreplaceable!—real one? More precisely, what did it prove to have been all along in the extremity that showed forth its truth?[13] One asks this, the "big" question, and arrives once more at insanity. To be sure, they were all responsible decision-makers, not human flotsam carried into catastrophe by waves of "laws." The decisions themselves, however, were insane. Yet insanity, as we already know, is too "small" an answer to the "big" question.

We thus have reached an impasse once more—or would have reached it were it not for the *nationalsozialistische Weltanschauung.*

Hitler's *Weltanschauung*

Back in 1938 Hermann Rauschning, a one-time Hitler supporter but now resolute foe, advanced the thesis that Nazism was a "revolution of nihilism" that aimed at nothing but naked power. He would not destroy the Jews, Rauschning reports Hitler as saying, for he needed a visible enemy for Germans to focus their hate on; indeed, if Jews did not exist, he would have to invent them.[14] But then came the Holocaust. And since, moreover, there is nothing to suggest that, had Hitler won the war and made the world *judenrein*, he would have "invented" new Jews to take their place—Slavs, blacks, to say nothing of Englishmen[15]—the Rauschning thesis is destroyed by the facts. Yet it survives.

An explanation emerges, strangely enough, from a work aimed at refuting that thesis. As is well known, there was a *nationalsozialistische Weltanschauung*. Equally well known is, or ought to be, that it was formulated authoritatively by Hitler himself, and solemnly invoked on all proper occasions. Yet, Eberhard Jäckel argues,[16] historians have neglected that

Weltanschauung, and in a brief but powerful book he sets out to remedy that defect. In so doing he puts forward a thesis of his own but, to his credit, does not hurl it at the reader, proceeding instead to examine the evidence. Hitler, ruthlessly Machiavellian in his means, Jäckel asserts, was by no means Machiavellian in his ends: he aimed, not at power for power's sake, but rather at goals set forth in his *Weltanschauung*—the "granite-like foundation of . . . [his future] actions."[17]

What were these goals and that *Weltanschauung*? To cite only aspects presently relevant, the German *Volk* needs *lebensraum*, and armed conquest is a just way of getting it: such are "nature's" social-Darwinist "laws." Armed conquest is practical as well as just, provided the aim is pursued in alliance with others. Natural allies are Italy and Britain, both *Völker* with *Lebensraum* needs of their own, with the British being fellow "Aryans" to boot. Italy would expand in southern Europe and Africa, Britain overseas; and in return for a free hand in those parts of the world, these two powers would let Germany expand eastward. They would do so gladly, moreover, since, in destroying Russia, Germany would destroy also the world citadel of Marxism, the common enemy of them all. Only two further aspects of the *Weltanschauung* need to be mentioned here: the *Führerprinzip* and anti-semitism. Hitler would not merely happen to be Führer: it was a *Prinzip* that there should *be* a Führer, and that Hitler himself would be he. This one principle emerged together with the other, for in his own mind (if not yet outside it) Hitler became Führer with his Vienna "conversion" from "cosmopolitanism" to "antisemitism."[18] To be sure, the account of that process in *Mein Kampf*—theatrical and self-inflating as it is with all that talk about "greatest inner soul struggles"—deserves little credit: in all likelihood Hitler was an antisemite since childhood. The account does deserve credit, however, insofar as it marks the birth of a *Weltanschauung*. Nor may one take lightly the theatrical self-inflation that accompanies the retrospective account—a retrospect that was to last till Hitler's death.

Such, then, was the *Weltanschauung* that was to be the "foundation" of the Führer's subsequent "actions." But what happened when, with actions in full swing, the actors failed to play their preassigned roles: when Britain turned enemy rather than ally; when Italy, no heroic victor, became instead a defeated coward; and when Russia, easy prey though it was to be by dint of its "Jewish Marxism," refused to expire? What of the *Weltanschauung* remaining "granite-like" then?

Jäckel keeps asking this question. He also keeps looking for the *Geschlossenheit*—comprehensive unity—that, as he rightly insists, a full-blown *Weltanschauung* requires. He does find the necessary *Geschlossenheit*, but only after much labor and in the book's last few pages. Yet the reader seems to have guessed it—the great mystery—all along, for he has read the book with care, and has been startled by the unique character of its third chapter.[19] Why, *das Judentum* gives the *Weltanschauung* its needed

Geschlossenheit.[20] It solves the large problem, showing what Hitler is *for* by showing what he is *against*—internationalism, pacifism, and parliamentary democracy, poisonous Jewish inventions all! *Das Judentum* also solves the small problem—why the actors failed to play their preassigned roles. Why had Britain turned hostile? Because Churchill was Jewified! Why was Russia winning? Because Stalin, no Jewish Marxist after all, deserved to win! The *Weltanschauung*, then, had been right, and remained right even *in extremis*: only in Italy's case does Hitler admit to a mistake, and even that one was due, not to his *Weltanschauung*, but merely to misguided personal kindness.

In the extremity that showed forth its truth, then, the *Weltanschauung* survived, but in part only. Not among the surviving parts was the thousand-year-Reich, its right to ever more *Lebensraum*, or even to *Leben* itself. All these, the *Führer* himself included, went down in a self-destructive, nihilistic fury that confirmed what had been true all along in the Rauschning thesis, after all.[21] Rauschning had been wrong all along, however, in two respects: the Jews were the poisoners of the world, and—except for acts of mistaken kindness—the *Führer* was always right. These two parts of the *Weltanschauung* were veritable pillars. They remained standing to the end. And they were "granite-like" because they confirmed each other: *that the Führer was always right was proved by the Jews being the poisoners of the world; and that the Jews were the poisoners of the world was proved by the Führer being always right.*

Evidently we have, for yet a third time, arrived at insanity; indeed, if the mind's self-enclosure in its own circle, immune to all external evidence, is what *constitutes* insanity, we have reached a classic case of it. We must therefore, at this late point, alter the strategy we have followed thus far. Earlier we simply dismissed "insanity", as "too small" an answer to the "big" Holocaust question. Simply to dismiss it is possible no more. Instead, we must think again.

Does history lack in mad, megalomanic dictators? With his "Heil Hitler," his "Hitler youth," his *Führerprinzip*, and all the rest, does Hitler not rank with the maddest of them? Way back in ancient times Nero fiddled while Rome burned, having set the city on fire himself in order for his musical genius to be inspired by the sight.

But the parallel fails. Nero fiddled alone; no quasi-Neros fiddled with him or under him. In contrast, if Hitler was insane, so were Eichmann, the S.S., Himmler until he became *treulos*, and indeed—in the extremity that showed forth its truth—the whole Nazi Reich. This, however, is the crux: *whereas a mad Nero is an explanation, a whole Reich-as-madhouse is not; whether or not recognized as such, such a purported "explanation" is but an admission on the historian's part, witting or unwitting, that nothing has been explained.* The "why" of the Holocaust, then, is a truly great predicament for the historian in the practice of his craft.

He may be helped somewhat by pondering the second difference between Nero's Rome and Hitler's Berlin; indeed, by pondering it ourselves we reach at length the goal of the present inquiry. When Nero's Rome burned, nothing remained sacrosanct, not even the emperor's fiddling. In contrast, two things—but two things only—remained sacrosanct when Hitler's Berlin was aflame: the *Führerprinzip*, and the murder of more, and ever more, Jews. Indeed, if Hitler's "political testament" is taken seriously—and this it must be—these two things were to remain sacrosanct not only unto death but, in Nibelungen-like *Treue*, even beyond. This difference exists because Hitler's Berlin, unlike Nero's Rome, had a *Weltanschauung.*

What *Weltanschauung* Means in German History

As used in languages other than German, the word *Weltanschauung* has lost its German meaning. On their part, Germans are too close to their own history to reflect on that meaning and its role in their history. Even Jäckel, among the most perceptive, refers to *Weltanschauungen* other than Hitler's, but never stands back to ask—ask in depth—precisely what *Weltanschauung* means in German history.

An ideology is confined to history. Hence such crimes as Stalin's murder of the peasants and the Cambodian genocide shatter the imagination, to be sure, but remain within the limits of intelligibility. That it was to be otherwise with Hitler's *Weltanschauung* is evident as early as in his 1924 "dialogue" with Dietrich Eckart which, though still confined to history, is already "world-historical" enough—as well as world-historically anti-Jewish enough—to make Moses into a Bolshevist and Lenin into a Jew.[22] That the as-yet-not-*geschlossene Weltanschauung* was to transcend history altogether is announced in a much-quoted passage of *Mein Kampf:*

> If, with the help of his Marxist creed, the Jew is victorious over the other peoples of the world, his crown will be the funeral wreath of humanity, and this planet will, as it did thousands of years ago, move through the ether devoid of men.[23]

Much quoted, this passage is little understood, even though Hitler himself, so to speak, lends a hand when, in the second edition, he "corrects" "thousands" into "millions." *Millions* of years in the past? Perhaps millions *again* in the future? Why did such passages not mark their author as a raving madman? Nothing is explained by the fact that *Mein Kampf* was the world's least-read best-seller, for Hitler said much the same often enough in his speeches. Nor by the fact that antisemitism was rife in Germany: except in Germany, few antisemites, however extreme, ever made Jews into a cosmic principle.

Historians may never succeed in answering this question satisfactorily. They will fail entirely unless they understand—understand in the depth that the subject requires—that whereas an ideology remains with history, the scope of a *Weltanschauung*, in the context of German history, goes beyond things historical and extends to the cosmos. An encyclopedia article, published in Germany in 1931, declares that the "true problem" of a *Weltanschauung* is to find "a firm, unified framework for life that transcends the achievement of the senses, of thought, of the sciences—to find it with the help of other powers."[24] The author, himself a Christian, will not have guessed how—and how soon—the 'problem' would be "solved."

Nothing in history quite compares to the role of *Weltanschauungen* in nineteenth- and early twentieth-century Germany. Like people elsewhere, Germans had opinions, beliefs (religious and/or other), interests, belonged to clubs and political parties. To have a *Weltanschauung* was something special. It deserved respect, even awe, if only it had the three characteristics a *Weltanschauung* requires: cosmic scope, internal coherence or *Geschlossenheit*, and a sincere commitment on the part of its devotees. (Whether it was right or true by external criteria—such as, in Hitler's case, elementary decency or facts about Jews—mattered little or not at all.) Hence when the *nationalsozialistische Weltanschauung* appeared, it was respected simply *because* it was a *Weltanschauung*: not despite the fact that it was cosmic but because of it; not despite the fact that it slandered "good" as well as "bad" Jews but—indiscriminate attacks on *das Judentum* being necessary for *Geschlossenheit*—because of it. And the pimp Horst Wessel became a saint, not despite the fact that he died needlessly but, having died because he had refused a Jewish doctor's aid, because of it.

Who had a *Weltanschauung* in Weimar Germany? Even the communists had only an ideology. As for the others on both right and left, they had at best a few principles, i.e. fragments of a *Weltanschauung*. The fragments of the Weimar "traitors" on the left, of course, were held in contempt, and not by the Nazis alone. But right-wing would-be restorers of the Kaiser's *Reich* did not fare well, either. It was for lack of a *geschlossene Weltanschauung*, Hitler claimed, that the Kaiser had lost his war—and won over many hankering for the Kaiser's return. Once in pre-Nazi days an argument erupted in my high school class. The subject was German wartime policy toward Belgium. The Kaiser's government had violated Belgian neutrality but subsequently apologized. The handful of Weimar democrats in the class attacked the violation and lost. But so did the Kaiser's defenders, and they were the great majority, who usually set the tone. It was the handful of Nazis that won the argument: the Kaiser had been right in violating Belgian neutrality—but should have blamed the violation on the Belgians. The Nazis won because they—and they alone—had a *geschlossene Weltanschauung*. They continued to win. And their *Weltanschauung* continued to remain *geschlossen* when Hitler started his newer and better war on Poland; and when his war ended, with Eichmann keeping on sending his trains, with the S.S. force-marching the Auschwitz survivors westward, and with the Führer himself composing his "political testament."

Arguably this end marks the nadir of all history. One must understand it, however, as the nadir of *German* history—and hark back from this to its zenith, for then the German notion of *Weltanschauung* was born. Their best age once earned Germans the title of *Volk* not only of *Dichter* but also of *Denker.* Their worst age came when Hitler was not only their *Führer* but also their *Denker. Corruptio optimi pessima est.*

The greatest German age began when Kant—*der Alleszermalmer*[25]—having smashed metaphysics, placed moral duty into the vacated place, thus giving it cosmic significance. Two decades later, in 1807, what for Kant was absolute was described by Hegel[26] as *die moralische Weltanschauung,* i.e., first, a *Weltanschauung,* and second, only one among others. This was no whim on Hegel's part but rendered inevitable by intervening developments. In 1797 Fichte[27] wrote, "What philosophy one chooses depends on what kind of person one is. A philosophical system is not a dead piece of furniture that one can accept or reject at will, but is rather animated by the person that holds it." This well-known statement is widely taken to mean that philosophy is a cluster of personal idiosyncrasies, something that Fichte would not have dignified by the name of philosophy. The philosopher rather faces up to a serious but new philosophical problem. Since Kant, the philosopher can—and therefore must—choose between two philosophical systems, the one—realism—making objective reality ultimate, the other—idealism—subjective freedom, with each reducing to appearance what to the other was reality. Though coherent, however, neither system sufficed by itself to lay claim to truth. The new problem is that whereas both are coherent neither can refute the other and therefore demonstrate its own truth. Hence —lest the choice be arbitrary—the claim to truth made by either must be backed by the person that affirms it. The word *Weltanschauung* doubtless existed before in the German language. But this is how it became a respected notion in philosophical discourse—and, Germany being Germany, in German discourse as a whole.

What Fichte showed to be a problem quickly turned into a predicament. In 1797 he affirmed two possible *Weltanschauungen,* a "realist" suffused with a weak freedom overwhelmed by cosmic necessity, and an "idealist" with a freedom so strong as to maintain itself against the whole universe. In 1799 Schleiermacher followed with yet a third, the religious *Weltanschauung,*[28] and only one year later Schelling with yet a fourth, the aesthetic one.[29] With the exception of the soon-forgotten "realism" (acknowledged but not held by Fichte), these *Weltanschauungen* all were supported by philosophical argument, as subtle as it was honest, for their *coherence;* they also all culminated in the noblest of human experiences affirming their *truth*—respectively, moral freedom, religious devoutness, and the aesthetic creativity by which truth is wedded to beauty. By dint of their very plurality, however, they also willy-nilly introduced arbitrariness into philosophical discourse. Even so, however, there was yet no reason to fear the specter of

Holocaust and *Weltanschauung*

Weltanschauungen that would owe their *Geschlossenheit* not to philosophical honesty but to lies and slander; and that would affirm their truth not through noble experiences but mass murder.

Then came Hegel. A philosopher of unequaled modern greatness, he confronted the predicament of the plurality of *Weltanschauungen* with unmatched integrity, but sought to overcome it with an all-comprehensive system of thought in which all *Weltanschauungen* were accorded partial truth, and none more than a partial one. However, as every German *Privatdozent* worth his meager stipend was to intone for the rest of the nineteenth century and well into the twentieth, the Hegelian synthesis has "collapsed". Not many have added that, with this collapse, the great age of German *Denker* came to an end.

No end came, however, to the multiplicity of *Weltanschauungen*, with few Germans deterred from giving them respect by the fact that the level of humane culture and philosophical subtlety were rapidly declining. Count Gobineau was a Frenchman, Houston Stewart Chamberlain an Englishman. Yet the coarse trash of both became *Weltanschauungen* only in Germany. Nor was respect paid to the trash only by the coarse. The chief German booster of the Frenchman was Richard Wagner, and the Englishman became his son-in-law. Nothing influenced the young Hitler quite as much as getting drunk on Wagner's music.[30]

A wide gulf still exists between Hitler and Wagner, to say nothing of the vast one between the darkest period in German history and the brightest. Our task is not to explore this gulf, but merely to point to it, for future historians concerned with the "big" Holocaust question to ponder and explore. In doing both they are given food for thought by the fact that Schelling's call for a future union of beauty and truth—a "new mythology" in which music and drama, dance, poetry, and philosophic thought were all at one—found a response in Wagner's musical dramas; and on these the young Hitler got drunk.

Pondering the twofold gulf ourselves, we on our part say only this: if *der Nationalsozialismus* was the acting out of a *Weltanschauung*, and if antisemitism was the "granite-like" core of it,[31] then neither the Führer nor his "decent" followers could be satisfied with a *Halbheit* that would have *Geschlossenheit* but stop short of confirming its truth. The "solution" of the "problem" posed by the Jewish "poisoners" of the world, in that case, had to have *Ganzheit*, i.e., be "final," and remain so to the end. Not even Bertchen Bacher, in that case, could be allowed to die in bed.

Reality and Theater

Did Hitler believe his own *Weltanschauung*? Some say that nobody dies with a lie.[32] A dubious thesis, in Hitler's case this may be wholly false. An actor, Hitler was a nobody who became a somebody when he found his

Weltanschauung. In order to die a somebody, he may well have played to the end a role in a tragedy that he himself had had the main share in writing. If so, the Holocaust, unique in any case, is also a unique tragedy. Like other tragedies, it inspires terror and pity—terror because of the criminals, pity because of the victims. But enacted on no mere stage, it offers no way for us, no mere spectators, of purging these emotions.

Epilogue

When Hitler died, did German *Denken* come to an end? An understandable reaction, it offers no way out, however, for the specter of Hitler, his Reich, his Holocaust, all keep on haunting the world and will keep on haunting it.[33] The times therefore call for a new generation of *Denker*—they can only be German—who will not escape into rarefied realms of "Being" or generalized "revolts against transcendence,"[34] but rather assume responsibility for their history, pondering the history of German *Denken*, from its bright beginning to its catastrophic end.

PART III

Jewish Philosophy

Introduction to Part III

The Holocaust and philosophical reflections on it—its uniqueness, its evil, its challenges to ideas of human nature, these are stages on the way to Jewish philosophy today, but they are not yet it. In the essays in this part, Fackenheim ponders the following question and its relevance to his own identity: what today, in the age of Auschwitz and the new Jerusalem, is Jewish philosophy? The Jewish philosopher is both a philosopher and a committed Jew; the issues he or she faces are Jewish ones faced philosophically and philosophical ones faced Jewishly. His or her experience is deeply particularized historically, religiously, and conceptually. Timeless philosophical transcendence is gone, replaced by a tradition read and appropriated in a very particular way. Gone too is a set of timeless religious truths. What remains is a finite, historical episode, a place at which two complex historical roads intersect, conflict, overlap, and complement. That episode, that venue, is, in this case, the identity of Emil Fackenheim. It is no accident that this part, and this book as a whole, culminate in a newly written autobiographical fragment. There is no substantive and general portrait of Jewish philosophy today; what there is are particular Jewish philosophers.

In the first chapter of *To Mend the World*, Fackenheim recalls the journey that led him to confront the demons of Auschwitz. His initial engagement occurred in 1966–1967. From that time to this, his efforts to articulate a post-Holocaust Jewish thought have centered on three problems. The first is: is there a necessity to post-Holocaust Jewish existence and if there is, what is its ground? The second is: if there is such a duty, an obligation, what makes it possible for Jews today to fulfill it? And finally, what is the content of such an obligation? What, in other words, are the standards for authentic post-Holocaust Jewish life? In six books and dozens of articles Fackenheim has thought and rethought these questions, laboring to find answers, or at least responses that forge the outlines of a Judaism of the future. Often these efforts are aimed at specific content, but just as often they incorporate philosophical reflections of a fundamental kind. These philosophical reflections are for Fackenheim today the work of Jewish philosophy.

In the introduction to this volume I discussed the first two essays in this part (chapters 13 and 14), both of which focus directly on the nature and possibility of Jewish philosophy. In the second, Fackenheim turns to a concrete example, the nature of Jewish identity, of antisemitism, and more. But the core of this part lies in the next three essays, two on Israel (chapters 16 and 17), the third a more general discussion of the duties of contemporary Jewish life (chapter 15).

Much of Fackenheim's notoriety comes from the way in which a single formulation—the 614th Commandment—crystallized the self-conscious pride and militancy of American Jewry in the wake of the Six-Day War in June 1967. It is a statement so famous that I have heard it misquoted and even misidentified, as the 11th Commandment or the 366th Commandment. Here, in this short reconsideration of that formulation, we have a very important product of Fackenheim's Jewish philosophy. It is a reaffirmation of his convictions, first endorsed and articulated in the years from 1967 to 1970, that contemporary Jewish existence, if authentic, was grounded in necessity, that the necessity itself arose out of the encounter with Auschwitz, and yet that the content of the necessity was a ramified set of obligations to deal honestly and genuinely with both the darkness itself and the entire Jewish world—texts, ideas, practices, and more—that it threatened to occlude. At its core, the 614th Commandment—thou shalt give Hitler no posthumous victories—was a mandate of honesty, of probity, of integrity. It said to Jews: Our identity is shaped by a richly textured past and by a horrific present. To be genuine we must confront both, the constituents of continuity and the risk of discontinuity, and yet go on. To yield wholly to either one is to court anachronism or self-destruction. Neither is authentic. It is hardly surprising that a jubilant Jewry, celebrating victory in 1967 and at the same time recalling the past in the light of that victory, passionately appropriated Fackenheim's formulation as its slogan. Whatever distortion that appropriation involved, it was grounded in a true insight, that the 614th Commandment incorporated a sense of honest threat and committed affirmation all at once.

After *God's Presence in History*, published in 1970, the 614th Commandment virtually dropped out of Fackenheim's vocabulary.[1] A careful reading of his essays and books, however, shows that it never was abandoned. For most of this period the role of God and revelation was set aside; hence, the notion of a 614th Commandment was replaced by a more generic notion of necessity or duty. The recent reconsideration reprinted here (chapter 15) marks its explicit return to Fackenheim's discourse (or at least its explicit acknowledgment), complete with a rethinking of its specific content for today, more than twenty-five years after its first formulation.

If the articulation of this general framework for Jewish existence today is one task of a contemporary Jewish philosophy, another is the more specific task of formulating "a political philosophy for the state of Israel." For two decades Fackenheim has pondered the significance of Israel, the Jewish state, for post-Holocaust Jews and Judaism. Its reality exemplifies the polarities of all genuine Jewish response to Auschwitz, a complex blending of religious purpose and secular self-reliance.[2] Most brilliantly of all, the essay "Israel and the Holocaust: Their Interrelation" ties the contemporary state of Israel to age-old Messianic reflections and to authentic response to Nazism and the death camps. But if Israel is bound to religious hope and destiny, it is also burdened by political contingencies—its particular history, Arab-Israeli conflict, world politics, conceptions of the modern liberal state, and much else. A political philosophy for the state of Israel must respond to all of this and more. Here, in two essays, Fackenheim sets out to do just that, a fragmentary beginning for a central project. These twin essays (chapters 16 and 17) both focus, in one way or another, on Jerusalem. It is, and has been for a decade, Fackenheim's home.

The final essay returns to beginnings and takes us on a brief tour of the stages on life's way for this, the greatest Jewish philosopher of our generation—from Halle to Berlin to Aberdeen to Toronto and then, once more, to Jerusalem. It is a personal, autobiographical reflection. But it is more, for in this short piece Fackenheim identifies strands that combine to weave the fabric of Jewish philosophy today.[3]

The essay ends on a moving note. In his seventies, Fackenheim writes about his life, about Judaism, and about Jewish philosophy no longer as a young man but now as an old one, as he puts it. Even now, however, the sense of urgency and of crisis persists. As he reminds us, Hegel could think of the Absolute Idea as an old man for whom all of life had been lived and whose attitude must be one of satisfaction, resignation, and perhaps even joy. No such posture comes easily today; Fackenheim's thought—neither philosophy nor Jewish philosophy—cannot enjoy its years of maturity in Hegel's way. For history has shattered the Absolute Idea and forever fragmented the whole in which we live. Fackenheim may live in his old age, but for all that his thought cannot be complacent or self-satisfied. The urgencies still exist; the need is still great; the times demand new and creative reflection on the necessities and possibilities of authentic Jewish existence—from us all, no matter what our age.

Thirteen

What Is Jewish Philosophy?
*Reflections on Athens, Jerusalem,
and the Western Academy*

I

Thoughts on Jewish philosophy should begin with philosophy, and begin with an exemplary teacher. In the West, there is none to compare to Socrates: he taught Plato. But who taught Plato's teacher?

The story is told in Plato's *Apology*. A curious person inquired of the Delphic oracle: who is the wisest of humans? And the reply was: Socrates. Incredulous when hearing of this, but unwilling to dismiss the oracle, Socrates embarked on a venture that was to be of great consequence. He sought out people he considered wiser than himself, asking them questions he could ask but not answer. What is art? he asked of artists. What is the state? he asked of statesmen. But what did he find? The people he visited were good at their pursuits, the artists at art, the statesmen at statecraft; they were at a loss, however, to answer his questions. Either they had thought all along that they knew but, on being asked, did not; or, more typically, they had never given thought to what yet was so great a part of their lives.

Socrates' venture had three results. First, the Delphic oracle had been right after all, for while he too did not know, any more than the artists and statesmen, he *knew* that he did not know: his was—to use a term that came into use much later—a *docta ignorantia*, a learned ignorance.

Second, and more importantly, Socrates discovered that he was a philosopher. For while only the gods were wise, he strove after the wisdom of which the gods were in possession. This striving was inspired by love, nay, it *was* love: "lover of wisdom" is what "philosopher" means. How does this love originate? Socrates wondered about what nonphilosophic opinion either ignores or takes for granted. He discovered that philosophy, the love of wisdom, begins with wonder.

His venture had yet a third result. In going about, a "gadfly," asking artists, statesmen, others, questions they had not asked, and that they would rather have left unasked, he had aroused a good deal of hostility, and for this he eventually paid with his life. He paid that price, however, without regret. Would the unexamined life have been worth living? Not for Socrates. And if to this day he has remained the paradigm of a teacher of philosophy, it has been for what he taught, not only with his life but also with his death.

Who then taught Socrates? A great many centuries later—philosophy was by then well on its way—Augustine wondered about time. "If nobody asks me what time is," he confessed, "I know. But if someone does ask me, I do not know." But who did the asking? Surely it was Augustine himself, and what is surely true of him is indisputably true of Socrates.

Who then *did* teach Socrates? None other than Socrates himself. To go further, if Plato was not merely to learn about other people's philosophy but was himself to become a philosopher, then all Socrates could really teach him was how to teach himself, how to ask his own questions: to do his own wondering. For Socrates philosophy had begun with wonder. Plato reaffirmed it, as did Aristotle after him. And this is one characteristic of philosophy that has never been successfully denied—that wonder is not a one-time-beginning of philosophy, way back in ancient history. So long as there is and will be philosophy, the wondering must be done and redone.

But where go from there? If only the gods are wise, if they alone have achieved wisdom, this question is difficult to answer: different philosophers travel different roads. Hence "what is philosophy?" is itself a philosophical question. And philosophers can often agree only on a circular definition: "Philosophy is what philosophers are doing."

II

Philosophers ask what philosophy is. Of Jewish philosophy it may well be asked whether it exists at all or, perhaps more precisely, whether such existence as it does have is legitimate. This has often been denied on both sides, in behalf of Judaism, on the one hand, in that of philosophy, on the other. For the present purpose the objections coming from philosophers may be more relevant. But those coming from the Jewish side are not to be ignored.

On the latter side, the most clear-cut objections have always come from Orthodox Judaism, based as it is on Halakhah, "the way" as prescribed by the 613 commandments divinely revealed on Mount Sinai. At worst, what could philosophy do to the Sinaitic Word except call into question—if indeed not deny altogether—the divine authority on which Jewish orthodoxy claims it rests? At best, what could it do except endorse that Word, as if its authority required extraneous endorsements? Not accidentally the greatest work in Jewish philosophy, Maimonides' *Moreh Nebukhim* (Guide of the Perplexed), was under Orthodox attack for well over a century, with here and there a *herem* (ban) hurled at it. Indeed, if Maimonides himself escaped Spinoza's fate—excommunication by an Orthodox rabbinic court—it was arguably because the author of the *Guide* also composed the *Mishneh Torah*

What Is Jewish Philosophy?

(Repetition of the Torah), one of the most important codes, influential to this day, of Halakhah—the very 613 Sinaitic commandments.

At length, however, not only Maimonides himself but also his *Guide* became pillars of Orthodox Judaism. It is thus not obvious, after all, that, even for Jewish orthodoxy, philosophy must be beyond the pale of Judaism.

But if Maimonides is not beyond the pale, Spinoza can hardly be within it. Moreover, that this view is not necessarily limited to Orthodox Judaism is illustrated by the Jewish but nonorthodox philosopher Hermann Cohen. As a liberal proponent of free speech, Cohen was a principled opponent of the practice of excommunication. Yet, to judge by what he wrote on Spinoza, he must have thought that, if the Amsterdam rabbinate had to single out a foe of Judaism, they got the right man. The liberal Cohen, no less than the Orthodox Amsterdam rabbinate, viewed Spinoza as an enemy of the Jewish religion.

But must a Jewish philosophy necessarily be religious? Ever since Moses Hess, Zionist thinkers have labored at reclaiming Spinoza as a Jewish philosopher. And, at this writing, a work that makes that unique heretic into the philosophical founding father of modern Jewish secularism is a bestseller in Israel.[1] Thus questions about the concept "Jewish philosophy"— whether it is a legitimate discipline, and if so, just what it is—do not have obvious answers from the Jewish side.

It ought not to be otherwise also from the side of philosophy. This, however, is not always conceded in the academy, even now when the spirit of the age calls for "multiculturalism." The argument of the modern academy against a Jewish philosophy has long been firmly entrenched, so much so that few academics have ever found it necessary to take the trouble of spelling it out.

The entrenched argument may be spelled out as follows. The Socratic wonder with which philosophy begins is surely rational and, equally surely, so is the examination of life to which it gives rise. The hallmark of rationality, however, is detachment from partisanship, an objectivity that seeks a truth as universal as reason itself. How then can "philosophy" be qualified by "Jewish," when that adjective seems to signify commitments that are subjective, partisan, particularistic—even tribal and parochial? Is there a Jewish mathematics or physics? Then how can there be a Jewish philosophy?

Arguments entrenched in the academy are rarely entirely without substance: a philosophical work is not Jewish by dint of the Jewish birth of its author. Books such as Edmund Husserl's *Logical Investigations* and Henri Bergson's *Creative Evolution* did not "become" works in "Jewish philosophy" until they were defined and ostracized as such by Adolf Hitler's *Weltanschauung*. Few facts show quite as glaringly how utterly antiphilosophical that *Weltanschauung* was, and how disgraceful was the surrender to it by quite a few once-respected professors of philosophy, not excluding some distinguished philosophers who, somewhat surprisingly, are respected still.

The works of Husserl and Bergson, then, are clear-cut cases of *what Jewish philosophy is not.* In contrast, the cases of Maimonides and Spinoza are not nearly so clear-cut. Why has the first traditionally been kept out of philosophy departments, whereas the place given to the second had always been unchallenged until the advent of the Third Reich? Have the academy and its philosophy departments kept Maimonides out because, so far as Judaism is concerned, he remains inside? And have they let Spinoza in because, so far as Judaism is concerned, he opts out? To press this question further, have the doors of the academy been wide open to Spinoza because, in opting out of Judaism, he "outgrows" or "transcends" a heritage that is "narrow" or "parochial"? Spinoza scholars have often written in this vein, and at times have not hesitated to use these and similar words. *But is Judaism "narrow" or "parochial," and is to opt out of it to "outgrow" or "transcend" it? And is "Jewish philosophy" nothing less than a contradiction in terms— "Jewish" being "narrow" and "particularistic" and "philosophy" being "wide" and "universalistic"?* These questions, raised here at the very start, will stay with us, through medieval, modern, and "postmodern" Jewish philosophy, to the end.

III

Once, modern academic curricula typically would leap from the last of the ancient philosophers—Neoplatonists, Skeptics, Stoics, and Epicureans —to the first of the moderns—Descartes, Spinoza, Bacon, Locke, and others equally modern-minded. The entire Middle Ages were simply skipped. Implied in this practice was an argument as entrenched as the one already referred to, this one also so seemingly obvious as hardly to need the bother of being spelled out until, in more recent times, it was dislodged.

There was some substance to this argument as well. Medieval philosophy may be viewed purely as a developmental stage within philosophy, or else, more comprehensively and also more profoundly, as an effort to relate philosophy, the work of a "reason" merely human, to "Revelation," the more-than-rational, more-than-human act or acts of God. The latter task could not be considered by Socrates and—except for Philo of Alexandria—by other ancient philosophers, for it presupposes the exposure of philosophy to one of the religions of Revelation—Judaism, Christianity, Islam. This exposure having become a fact, however, the theme appearing on the scene, not ever to disappear, may be summed up as "Athens and Jerusalem."

But "what indeed has Athens to do with Jerusalem?"[2] This question, as asked by the Christian Tertullian from the side of Jerusalem, is purely rhetorical. And when asked in the modern Academy from the side of Athens— with "Athens" standing for all philosophy, modern as well as ancient—it is no less rhetorical.

The once-entrenched argument may be spelled out as follows: What originality can be found in medieval philosophy when it very nearly remains within the confines of the Aristotelian-cum-Neoplatonic tradition? Further, is medieval philosophy philosophical at all when sooner or later—in some cases sooner, in others later, but always somewhere—philosophical reason is fettered by the limits imposed by divinely revealed Scriptures, the Jewish Bible, the Christian Bible, the Qur'an? *Is* the Christian Thomas Aquinas a philosopher when he writes that "although the argument from authority based on human reason is the weakest, yet the argument from authority based on divine Revelation is the strongest"?[3] And *how much* of a philosopher is the Muslim Ibn Rushd ("Averroes" in Christendom) when he believes, and acts on the belief, that Aristotle is a gift of "divine grace," bestowed on humanity in order that it may "know what is knowable"? Is not, then, authority the great stumbling block for philosophy in the Middle Ages—on one view of it, that of an Aristotle, on the other, that of a sacred Scripture?

With these two views of medieval philosophy prevailing, it comes as no surprise that, whichever is adopted, the question of a place for medieval Jewish philosophy in the academy simply did not arise.

The more recent academic welcome accorded to medieval philosophy shows its former exclusion, for all its superficial justice, to have been riddled with prejudice that may be called modernist, crypto-Protestant, or neo-pagan. If truth and not originality is the goal of the "love of wisdom," is it self-evident or even plausible that such wisdom as is attainable had to wait for attainment for modernity, for the twentieth century, for the 1990s, or even for the year 2000? May it not be worth a philosopher's while to "reopen dusty old books" (Leo Strauss) in pursuit of truth, so that even Averroes is not beneath modern philosophical contempt when, typically, he does his philosophizing not in "original" treatises of his own but in commentaries on Aristotle? Averroes viewed the Stagirite as "*the* philosopher": was this view necessarily due to slavish obedience to authority, rather than to serious, critical—nay, *self*-critical—thought?

A prejudice is "modernist" when it rests on the unexamined belief in the superiority of present wisdom over that of the past. It is "crypto-Protestant" when resting on the unexamined belief that, as a ground on which would-be believers may stand, a Luther-style "here I stand, I can do no other" is superior to a time-honored tradition.

Lastly, and in the present context most importantly, while no prejudice is implicit in the "paganism" of Socrates and his ancient followers (for an exposure to religions of Revelation had yet to occur) prejudice *is* involved when, *after* such exposures, philosophers resort without examination to "*neo*-paganism," as if the rejection or "overcoming" of Revelation were a self-evident necessity for modern philosophers. Should they not ponder the fact that, of the great speculative philosophers of the earlier modern period—Descartes, Spinoza, Leibniz, Kant, Fichte, Schelling, Hegel—only Spinoza and Fichte rejected Revelation in behalf of modern "autonomy"?

Should they not also ask whether, of the more recent anti-speculative philosophers, such foes of Revelation as Karl Marx and Friedrich Nietzsche are truly better and more solid guides to modernity than the Christian Sören Kierkegaard and the Jew Franz Rosenzweig?

It was Rosenzweig who coined the terms "old" and "new paganism," and this, note well, vis-à-vis Revelation defined as the "incursion" of a "higher [i.e., divine] content" into a [human] "vessel unworthy of it". *Simply in being*, Revelation is an "insult" to "paganism" whether "old" or "new"; and, with the appearance of the theme "Athens and Jerusalem" on the scene, a pride "insulted" by the "incursion" of a "higher content" stands in need of philosophic examination. With the demand for just that examination, the modern Jewish philosopher Rosenzweig storms, in the twentieth century, into the bastion of modern philosophy.[4] In different language and with a different emphasis, Kierkegaard had done likewise in the nineteenth century, leaving a significant mark, however, only in the twentieth.

With the exposure of the above three prejudices—modernist, crypto-Protestant, neopagan—the once-entrenched argument for leaping from the last of the ancient to the first of the modern philosophers collapses: medieval philosophy must be given its academic due. With this established, are any grounds left for admitting medieval *Christian* philosophy and yet continuing to keep its *Jewish* counterpart out? Reason in Maimonides' philosophy may be "fettered" by the limits imposed by revealed authority, the characteristic medieval-Jewish argument for authority being that no fewer than 600,000 Israelites witnessed the Sinaitic Revelation; that so many could not have been mistaken; and that an unbroken line of trustworthy witnesses leads from Sinai to the present. But then (as has been shown), with his reliance on "sacred" authority, reason in Thomas Aquinas's philosophy is equally fettered. With Aquinas given a secure place in the academy, what, other than surviving prejudice, is at work when Maimonides is ignored, or else reduced to background material for understanding the Angelic Doctor?

Just one argument for excluding Jewish philosophy deserves consideration and indeed, in the present context, requires it. In medieval (and almost all) philosophy, the scope of "reason" is universal and, in both Christianity and Islam, the scope of "Revelation" is universal as well. In contrast to both, "Revelation" in Judaism is focused on, or even limited to, just one particular people. What if, in medieval times, this shared universalism had given rise to genuine "Christian" and "Muslim" philosophies; would the academy still need to bother with the empirical study of *Jewish* philosophy in order to dismiss its claim to genuineness? Does the "universalism" of philosophy not of necessity clash with the "particularism" of Judaism? If Christians or Muslims can become philosophers and still remain Christians and Muslims, must not, in contrast to both, Jews aspiring to philosophy "outgrow" or "transcend" a "background" shown by that very "universalist" aspiration to be "narrow" or "parochial"? Indeed, precisely with prejudices against medieval philosophy as such removed, does not what once may have been riddled with prejudice purify itself into a well-founded judgment—that there is not and cannot be a medieval-Jewish, nay, a Jewish philosophy? Is the view not confirmed that Maimonides, who remains within Judaism, is *ipso facto* not a philosopher, whereas, in order to *become* a philosopher, Spinoza must opt out of it?

Philosophers often can give none but a circular definition of their discipline, namely, that philosophy is what philosophers are doing. A point has now been reached for a look at what Jewish philosophers are doing; better still, at what Jewish philosophers were doing in the Middle Ages; best of all, at what was being done by that medieval Jewish philosopher whose bold "particularism" has never been matched, namely, Yehudah Halevi. Even in modern "tolerant" rather than medieval "intolerant" times, only Rosenzweig ever comes close to it.

In the eighth century, the Khazars, thought to have been a Tartar people, converted to Judaism. Halevi's *Kuzari*, written "in defense of a religion held in contempt," is based on this event. The work has the Khazar king consult in turn a philosopher, a Christian, and a Muslim; then, dissatisfied with all three, he speaks last but at length with a rabbi—*last* because his religion, after all, is held in contempt, and *at length* because, step by step, he discovers that the contempt meted out to Judaism by Christians and Muslims is utterly undeserved. When speaking with the Christian and the Muslim (the philosopher is not relevant in this context), he begins to make three discoveries, subsequently to be confirmed in his dialogue with the rabbi. Both the Christian and the Muslim base their claims on the Scriptures of Judaism; both despise the very religion on whose Scriptures their own claims are based; and although, admirably, they are sincere believers in love, both human and divine, they are always at each other's throats. (Rediscovering the Khazar king's first discovery, the debt of Christianity and Islam to Judaism, subsequent thinkers were sometimes to speak of Christianity and Islam as "daughter religions" of Judaism.) With his three discoveries taken together, the king may be paraphrased as asking, "What universalism is this on the part of the 'daughters,' that does not extend even to the 'mother'; and what love is this on the part of the 'sisters,' that expresses itself in warfare between them?"

The Khazar king shows grave doubts about Christian and Muslim "universalism." On his part, although an unabashed "particularist," the rabbi gives striking proof of his "universalism" when he, the Jewish teacher, takes instruction from his pagan pupil. He has previously taught the latter that even though Jews are in exile and the Holy Land is in ruins, it is a Jewish duty to dwell amid the ruins rather than in comfort elsewhere. Having listened and learned, the pupil reprimands the teacher:

If this be so, thou fallest short of the duty laid down in thy law, by not en-
deavoring to reach that place, and making it thy abode in life and death, although thou sayest, "Have mercy on Zion, for it is the house of our life."
(*Kuzari* II 23)

This reprimand occurs early in the dialogue between the two. Yet so
deeply is the rabbi disturbed by it that the whole work ends with the teacher
obeying the pupil: he sets out for the Holy Land. Apparently the Jewish
teacher needed his pagan pupil to remind him of the teaching of his own
religion that "Jerusalem can only be rebuilt when Israel yearns for it to such
an extent that they embrace her stones and dust" (*Kuzari* V 27). Thus, although a "universalist" in that he examines *everything* prior to his commitment to Judaism, the pagan king endorses, far back in a medieval Jewish
philosophical work, what has become in this "postmodern" age the most
dramatic expression of a "particularistic" Jewish destiny.

The "postmodern" relevance of yet another text in the *Kuzari* may well
be even greater. Here too the Jewish teacher takes instruction from the
pagan pupil, and in this exchange the "universalism" inherent in Jewish
"particularism" is wider still, in that its stance toward the two "daughters"
of Judaism is not negative and critical but and positive and affirmative.

Quite early in the dialogue, the king has touched what the rabbi admits
is a "weak spot" in Jews: while Christians and Muslims have saints who actually choose humility, poverty, and even degradation, Jews assuredly suffer
humiliation, poverty, and degradation at the hands of enemies, but rarely
if ever convert necessity into virtue (*Kuzari* I 113–115). Returning to the
theme, because of its importance, later in the dialogue, the rabbi once
again pays tribute to the saintliness of some Christians and Muslims, and
once again concedes that the king rightly blames Jews for "bearing degradation without [spiritual] benefit." Yet then he states that "thoughtful men
among . . . [Jews] could escape this degradation by a word spoken lightly"
—the "word" of conversion to Christianity or Islam, "spoken lightly" because not from conviction. They could do it but, because of fidelity, they
do not. If Christian and Muslim virtue is saintliness, Jewish virtue is fidelity
(*Kuzari* IV 22, 23).

To become wholly up-to-date, this medieval Jewish philosophical teaching needs changing in but one respect. In order to opt out of Jewish history, its fate and its destiny, in the "postmodern" world, even a word spoken lightly is no longer required, nor is the possibility confined to the
"thoughtful": in "enlightened" societies Jews can simply drift away. In consequence, the "postmodern" world—which is also the post-Holocaust world
—discloses this stark difference between Christians and Muslims, on the
one hand, and Jews on the other: Christianity and Islam do not fully lose
credibility so long as they have even a few saints; without fidelity, however,
Jews cannot—never did, never will—survive at all.

IV

The Jews among whom Spinoza grew up descended from Portuguese Marannos, i.e., forced converts to Christianity, and, as "new Christians," were subject to inquiry as to the bona fide of their conversion. From the standpoint of the inquisitors this was consistent, for, while forced to make a show of their new faith, these former Jews had inwardly remained true to their old one, so much so as to keep on practicing secretly—in view of the methods of the Inquisition, *very* secretly—such fragments of Judaism as circumstances permitted, and as they themselves kept on remembering. Spinoza's ancestors had fled from the Inquisition but also, more profoundly, from having to be Christians. Hence, once having reached tolerant Holland, they had returned openly to their old faith. But scars of the past had remained, and affected their present consciousness.

This background helps explain the Amsterdam rabbinate's unwonted harshness toward the renegade in their midst: it was feared that, even in tolerant but not omnitolerant Holland, his presence among them threatened the repute, or even safety, of the refugee community. So some say. Others say that this background helps explain Spinoza himself. Carl Gebhard has written:

> Everyone else in Europe was born into predetermined categories of thinking, Jews into the categories of law and justice, Christians into the categories of sin and redemption. Here, however, there is for the first time a group of people without predetermined categories of their own, a people with a ruptured consciousness. A people looked for the coasts—and Spinoza discovered a new world.[5]

This judgment is far removed from the academic prejudices hitherto encountered. ("Academic prejudice" may be a contradiction in terms, but often it is real enough.) If the Jew Spinoza had a "narrow" background, so did his Christian contemporaries. If the "new world" discovered by such as Columbus, Copernicus, and Galileo required philosophers among Jews to "outgrow" or "transcend" their "background," it made the same requirement of philosophically minded Christians, with respect to theirs. Indeed, what with his "ruptured" post-Marrano Jewish "consciousness," Spinoza may be said to have faced the "new world" more radically than, say, René Descartes or Francis Bacon. The modern *cogito* of the former is never made by him to clash with the premodern claims of revealed authority. And the latter's modern war on "four idols" is not extended by him so as to make premodern revealed authority into yet a fifth. In contrast with these Christian contemporaries, Spinoza writes a *Theologico-Political Treatise* that includes a modern wrestling with pre-modern authority, and that extends this wrestling—circumspectly, to be sure—to authorities that claim to be divinely revealed. The *Treatise* Spinoza dares to publish. His *Ethics* he prudently leaves unpublished for, to readers who understand both its teaching and what Revelation implies, the work is incompatible not merely with revealed *authority* but with nothing less than the truth claim *of Revelation itself,* whether Jewish, Christian, or Muslim.

Spinoza, Descartes, Bacon: these are three modern philosophers—one a Jew who "opts out," the other two Christians who "stay in." Descartes, Bacon, Moses Mendelssohn: these, modern philosophers all, "stay in"—the first two in Christianity, the third to emerge as the first modern philosopher to remain, not casually but most emphatically, within Judaism. However, it is worthy of note that whereas the Christians avoid a clash with premodern revealed authority the Jew expressly invokes that very authority. As Mendelssohn writes,

> The [revealed] law [of Judaism] can perhaps . . . be changed according to
> the requirements of a particular time, place, and set of circumstances, but
> only if and when it pleases the supreme Lawgiver to let us know His will—
> to make it known to us just as openly, publicly, and beyond any possibility of
> doubt and uncertainty, as He did when [at Sinai] He gave us that law itself.[6]

Why and how are the "staying in" of Descartes and Bacon on the one hand, Mendelssohn on the other, not on a par? The fact of difference is undeniable. The two Christians, and many others after them, avoid a clash between the philosophy of the "new world" and the revealed authority of the "old." They do so—can afford to do so—quietly and perhaps even hypocritically. Why, in contrast, and in a work committed to the "new world's" philosophy, does the Jew Mendelssohn expressly *hark back* to the "old world's" revealed authority? In order to "stay in" Judaism, why can he not afford his Christian counterparts' luxury—or hypocrisy—but *must* do his harking back? Mendelssohn, the first modern Jewish philosopher, must have suspected if not known that premodern authority fails in the modern world. That it does in fact fail was to be shown clearly in his own descendants, the most famous of whom was Felix Mendelssohn-Bartholdy, the Christian composer of the oratorio *Paul.* The simple but weighty answer is this: *Descartes, Bacon, and all their spiritual children, while entering a "new world," continue to live in one world. Mendelssohn's, to be sure, is no "ruptured consciousness": he is no Maranno and no son of Marannos. However, he and his children live in two worlds:*

> Even now, no better advice than this can be given to the House of Jacob:
> Adopt the mores and constitution of the country in which you find yourself,
> but be steadfast in upholding the religion of your fathers, too. Bear both
> burdens as well as you can.[7]

Such is the advice given by the first modern Jewish philosopher. Practicing what he preaches, he bears the two burdens, as a way of thought as well as of life. Mendelssohn's was a privileged position, dramatized by his "right of residence" in Berlin, a right rarely granted by the great Frederick of Prussia, despite his enlightened and broad-minded attitude toward matters religious-in-general, to Jews-in-particular. Yet Mendelssohn remained with Orthodox Judaism in both practice and belief.

Privileges were granted this Jew and praise showered on him, as a man. Among the philosophically minded, he earned the title of "German Socrates"; nor was this title without justice, for among his numerous contributions to German thought and letters is *Phaedon*, an argument for the immortality of the soul. Yet untempted by the privileges granted him and the praise showered on him, he never ceased to think of himself as a Jew, practicing solidarity with his unprivileged fellow Jews, and doing what he could to improve their social and spiritual condition. In due course this "new Socrates" was also thought of, by his own people, as yet another Moses—after the original one and Maimonides.

Mendelssohn, then, lived in two worlds. However, the philosophically minded who celebrated him and had discourse with him lived in one world. This was shown dramatically by the so-called Lavater Affair. A Swiss clergyman named Johann Caspar Lavater admired Mendelssohn for his wisdom and learning, and especially for the broad-minded views on Christianity he had expressed in private conversation. When Lavater published a German translation of a French Calvinist tract, he dedicated it to Mendelssohn and, forgetting or ignoring the private nature of their earlier conversation, publicly challenged him either to refute the work's argument in support of Christian truth or else "to do what wisdom, love of truth, and honor require, and what Socrates would have done had he read the treatise and found it irrefutable."[8]

That a person could be wise, noble, learned, enlightened, broad-minded, modern-minded and still remain a convinced Jew rather than become a Christian the theologian Lavater could not imagine. His philosophical contemporary, none other than the towering Kant (a lukewarm Christian at best) presumably *could* imagine Mendelssohn's not becoming a Christian—not a convinced one because of his rationalism, and not an opportunistic one because of his integrity. But Kant's views on Mendelssohn's Judaism were much the same as Lavater's, as is shown by his expressed hope for the "euthanasia" of Judaism. Even in the "dark" Middle Ages, Christian theologians would sometimes go to school with rabbis. Now that the "bright" Enlightenment had arrived, and along with it the first modern Jewish philosopher, the idea that admirers of his philosophy should be curious about his Judaism, and ask him to teach them some of it, did not occur even to Kant and certainly not to Lavater.

Presumably the "Berlin Socrates" would have had little trouble refuting the arguments presented in the book dedicated to him: were it not for "the affair," not even the name of its author—it was Charles Bonnet—would still be remembered. In publicly refusing to take up Lavater's challenge,

Mendelssohn lists among several reasons that he is part of "an oppressed people," and that for him to engage in public Jewish-Christian polemics would be to risk making things worse. A privileged Jew and an apostle of modern Enlightenment, Mendelssohn had, nevertheless, always viewed himself as sharing the exile of his unprivileged fellow-Jews. Lavater's challenge proved that he had been right all along.

At the time, the Lavater affair created a sensation. In retrospect it would be a tempest in a teapot were it not for one important result: it occasioned the first work in modern Jewish philosophy. At one time Mendelssohn had "wanted to refute the world's derogatory opinion of the Jew by righteous living, not by pamphleteering": he had refrained from Jewish-Christian polemics for the reason subsequently given to Lavater. This was before "the affair." After and on account of it, he saw himself duty-bound, no matter what the risks, to write *Jerusalem*. Little wonder that, given these circumstances, the first work in modern Jewish philosophy could come nowhere near the militant particularism of the medieval *Kuzari*. Little wonder, too, that, in defense of the continued survival of Jews and Judaism in the "enlightened" modern age, it had to fall back for support on a revealed authority which was no longer defensible. It is also perhaps not too much of a surprise—although better might have been expected—that, having read the work, Kant did not change his mind about Judaism.

The circumstances in which the first work in modern Jewish philosophy was written ought to give pause to modern and "postmodern" philosophers even now, seeing that they like to think of their discipline as continuing the war on the idols of prejudice and "blind authority" begun by such as Descartes and Bacon. While this self-understanding may generally be justified, one must ask whether general virtue has manifested itself in particular justice in at least one case—a fair and even-handed stance toward Christianity and Judaism. The answer, it must be said, is not encouraging, and great philosophers have been little better in this respect than mediocre ones. Thus even as lukewarm a Christian as Kant manages to save quite a lot of Christianity, by making Jesus into a great and, possibly, unique teacher of morality; but to conduct a similar rescue operation for Judaism—say, by linking Mendelssohn with Isaiah—never enters his mind.

In this as well as other respects, Hegel towers above the towering Kant. He enters into Biblical—if only Biblical—Judaism deeply enough to achieve some remarkable insights. Also, he firmly supports the emancipation of Jews, at a time when philosophical or generally academic support was far from the rule. And since in his view an ancient meeting between Jewish "East" and Greek-Roman "West" is the basis, directly of the medieval and indirectly of the modern world, much in Hegel's work gives rise to the thought that a place might be left, or even required, for a vital Judaism in just that modern world. The thought comes to his reader's mind, in our time. But it does not come to Hegel's mind, in his time. As he moves

What Is Jewish Philosophy?

through the ancient, the medieval, and at length to the modern world, the theme "Athens and Jerusalem" becomes an anachronism; and so, along with "Athens," do both "Jerusalem" and its manifestation in Judaism.

Hegel enters into the Judaism of his Old Testament. Kierkegaard's self-immersion in his Old Testament is so total as to make him see as his "knight of faith" none other than Abraham, none other than the patriarch whose descendants are Kierkegaard's own Jewish contemporaries, the ones who to this day invoke the God of Abraham in their prayers. Unlike Hegel (to say nothing of Kant), Kierkegaard is indisputably a Christian or struggling to become one. Equally indisputably, he is in and of modernity, for his Abraham is his own spiritual contemporary, rather—to put the contrast as starkly as possible—that of Torquemada. For any reader of the text, Abraham—he who sets out to sacrifice Isaac (Gen. 22: 1–19)—is prepared to do what would make him a criminal were it not for the divine commandment. In setting out to do it, however, Kierkegaard's Abraham—unlike, say, Torquemada's—is not serene in spirit and in much company, relying on infallible authority. Rather, he acts in "fear and trembling," and is utterly alone. Is what appears to be the will of God in fact that will? In obeying, will he be God's faithful servant or a common criminal? Kierkegaard's Abraham cannot, does not, rely on an authority, human or divine. All he has to rely on is his own, solitary, all-too-human, all-too-fallible, "existential" commitment. This is Kierkegaard's "knight of faith"—the only Abraham that *can be* that knight.

Kierkegaard, then, as well as his Abraham, are of postauthoritarian modernity. Moreover, his modern-Christian focus on Abraham makes Kierkegaard the foremost pioneer of a modern Christian philosophy. His Christian commitment, we have stressed, is focused on Abraham on the road to Mount Moriah rather than, say, on Paul on the road to Damascus. To be stressed now is that the commitment of Jews is focused on the same event in their ancestor's career, most clearly so when on Rosh Hashanah they read the Biblical text in the synagogue. The door is thus opened, directly, to an encounter between the two commitments and, indirectly, to a Christian philosophy that "circumnavigates" human existence as a whole, and "leaps" into a particular Christian "immediacy" only "after" a universal philosophical "reflection" has done its work.[9]

Kierkegaard makes many forays in the direction of such a philosophy. Yet he only paves the way for it, and the justice he accords to Judaism remains limited. His Abraham turns out to be a proto-Christian—a Christian-before-Christ; and when elsewhere he has Christianity "invent martyrdom," he either forgets the Maccabees or else makes them, too, into Christians-before-Christ.[10]

Uneven justice to Judaism and Christianity is not confined to pre-twentieth century or to Christian philosophers. Jean-Paul Sartre's atheistic existentialism recognizes a Christian existentialism but, Martin Buber and

Jewish Philosophy

Franz Rosenzweig notwithstanding, not a Jewish one. Sartre is no Christian and is of the twentieth century: the same is true of Martin Heidegger. Heidegger recognizes theology but makes it Christian by definition; and of what he says of Judaism—of Biblical prophecy—Buber writes: "I have never in our time encountered on a high philosophical plane such a far-reaching misunderstanding of the prophets of Israel."[11]

Is uneven justice to Judaism and Christianity confined to the "prejudiced" Continent? Crossing the channel, one comes upon Cambridge philosopher John Wisdom's "Gods."[12] Like Kierkegaard, he is a Christian and a modern. And, like him also, he chooses for a paradigm an Old rather than a New Testament figure. There, however, the resemblance ends. The existentialist Kierkegaard views the Biblical Abraham as nothing less than his spiritual contemporary. Wisdom, the scientifically minded empiricist, sees in the Biblical Elijah nothing more than a figure from the primitive, prescientific, religiously irrelevant past. He singles out the well-known incident on Mount Carmel. The people have fallen away and worship Baal. All alone, Elijah challenges the priests of Baal, no fewer than 450 of them, as it were, to a duel, to be watched by the people. The priests are to offer a sacrifice to their god, to Baal, whereupon he, Elijah, all by himself, will act likewise toward his god, the God of Israel. Accepting the challenge, the 450 beseech their god all day long to accept their sacrifice, without anything happening. But when Elijah, having been abandoned by men, implores his God not to abandon him also, a fire falls from heaven to devour his sacrifice, and the people, overwhelmed, exclaim, "Adonai, He is God" (I Kings 18:20–39).

Elijah's act is celebrated in Judaism, but not in John Wisdom's "Gods." The Jewish Elijah risks the meaning of his life, nay, life itself and, beyond his own life, that of the covenant, acting at a crisis moment when it is all but extinct. For Wisdom the action is a mere "experiment" to settle "what god or gods exist"; and risked by it is only what is risked, say, by scientists peering through a microscope. Wisdom does manage to rescue some of Elijah, not his Mount Carmel "experiment" but the "still, small voice" that subsequently speaks to him. But his rescue is at a price: "The Kingdom of Heaven is within us, Christ insisted."[13]

How does Wisdom's Elijah compare with Kierkegaard's Abraham? Kierkegaard's is a genuine, painful struggle with a Christian text that is a Jewish one also, which is why modern Jewish philosophers, themselves struggling with that same text—no less genuinely, no less painfully—must struggle also with Kierkegaard.[14] So much for Kierkegaard and his text: what of Wisdom and his? He does not struggle with his text but merely plays fast and loose with it. What does the actual text's still, small voice say to Elijah and—no less important—when does it say it? The Mount Carmel duel is won, but its effect has not lasted: once more the people have fallen away; once more God's prophets are being slain; and once more Elijah is alone, this time as sole survivor of a slaughter. At last gripped by despair, the prophet is left with one wish only, that his God take away his life. It is then that the still, small voice speaks, uttering a promise and a commandment. The promise: a remnant will survive. The commandment: Elijah is to appoint a successor; he will no longer be alone. His faith and strength thus revived, Elijah goes forth to appoint Elisha (I Kings 19:15–18).

One may doubt that since Elijah's own time a still, small voice ever spoke as urgently, as insistently, to the Jewish people as just a year or so after Wisdom lectured on gods. The war against Hitlerism was over. The murder camps were revealed. Jews the world over—those who could bear to look rather than look away—saw the covenant as all but extinct. Just then a voice uttered a promise and a commandment. A still, small voice, it was not heard by too many but heard by some. A new page was to be opened in Jewish history. There would be—would have to be—a rebirth of a Jewish state, a Jewish return to Jerusalem.

Wisdom addressed himself to members of the Aristotelian Society. His thinking did not move outside his country, to what was happening across the channel. It did not even move outside his academic circle, to inquire what Elijah's "experiment" might mean to observant Jews. The confession "Adonai, He is God" concludes the Mount Carmel incident: it also concludes the liturgy of Yom Kippur, the holiest day in Judaism. Does Wisdom know? Would it shake his thought if he knew? One need not say Wisdom's "Gods" is shot through with prejudice; one cannot but say that it is insular. If "empirical" denotes something more than what is seen through a microscope, this British empiricist is insufficiently empirical.[15]

Medieval Jewish philosophy is an encounter with Greek philosophy; its modern successor, an encounter with Lessing, Kant, Fichte, Schelling, Hegel, Kierkegaard, even Nietzsche and even Heidegger, except for Kierkegaard Germans all, and Kierkegaard himself encounters Hegel and Schelling. The last word on modern Jewish philosophy therefore belongs to Germany. Rich in distinction and promise, its career in that country ended with catastrophe. Arguably the last modern German-Jewish philosopher was also the greatest. Franz Rosenzweig died in 1929. But had he lived through the twelve Hitler years that were soon to follow, he would have had to write his *Star of Redemption* differently, or been unable to write it at all.

Not until after the catastrophe did German philosophers discover Rosenzweig. Rosenzweig himself had come upon Heidegger's *Being and Time* just prior to his death, and had not failed to recognize its significance. On his part, Heidegger survived Rosenzweig by a whole generation, but ignored the *Star of Redemption*; and except for the maverick Karl Löwith, Heideggerians have acted likewise. Not until a 1985 did a conference on Rosenzweig's thought take place, in his native city of Kassel.[16] Many German philosophers attended, among them, possibly, some who, let down by Heidegger during the catastrophe, now looked to this Jewish philosopher who had died before it had occurred. Many German philosophers were present. But, except for a small remnant, Jewish philosophers had to be imported, and those still of German origin, few and old, would soon pass from the scene. The conference was a great and noble occasion but also a melancholy one.

Jewish philosophy in Germany began when Moses Mendelssohn translated the Jewish Bible into German, so as to teach the language to German Jews. It ended when Buber and Rosenzweig translated the book once more, this time in order to teach Hebrew to the German language. But when Buber completed the translation—in 1961; Rosenzweig, as mentioned, had died in 1929—he must have been at a loss as to who would be the work's readers. German Jews had been expelled or murdered. German Judaism had been expelled or murdered. And the Kassel conference was unable to initiate a new Jewish philosophy in Germany.

Jewish philosophy in Germany was murdered or expelled. What of the expelled philosophy? Hegel once guessed that the World Spirit might emigrate to America. He also asserts that it does not return where it once was. The twentieth century suggests that on the second if not the first point a contemporary Hegel would change his mind. In his thought the modern world arises from a meeting between Jewish "East" and Greek-Roman "West." What if "postmodern" Jewish philosophy were to return to one of the two places in which the theme "Athens and Jerusalem" originated—to Jerusalem itself?

V

The adjective *postmodern* ought to attach to philosophy in Germany today. Hitherto in this essay that term has been used only in quotation marks, for it was defined neither generally nor philosophically. From now on the quotations marks are omitted. Surely the most celebrated German philosophical contribution to philosophy—to humanity!—is Immanuel Kant's categorical imperative, to the effect that human beings owe others the duty of treating them never as means only, but always also as ends-in-themselves: the doctrine that all members of the human species have dignity. But, as emerged in his 1961 Jerusalem trial, during the Holocaust Adolf Eichmann acted to destroy human dignity, as well as human lives, as he was, dutifully, part of a world that made human corpses, not into by-products, but into *the* product. During his trial he claimed to have followed the Kantian imperative, but it had been the following new version of it: "Act so that, if the *Fuehrer* knew of your action, he would approve!" In postmodern, post-Holocaust Germany, the first, fundamental philosophical question ought to be: how was the Hitlerization of the categorical imperative possible? To paraphrase Kant, at least one philosopher ought to consider himself "solemnly exempt" from all his other tasks until he had, if not answered this question, at least deeply wrestled with it.[17]

What Is Jewish Philosophy?

But that one philosopher can only be German. Left for a Jewish philosopher is to note a fact and to ask a question. Once, when modern Germany had Jewish philosophers, its academy all but ignored them; now that postmodern German philosophers seek Jewish philosophers they cannot find them in Germany—once the land, if not especially of "poets," so certainly and emphatically of "philosophers." This is the fact. What can be done by German philosophers is the question.

Done can be at least one thing, a belated philosophical justice to Judaism through a postmodern retrieval of great German philosophers. Hegel died in 1831. Samuel Hirsch's *Religionsphilosophie der Juden* appeared in 1841, and Moses Hess's *Rom und Jerusalem* in 1862. The epigones on the Hegelian Christian right ignored Hirsch, and those on the atheist left took notice of Hess, if at all, only so as to vituperate him. What if Hegel himself had been alive? Once Leo Strauss, an opponent of Hegel, said to me that he was bound to admire his philosophical *Rechtschaffenheit*, his rectitude. No opponent of Hegel myself, I can visualize him reading Hirsch on the Hegelian-anti-Hegelian religious right, and giving up his view of Judaism as an anachronism. No less can I visualize him reading Hess on the Hegelian-anti-Hegelian atheistic left, and giving up his view of Jews as a people that, with the loss of the Bar Kochbah war, also lost national courage forever.[18] There have been several Hegel revivals in the academy. What if the times called for yet another such revival, part and parcel of which were a belated Hegelian justice to Jews and Judaism?

A similar question might be asked of Kant. The modern neo-Kantian orthodoxy ignored, if not Hermann Cohen—they could not, for a while he was the greatest of them—at least the Jewish aspect of his thought that with advanced age became increasingly prominent. What if a postmodern "back-to-Kant" movement gave that aspect the prominent attention that it deserves? After Eichmann a retrieval of Kant's categorical imperative is in any case necessary. What if no less necessary were a belated Kantian justice to Judaism? Cohen restated Kant's ethics but added one element that he could not find in Kant nor, for that matter, in all philosophy. He had to "borrow" one doctrine from the prophets of Judaism, namely, the messianic hope. A rigorous logician, Cohen must have found this borrowing dubious as regards method. He did it anyhow because he considered it a moral-religious necessity. And the necessity was a philosophical possibility because it seemed endorsed by empirical history, because history itself seemed to move in a messianic direction. It must be borne in mind that Cohen wrote just before the Great War brought the nineteenth "century of hope" to an end, to initiate—a grim beginning!—the twentieth.

Rosenzweig, Cohen's disciple, was in and of the new century: his *Star of Redemption* was drafted in the war's trenches. In this awareness of the century—as well as in other respects—it is the only philosophical work to be mentioned in the same breath as Heidegger's *Being and Time*. "All cognition of the All originates in death, in the fear of death" are the opening words of the *Star. Being and Time* is informed throughout by a human Dasein that is authentic only if it is being-toward-death. Thus both works are equally removed from Cohen's messianic expectation. Yet while hope is absent from Heidegger's work, Rosenzweig's culminates with Yom Kippur and its Jewish testimony to the victory of life over death.

A retrieval by postmodern German philosophy of Jewish philosophy, culminating as it would have to with Cohen and Rosenzweig, could thus be a source of philosophical strength; but it would also be shot through with melancholy. There cannot be, in postmodern Germany in the foreseeable future, a Jewish philosophical presence. The best possibility is, instead of a sheer absence, what might be called the presence of an absence.

For German philosophy the years 1933–1945 ought to be a rupture; for Jewish philosophy the rupture is indisputable. Such, however, is the impact, directly of the Holocaust and indirectly also of the other indisputably postmodern Jewish event, the state of Israel, that the two have yet to find normative philosophical responses.

Perhaps it is no accident that the two post-Holocaust Jewish philosophers recognized by the academy deal with these events only obliquely and, moreover, would seem to move under their impact in opposite directions. Leo Strauss and Emmanuel Levinas have lived through and beyond the years 1933–1945. Neither philosopher has his thought focused on these years. "Progress or Return?" is Strauss's question, and his own quest for a return began prior to 1933. A much younger man, Levinas set out on his way only after 1945; but by his own confession his lifelong concern with "alterity" is inspired by Rosenzweig who had died in 1929. Surely both thinkers would have gone, each on his way if those twelve years of catastrophe had never occurred. Yet but for a radical failure of modernity displayed in those years, not only through Nazism but also the feeble philosophical opposition to it, would Strauss's "return" have carried him so relentlessly beyond modernity to the Middle Ages (he considered Maimonides as a greater philosopher than Spinoza), and beyond the Middle Ages all the way back to Athens and Jerusalem? Again, but for the radical failure shown by human beings and their philosophers, to be their brothers' keeper, as revealed in the years 1933–1945, would Levinas have pushed "alterity" so strenuously, in his endeavor to expose and oppose philosophical egotism?

If both philosophers are moved by the rupture that had occurred in their lifetime, back to the theme "Athens and Jerusalem," it would also seem that they are moved in opposite ways. For if Strauss turns to Athens—only ultimately, and on this even his disciples are divided—it is because Athens requires a reason that is accessible, whereas Jerusalem requires a faith that may not be. And if, ultimately, Levinas lets Athens be instructed by Jerusalem, it is because a Jerusalem that teaches the duty to be a brother's keeper never needed instruction about "alterity."

What Is Jewish Philosophy?

Perhaps this move in the same direction in opposite ways may be illustrated by two images of Socrates. Strauss's Socrates, discoursing as he does on immortality to the end, is the teacher of Eternity to the end, of the need to return to the eternally True, the eternally Good, the eternally Beautiful —in view of what has happened, above all to the eternally Good. Levinas's Socrates is one about to drink the cup of hemlock. The flaw which this post-Holocaust thinker finds in Heidegger, at the end of a long tradition that begins in Athens, carries him back to Socrates, with whom it begins. One can picture Levinas's Socrates as the husband and father who sends away wife and children, all weeping, so as to spend his last hour with fellow philosophers, in selfish pursuit of philosophy.

A rupture for German and Jewish philosophy: are the years 1933–1945 a rupture for philosophy as a whole? A thought-provoking recent discovery: the most ancient grave ever found is estimated to be 100,000 years old. How do archaeologists know that it is a grave? By bones. So long as prehistoric bodies were left lying where they had dropped dead, animals would devour the flesh, leaving archaeologists to find only scattered bones. These bones, however, are not scattered; a grave protected the body from the wild animals. Whose body is it? A Neanderthal man, who may or may not be the ancestor of *Homo sapiens*; 100,000 years ago the species *Homo sapiens* had yet to evolve. But even his precursors had discovered the awe of death, the difference between life and death, and thus the respect that is due to the dead.

With this discovery civilization may be said to have begun. It has continued ever since with the burial of relatives, friends, strangers. Even enemies so numerous and hated as to be denied individual burial were given mass graves: even the bones of such as these were left in peace. But something new happened when at Auschwitz, what was usable in victims' bodies having been used, their bones were ground into dust, and the dust was cast into rivers.

No Socrates a hundred thousand years from now will wonder at this fact, for archaeologists will find no bones. But knowing what has happened in this postmodern age, a Socrates today would be the same as his Athenian precursor but also different. His philosophy would continue to begin with wonder. But the age-old wonder would be mingled with a new horror.

VI

Let us conduct an experiment in the philosophical imagination. Let Socrates cross the Aegean, arrive in Jerusalem, and at length meet the prophet Isaiah. The meeting would give Socrates cause for new wonder. His own Delphic oracle was mysterious enough; its mystery is dwarfed, however, by a God—"holy, holy, holy, His angels proclaim" (Isaiah 6: 3)—whose thoughts and ways are as high above those of humans as heaven is above earth (55: 8–9). He, the one who hears of the Delphic oracle, is restrained from going astray by his *daimonion*; the other, the one who is to hear the thoughts of a God high above earth, is nothing better than a "man of unclean lips" (6: 5). How bridge that gap between that God and that man? This would be the wonder of Socrates, not in Athens but in Jerusalem. A glowing stone taken from the fire having touched Isaiah's lips, having cleansed them by angels at divine command (6: 6–7), the Word of the God who is Mystery becomes humanly speakable, a commandment so removed from mystery as to be humanly performable—and universally compelling.

The Athenian philosopher and the Jerusalemite prophet never met. But after them Athens and Jerusalem met often enough. What if the postmodern world were to demand a new such meeting? What if philosophy in the postmodern academy were compelled at last to give up its "universalist"-Athenian contempt for "particularistic"-Jerusalem? Let philosophers face up to the fact that it was from Isaiah and his Jewish Jerusalem, and not from Socrates and his Greek Athens, that this commandment and this promise came into the world: "And they shall beat their swords into plowshares and their spears into pruning hooks. Nation shall not lift up sword against nation, neither shall they learn war any more" (Isaiah 2: 4).

Fourteen

Jewish Philosophy in the Academy

In 1977 my wife and I went to the Soviet Union to teach Judaism to re-fuseniks. Our first stop was Riga. When I asked the leader of the local study group what he wished me to discuss with his group, he replied, "Jewish philosophy." And when I went on to ask what he meant by his term, he gave a classic response: "Our whole group knows that we must remain Jews," he said. "Jewish philosophy will tell us why."

What a response—and how quintessentially Jewish! Cut off by a tyrannical regime from knowledge of their Jewish heritage, refuseniks such as Arkady Tsinober, by the mere act of becoming refuseniks, commit themselves at great cost to a Jewish destiny—without yet knowing what it is. Is this not reminiscent of the generation at Sinai that said "na'ase v'nishma," "we shall do it and hear it"? So great was the faith of that first generation, the commentators explain, that they accepted the Torah before having heard what it contained, or what acceptance of it involved.

The Riga refusenik, who now lives in Israel, would be puzzled to learn of an incident that happened approximately fifteen years ago at a Canadian university that shall remain nameless. A small group of Jewish professors got together and decided that their university should have a chair in Jewish studies. In such cases the first choice is usually Jewish history; but with but one teacher of Judaism, what may vaguely be called "Jewish philosophy" is a good second option. A couple of years ago I gave a lecture to the freshman class at an American Catholic liberal arts college. On arrival, I was surprised to learn that the whole class had been required to read one book, and that book only: Victor Frankl's *Man's Search for Meaning*. The book is far from being the best introduction to the Holocaust, and it contains nothing at all about Judaism. Still, the compulsory reading of a book like that, for freshmen at a liberal arts college, clearly makes desirable the campus presence of a "Jewish philosopher."

So the Jewish professors at that Canadian university went with their request to the chairman of their philosophy department, who reacted as follows: "Jewish philosophy? There is no such subject!" The one of their number who phoned me to tell the story was hurt and humiliated.

Had there been a philosopher among the petitioning group, he might have asked the chairman kindly to define philosophy; since there is no professional agreement as to what philosophy is, this latter, if questioned

185

sharply and professionally, would have been pushed at length into the lame reply that philosophy is what philosophers are doing, whereupon the Jewish group could have shot back triumphantly that Jewish philosophy is what Jewish philosophers are doing. This, however, would have been a merely verbal victory. One can easily think of philosophers whose thought one rejects but whose philosophical credentials are impeccable all the same. One does the cause of Jewish philosophy in the academy no good unless one so defines the subject as to include only figures with equally impeccable credentials. Midrash is deep Jewish thought—in my view the deepest of all—but it is not philosophy. What makes Maimonides and Hermann Cohen Jewish philosophers and, say, Ahad Ha-am a significant Jewish thinker, no doubt, but not a philosopher? The answer is clear: in the case of the first two, unlike in the third, there is a thorough and disciplined involvement with general philosophy, in the one case with Aristotle, in the other, with Kant. In my view, therefore, a distinction is necessary that in Israel already exists: *Machshevet Israel* encompasses all "Jewish thought," from ancient Midrash to modern Zionist thought, including also Jewish philosophy. *Philosophia Yehudit* is the narrower category of the kind of thought that involves a disciplined, systematic encounter between the Jewish heritage and relevant philosophy.

If thus limited and defined, there is at least one Jewish philosophy—namely, the medieval; the Canadian chairman showed his prejudice or ignorance in not immediately making that limited concession. On this score, not so long ago prejudice and ignorance were standard in the academy; this was true despite the fact that "prejudiced" or "ignorant academy" are contradictions in terms. Thus, for example, the two-volume Scribner's *Selections from Medieval Philosophers*, edited by the well-known Chicago philosopher Richard McKeon and first published in 1929, contains selections from no fewer than fifteen medieval philosophers; but not a single Jewish (or for that matter Muslim) philosopher is among them. This was quite characteristic of the time: otherwise self-critical professors would not have batted an eyelash when alluding to Maimonides for one purpose only—to shed light on Thomas Aquinas when he quotes "Rabbi Moses."

However, as regards medieval philosophy on the campus, things have improved considerably. The Scribner's text is presumably still being used. But there now is also a text such as *Philosophy in the Middle Ages* (Indianapolis, 1973). It contains some five hundred pages of Christian philosophy, edited by James Walsh, and about one hundred pages and fifty pages, respectively, of Muslim and Jewish philosophy, edited by Arthur Hyman. Considering the small number of Jews philosophizing in the Middle Ages, compared to Christians and to a lesser degree also to Muslims, this is no mean Jewish philosophical presence. My 1978 copy of that text was already part of its fourth printing, and by now there are probably more.

This suggests a gradual overcoming of prejudice and ignorance in the

Jewish Philosophy in the Academy

academy. Actually, as regards medieval philosophy, there has been a far deeper, more radical change since the days when I was a graduate student of the subject; it is not merely academic but existential. My Catholic teachers at the famed Toronto Institute of Medieval Studies then included luminaries such as Jacques Maritain and Etienne Gilson, and the less well known but equally outstanding Gerald B. Phelan. In various and subtle ways, Thomism was for them all not merely a significant heritage from the past, but nothing less than philosophical truth for the present. This was in the early 1940s. When, in 1961, I was the first Jewish philosopher to give the annual Aquinas lecture at Marquette University, my subject, to be sure, was far removed from Thomism; yet both I and my hosts at that time felt it was fitting for me to make a laudatory introductory reference to the thinker in whose honor the lecture was given. Yet a decade or so later, when I was back lecturing at Marquette and made a similar introductory reference to Aquinas, my Catholic host told me afterward, only half in jest: "You could do it, but none of us would have gotten away with it."

Why this change? Ever since the turbulent sixties, Catholic thinkers have been in the throes of coming to terms with modernity, doing in the process what seems to me less than justice to their own medieval tradition. Ever since this period—more precisely, since the Six-Day War—Jewish thinkers have been in the throes of coming to terms with the Holocaust and a reborn Jewish state; from these throes has emerged a new relevance of some of the Jewish medieval philosophical heritage, to name but two parts of it, the political thought of Maimonides and the Zionism of Yehuda Halevi. As a result, what would have been unimaginable as little as twenty-five years ago is quite imaginable now: a classroom crowded with students studying Halevi or the Rambam, with another next door devoted to Aquinas's doctrine of being, attended by a mere handful.

Even so, Halevi or the Rambam will not secure Jewish philosophy a substantial place in the Western academy: this is obvious to all acquainted with current philosophy, with its search for "relevance" and with its consequently low esteem for things medieval. Is there, then, such a thing as a modern Jewish philosophy? With this question we come closer to our question, of whether there can or should be a place of substance for Jewish philosophy in the Western university.

The case is far less straightforward than that of Jewish philosophy in the Middle Ages. Doubtless, the eighteenth-century thinker Moses Mendelssohn was a philosopher—indeed, he is the "father" of modern Jewish philosophy. But by common consent his solution to the problems posed for a Jewish modernity was ephemeral. Again, doubtless such nineteenth-century thinkers as Samson Raphael Hirsch and Moses Hess were far from ephemeral: their influence is felt to this day, of the one on modern Orthodox Judaism, of the other on socialist Zionism. However, by the rigorous standards set above, not even Hess, and certainly not Hirsch, is a philosopher. Surely their thought should be studied in the academy, but not, most academics would insist, in departments of philosophy. What then of such nineteenth-century thinkers as Solomon Formstecher and Samuel Hirsch? By the standards set above, both are Jewish philosophers, for the one was a Jewishly inspired, yet philosophically sophisticated critic of Schelling, the other of Hegel. But with Formstecher and Hirsch, too, we have a problem. To be sure, it is characteristic of the long-prevailing anti-Jewish bias in the academy that its Schelling—and Hegel—scholarship has never so much as noticed these two Jewish thinkers; theoretically it is desirable for this past failing to be mended. But a substantial role for Jewish philosophy will not be achieved through the study of Hirsch and Formstecher. Their works have never been reprinted in German; while there now is a move afoot to have some of their thought reproduced in an anthology in English, their work never bore fruit, not only among philosophers but among Jews. It would be unrealistic to assume that their thought will ever engage the sustained interest of any except a few scholars.

In our search for substantial and relevant modern Jewish philosophers, we are thus driven from the nineteenth to the twentieth century. The single example of Hermann Cohen, had he known of it, should have proved to that department chairman that there is, indeed, a Jewish philosophy. Cohen was the greatest Kantian philosopher of his time before he became a Jewish philosopher; in his monumental *Religion of Reason out of the Sources of Judaism*, Kantianism and Judaism are profoundly intertwined. The work appeared in English in 1972. As far as I know, however, it is not being studied widely; certainly it has not secured a substantial place for modern Jewish philosophy, possibly because what is wanted is something more "relevant" and contemporary. Both could be got from Franz Rosenzweig, a Jewish philosopher by the most rigorous of standards; but whereas the latter's equally monumental *Star of Redemption* has been available in English since 1970, it too has yet made little impact. In this case, however, there is hope. The work of Martin Heidegger has begun to penetrate Western philosophical thought. Not yet perceived by those open to Heidegger is that Rosenzweig may be of equal importance to them, not despite the fact that *Star* is a Jewish book, but rather because of it.

This leaves us with Martin Buber. For my part, and in disagreement with some of my colleagues in philosophy, I would classify him as a Jewish philosopher, despite the fact that by his own confession he "philosophizes no more than necessary"; for his engagement with philosophy, if and when it occurs, is disciplined, and his thought as a whole has a remarkable consistency. Moreover, in his case one cannot complain about academic inattention. His very "success" in the academy, however, reveals as much about the problem of Jewish philosophy in the academy as it contributes to its solution. For the plain fact is that Buber's thought is being de-Judaized in the very process of being received as philosophy. Buber's *I and Thou* has been widely studied in philosophy classes at least for a generation. But is there ever a philosophy professor who stresses (let alone explores in depth) that the book's central thesis—an immediate divine-human relation, one without need of a mediator—is a Jewish thesis, profoundly at odds with Christianity? Jean-Paul Sartre was as good a philosophical friend as the Jewish people have had in recent decades. Yet he asserted that there were two kinds of existentialism, the atheist and the Christian. Had he never heard of Buber? More likely he was classifying him, consciously or unconsciously, with Christian existentialists. This story about Sartre is true. Probably apocryphal is the story about a Christian theology student who, having heard a lecture about Buber and liked what he had heard, complained only that Buber was a bit weak in Christology.

This brings me to the term *Judeo-Christian*. Experience has taught me to become suspicious whenever that term is used by a philosopher. Often one must pay close attention, but the following example is glaring. It is taken from Ninian Smart's *Philosophy of Religion* (New York, 1970, p. 115):

> Another necessary condition of the acceptability of revelation is a mixture of the ethical and the historical. Still confining our examples to the Judeo-Christian tradition: suppose that tomorrow a new document were turned up in the sands of the Negev, which was seen to be an account of the life of Jesus (or Moses), but by the usual historical criteria was much more reliable than the Gospels (or the Old Testament). Suppose that it showed conclusively that Jesus wantonly murdered one or two people (or that Moses did). Would it be easy to think of Jesus (or Moses) in the way in which orthodox believers do? Would it still be possible to treat this real (not just technical) criminal as *Son of God*? (Emphasis added)

What Jew ever thought of Moses as the Son of God? The upshot is clear: any philosopher using "Judeo-Christian" bears the burden of proof that his use of the term is more than mere tokenism.

The original question, then, is still with us: can a place be found for Jewish philosophy in the academy that will make it impossible for future philosophers to say, "Jewish philosophy? There is no such subject!"? Thirty-five years of experience in a Western philosophy department have led me to this conclusion: even with the strongest will in the world, and even when they have rid themselves of traditional prejudices, philosophers will never truly accept a subdiscipline within their subject if it can boast only a few practitioners; a proposed subdiscipline is bona fide only *if it can display problems that are genuinely philosophical*. Our question, therefore, must be rephrased: are there problems that, on the one hand, are distinctively Jewish and yet, on the other, are truly philosophical?

For a good many years I have been convinced that there are such problems, and a few years ago I devised a pioneer course that I am currently teaching for the third time at Hebrew University's School for Overseas

Students. The practice has thus far confirmed for me at least, the soundness of the theory.

Aristotle teaches the teacher to proceed from the known to the unknown. In my course I proceed from the less controversial to the more controversial. My first problem is Jewish identity. Approximately since Kant, the human self's "identity" has been a philosophical problem, and this has entered into general discourse with such terms as "self-determination" and "self-realization." What sort of being is this, post-Kantian philosophers ask, who does not reach his full destiny unless and until his freedom is more than the choice of one thing or another, i.e., unless what is determined is one's very own self, or what is "realized" is what presumably remains otherwise somehow lacking in reality? This is a deep problem with not only metaphysical but also moral implications, implying as it does that a person is not genuinely moral as long as he does what is right on someone else's authority rather than on his own conviction.

But does the problem of identity have a Jewish dimension? We need go no further than the institution of Bar Mitzvah. A Christian at confirmation age is confirmed if, and only if, he is prepared to make a commitment to Christianity. In contrast, a Jewish boy at age thirteen, to be sure, may or may not choose to have a Bar Mitzvah; but according to tradition, he becomes a "son of duty" at age thirteen anyway. Is there an unresolvable conflict between Jewish existence, as traditionally understood, and a truly modern concept of selfhood, or are there ways of resolving the conflict? The problem is distinctively Jewish yet also clearly philosophical. There has long been much talk among sociologists and psychologists about a variety of Jewish identity—problems and crises. In my view they are all ultimately reducible to the philosophical problem as just defined.

From the less controversial I proceed in my course to the more controversial: a Jewish state as a problem for political philosophy. The existence of that state is a fact. Its right to exist, if subject to legitimate controversy (which I do not think is the case), belongs to politics. What is philosophically controversial is the question of whether the Jewish state poses special philosophical problems in its own right. For the extreme secularist left, Israel is a state of Jews rather than a Jewish state, i.e., it is a democratic state the majority of whose citizens currently happen to be Jews: as such it poses no philosophical problems not covered in general political philosophy. On the extreme religious right, Israel is viewed as a Jewish state, "Jewish" being understood as governed by Halakhah, the traditional religious law: but as a theocratic state of this sort Israel falls outside the realm of philosophy altogether. In between these extremes, to be sure, conflicts abound within Israel, as well as in the Diaspora in its views about Israel. Even so, a normative view can be detected between the extremes. In that view the state, on the one hand, ought to be secular-democratic, its laws set down and enforced by elected representatives, not by religious authorities; yet, on the other hand, it must have at least one nonnegotiable Jewish commitment, the 1950 Law of Return, which gives Jews the world over the right to become Israeli citizens. Without that law, Israel would end exile for its citizens only; but of all Zionist commitments the most basic for a Jewish state is to do whatever lies in its power to end exile not for this or that group of Jews but for all Jews; it must end Jewish exile as such, and in principle. Any Israeli government that tried to revoke the Law of Return would be toppled overnight: the Law of Return is the core of the "civil religion" of Israel.

What then of Israel and political philosophy? The relation between "state and church" in democratic states is a problem for political philosophy. That problem in Israel is not simply one case among others. By virtue of a unique history of exile, a unique "ingathering" accomplished by a rebuilt state, and a unique commitment to the continuation of a process that the rebuilt state has begun, the Israeli philosophical problem of church and state is itself unique.

Finally, I present my students with the most controversial: the Holocaust. The subject should in any case be last, for two reasons: first, lest the notion that the Jewish state owes its legitimacy to the Holocaust be given aid and comfort; second, because the horror of it is so vast as to be very nearly incomprehensible. Aristotle's dictum about the known and the unknown also implies that a teacher should go from the more comprehensible to the less comprehensible, and leave the least comprehensible to the end.

Because of the sheer incomprehensibility of its horror, the subject for decades simply did not exist, either for Jewish or for general philosophy; it was ignored, blocked, repressed. It has begun to exist now in both disciplines, and it has given rise in both to much the same controversy. For Jewish thought it is a debate over whether the Holocaust is an unprecedented catastrophe, or rather one in principle no different from previous ones; for philosophy, it is a debate over whether the Holocaust is but one case of the species genocide, or rather, even within that grim category, sui generis and unique. Here it is necessary to stress one point above all others. In entering into this controversy philosophy must weigh *both* sides of it, and cannot do so without a profound self-immersion in the Holocaust in *its scandalous particularity*. To avoid doing just this is the philosopher's great temptation, for it is a philosopher's habit to generalize. In this case, he is therefore tempted a priori to reduce the Holocaust to genocide-in-general, or even to man's-inhumanity-to-man-in-general. He must resist that temptation. To avoid self-immersion in the Holocaust would be to lapse into escapism—to be unphilosophical.

It would be unphilosophical for Jewish and general philosophy alike. A Jewish philosopher may argue that since anti-Semitism is a gentile problem, so is the Holocaust, and that if any discipline must confront the Holocaust it is philosophy-in-general. However, Jewish philosophy must consider, if not the Holocaust itself, then at least a Jewish response to the challenge: a priori

Jewish Philosophy

to assume that the Holocaust is a problem for theodicy-in-general is escapist. Again, since Jews were singled out as victims, the general philosopher may wish to make the Holocaust into a Jewish problem. But if indeed philosophical probing should show "Planet Auschwitz" to have been a kingdom not of this world, a world of unparalleled evil, then grim philosophical honesty will require future philosophers to revise a quest as old as philosophy itself. As I said in what I believe to have been the first paper on the Holocaust given at a convention of the American Philosophical Association: "pursuing his age-old goal, the Socratic quest, 'What is Man?', the philosopher, now as then, is filled with wonder. But the ancient wonder is now mingled with a new horror."

Fifteen

The 614th Commandment Reconsidered

In 1967 I formulated a "614th commandment" for post-Holocaust Jews: they are forbidden to give Hitler posthumous victories. A generation later, my most fitting contribution to the present symposium would seem to be to spell out how this "commandment" might apply today.

In 1967 I already spelled out the following:

1. Jews are bidden to survive, even if unable to believe in a "higher" purpose.
2. Jews are bidden to remember, even though thereby compelled to wrestle with the threat that Auschwitz poses to Sinai.
3. Jews are forbidden to despair of mankind, even after the one-time division of the world, with all-too-few exceptions, into the perpetrators and the indifferent, when at the same time the crime of the Holocaust was unique, and the indifference, very nearly so.
4. Jews are forbidden to deny God, even though having to contend with the Divine in ways without precedent in their entire, four-millennial life with God.

These are fragments spelled out at the time. How do they fare today?

1. The first fragment has been the most widely-cited and also the most criticized. The criticism is: Must Jews not "go beyond mere" Jewish survival to a "higher purpose"? Can Judaism exist without Jews? Obviously not. Will Jews always exist? As premodern belief, this has been based on divine authority. Bereft of authorities, divine or other, the modern Franz Rosenzweig could, nevertheless, believe in "the eternal people": despite perpetual attrition—pogroms, assimilation, childlessness—a remnant would always survive, to witness its mission—to Eternity. Rosenzweig, however, taught before the Holocaust. After the event—the unheard-of attempt to murder *every last* Jew on earth—theology must think in new ways of the Jewish future: having once been a fact, a Holocaust is known to be a possibility; *precariousness therefore attaches henceforth to Jewish survival—and also to Judaism.*
2. As the survivors pass away, so does their searing experience. But, precisely with the experience fading, a task stands out more clearly for

reflective thought. In the wake of the catastrophe and too stunned to listen to the survivors, historians would bury the event in footnotes, while theologians and philosophers would flatten it out, in the one case into evil-in-general, in the other, into "the demonic"-in-general. A generation later, Holocaust-history is a respected discipline, and some philosophers and theologians have begun to face up to the truth. With what result? *The more and better the Holocaust is explained, the more unfathomable it becomes.* Why did the criminals do it? is the key question for historians. How to respond to the fate of the victims? is the key question for theologians. Both questions become more baffling with the passage of time. A miracle, Martin Buber has said, is an event that, the more it is explained, the more astonishing it becomes: among believers it evokes—as does the salvation at the Red Sea for Jews to this day—"abiding wonder." *The Holocaust is an anti-miracle, if not the anti-miracle par excellence; and it is bound to evoke, among believers and unbelievers alike, an abiding horror.*

3. Is Hitler winning posthumous victories? Cambodia, Somalia, "ethnic cleansing"—the genocidal list is long. And, but for her military prowess, added would be today one politicide, that of Israel. Hitler launched the most radical attack ever on the divine image in humanity. The belief stems from the Jewish Bible. Post-Holocaust Jews are heir to Hitler's most singled-out victims. *Even if unable to believe in God, they are commanded to rebuild the belief that humanity—every member of it—is created in the Divine image.*

4. Can post-Holocaust Jews live with God? Can they live without Him? A prior question is how they can live at all. In the Holocaust—so survivors have testified—along with Jews themselves, Jewish hope died. After this, the two key Jewish questions are: How to bring up Jewish children? And how to open a new page in Jewish history, with the Jewish state? There is but one answer: *Whenever Jews bring up Jewish children, and whenever they take actions that help secure the Jewish state and make it flourish, the agents, even if unaware of the fact, participate in the resurrection of the hope that died.*

Jewish survival today, then, is not "mere" after all, but rather a testimony to a hope without precedent in the annals of history. *In a world that often seems on the verge of despair, is not this Jewish testimony, more perhaps than any other mitzvah that Jews are bidden to perform, what makes them a light unto the nations?*

How to relate this resurrected hope to the age-old Jewish God of hope? To contend with this question is a task still ahead, perhaps only for generations yet unborn.

Sixteen

A Political Philosophy
for the State of Israel
Fragments

"**W**hen philosophy paints its grey in grey, then has a shape of life grown old. By philosophy's grey in grey it cannot be rejuvenated but only understood. The owl of Minerva spreads its wings only with the falling of dusk." This is a famous passage.[1] Reacting to it as expressing Hegel's view of philosophy, a good many of his left-wing followers have opposed to his "owl" a philosophical "rooster," i.e., a bird announcing, and thus paving the way for, a new day. The most influential of these was Karl Marx. Were Marx alive today, he would surely be shocked by some forces his "crowings" helped loose upon the world. He failed to foresee the future. (So did his fellow-leftist contemporary Moses Hess, the first modern Zionist philosopher.) In fairness to such as these, the attempt to predict the future, in the grand manner a philosophical "rooster" would require, must always fail. Of this philosophical limitation Hegel himself—his own attempts to fathom the future were few and hesitant—was well aware.

According to his left-wing followers Hegel's "owl" is a gravedigger. They misunderstand him. He sees philosophy as the self-consciousness, not of a dying, but of a mature "shape of life." That in some cases philosophy might even help "rejuvenate" such a "shape" he hints in some cryptic remarks about America. A rejuvenation was dreamt of by Martin Luther King, Jr. My only conversation with this great American was about the present relevance of Hegel's philosophy.

These cases, however, are exceptional. Hegel's chief teaching is that philosophy cannot arise so long as a "shape of life" still undergoes the storms and stresses of its growing pains.

Of no contemporary case is this as true as of Israel. The Jewish polity is no Khomeini-type tyranny that expels or slaughters philosophers, nor a Soviet-type one that "reeducates" them. It is a free modern state, hospitable to philosophy and in need of its wisdom. Yet while it has much ideology and political passion, such continue to be its storms and stresses that the wisdom of philosophy is little in evidence. Nor, if Hegel is right, can it be otherwise.

Then why seek a philosophy for Israel now? Numerous states have arisen in the wake of the Second World War. Among few are there signs of the owl of Minerva beginning its flight. Israel, however—and she alone—cannot wait for the still-elusive wisdom. Only fragments can yet be had. These, however, must be gathered.

The Present Storm and Stress

The Storm from Without

Alone among currently existing states, Israel has been under siege since the day of her birth. To the world this has become a fact of all-but-natural life, much as once were slavery in America, colonies in Africa, and Jewish homelessness. Among these all-but-natural facts of the siege of Israel are Iraqi nuclear weaponry, Syrian missiles and poison gas, the unyielding PLO demand for the death of the "Zionist entity," the Iranian lust for Jerusalem, and, last but not least, an economic boycott participated in even by "moderate" states near and far. An all-but-natural fact, the siege is not new, nor does it make the news.

This is true of the world. On their part, however, the besieged cannot take so nonchalant a view of their own condition, nor can they accept it as all-but-natural. Neither was this possible in times gone by for slaves in America, the colonized in Africa, or homeless Jewish refugees.

Frantz Fanon's *The Wretched of the Earth*[2] teaches that, so long as the power of the colonizers is overwhelming, the colonized fight not them but each other. What was once true of colonized Algerians is true today of besieged Israelis, and a quantum jump occurred in this regard when, following the Six-Day War and more energetically the Yom Kippur War, those conducting the siege transformed the war into one of words and transferred its chief locale to the Western democracies. This was accomplished by means of three rules:

1. "Israel vs. the Arab nation" had made Israel into David; "Israel vs. the Palestinians" would not make it into Goliath.
2. "The Jews into the sea" had aroused sympathy for Israel; "self-determination for Palestinians" would not shift it to Israel's enemies.
3. This above all: the "self-determination" demanded would be unspecified and must remain so at all costs, for whereas the means of warfare had changed, the goal had not—the eventual destruction of Israel. The PLO National Covenant that seeks Israel's demise has not been amended.[3] Nor has an amendment been asked for by those who, in one way or another, have raised the prestige of that organization. Not by the United Nations when it gave the PLO observer status. Not by the countries that have permitted PLO offices on their soil. Not by the current pope when he granted an audience to Yassir Arafat.

A Political Philosophy for the State of Israel

This strategy, simple and indeed transparent though it is, has proved to be extraordinarily successful. That those who shared the goal all along accepted the new strategy was not surprising. Some surprise was caused by the ease with which states not hostile to Israel submitted to blackmail. The truly astounding fact, however, has been the headway the new warfare has made among Israel's friends, i.e., the Western democracies. Yet for an explanation one need not turn to residual antisemitism, survive though it surely does; their weariness of the "Arab-Israeli conflict" is explanation enough. Already disposed to view the siege as an all-but-natural fact of life, they have widely responded to the new war of words as though the siege did not exist. In this—unwittingly, one hopes—they have helped those who continue to lay the siege with few signs of tiring.

That this is explanation enough is shown by the fact that the besieged are tired of the siege themselves. The Israeli Right cries that Israel cannot withdraw from Judea and Samaria, that demands for evermore withdrawals would not end until Israel is destroyed. The Left cries that Israel cannot *not* withdraw, that nonwithdrawal must destroy the hope for Arab-Jewish coexistence, as well as Israel's own soul. In this way both make light of the siege itself; the one acting as though those conducting it would be the first to tire, the other as though the siege would be lifted if only Israel behaved more nicely—thus, in Fanon style, the two fight each other. There is, however, one big difference. Colonized Algerians at length expelled the colonizers; besieged Israelis cannot end the siege even by mighty military victories. This was proved when, after the Six-Day War, the Arab states—for once united as they seem to be in no other cause—pronounced their three "No's" at Khartoum; when the peace with Egypt did not end the siege; and when the Israeli attempt to break it by unilateral action—the Lebanon war—ended in failure. The true cause of the polarization of the besieged, then, is that each side fears—*has reason* to fear!—that the policy advocated by the other will lead to the destruction of Israel.

As these words are written the siege is undergoing yet another transformation, with warfare returning to the Middle East in the form of unrest in the occupied territories. Unless checked, the unrest will surely spread; and for it to lead to a Khomeini-style destruction of Israel is doubtless the aim of many who do the spreading. Yet this new version of the siege has divided the besieged more sharply than ever. At one extreme it is held that no political concessions are possible unless the violence has first been put down by whatever means necessary; that even then the concessions possible are more problematic than ever; and that in any case to yield now would be the beginning of the end of the Jewish state. At the other extreme it is held that, if Israel is to survive—by no means only "spiritually" but physically as well—not a day is to be lost for the most far-reaching concessions.

Only the ideologically blinkered can be sure which of these extremes is closer to a safe course that the besieged ought to pursue. In the present situation only one thing is certain: wholly wrong—and this morally as well as politically—are those who, far away and safe, supply Israel with moral advice as to what she may not do if she is to save her soul, but have no advice worth taking seriously as to what she should do to assure her survival. Their moral blinkers are due to the fact that they too ignore the siege —more so now that it is escalated. Hence they also neglect their own foremost duty—to do what they can to bring that forty-year-long siege, at long last, to an end.

Such is the storm from without that has assailed the Jewish state since its birth. Such are the stresses within—or some of them—that continue to be caused by it. The above account has aimed at objectivity. Yet so great is the storm, and so deep the stresses, that it will inevitably be viewed as partisan even by friends. As for enemies, they will dismiss it as "Zionist propaganda."

The Stress Within

That the stress within caused by the storm from without is not the only one is expressed in an Israeli joke: if there were no Arab-Israeli war, there would be a *milchama* (Hebrew for war) in Israel itself. Recently Israel has had much of the "*milchama*" even while the "war" is still on—the joke has ceased to be funny.

One *milchama* is implicit in the Zionist enterprise itself. This began with the decision to stop waiting for God or Man to end Jewish homelessness— the decision to make the project of Jewish emancipation into one of auto-emancipation. Without this decision exiled Jews would be exiled still—in Poland and Russia, Iraq, Iran, and Ethiopia—waiting for redemption by God or emancipation by Man. Hence, if the taking of one's destiny into one's own hands is a modern secular project, Zionism is a most striking version of it. Yet if it were this alone, Jews might have built themselves a state in Uganda, not in Eretz Israel. The failure of the Uganda project and the success of the Eretz Israel one bespeaks an ancient religious yearning that, long dormant, has come powerfully alive. Having a religious as well as a secular aspect, then, a tension between the two is built into the Zionist project as well as into the state that is its product. A future of it was to be anticipated. Hardly to be anticipated, however, was the current polarization in which, at one extreme, there is fear—and reason for fear—of a creeping theocracy and, at the other, fear—and reason for fear—of a creeping and in the end all-encompassing secularism. This current polarization may or may not be yet another effect of the storm from without. This is a moot point. The polarization exists. It cannot be wished away. It calls for philosophic wisdom, at a time when only fragments of it can be had.

There are other stresses within, the most obvious being that between Jewish and Arab Israeli citizens. These may or may not have parallels elsewhere. One stress within, however, is indisputably unique. Every other state

A Political Philosophy for the State of Israel

obligates would-be immigrants to show cause why they should be admitted. By virtue of its 1950 Law of Return the Jewish state obligates *itself* to show cause why would-be Jewish immigrants should *not* be admitted; and not among grounds for refusal is their refusal to recognize the very state that bids them welcome. Of all of Israel's internal stresses this is the most profound. It stands most in need of philosophical wisdom; yet, as will be seen, it is also philosophically the most intractable.

Gathering Fragments of a Political Philosophy

Israel as a Modern Democratic State

Legitimacy The state is a social structure endowed with power. The first topic of political philosophy is therefore whether a distinction between legitimate and illegitimate power is possible and, if possible, how far to stress it as just, prudent, or otherwise desirable. No century matches the present in demonstrating both the importance of the distinction and its difficulties. On the one hand, philosophers since Plato have insisted that without it a state does not differ from a band of robbers. On the other, this century has yielded more completely than any other to a social Darwinism that would collapse the distinction between right and might, thus legitimizing the strongest band of robbers. The most extreme proponent of social Darwinism, of course, has been Nazi Germany: had she won the war, a world cowed or conquered would doubtless have long bestowed legitimacy on her, murder camps and all. Yet despite the specter of a Nazified earth, the world continues to compromise with social Darwinism—and cannot do otherwise. Why is the Soviet conquest of Latvia, Lithuania, Estonia (not to mention other cases) considered legitimate? Because no one dares to question it, lest doing so lead to World War III. Indeed, whereas the legitimacy of many current *regimes* is being questioned, this is the case with no existing *state*—none except Israel. "Wo kein Klaeger ist, ist kein Richter (Where there is no accuser, there is no judge)." Armenians, Kurds, and others do not rise as *Klaeger* against those who deny them self-determination for, knowing the power of their oppressors, they also know that no *Richter* would stand up and be counted on their behalf. Only against Israel's existence have *Klaeger* risen; and, whatever the differences among the states of the world, they nearly all act as though they were qualified *Richter*. This would not be so if either there were no *Klaeger*, or if the *Klaeger* were fewer and less intransigent, or if the accused were powerful enough to ignore them. With regard to the very first topic in political philosophy—the legitimacy of the state—we are thus driven back to the most basic fact of Israel's condition since the day of her birth: that wearisome siege which the world treats as an all-but-natural fact of life.

When there is a *Klaeger* it is natural for the accused to wish to rise in their defense, i.e., in this case, for thinkers among the besieged to invoke this or that ground of the legitimacy of their state, and in so doing to act as if there were qualified *Richter*. (If questioned on this point, they might refer to world-conscience-in-general or the United Nations-in-particular.) But the philosophically reflective among the besieged must recognize this wish-to-self-defense as a temptation to be resisted. When no other state's right to exist is in debate, to debate that of Israel—*and it alone*—is to act as if her case alone were debatable, i.e., to fall into a trap set by those laying the siege. I have tested this trap many times in America—whenever some well-meaning person would intone that Israel has a right to exist, and I would respond that yes, and so did Canada and the United States. The invariable reaction has been surprise, and on many occasions resentment.

How then can the owl of Minerva rise to flight on this very first subject in political philosophy? Either not at all or else by dint of great and bold sophistication. The first choice is a principled refusal to debate the whole subject, i.e., an unyielding insistence that Israel's right to exist is no more to be questioned than that of any other state. The second is to initiate a debate on the legitimacy of states-in-general. Maximally, this would aim at a universal inquiry into the multifarious grounds on which the legitimacy of states has been asserted and may reasonably be asserted. A good minimal beginning might be to broaden the debate so as to include neighboring Jordan, a state established on two-thirds of Palestinian soil by a now-defunct empire that, some sixty years ago, imposed an alien monarchy on the native population.

The State as a Moral Entity The temptation just warned against would exist for any state singled out for siege. It has a dimension all its own when it is a Jewish state, i.e., one that is heir to nearly two millennia of statelessness, and heir also to a long experience profoundly ambiguous about Jewish statehood. This ambiguity was well illustrated in a 1916 debate between the then greatest Jewish philosophers, Hermann Cohen and Martin Buber.[4] Ascribing the highest value to the state and indeed viewing it as the "hub of all human culture," Cohen, an anti-Zionist, was firmly opposed to a Jewish state. On his part, the Zionist Buber could hardly oppose a Jewish state absolutely, but he viewed statehood as such as of little or no value, and his Zionism aimed at something more exalted than just "one more trifling power structure." At a time when the soldiers of the most civilized states were shooting at each other, one might have thought that Cohen would write in somewhat less glowing terms about statehood. And while Jews were prey to tsarist (though not yet German and Austrian) persecution, one might have thought that Buber would ascribe at least a minimal value to a Jewish state, i.e., an institution endowed with enough power to protect Jews living within its borders. One of these Jewish thinkers took a high view of the state, the other a low one—neither took a high view of a

A Political Philosophy for the State of Israel

Jewish state. In this they doubtless were influenced by a tradition in Judaism that makes power forever subject to criticism by prophetic spirit. But mixed with this was quite another tradition, this one stemming not from Judaism but from the experience of exile. Extended misfortune tends to give rise among the unfortunate to all sorts of ways of living with it. One Jewish way of living with powerlessness has been to make it into a virtue. At the time Cohen and Buber were arguing about Zionism, it was a widely accepted view that the destruction of the ancient Jewish state had been a blessing in disguise, that Jewish powerlessness made for greater moral purity. Reflecting on that 1916 debate in the light of present realities, is one to conclude that it was acceptable for Germans and Frenchmen to shoot at people, but that for Jews to do likewise was acceptable only if they did it as Germans and Frenchmen, but not as Jews? To ask this question is to see that, whereas in some circumstances powerlessness may indeed be made a moral virtue, in others it is indulgence in a moral luxury.

That despite forty years of Jewish statehood this ambivalence about Jewish power has not vanished, even within the confines of the Jewish state itself, was expressed in a moving Jewish *cri de coeur* in the midst of the unrest that at this time of writing has not yet ended. "We used to suffer the anguish of powerlessness," a Jewish woman wrote in the *Jerusalem Post*. "Now we suffer the anguish of power." This statement is completely false. That there is deep Jewish anguish as Jewish soldiers club stone-throwing Arab youths is evident on every side. (It speaks well for the moral fiber of the state that it should be so, even after forty years of siege; whether there was moral anguish among Syrian or Iraqi soldiers who recently killed thousands of their fellow citizens is not known to the media, nor do they seem interested.) The anguish is caused, however, not by Jewish power but by an insufficiency of it. A few years ago, the Canadian province of Quebec seemed to seek national independence. In response there was some illegal governmental violence, but it was little noticed and soon passed. (So, incidentally, did Quebec separatism itself.) This was not accidental. Like Israel inhabited by two peoples, unlike Israel, Canada is not a small country but one of the world's largest. Unlike Israel, too, far from besieged, she boasts the world's longest unguarded frontier. Most important of all, unlike the PLO, not even the most radical Quebec separatist ever dreamt of wishing to destroy the country from which it sought separation. Had Quebec decided on separate statehood, then, the procedure, though causing much upset, would and could have been peaceful and orderly, for it would not have threatened Canada's survival.

The Social Contract If the state is a moral entity, the idea that comes next to the philosophical mind is that of a social contract. It does so if the state, being modern, rests not on the divine right of kings but on the presumed consent of its citizens; and if the modern idea of consent is not perverted, as it is in communism, fascism and—unsurpassably!—in the S.S. "consent" to the whims of a *Fuehrerbefehl.* The modern state's minimal moral nature derives from its minimal duty, i.e., the legally enshrined protection of its citizens. On their part, citizens test their state's purported moral pretensions (as well as fight against their perversions) when they assert their rights, minimally, to legal protection. In asserting rights, however, they *ipso facto* assume duties, both to other citizens and to the state itself. Thus arises the philosophical idea of a social contract. It is indispensable in the political philosophy of every minimally decent modern state. But while Israel is a more-than-minimally moral state, the social contract idea has yet to enter significantly into her political discourse. To let it enter, even in the current period of storm and stress, is not impossible. Moreover, it is desirable, for it might make for an easing of some of the current tensions.

This is most clearly so with the secularist-religious tension, the exacerbation of which has made so much recent news. The tension itself was recognized as early as when the signers of the 1948 Proclamation of the State failed to agree on the inclusion of God in their document, but managed to compromise. Numerous further compromises followed, resulting, not unnaturally, in a status quo. Equally natural, however—especially in rapidly changing circumstances—has been the wish to change the status quo in one or another direction, as well as the suspicions of those who, opposed to the change in question, hang on to the status quo for dear life.

This tension would be eased if the status quo, to be either maintained or altered, were viewed as deriving from a social contract, i.e., not as an armistice between enemies but as an agreement between parties sharing the same project. Once viewed in this light, a distinction might be accepted that is vital: that it is one thing to wish to *change* the terms of the social contract and to engage in a process of trying to change it, but that to *break* the contract is quite another.

This distinction should be brought to bear also on another tension within, this one bound to loom large if the current unrest does not soon come to an end, that between Jewish and Arab Israeli citizens. In some respects this resembles tensions between other national groupings within single states. The difference is due largely (though of course not entirely) to the ongoing siege, spearheaded as this after all has been all these years by other Arabs. The status quo in Jewish-Arab coexistence within the state, arrived at in these circumstances, is inevitably unsatisfactory. That it has not been unmanageable, however, is shown, for example, by the exemption of Israeli Arabs from military service, freeing them as it does from the contingency of having to shoot at non-Israeli Arabs.

The current turbulence in the occupied territories is upsetting this status quo. At this time of writing neither the purpose nor the outcome of the turbulence is clear. Crystal clear, in contrast, is that the purpose of many engaged in the turbulence is not confined to Palestinian Arab autonomy

A Political Philosophy for the State of Israel

or even statehood, but includes the destruction of Israel; crystal clear too is that a mortal threat to Israel could in any case be the unintended outcome. Yet in this situation responsible Israeli Arabs have claimed a right to two loyalties—one to their state, the other to fellow Arabs in revolt against it—insisting at the same time that between these two loyalties there is not and cannot be a conflict.

Much is gained by examining these claims in the light of the social contract idea. That this must in principle include the right to two loyalties Jews should be first to concede, for they have a long history of claiming that right themselves. Whether to make such a claim is to reinterpret the social contract or to break it, however, depends on the circumstances. One could not deny Israeli Arabs the right to solidarity with Palestinian Arab claims to autonomy or even statehood, even though they are made against the state to which they, the Arab Israelis, profess loyalty. The purpose of many engaged in the current turbulence, however, includes the destruction of Israel; a mortal threat to Israel could even be its unintended outcome. In these circumstances unqualified claims to dual loyalty made by Israeli Arabs are therefore a luxury to which they are not entitled; indeed, so long as it is vague and unspecified, Israeli Arab solidarity with Palestinian Arab aspirations is tantamount to a break in the social contract with their own state. Their heightened solidarity with these aspirations can be understood as a change in the social contract, rather than a breach of it, only if it is clearly limited—and matched by a heightened concern for the security of their own state.

In the current situation, harsh though it is, there is still room for dreamers. These might envisage a future in which Israeli Arabs, freed of the duty to defend their state by force of arms, feel morally impelled to defend it in every other way; or even one in which the end of the long siege of Israel is demanded most eloquently by those who can demand it most powerfully—Israel's own Arab citizens.

These, however, are dreams. What applies to Israeli Arabs in the harsh present is something Jews have always discovered and rediscovered, often not without pain: that the right to dual loyalty has limits—and that it exacts a price.

Arab-Jewish tensions within will be manageable once the siege has ended. Another tension within would be unmanageable even if the siege had never begun. This is not between Jew and Arab but between Jew and Jew. Indeed, one brings the social contract idea to bear on it only to fail. Yet in philosophy to fail is to succeed in part. To succeed in part is to display a problem, even when no solution is in sight.

The social contract idea runs into difficulty with sundry anarchist sectarians who do not recognize the state. In general, however, political philosophers can make light of such groups, or even ignore them altogether. If a political philosophy of Israel cannot enjoy this luxury, it is because of its own Law of Return. We have already referred to this law as obligating the state to receive Jewish immigrants without restriction. Being without restriction, it is not restricted to Jews who, recognized by the state, are willing to recognize it in turn. Thus arises a dilemma for the social contract idea that, unprecedented in political philosophy, deserves close attention from Jewish political philosophy and indeed from political philosophy as a whole. The Jewish state cannot limit the scope either of the social contract or of the Law of Return to those prepared to recognize it. Not the first, for this would legitimize anarchy; not the second because Israel is not only a modern democratic state—it is also a Jewish state.

Israel as a Jewish State

The Return In a "state of Jews," Jews are the majority of citizens, now and in the foreseeable future. A "Jewish state," in contrast, is Jewish in essence, and aims at remaining so also in the future beyond the foreseeable. In principle, a Jewish essence is already implicit in the choice, made long ago, against some new land, and for a return to the old land, making it into an "old-new land."[5] This choice was made by no means in Zionist congresses only, but more authentically when Jewish farmers failed in Argentina, Canada, and other places, but succeeded, against formidable odds, in Eretz Israel.

When a state is singled out for siege, philosophers can debate its legitimacy only if they broaden the debate; this has already been shown. If the state is not merely one of Jews but also a Jewish state, the broadening cannot be random, so as to include this or that other state, but must focus on a new *category* of legitimacy—the return to its ancient land, of a people cut off from it by the power of enemies for nearly two millennia.

In a debate of legitimacy under this head many facts may be adduced. The second-century Roman emperor Hadrian emptied "Judaea" of Jews and renamed it "Palestina" (i.e., "the land of the Philistines"), thus doubly delegitimizing the Jewish claim to it; Christians, Muslims, and Turks followed in his path; on their part, however, Jews never renounced their claim. Again, enemies through the ages have jeered that "Jerusalem is destroyed"; on their part, however, Jews came to die even when they could not live amid the ruins; and those staying away ignored the jeers and prayed for a great rebuilding—and at length came and did it. The political philosopher may adduce all this. He may even invoke Jewish faith in a divine promise. He must stop short, however, of invoking a divine promise. This would invite a clash between "the religious" who believe in divine promises and the "non-religious"[6] who reject them; between "the religious" themselves, i.e., those who see the state as fulfilling the divine promise, and those who see it as an antidivine rebellion; last but not least, between Jew, Christian, and Muslim, each appealing to a divine promise of his own. To be sure, the belief,

A Political Philosophy for the State of Israel

once widely held, that "in this modern age" resorts to Divinity no longer have political power, is refuted in our time, and for philosophers to attempt to proscribe them would be futile. One cannot, however, invoke divine promises and remain within the limits of philosophical discourse. Such unargued and unarguable invocations—Franz Rosenzweig termed them "fanatical"—shatter it. On a subject in any case beset by storms and stresses, we here seek the help of philosophy. Yet once it invoked divine promises, the philosophical, attempting to rise above the war of weapons, words, ideologies, would itself be fragmented into ideologies, at war with each other.

Belief in the Jewish state as a divine promise fulfilled—Christian as well as Jewish—must therefore, as it were, be privatized in the context of philosophical discourse. This concession to political philosophy *qua* philosophy must be matched, however, by a demand made upon it—the broadening of its categories of political legitimacy which has already been described. Political philosophers may object that this would be to allow a *novum* into their discipline, one all the more dubious because—thus far!—it would apply to but a single state. Consciously or unconsciously, their resistance may be motivated by the wish to stay out of a clash between two claims to the same land, i.e., that of Jews "returning" to it and that of "Palestinians" who have lived in it—so they affirm—"since time immemorial." In rejecting or ignoring the new category, however, they do not stay with the neutrality to the serenity of which they are so often accustomed. The medieval Crusaders came, went, and left behind only ruins surrounded by sand. To predict the same fate for modern Israel is the stock-in-trade propaganda of Israel's enemies. As a serious case, it rests wholly on blotting out the difference between the Crusaders who *came* and the Jews who *came back*. Philosophers are not true to the impartiality that is required of them by the canons of their discipline when they reject this coming back as a legitimizing category; they are false to them even if they just ignore it. Whether wittingly or unwittingly, they in either case cease to be philosophers and become tools of the PLO.

The Law of Return A state that is Jewish in essence requires Eretz Israel, though not necessarily all of it. That the state itself must be Jewish (rather than binational) emerged as early as in prestate days, and precisely among that brave handful of souls—quite a few Jews, at least a handful of Arabs—who, wishing a binational state, devised plans for an institution in which Arabs and Jews, equal in number, would have an equal share in state power. Their ideas were brought to naught by the storm and stress of subsequent events. Even if this had not occurred, however, they would have foundered on a moral dilemma; wanting a democratic state, the Jewish planners did not wish to reduce what was then an Arab majority to a minority. Yet they could not concede a halt to Jewish immigration, once Arab-Jewish parity was reached, without a breach of trust of what had to be, even to them, the future state's Jewish essence. Once a state had come to be, this commitment was enshrined in the 1950 Law of Return, next in importance to the state's Jewish essence only to the Return itself.

The Law of Return was passed, not by a council of rabbis interpreting the Halakhah (Jewish religious law), but by the democratically elected Knesset.[7] When the need arose to amend the law, it was—though taking note of the Halakhah—once again the Knesset that did the amending. What was, and was not, of the state's Jewish essence was thus democratically decided. Yet a storm and stress surrounds current pressures for still another amendment, for this one is a threat to the Jewish state's democracy. The content of the proposed amendment, however, is a betrayal of it. What convert is a Jew? What converting agent is a rabbi? Only one converted under the Halacha is the proposed amendment's answer to the first question; only an Orthodox rabbi is its answer to the second. A Knesset that passed this amendment would doubtless act democratically, but in passing it it would cause the democratic state at home to show a theocratic face abroad.

If at the "religious" extreme there is a wish to theocratize the Law of Return, at the "nonreligious" extreme there is a wish to abrogate it. After all, the argument here is, most Jews wishing to come have already come. Moreover, though not "racist"—the coming of the Ethiopian Jews should have ended this slander once and for all—the Law is obviously discriminatory, if not against other would-be immigrants, so in favor of Jewish ones. Then why not erase the outdated law from the books, in behalf of democracy, as well as of good will at home and abroad?

But if amending the Law of Return, in the manner pressed for by the "religious" extreme, would undermine Israeli democracy, the abolition of the law, as suggested by the "nonreligious" extreme, would do away with the historic—nay, heroic—character of the state's Jewishness. In coming to be, the state ended exile for its Jewish inhabitants. In passing the Law of Return, it called for an end of Jewish exile in principle and everywhere, and also committed itself to ending it to the extent of its power. On the part of a small state barely born, this was a heroic act. The stance behind the Law of Return remains heroic to this day. And it has inspired Jewish heroism in many quarters. In the storm and stress of the growing pains of their state, Israelis often forget its Jewish commitments. They remember them in moments of truth. Such moments occur whenever a prisoner of Zion, having defied the world's most powerful dictatorship for endless years, at last arrives in Jerusalem.

Jerusalem The 1948 Proclamation of the State of Israel contains in nucleus the state's most profound social contract of all. Its secularist signatories could not in good conscience sign a document containing a reference to the God of Israel; its religious signatories, not one not containing it. A formula was found that resolved the dilemma. We have already mentioned this compromise. What made it more than a compromise was the commitment

A Political Philosophy for the State of Israel

to a shared project, coupled with respect by each side for the conscience of the other. A social contract was implied.

Philosophically to explicate this contract is to recognize that Israel is neither a "religious" nor a "nonreligious" state, that the deepest ground of its Jewish essence lies in a bond between the two. Obscure for the most part, this bond became a powerful experience when on June 7, 1967, the Old City of Jerusalem, after 1,832 years, was recovered for Jewish sovereignty.

The Roman emperor Hadrian had tried to cut the bond between the people and the land. He had gone for the jugular when he forbade on pain of death Jewish residence in Jerusalem. Christians, Muslims, and Turks were to follow his example, sometimes more closely, sometimes less so. And whereas, defiantly, Jews kept on coming, they always had to come, cap in hand, to ask someone—Christians, Muslims, Turks, even the British—for permission to wail at the Wall. And then, in 1948, came Jordan and, ignoring solemn agreements, it denied Jewish access to the Old City entirely. For good measure they also destroyed most of her synagogues and desecrated her Jewish cemeteries.

But then came June 7, 1967, causing "nonreligious" Jews to speak of miracles and "religious" Jews to praise military valor; the whole people was united by a religious-secular wonder. This wonder was given political expression a mere three weeks later. Having regained Jerusalem after centuries composed of longing and mourning, the Jewish state decided that it would not lose her again.

Jerusalem is a city of dreams. Although the long siege shows few signs of ending, there is room for political dreams about her even now, such as an Arab-Jewish sharing of Jerusalem, of brotherliness overcoming ugly political realities. Such dreams must not, however, obscure a commitment that is at the heart of the Jewish state's Jewish essence: that never again will Jews come cap in hand to someone—*anyone*—for access to the supremely symbolic place, national to some, religious to others—a place called the Wailing Wall through the long centuries of exile, but to be called by that name no more.

Beyond Politics and Political Philosophy

Jerusalem is a city of dreams—the city also of the Messianic dream. Afraid of Messianic dreaming about miracles, the sober Maimonides cited the Talmud to the effect that "the sole difference" between those days and the present would be "deliverance from servitude to foreign powers." But how, short of a miraculous transformation of history itself, such a deliverance could be assured in perpetuity, he was unable to say.[8]

The Messianic Jerusalem is beyond the sphere of the political. It is therefore also beyond the scope of political philosophy. History, in contrast, remains in the sphere of the political. Just how far the present Jerusalem is from the Messianic Jerusalem, prayed for by Jews through the ages, is a daily, painful experience for Jews everywhere. It is so especially for Jews besieged in Jerusalem.

Yet they are sustained by Messianic fragments, in the midst even of the siege. A fragment is found wherever there is a building of buildings—and more so of human lives and relations. A Messianic fragment was found in Golda Meir's remark that Jews could forgive everything to their Arab enemies, except the necessity to shoot at them. The remark implied the hope that, even short of the Messianic end, the shooting would come to an end.

The realm of the political exists where there is power, and where there is power there is conflict and fear. The political is therefore a burden, as is political philosophy. One would wish to be rid of both—no one more so than the Jew who has dreamt Messianic dreams through the ages. The burden, however, must be borne. Even in bearing it, however, one may be sustained by the transpolitical vision of all nations flowing to Jerusalem, of each sitting under his vine and fig tree, with none to make them afraid.

Seventeen

Pillars of Zionism

I

Jerusalem is a city of dreams, at nearly all times. At this time, however, Jerusalem is well advised to be wide awake rather than to dream, indeed, to be wary; and the same advice must be given to her friends at home and especially abroad. The Jerusalem I speak of is not the "heavenly" one "above" but the "earthly" one "below," and this is neighbor to nearby Syria and not-so-far Libya, Iraq, and Iran. A nearby neighbor, too, is Jordan. Never since the 1967 Jewish return to Jerusalem have these neighbors borne closer watching than at this time.

Not long ago Jerusalemites *were* wide awake and wary. The scud missiles had been falling on Israel and, although unlikely to be dropped on Jerusalem—could the Iraqi ruler risk hitting the al-Aqsa Mosque and still pose as the new Saladin fighting infidels?—one never knew. Night life in Jerusalem—restaurants, concerts, lectures—was dead, as people stayed at home, ready, gas masks and all, to scurry into their sealed rooms the moment the sirens sounded. Was it two or three minutes we were given? I already forget. I do remember, however, that our son Yossi often had trouble finding the cat in the nick of time.

The scuds were not all. PLO leader Yassir Arafat had promised to ride on horseback, side by side with his friend Saddam Hussein, not into Hebron or Nablus, and certainly not—note this, Western media!—into Bethlehem, but into Jerusalem. This was big publicity. Little publicized but well known to Jerusalemites was that at 10:00 night after night, Jordan TV praised the moral excellence of that other great Mideastern survivor's support of the Iraqi Hitler (as he then was called), the praise often being voiced by King Hussein himself.

The king did more: in an interview he instructed the West in the deeper meaning of the Gulf War—the need for a quick Western withdrawal from Saudi Arabia, the guardian of two of Islam's three holy places, and the equally great need to liberate "illegally occupied Jerusalem," the city containing not only the third holy place of Islam *but the holy places of Christianity as well.* This last bit was arresting for Jewish Jerusalemites: what was this but a call for a new crusade, this time with Muslims and Christians as allies rather than foes, against the Jewish return to Jerusalem?

Lectures given at the time were confined to daytime and, after one of mine, the kind of left-right argument erupted that never stops among Israelis: "Which way toward *both* peace *and* survival?" As a philosopher, I find the soul of Israel located not on either side but *between* the antagonists, so I listened for a while. Then I grabbed the microphone with this question: "Is anyone in this room prepared to go back on the Jewish return to Jerusalem?" There was a hushed silence: it was a moment of truth.

The group had discovered—more precisely, *re*discovered—a pillar of Zionism. If a pillar collapses, so does the building that rests on it.

II

To understand the emerging essence of Zionism one must attend to its moments of truth. One such moment seemed to have arrived when Martin Buber, the Zionist philosopher most widely respected by the world, made an authoritative statement, a few weeks after the November 1938 *Kristallnacht*, when in Germany and Austria synagogues were burned, Jewish store windows smashed, Jewish possessions stolen, Jews themselves murdered, beaten, carted off to concentration camps—all this with the civilized world not reacting except with feeble protests and a slight opening to some refugees of a few borders. That was the time. The occasion: none other than Gandhi *had* reacted—by denouncing Zionism, by declaring that Palestine belonged to the Arabs, and by advising German and Austrian Jews to resist the Nazis, Indian-style, with *satyagraha*, "soul power": Gandhi's Jewish admirers must have suffered in silence. Buber suffered, but not in silence. He responded with a public letter, militant in that it challenged the revered Mahatma (who never replied), but also, more importantly in what it said. A land "belongs" to those who are there? If matters were that simple, a land's most ruthless conquerors would be, in due course, its sole legitimate possessors. Buber made this and other points but the Zionist essence of his reply was elsewhere. For Gandhi "the Palestine of the Biblical conception"—a nonsensical expression, of course, for the word "Palestine" is not Biblical—was not a "geographical tract" but located in "hearts." Buber responded:

> Zion is the prophetic image of a promise to mankind but it would be a poor metaphor if Mount Zion did not actually exist. This land is called "holy";
> but it is not the holiness of an idea, it is the holiness of a piece of earth.
> That which is merely an idea and nothing more cannot become holy; but a piece of earth can become holy.

This passage takes Zionism back to its past. On Easter 1903 forty-nine Jews had been murdered in the city of Kishinev. Hard-pressed by the pogrom, the 1905 Basel Zionist Congress considered replacing its long-term goal of Palestine with a tract in Uganda, offered for immediate possession by the British government. But the Uganda alternative was rejected

—among others by the delegates from Kishinev. This vote for *the* Land was a Zionist moment of truth, a vote for the first pillar of Zionism; and when in 1939 the philosopher Buber pitted against Gandhi's spiritualized, quasi-Christian "conception of Palestine" the "actual existence" of the "piece of earth"—*Eretz Israel* and Mount Zion—he confirmed what had already been recognized by *amcha*, i.e., ordinary Jewish folk, decisively so by the delegates from Kishinev.

However, despite *Kristallnacht* and its revelations—Jewish defenselessness, homelessness, abandonment—Buber did not yet recognize another pillar of Zionism: there is no mention of a Jewish state in his letter to Gandhi.

III

It took the advent of Nazism, the Holocaust, and the total Arab rejection of the [Balfour Declaration's] national home [of the Jewish people in Palestine] to convert the Zionist movement to the belief in [Jewish] statehood.

Thus writes the historian Walter Laqueur. On November 29, 1947, the United Nations had voted for partition of Palestine and Jewish statehood in it. But when Arab violence followed, the new world organization had reacted as feebly as had the civilized world to *Kristallnacht*. Endorsing that feebleness, on March 18, 1948, U.S. delegate Warren Austin rose in the General Assembly to suggest that, since partition could not be implemented peacefully, it be replaced temporarily by a U.N. trusteeship. Further endorsement came from the U.S. secretary of state, General George Marshall, no mean military expert, who advised Palestinian Jewry against proclaiming their state after the British army departed, lest it be strangled at birth by the seven Arab armies poised to strike at just that moment. Then Chaim Weizmann phoned Tel Aviv from his New York sickbed, urging his colleagues "to found the state, now or never." (Who doubts today that Weizmann was right?) Thereupon eight men and one woman in Tel Aviv, having heard both Marshall and Weizmann, having weighed both the compelling imperative and the mortal threat, made the gravest Zionist decision ever made. On May 14, 1948, a moment of truth occurred when David Ben-Gurion proclaimed the Jewish state—the first in 1,813 years. They danced in the streets of Tel Aviv with this commitment to the second pillar of Zionism. However, by his subsequent confession, Ben-Gurion himself was filled with foreboding.

IV

A Jewish state had been called for by Theodor Herzl back in 1896. It is unmentioned in Buber's letter, more than four decades later. Statehood

Jewish Philosophy

involves power, and power corrupts: Buber thought little of statehood. He thought less of Jewish statehood in Palestine out of concern for its Arab inhabitants. Hence, when after the war Palestinian statehood became inevitable, Ichud, the group of which Buber was a leading member, suggested a binational, Jewish-Arab state. That the Arab leadership would reject this Zionist compromise as much as all others the Ichud leadership refused to accept; that Jewish immigration into the bi-national state would stop once Jews had reached parity with Arabs, Ichud was itself prepared to accept.

The war was over. The horror of the murder camps was revealed. So was the fact of millions of "displaced persons"—and that, except for Gypsies, Jews alone were displaced permanently. Were German-Jewish survivors expected to "go back home"? Some Polish Jews did just that—and were greeted by a pogrom in Kielce.

This time the world reacted: countries that had shut their borders during the Nazi regime opened them wide after its demise. (My own Canada was one of them.) What if the Ichud's binational state had become fact? It would not have limited Arab immigration; it might have accepted also some non-Jewish "displaced persons (D.P.s)": but at the precise moment that other states opened their borders, the Jewish-Arab state, and it alone, would have imposed for Jews, and them alone, a *numerus clausus*. This scandalous implication caused the binational state idea, never taken seriously by the Arabs, to die a quiet death among Jews.

The Jewish state was two years old when its Knesset passed the Law of Return, committing the state to Jewish immigration without restriction. Soon it found itself swamped by refugees, penniless "D.P.s" if from Europe, but hardly less penniless if from Algeria, Yemen, and other Arab countries that had stripped them all but naked. (Among them were Jews who had lived in Iraq since the Biblical Babylon.) The refugees were penniless, and the state all but bankrupt: yet any government with second thoughts about the Law of Return would have collapsed overnight. Thus in 1950 Zionism had another moment of truth, recognizing the third pillar without which the whole building would collapse.

As these lines are written the 1950 Zionist moment of truth is reenacted. The bulk of black Ethiopian Jewry has been brought to Israel. Jews from the former Soviet Union are arriving in unexpected multitudes, constituting "one of the greatest peace-time migrations of the century" (thus the respected *National Geographic*). And if the state is near bankrupt once more, it is because it cannot compromise its sovereignty by letting foreign states, however friendly, dictate its policies. In the election campaign currently under way these policies may be hotly debated; not in debate, however, is the state's sovereignty: and still less its Law of Return.

In 1992, what would be happening before our eyes were there no Jewish state, and hence no Law of Return? What but a repetition of the unholy spectacle of the 1930s: increasing numbers of Jewish refugees from antisemitism or the justified fear of it—and the closing of borders by civilized states, exactly in proportion to the need.

The great Zionist philosopher Martin Buber had taken too low a view of the state (which, after all, can protect its citizens only by dint of power) and much too low a view of a Jewish state.

V

I hark back to the time when the scuds were falling; when Arafat and King Hussein had their say, the one about riding with Saddam Hussein into Jerusalem, the other about the Muslim-Christian necessity to "liberate" the "illegally occupied" Holy City; and when, after a lecture of mine, that moment of truth occurred which has led to these present reflections.

Much earlier Martin Buber and David Ben-Gurion, otherwise far apart in their Zionism, had been at one on Jerusalem. In 1939 the first, a religious philosopher, had affirmed Mount Zion's "piece of earth"; in 1948 the second, a philosopher-statesman, having proclaimed the state but filled with foreboding, had expressed faith in the state's survival if it could hold two of its three cities—but only if one was Jerusalem.

In 1967 occurred the Jewish return to Mount's Zion's "piece of earth" and the Jewish decision to stay. What of a Zionism that, having returned, were prepared to leave once more? A Zionism abandoning Zion—can one doubt that the whole building would collapse? Zionists know it. But so do their enemies. Soon after the Jewish return, King Saud complained that, with the al-Aqsa Mosque under Jewish control, he could not worship there: in the nineteen years it had been under Muslim control he had never bothered to go.

Few foreign embassies are located in Israel's capital: the world has yet to accept the Jewish return to Jerusalem. If since 1967 the Jewish state and Jerusalemites have been able to live with this fact, it has been because of a silent compact with friendly states: *Confront the Jerusalem issue first, and nothing will result but head-on conflict. But tackle and resolve first all other aspects of the Arab-Israeli problem, and who knows, an understanding may be reached also about Jerusalem.* During the Gulf War such as Arafat and King Hussein made obvious and crude attempts to undermine that compact. Now that the war is over, peace discussions are under way, and there is talk about reunited Jerusalem containing "occupied territory," Zionists must wonder whether the silent compact is still in force with Israel's friends. This is indeed a time for Zionist wariness, for none as existentially so as for Jews in Jerusalem.

VI

Way back at the time of Cyrus the Jewish people returned from Babylon to Jerusalem. Had this return never occurred, there would be neither Christianity nor Islam today. Do Christians and Muslims ever ponder this fact? Will the time come when they ponder it ever more deeply, this in the light of the second Jewish return that is still taking shape as these lines are written?

When will the time return for dreams about Jerusalem, dreams in Jerusalem? Perhaps this is the best answer available: when Christians and Muslims come to worship in the city, not despite the fact that Jews have returned but because of it.

Eighteen

A Retrospective of My Thought

From Halle to Berlin

I completed high school in 1935 in Halle, the German city in which I was born. Then I moved to Berlin, for the study of Judaism at the *Hochschule für die Wissenschaft des Judentums*. I begin this retrospective with that move to Berlin, for with it began my Jewish thought. Also, it was to determine much of my life. What started with a move to Berlin ended—perhaps better, culminated—with a move, in 1983, to Jerusalem.

Why did I go to Berlin? With so much hindsight and after all these years, this is no easy question to answer truthfully. The liturgy of the German-liberal synagogue; the reflective piety of my mother; the rather more simple piety of my father, who, busy lawyer though he was, never failed to recite the lengthy morning prayers, and this despite the fact that, while able to read Hebrew fluently, he understood little of it; a dry but knowledgeable and thought-provoking rabbi: all these doubtless had a share in my wanting to become a knowledgeable Jew. (To become a rabbi was only vaguely in my mind, if at all.) However, if there had been no Nazi regime, who knows, I might never have left home, and eventually become a professor of philosophy at the local *Martin Luther Universitaet*. Or perhaps of classics: my Greek teacher at the *Stadtgymnasium*, Adolph Loercher, had been a powerful influence, and on leaving school I still listed among plans for academic study, in addition to Jewish theology, classical philology.

But a Nazi regime there was. Hitler had come to power in 1933. By 1935 I understood Nazism as an unprecedented assault, not only on the Jewish people but also, and for me then especially, on the Jewish faith. I went to Berlin, then, in search of an answer. And, odd or even dubious though this may seem to today's reader—of another time, at other places—crystal clear in my memory is this: before I ever got to the *Hochschule* I was convinced that what I was looking for was to be found in the sources and resources of Judaism.

That conviction may well be the best clue to my Jewish thought ever since: I *brought it to* the study of Judaism, and it has never left me, not to be destroyed even when holding fast to it became precarious as never before. Midway in my life as a thinker and writer, the bond between Jewish present and the past faith became itself precarious, made so by the Holocaust. A

215

"614th commandment" reaches Jews from Auschwitz, forbidding them to give Hitler posthumous victories: this was my first, much-quoted (and also misquoted) statement, when in 1967, having evaded for so long what the Holocaust really was, I could evade it no more. Some readers have viewed that "commandment" as tantamount to replacing Judaism with what one of them has called "Auschwitzism." They did not read carefully: a 614th commandment—not a "new-and-first," all previous "tablets" having been "broken" or crying out to be broken (Nietzsche)—can only be added to 613 others, and these are traditionally said to reach Jews from Sinai.

What did I find in Berlin? Good teachers and lifelong friends, but the teaching looked for came from three thinkers who were not there. What if—so I found Leo Strauss ask—premodern Jewish philosophy were more truly critical, hence more truly philosophical, than that of modernity? The latter typically comes on the scene as an "autonomous" critic of all things, hence also of all Jewish things: but what if this rules out *ab initio* the possibility that *some* Jewish things—Torah—are *min ha-shamayim*, "from heaven," divinely revealed? What if that possibility were done greater justice when premodern Jewish philosophy, self-critical as well as critical, is prepared to subordinate philosophy—after all, for most philosophers no more than the word of man—to Torah, received as the Word of God? Strauss called for a reopening of those "dusty old books" of medieval philosophy, in behalf not merely of scholarship but also of truth. For the next decade I was to focus much attention on such as Augustine and Aquinas, al-Farabi, Ibn Sina and Ibn Rushd, Yehuda Halevi and Maimonides. I even published an article on the *Ikhwan as-Safa*, the—putting it mildly—rather obscure Muslim "Brethren of Purity."

My concern with medieval philosophy did not last. The concern with revelation, in contrast, has been lifelong, and over decades I was to follow in the footsteps of Martin Buber and Franz Rosenzweig, both first discovered in Berlin. I remain indebted to them to this day: "The theme of the Bible is the encounter between a group of people and the Lord of the world in the course of history." This teaching of Buber's is basic still in *The Jewish Bible after the Holocaust: A Rereading* (1991).

As for Rosenzweig—in the long run the profounder influence—without his *Star of Redemption*, my own book *To Mend the World* (1982, 1989) would have had to be a different book. And if, *with* the *Star*, it is a book quite other than Rosenzweig's magnum opus (*To Mend*, such as it is, being my own magnum opus), the break with Rosenzweig is by no means due to this or that idea that has appeared in the half-century between him and ourselves, but *by that half-century itself:* were Rosenzweig alive in the age of Auschwitz and of the Jewish return to Jerusalem, he would have to write a quite different *Star of Redemption*—if indeed he could write any such work at all.[1]

A Retrospective

Sachsenhausen

That I would not have the six years required by the *Hochschule* curriculum I knew from the start: in my first week in Berlin the Gestapo arrested my father. Having thus begun, my studies ended three-and-a-half years later, with my own arrest, also by the Gestapo. (This was after the November 1938 *Kristallnacht*, during which they burned synagogues, smashed Jewish store windows, beat up a great many Jews and murdered quite a few, and carted into concentration camps thousands of Jewish males, of whom I was one.) The time between the beginning and the end of my *Hochschule* days thus made Nazi Berlin the most absurd place for the study of Judaism—and the most appropriate. At the time I was asked by my cousin Lisa how I could study in these circumstances. "We know that we are sitting on a powderkeg," was my reply, "but we must be calm enough to smoke a cigar while sitting on it." I told that story to a neighbor, over half a century later, when the scuds were falling on Israel, but added that there were two differences now: I was no longer smoking cigars, and I had no intention to run from Jerusalem.

Some lessons of the three months in Sachsenhausen were to become part and parcel of my thought. The concentration camp first taught me to dislike theologies (Christian as well as Jewish) that are concerned with the fate of Judaism but are indifferent to—or so high-minded as to be above concern with—that of Jews. "What is the point of mere Jewish survival?" a theologian asked at a Jewish conference held in the Quebec hills in the mid-1960s. Milton Himmelfarb exploded. "After the Holocaust, let no one call Jewish survival 'mere'!" I have thought fondly of Milton ever since. At a Tel Aviv conference in the late 1980s—on the film *Shoah* yet!—Isaiah Leibowitz asserted that what mattered was the survival of Judaism, not that of Jews. Claude Lanzmann, the guest of honor, was scandalized. He would ask just one question of the professor, he said, but would have nothing more to say to him after that: "Where were you during the Shoah?" Leibowitz replied that he had been right there in then Palestine, with Rommel at the gates, and that if the Shoah had wiped out the Yishuv also he would think no differently. With Lanzmann not saying any more, it fell to me to answer and this, I felt, should be in behalf of Judaism as much as of Jews. "If Professor Leibowitz says that Judaism would survive the murder of the last Jew he cannot be serious. He is joking about a desperately serious subject." I was booed by his supporters, and the two of us have not spoken to each other since.

I learned something else in Sachsenhausen: to love *amcha*, ordinary Jewish folk, its courage, decency, and good humor in adversity, but also, and especially, its wisdom. Decades after Sachsenhausen a reviewer wrote that my views would be liked by "Jewish shoe salesmen and taxi drivers." This delighted me, for *amcha* has in fact often understood me better than quite a few theology professors. "If a mad dictator wanted to kill all stamp collectors, one would have to stop him, but this would be the end of the matter; there would be no posthumous consequences." In words such as these Professor Michael Wyshogrod once disposed of the possibility of posthumous victories for Hitler, and over two decades later he is still being quoted by other professors.[2] No member of *amcha* of my acquaintance would fail to notice that there has been no bimillennial tradition of people trying to kill stamp collectors—or that post-Hitler anti-Semitism exists both in spite and *because* of Hitler.

Yet a third lesson I learned in the concentration camp, but this one I am fully conscious of only now, as I write these lines. Three *Hochschule* friends shared my fate in Sachsenhausen: Karl Rautenberg (later Rabbi Charles Berg in England), Heinz Fischel (later Henry Fischel of Indiana University), and Hans Harf (later a rabbi in Buenos Aires), the first now deceased, the other two retired and friends to this day. The four of us would meet often if hastily, exchanged views and jokes, and doubtless here and there talked about Judaism. But never once did any of us ask how God could let this happen to us.

As I reflect on this now I am not sure what to say. Our Jewish faith was unaffected; for me the experience, if anything, confirmed the view toward Nazism that I had held since 1935. But was it from friends we all had in *amcha* that we rabbinical students learned to focus on two things—that the unscrupulous enemy would shrink from nothing, and that we must husband our strength for the task of survival?

Of one thing I am sure: ask how God can let this happen to you—*to you personally*—and the danger is that you will end up feeling sorry for yourself; and once you give in to self-pity in Sachsenhausen—to say nothing of Auschwitz—you are finished.

The University of Toronto

"I am sorry I am so late," I said to Dean G. S. Brett of the University of Toronto Graduate School when I arrived at his office at noon on December 15, 1941. (Released from Sherbrooke internment camp, I had arrived in Toronto four hours earlier.) "I cannot expect to get credit for this academic year." "You can show what you can do," the dean replied. "There is another problem," I went on. "I have no academic degree, only a rabbinic diploma, but on the basis of that Aberdeen University admitted me to their Ph.D. program." "What is good enough for Aberdeen is good enough for us" was Brett's reply and, having huffed that he wished to be done with all that stuff and nonsense, he launched on a discussion on Aristotle, and I felt that I had never left home.

Home the University of Toronto was to become—not, however, without either delay or one significant interlude. I was released from Sachsenhausen on February 8, 1939. After this came a hair-raising two months until, having

A Retrospective

passed my rabbinical exams at the *Hochschule* with breakneck speed, I got out of Germany on May 12, one week or so ahead of the Gestapo. (I still owe the *Hochschule* one of two theses, the one on rabbinics, but like to think that my writings on Midrash would do.) Then came Aberdeen, Scotland, a year's quiet study before the storm—the war that was sure to come—and after that some twenty months of internment, first in Britain but then and mostly in Canada—a country that at that time was far less prepared to welcome such as me than, subsequently, its own University of Toronto.[3]

These were the delays. The interruption was five years as a rabbi in nearby Hamilton. The period 1943–1948 included the worst years of the Holocaust; and the most powerful memory that remains is an overwhelming sense of Jewish impotence. There were long meetings of community representatives nearly every night, with one speech after another, either on trifling subjects or with trifling results. There was no mistaking the depth, either of *amcha*'s concern, or of its sense of impotence. Once I thought I could do something, so for every Shabbat I prepared a prayer for the Jews murdered during that week, and read it at services. After a few weeks of this the congregation's president, Jack Mandell, himself of Polish origin, asked me to stop it. "We all know what is happening. Why twist the knife?" I reflected on this as a serious young rabbi would, and at length followed Jack's advice—but to this day do not know whether I did right.

The texts of the great Western philosophers are inexhaustible: this was the principle of philosophy at Toronto in my time. (In some ways—although of course not in others—this principle resembles the rabbinic stance toward the Torah.) The theory had its praxis: staff members would take their time eyeing subjects for graduate teaching and, once they knew what they wanted and succeeded in obtaining it, would keep on teaching it. But who are the great ones among Western philosophers? My colleague Bob McRae once chose British empiricism, got tired of it after three years, then turned to Descartes, Spinoza, and Leibniz, never to get tired again.

Luckily for me no graduate course on Hegel was being taught when I joined the staff, so after biding my time I gathered my courage—needed to take on Hegel but hardly less to take on F. H. Anderson, the formidable head of the department and its *spiritus rector*—and asked to teach German Idealism. "Do you understand Hegel?" Anderson asked. His question was more like a bark. "Yes," I lied, and began my career of teaching Kant, Fichte, Schleiermacher, Schelling, and Hegel for the coming decades.

But mostly it was Hegel's *Phenomenology of Spirit*. "The time is ripe for philosophy to become *Wissenschaft*": what a promise in the opening pages! Philosophy acknowledges the facticity of what-is, but seeks to rise to comprehension of it: this at its boldest. A philosophy-become-*Wissenschaft* would acknowledge all past philosophies also, view them as partial comprehensions of what-is, and rise above all partiality to all-comprehensive totality. And as for the ripeness-of-time for this monumental achievement, this would be the work of history, with the *Wissenschaft*, however, being *in* history but, having risen above it, also not *of* it. The reader even slightly familiar with my work will detect my own involvement in these themes, and above all in the theme "Metaphysics and Historicity."[4]

I had heard lecturers mention Hegel before and had read surveys of his thought in histories of philosophy. But when I first opened a book of his— for me his greatest, the *Phenomenology*—it bore little resemblance to any of that. This happened during an unforgotten, unforgettable Berlin evening, when a few of us, invited to his home by the former Husserl assistant Arnold Metzger, pondered Hegel's preface to his work deep into the night. During that evening I did not understand too much of the text; but it gripped me at once, and with it came an inkling that, if ever I was to be serious about philosophy, with that book I would have to struggle. And how be serious about Jewish philosophy without being serious about philosophy?

That evening in the Metzger home was all the Hegel instruction I ever got; but soon after, in Aberdeen, I spent one hour every day studying the *Phenomenology*, alone.

What makes the work unique in German Idealism—in philosophy!—is not its opening promise or even its unfolding plan, but the fulfilment of the promise, the "labor of thought" through which the plan is carried out; and the labor is unrelenting until the "absolute knowledge" necessary for *Wissenschaft* is reached.

In my own labor with the text, I never exhausted Hegel's, thus tiring as little of the *Phenomenology* as my colleague did of Descartes, Spinoza, and Leibniz. Hegel begins by immersing himself in a consciousness barely emerged from animal life, to see it—to-be-human is more than to-be-animal!—dissipate and transcend itself; then moves on to a higher, next-emerging form, at length to self-consciousness, only to watch the self-dissipation and self-transcendence of *that*; and moves on patiently, relent-lessly, in ever-richer contexts, until a goal is reached that is goal because to go beyond it is neither possible nor necessary.

To follow the *Phenomenology*'s road, however fragmentarily, is forever to discover new byways, and often to see why some are taken and others not.

Hegel's own dialectical move toward absolute knowledge is necessary, inexorable, unstoppable. But famous readers, much prior to my students and myself, have often stopped, in protest against the purported necessity, at junctures significant to them, jumped off, and gone elsewhere on their own. In my earlier years of teaching I was often tempted to do likewise. Were these earlier, famous, influential readers wrongly deficient in philo-sophical patience when they jumped off? Or, on the contrary, did they jump off rightly, and move rightly on to different goals? Sören Kierkegaard quips that Hegel's *Wissenschaft* is a castle in the air, with the flesh-and-blood Hegel living in a mud hut on earth. In my earlier years I often quoted this quip in class.

A Retrospective

In Hegel's necessary progression that begins with consciousness and ends with absolute knowledge, what happens to existence?

The following is what Karl Marx saw happen when he came to Hegel's master-slave dialectic. (Having seen, he jumped off and went on ways of his own.) *In extremis* the *Phenomenology*'s slave loses his fear of the master and transforms his forced labor into self-activity: with this revolution he liberates himself, attains free self-consciousness, and paradigmatically becomes a Stoic who is free whether (like Marcus Aurelius) he sits on the throne or (like Epictetus) he is in chains: slavery is overcome, has become irrelevant. For Marx, however, slavery was not overcome, was not irrelevant. He stopped reading on, or acted as if he had, when he sided with *actual* slaves *still existing*—the proletariat—whose liberation he saw as requiring a revolution, not of consciousness but of existence.

If Marx invoked existence against Hegel, so did Kierkegaard, for me always more powerfully because I have always considered him the deeper thinker. Hegel's free self-consciousness becomes "unhappy" when, discovering Infinity (equaling Divinity) and with it its own finitude, it acts to surrender itself in worship; and when yet, by its very acting, it reaffirms the very finite self-consciousness it would surrender, against Infinity. In its ongoing dialectic the *Phenomenology* sees this self-division overcome in a "Reason" that reconciles finite and infinite self-consciousness; but Kierkegaard protests in behalf of the "existing individual"—*is himself* the existing individual—who, with his task of "becoming a Christian" ever precarious, ever yet ahead, continues to stand, in solitary fear and trembling, and "edified" only by the knowledge that vis-à-vis God humans are always wrong, *over against* a divine Other *that remains* Other.

Kierkegaard too stopped reading on in the *Phenomenology*, or acted as if he had.

Over the years of teaching Hegel's work, my own philosophical patience deepened. Hegel's absolute knowledge, even as it transcends all less-than-absolute knowledge, must contain and preserve all *within* itself, lest some finite knowledge, uncontained and unpreserved, lashes out *against* it, destroying its absoluteness. That culminating standpoint having been reached, the *Wissenschaft* for which "the time is ripe" can hope to accomplish its monumental task only if it *preserves difference* within unity, nay—to go further—preserves *even discord and disharmony* within the all-comprehensive harmony. Hegel's nutshell formula is an—admittedly mind-boggling—"Union of Union and Nonunion." Right-and left-wing Hegelians never allowed their minds to be boggled, the first making light of "nonunion," the second, of "union." But in my own work in philosophical scholarship, no harder, time-consuming, patience-demanding task was ever mine than to lay hold of, not let go of, not to lose, *Hegel's own middle*. The "left" discord, struggle, historicity, earth-bound secularity of "nonunion" is to be acknowledged: Hegel is no less concerned with liberating still-existing slaves than

Marx. To be acknowledged too is the "right" harmony, eternity, heavenly-religious "union": Hegel is no less a Christian than Kierkegaard. But the whole power of Hegel's unique, mind-boggling thinking is concentrated on the "middle" that is the union of both.

To grasp that Hegelian middle was the chief work in my career as a scholar of philosophy.[5] Most fortunately, I completed it just before the turmoil of the Six-Day War, for with this the period of tranquillity in my life, with the University of Toronto as home, came to an end. The restlessness that has followed ever since has left little leisure for detached scholarship.

As a scholar I sought to understand the Hegelian middle; as a philosopher—indebted to Hegel but never a Hegelian—I concluded that Hegel's absolute knowledge is fragmented, that the Hegelian middle is broken. I had reached that conclusion already prior to 1967, the year of turmoil which forced me to face up to the Holocaust; thereafter, the conclusion was confirmed, but with a wholly new dimension.[6]

In a way, I may be said to have dwelled in the broken Hegelian middle ever since. While Hegel's enterprise was perhaps always foredoomed to failure, the whole Western tradition—both philosophical and religious, both reason and revelation—amounts to a demand that it be attempted. Moreover, the attempt having been made and failed, it has dialectical consequences. Fragments remain, and these, as Hegel himself might have put it, seek each other and flee each other, flee each other and seek each other. Rosenzweig rightly spoke of an age *post Hegel mortuum*; but perhaps he did not live long enough—or was not concerned enough—to pay sufficient heed to the secular fragments. As for such as Marx and Kierkegaard, in retrospect I regret their impatience with the *Phenomenology*. Had they suspended their protests and kept pondering to the end of the work, Marx might still have sided with the proletariat, without an atheism, however, that put the proletariat in the place of God and justified its dictatorship: his philosophy might have understood itself as a secular fragment seeking a religious one, even while finding itself obliged to flee it. As for Kierkegaard, he might still have sided with—himself have been—"the individual" existing over against a divine Other that remains Other, without committing himself to a one-sided fideism that made him all but indifferent to secular society, even to his moral duties toward it, as a Christian.

I reached these views of Marx, Kierkegaard (and others) while still in Toronto. But not until I had moved to Jerusalem, and had lived in the city long enough to attempt a sketch of a political philosophy for Israel did I find myself—to my surprise and in unexpected ways—plunged once more into something resembling the broken Hegelian middle. The extremes of Israeli political life—right and left, "religious" and "nonreligious"—I understand as fragments that flee each other and seek each other. Any journalist can see and report that the extremes flee each other, and the Israel-bashing press delights in dwelling on the fact. But the extremes also seek each other, for in rebuilding a Jewish state, in returning to Jerusalem—after nearly two millennia of statelessness, of only praying for Jerusalem—they are committed to a shared project.[7]

Only once in my career in the academy was I overcome during a lecture, so much so that for a few moments I could not go on. In Toronto, I had lectured on Kant and Fichte, Schleiermacher, Schelling and Hegel, giving only passing attention to Jewish philosophers and lay people whose love for German philosophy was never really returned. In Jerusalem, I lectured on the same period in philosophy, but now with emphasis on these Jews. I came to Schleiermacher's *Addresses on Religion,* and with it to the astonishing fact that this great and liberal-minded Christian theologian was helped in the composition of his work by Henriette Herz, an intimate Jewish friend. She was a proud Jewess, but her education in Judaism had been sterile, and eventually she was to undergo baptism. With her consent, Schleiermacher wrote that, once a living faith, Judaism was long dead: "Those who yet wear its livery are only sitting lamenting beside the imperishable mummy, bewailing its departure and its sad legacy."[8] I cited this passage in class, and an incident flashed into my mind. The twentieth-century American-Jewish thinker Will Herberg had been a follower of secularism and of Marxism. Having become disillusioned with both and being of religious bent, he sought out the Christian theologian Reinhold Niebuhr with the request to be baptized, only to be sent by Niebuhr back to the study of Judaism, of which Herberg was ignorant. Eventually Herberg became a major Jewish thinker. What a tragedy that the liberal-minded Schleiermacher did not do likewise to Henriette Herz! What a flaw in German philosophy—in its golden age!—its ignorance of, even contempt for, the vital continuity of a Jewish tradition! Might German-Jewish history have become different if such as Schleiermacher had anticipated Niebuhr?

On the Road to Jerusalem

In the early 1970s Rabbi Yechiel Poupko, then of the Ann Arbor Hillel Foundation, kept inviting me to share Holocaust seminars and observances with him: ours were much the same convictions as to what, with regard to the Shoah, was possible and necessary. But then one day he went on a pilgrimage that took him first to Jerusalem and then to Auschwitz. In 1970, Rose and I had joined Bergen Belsen survivors on their own pilgrimage, first to Belsen and then to Jerusalem. On this issue, how could the survivors be wrong?

The question has been important in our personal lives. After the 1970 visit, our second to Jerusalem, Rose refused to go on any third visit to Israel without the children, and once we started taking Suzy and David—after he was born in 1979, also Yossi—the process had begun which led to our eventual move.

Jewish Philosophy

A Jew visiting Israel cannot but relate its present to the Jewish past. The Jewish state and heroes: in 70 C.E. Titus destroyed Jerusalem, its Temple, the Jewish state, but Masada fell only after a heroic defense of another three years. That was then: now "Masada shall not fall again" is the vow of Israeli soldiers, aware as they are of enemies who would if they could follow in Titus's footsteps. The Jewish state and martyrs: in 135 C.E. Hadrian, having defeated the Bar Kochba revolt, sought to destroy the Jewish religion also, and made its practice a capital crime: but such as Rabbi Akiba defied him, were caught, tortured to death, and through their martyrdom gave Judaism a new lease on life. Without martyrs, then, Judaism would not have survived in exile; and without heroes—the memory of old ones and the reality of new ones—there would be no Jewish state now.

Can one fit the Holocaust into this Israeli history of heroism and martyrdom? Perhaps it was in protest against such attempts that Poupko took the route he did on his pilgrimage, and as such it would be right. Titus waged a Roman-Jewish war: Hitler's assault on the Jewish people is improperly described as a war, for it was unilateral, and the Jewish people was defenseless. Again, in outlawing the Jewish faith Hadrian, if unwittingly, created martyrs: in making birth and not acts or beliefs of the Jewish people into a crime, Hitler set out to murder, along with Jews, Jewish martyrdom. This then is the scandal of the Holocaust: heroes and martyrs have choices, the ones between surrender and resistance, if necessary unto death, the others between apostasy and death; but in the Nazi assault on the Jewish people the overwhelming aim was choicelessness, beginning with paragraphs in law and ending with Jewish death.

With Jewish children thrown into the flames without being killed first— how can one rehear their screams at Auschwitz and then hear a redeeming voice when one reaches Jerusalem?

At Bergen Belsen we heard an address by Norbert Wollheim, a leading figure among the Belsen survivors. He spoke in German, the language of the enemy, and his and my own mother tongue. "*Spottgeburt von Dreck und Feuer,*" "monstrous offspring of filth and fire": thus Goethe once described the devil, thus Wollheim at Bergen-Belsen described Hitler. His words continue to resound in my ears, well over two decades after. Filth and fire, feces and fire, monstrous offspring of both: can there be anyone who ever seriously thought about the *Fuehrer*—his mind, his life, his spell over millions, the murder camps as his ultimate self-expression—who does not understand that Goethe description, terse as it is, as chillingly accurate? I understood it the moment I heard it at Belsen. What I do not understand to this day is how, well over a century before, the greatest of Germans had found the right description for the most depraved. But then, the task of understanding is not really mine, but much more appropriately that of German philosophers.

For another word in Wollheim's address—this of a wholly different order —I also lack adequate understanding. *K'doshim,* "Holy Ones": thus he, a survivor, referred to the millions who did not survive—young and old, religious and secularists, saints and villains. That even villains among them were innocent is obvious, for they were murdered for birth and not deeds, and birth, even if Jewish, is innocent. But *k'doshim*? That there is a connection between *k'doshim* and the "monstrous" murderer one recognizes, is haunted by, for what the devil hates above all, wants to destroy above all, is holiness. But further than this I have not come, in the more than two decades since the Belsen visit. At length a letter to Wollheim got this reply: *k'doshim* was the name given those who did not survive by those who did, by the *she'erit ha-pleita*, the "remnant of the devastation." They, the survivors, were in their own eyes a remnant, but not a holy one. *As name for the murdered millions, then,* k'doshim *is a legacy bestowed for explication by* amcha *on future theological thought.* I can think of no more sacred task for theologians, Jewish, Christian, Muslim.

Who founded the state of Israel? One answer is Theodor Herzl, but to leap from the *Judenstaat* straight to May 14, 1948 is to ignore the Holocaust. Another answer focuses on that date itself, the day the state was proclaimed, and names Ben-Gurion and his associates; but not to go behind that is also to ignore the Holocaust.

Among those who do not ignore it, some do not hesitate to make Hitler into the grandfather of the Jewish state, a view that may be dismissed without thought as an obscenity. Not to dismiss it, to give it thought, is to turn the obscenity into an insult. Hitler did evil to the Jewish people in the Holocaust; in compensation, world conscience did good to it, presenting it as it did, through a United Nations vote, with a state of its own. The insult? Other peoples are subjects in history, and genuine (rather than shadow) peoples only because they *are* subjects. Jews, in contrast, are objects, whether as victims of Nazi enmity or as recipients of world charity.

Not Hitler was the grandfather of the Jewish state; its grandparents were Jews who formed a wide spectrum of resistance.[9] No more relentless, systematic, diabolical attempt to make humans into objects was ever made than in the Holocaust. No self-assertion as subjects was ever more heroic than that shown by those who resisted that project in whatever way possible. Even as hope suffered death for them, the men and women of the Warsaw Ghetto resistance fought to the end. With their fight they resurrected hope for the Jewish people, and bestowed the memory of the *k'doshim* on Jerusalem.

Philosophy and the Shortness of Life

At Toronto I was friendly with a classical scholar. His name was Wallace. (We called each other by our last names, so I have forgotten his first name.) On his fiftieth birthday he invited me to his house for a few drinks. "I want to tell you something, Fackenheim," he said to me. "The most striking thing about life is that it is so short." He was dead before he was fifty-one.

I have written retrospectives of my thought previously, but this is the first one that is permeated with a sense of the shortness of life.[10]

In 1958 Rose and I, recently married, visited Martin Buber in his temporary Princeton home. Our conversation of three hours or so touched many subjects, but only in one did we get into an argument. We had talked about Kant and Schelling and, using them as examples, Buber argued that in old age philosophers question all things all over again. With this I took issue. But I was then forty-one years of age, whereas Buber, as I am now, was in his seventies.

That Buber even in old age called into question his most basic teaching—the I-Thou doctrine—I cannot believe; in any case the published record shows only that he subjected it to ever more radical tests. For my part, having most recently inquired whether, in reading the Jewish Bible in the light of new realities—the Holocaust and the state of Israel—Jews of today must not shift the book's center from Exodus to Esther,[11] I now ask the more radical question by focusing on Ecclesiastes. To focus on Esther is radical enough, for it is to allow for a secular reading of the book as well as that for which Sinai is the core. To focus on Ecclesiastes is to question Sinai itself, if not to deny it outright. "There is nothing new under the sun": what even of lesser events, such as the Temple of Solomon, the traditionally reputed author of Ecclesiastes? What, above all, of Sinai? In response to this question of extreme awkwardness to any orthodoxy, its traditional defenders may resort to Platonizing, affirming as they do a prehistorical Torah that is above and not under the sun. But for Jews in the age of "the Jewish return into history,"[12] this is an evasion. Why, for the Jewish reader who lives in the age of Auschwitz and the Jewish return to Jerusalem, is Ecclesiastes in the Jewish Bible? Whatever the answer, it must contain that the possibility of radical doubt is built for them into the book itself.

This theme, if granted the strength and the years, I would wish to explore in the future. The outcome of the exploration I cannot predict or anticipate. But by past experience it would not surprise me if I would find myself once more located in the broken Hegelian middle. Hegel's own middle is broken, will surely remain broken, with what he called his "absolute Idea" shattered. Fragments of it, past experience assures me, will continue to remain for me. Of the absolute Idea Hegel himself writes:

> The absolute Idea may be compared to the old man, who utters the same
> religious doctrines as the child, but for whom they signify his entire life.
> The child in contrast may understand the religious content. But all of life
> and the whole world still exist outside it.[13]

Notes

Introduction

1. Philosophy does not always agree with this picture without qualification. According to Plato's conception of inquiry and knowledge, for example, at least in the *Phaedo* and probably also in the *Republic* and *Phaedrus*, inquiry and learning require that the truths to be apprehended and understood already exist, in a sense, in the soul. Hence, learning as *anamnesis* (recollection) does require that the truth is already possessed, in a sense, and then is clarified or illuminated by inquiry.

2. See chap. 11 in this volume.

3. See chap. 18.

4. Chap. 14.

5. Chap. 8.

6. Ibid.

7. For Fackenheim's engagement with the philosophical tradition, see his *Religious Dimension in Hegel's Thought* and his essays on German Idealism in *The God Within*, ed. John Burbidge (University of Toronto Press, forthcoming). For his involvement with Jewish texts, see his *Jewish Bible after the Holocaust: A Re-reading* (Bloomington, 1991) and *The Jewish Thought of Emil Fackenheim*, ed. Michael L. Morgan (Detroit, 1987).

8. This is true of all of the essays in part I except the tribute to Pinchas Peli, which is an essay on Peli's work and the nature of Jewish philosophy in our day.

9. Chap. 14.

10. Ibid.

11. See *The Jewish Thought of Emil Fackenheim*, where I have collected various relevant discussions.

12. Though not for Stephen Katz, who argues in *Post-Holocaust Dialogues* and *The Holocaust in Historical Context* that the uniqueness of the event is an historical issue but not a theological one.

13. In the short chap. 15 in this volume, Fackenheim outlines concerns about an authentic contemporary Jewish existence. One should also look at Fackenheim's *What Is Judaism?* (New York, 1987). An authentic post-Holocaust Jewish philosophy would have to be situated, as Jewish, within these parameters.

14. See also *The Jewish Thought of Emil Fackenheim*.

Introduction to Part I

1. For a serious and thoughtful account of Strauss as a Jewish thinker, see Kenneth Hart Green, *Jew and Philosopher: The Return to Maimonides in the Jewish Thought of Leo Strauss* (Albany, 1993).

2. See Emil Fackenheim, *To Mend the World*, chap. 3, and *What is Judaism?* as well as various essays in *Quest for Past and Future* (Bloomington, 1968) and *Encounters between Judaism and Modern Philosophy* (Basic Books, 1972). See also *God's Presence in History*, chap. 2.

3. Emil L. Fackenheim, "Mediaeval Jewish Philosophy," in Vergilius Ferm, ed., *A History of Philosophical Systems* (New York, 1950), 179–180.

1. The Possibility of the Universe in Al-Farabi, Ibn Sina, and Maimonides

This chapter first appeared in the *Proceedings of the American Academy of Jewish Research* (1947), pp. 39–70. It is reprinted with the permission of the Academy.

1. Al-Farabi, *Philosophische Abhandlungen*, ed. F. Dieterici (Leiden, 1890), 57; cf. also 66 ff., esp. 67: "The existence of a thing which is due to a cause outside itself is neither impossible *per se*—for then it could not exist—nor is it *per se* necessary—for then it could not owe its existence to an external cause: the existence of such a thing is *per se* possible."

2. Ibn Sina, *an-Najjāh* (1938), 224 ff. (N. Carame, *Avicennae Metaphysices Compendium* [Rome, 1926], 66 ff.). Cf. also M. Horten, *Die Metaphysik Avicennas* (Halle, 1907), 61 ff., 496, 601 ff.; *Metaph.* (ed. Venet. 1508), tr. I c. 7, f. 73 A; and A. M. Goichon, *Lexique de la langue philosophique d'Ibn Sina* (Paris, 1938), 381 ff.

3. See notes 4 and 55.

4. There is in both al-Farabi and Ibn Sina a certain ambiguity in the use of the term "necessary *ab alio*" (wājib al-wujūd li-ghagrihi). Its first meaning is well expressed in Ibn Sina, *an-Najjāh*, 226 (Carame, 69 ff.): "It is evident . . . that everything that is necessary *ab alio* is *per se* possible. But this is convertible. . . . Everything possible *per se*, when it exists actually, is necessary *ab alio*." Cf. also al-Farabi, *Philosophische Abhandlungen*, 67; Horten, *Die Metaphysik Avicennas*, 64 ff.; and Goichon, *La Distinction de l'Essence et de l'Existence d'après Ibn Sina* (Paris, 1937), 162. In this sense, the term "necessity *ab alio*" signifies the full determination toward existence of any being, temporal or eternal. In this sense, any substance which actually exists has "become" necessary; the full presence of its causes has necessitated its existence (cf. Aristotle, *Metaphysics*, 1065 a 6 ff.). Cf. also note 52. The second meaning of the term "necessary *ab alio*" is that "impossibility of being otherwise" (Aristotle, *Metaphysics*, 1026 b 29; cf. H. A. Wolfson, *Crescas' Critique of Aristotle* [Cambridge, 1929], 681) which is possessed by such beings as exist unchangeably through an eternal and necessary nexus with the First Cause. In this sense only the eternal and immaterial beings beyond the lunar sphere are "necessary *ab alio*" in addition to being possible *per se*, whereas the sublunary temporal beings are simply possible (cf. Wolfson, *Crescas' Critique*, 110 ff., 680 ff.). These two meanings are not always clearly distinguished. Throughout these pages, we are chiefly concerned with the second meaning.

5. For our needs it is unnecessary to pursue the classification of beings down to the species of the sublunary beings. Cf. Ibn Sina's complete classifications of beings in Horten, *Die Metaphysik Avicennas*, 322 ff., and Carame, *Avicennae Metaphysik Compendium*, 7. On the different principles governing these two classifications, cf. E. L. Fackenheim, *Substance and Perseity in Mediaeval Arabic Philosophy, with Introductory Chapters on Aristotle, Plotinus and Proclus*, (Toronto, 1944), 218 ff.

6. Cf. esp. Goichon, *Distinction*, and Wolfson, *Crescas' Critique*, 109 ff. and 680 ff. Wolfson interprets Ibn Sina's distinction within the celestial spheres between their possibility *per se* and their necessity *ab alio* in terms of problems arising from

the *Physics*, an interpretation he corroborates through the testimony of Ibn Rushd. However, Ibn Rushd gives different testimony also (see note 8); moreover, the physical problems analyzed by Wolfson would not fully explain the *a priori* and metaphysical character these notions possess in al-Farabi and Ibn Sina. The physical aspect of the problem analyzed by Wolfson and the metaphysical aspect dealt with here support each other.

7. Cf., e.g., L. Strauss, *Farabi's Plato* (New York, 1945), 359, 389 ff.

8. Ibn Rushd reports: "The Mu'tazalites used the term 'possible' to signify that which is really possible, and they held that everything except the First Principle belonged in that category" (Ibn Rushd, *Tahāfut at-Tahāfut*, Beirut, 1932, 320 ff.). In reply to an argument quoted by Ghazzāli ("The decisive proof for the impossibility of an infinite regress of causes is said to be the fact that each cause is either possible *per se* or necessary *per se*. If it is necessary, it is not in need of a cause; as for the possible, each possible being needs a cause in addition to its essence. . . . [If there were an infinite regress] everything would need a cause outside itself" (Al-Ghazzāli, *Tahāfut al-Falāsifah*, Beirut, 1927, 138), Ibn Rushd replies: "The first who introduced this proof into philosophy was Ibn Sina, who believed that it was a better form of proof than that of the ancient philosophers and that it touched on the very substance of being. . . . This method Ibn Sina adopted from the *Mutakallimūn*. These men believed it to be self-evident that being is divided into possible and necessary, and they postulated that the possible must have an agent cause and that, since the world as a whole is possible, it must have such an agent cause which is necessarily existent. Such is the doctrine of the Mu'tazilites who taught prior to the Ash'arites. This is sound and true reasoning except for their postulate that the world as such is possible. For that is not self-evident . . . " (*Tahāfut at-Tahāfut*, 276; cf. also 54, where al-Farabi is included in the more general charge). Al-Farabi and Ibn Sina may well have been led to accept the postulate of the Mu'tazilites, which was rejected by Ibn Rushd on account of the physical problems analyzed by Wolfson (see note 6).

9. Cf., e.g., Aristotle, *Metaphysics*, 1050 b 5 ff.

10. Cf. *De Gen. et Corr.*, 337 b 35 ff. (Oxford trans.): "What is 'of necessity' coincides with what is 'always,' since that which 'must be' cannot possibly 'not-be.' Hence a thing is eternal if its 'being' is necessary: and if it is eternal, its 'being' is necessary. . . . " Cf. also Aristotle, *Metaphysics*, 1026 b 27 ff., and *De Gen. An.* 731 b 25 ff. Ibn Rushd emphatically reasserts this doctrine: "Everything which is possible, be it moved or unmoved, may be or 'not-be,' for this is of the very nature of the possible and potential. But we say of some things that they have existed from eternity and will exist eternally and that their nonexistence is absolutely impossible, because they would have to have a potency for nonexistence. . . . Therefore the nature of the possible and that of the necessary differ basically . . . " (Ibn Rushd, *Die Epitome der Metaphysik des Averroes*, trans. S. van den Bergh [Leiden, 1924], 79). Cf. also Ibn Rushd *Tahāfut at-Tahāfut*, 98: "Possibility is in the case of eternal beings identical with necessity."

11. See Aristotle, *Metaphysics*, 1072 b 6 ff., 1050 b 20 ff., and *De Gen. et Corr.* 338 a 4 ff.

12. Plotinus, *Enneads*, VI 8, 15, trans. S. MacKenna, vol. 5 (London, 1930), 230.

13. See, e.g., *Enneads*, II 5, 3, vol. 2 (London, 1921), p. 200: "What possesses, of itself, identity unchangeable forever is in actualisation: all the Firsts then are

actualisations, simply because eternally and of themselves they possess all that is necessary to their completion" (panta oun ta prota energeia. echei gar ha dei echein kai par hauton kai aei). The self-sufficiency of the beings of the intelligible world must not be confused with the aseity belonging to the One only (see *Enneads*, VI 8, 16; for terminology, see II 5, 3; V 1, 7, 6, 3, 6, 6; and VI 3, 4, 3, 5, 3, 6, 8, 14: "He is the Cause of Himself, *a se* (par hautou) and *per se* (di hautou)"). Nevertheless, the existence of those emanated beings which last forever in perfection is an unqualified necessity. Because of the necessary nexus between the One and the beings of the immaterial world, the Aristotelian convertibility between necessity and eternity continues unimpaired. Plotinus's combination of this necessary nexus with the transcendence of it on the part of the One is well expressed in *Enneads*, V 5, 12, vol. 4 (London, 1926), 61: ". . . God has . . . (no) need of His derivatives. He ignores all that produced realm, never necessary to Him, and remains identically what He was before He brought it into being. So, too, had the secondary never existed, He would have been unconcerned, exactly as He would not have grudged existence to any other universe that might spring from Him *were any such possible; of course, no other such could be since there is nothing that has not existence once the All exists*. But God never was the All; that would make Him dependent upon the universe; transcending all He was able at once to make all things and to leave them to their own being, He above."

14. See *Die sogenannte Theologie des Aristoteles*, ed. F. Dieterici (Leipzig, 1882), 118: "Therefore he errs who claims that the spiritual world perishes. . . . For He who brings it into being does not cease to be. . . . Since He who brings the spiritual world into being is in this condition, the spiritual world can never perish . . . , but lasts forever, unless He who creates it wants to push it back into its former state, i. e., destroy it. *But this is impossible.* . . . " (See also 76 ff.) God "creates" by His very existence; far from reflecting on possibilities outside Himself, reflection and its objects are themselves the product of His emanation (168 ff.; also 55 ff., 60 ff.). In contrast with material beings, spiritual beings possess their "why" as implied in their "what" (58, 60, 62, 63). In other words, since there are no essences outside God which are not part of His emanation, the very analysis of the essence of a spiritual being leads of necessity back to its absolute Source. For the Plotinian origin of the *Theology of Aristotle*, see V. Rose in *DLZ* (1883), cols. 843 ff. For the emanation doctrine in the philosophy of the Ikhwān as-Safā, see E. L. Fackenheim, *The Concept of Substance in the Philosophy of the Ikhwān as-Safā*, Mediaeval Studies, vol. V (Toronto, 1943), 115 ff.

15. See *"Theology of Aristotle,"* 57 ff. and 168 ff., and *Die Abhandlungen der Ichwan as-Safa*, ed. F. Dieterici (Leipzig, 1886), 347, 536, 552.

16. See al-Farabi, *As-Siyāsah al-Madaniyah* (Hyderabad, 1346 a.h.), p. 34. See also the definition of creation in al-Farabi, *Philosophische Abhandlungen*, p. 58: "Creation (ibdāᶜ) is the preservation of the eternal existence of that thing whose existence is not *per se* eternally lasting" (also, for terms designating creation, see Goichon, *Lexique*, 18 ff.). Cf. also Ibn Sina, *Opera* (Venet. 1508), *Metaph.* VI 2, f. 92 a: "Si laxaverint nomen inceptionis circa omne quod habet esse post non esse, quamvis non sit haec posteritas tempore, tunc omne creatum erit incipiens." (cf. the testimony of Thomas Aquinas, *STh* I, 1 qu. 46 art. 2). Maimonides rebukes al-Farabi not only for maintaining that "it is clear and demonstrable by proof that

the heavens are eternal", but also for denying that Aristotle had any doubt in the matter (*MN* II 15).

17. From the "*Theology of Aristotle*" believed to be a genuine work of Aristotle (see al-Farabi, *Philosophische Abhandlungen*, 23 ff.)

18. See al-Farabi, *Der Musterstaat*, ed. F. Dieterici (Leiden, 1895), 16: "It is impossible that there should be anything, either within Him or without, preventing Him from emanating existences other than Himself." See also al-Farabi, *as-Siyāsah al-Madaniyah*, 17: "As soon as the being proper to the First exists, the rest of the beings of nature follow *of necessity*" (darūra).

19. See al-Farabi, *Musterstaat*, 17: "His substance is such that every being emanates from It, whatever its kind, and whether it be perfect or imperfect. His substance is of such a nature that, when all beings emanate from it in the order of their ranks, each receives from Him its share in being and its proper rank." (Cf. "*Theology of Aristotle*," 105.) See also al-Farabi, *as-Siyāsah al-Madaniyah*, 3, 7, 10 ff., 21 ff. To convey an impression of the detailed character of this "necessary" emanation, we may quote the following passage (*Musterstaat*, p. 19): "Insofar as the Second thinks the First, a Third necessarily emanates from it; insofar as it substantiates itself in its own nature, the being of the First Heaven necessarily emanates from it. . . . "

20. See al-Farabi, *as-Siyāsah al-Madaniyah*, 18: "The First exists in and by Himself, and it is part of His very substance to bestow existence on something outside Himself. Therefore that being in Him from which existence emanates on something else is in His very substance, and the being wherein He substantiates Himself in Himself is the very being from which the existence of something else results. It cannot be divided into two things, one of them being the part wherein He substantiates Himself in Himself, the other that from which the existence of another thing results." See also al-Farabi, *Musterstaat*, 16; Horten, *Die Metaphysik Avicennas*, 595 ff.; and "*Theology of Aristotle*," 118, 136, 143, 152, and esp. 168 ff.

21. Al-Farabi, *as-Siyāsah al-Madaniyah*, 26 ff.

22. Ibid., 34 ff.

23. See al-Farabi, *Musterstaat*, 5: "Nonbeing and the possibility of opposites can be only among sublunary beings. Nonbeing is the absence of that which ought to be present." The forms of the spheres have no opposites, and their substrates cannot accept other forms or be devoid of form (*Musterstaat*, 24). Many passages can be adduced also from the *as-Siyāsah al-Madaniyah*; see 10 ff.: "The incorporeal substances do not have the kind of defect characteristic of form and matter. They do not subsist in a subject, nor is their being for the sake of something else, as is the case with matter or that kind of being which serves as a tool or instrument subservient to something else. They have no need for an increase in being which they could derive in some future time from their actions on something else, or from the action of something else upon them. They have no opposites and cannot receive nonbeing. . . . " See 34 ff.: "Those things which are separate from matter are *per se* and from all eternity in their ultimate state of perfection. Their existence cannot be divided into two states, that of their first, and that of their last perfection. For neither they nor their subjects have opposites. . . . " See also 21 ff., 29 ff.

24. Al-Farabi, *as-Siyāsah al-Madaniyah*, 37, 26: it is of the very nature of the "possible" to be capable of nonbeing and change.

25. Ibid., 37.

26. See al-Farabi, *Musterstaat*, 8: "That which may possibly 'not-be' cannot possibly be eternal" (mā amkana an lā yūjad fa-lā yumkin an yakūn azalīyan). See also his *as-Siyāsah al-Madaniyah*, 10: "What may 'not-be' or has an opposite cannot have eternal existence" (ma lahu 'adam aw didd fa-laysa yumkin an yakūn dā'im al-wajūd). Cf. *Die Metaphysik Avicennas* p. 497: "Seine Erschaffung (i.e. of the universe), nachdem sie von dem ersten Seienden augscht, ist nicht ein solches Hervorbringen, das das Nichstein in irgend welchem Sinne ueber die Substanzen der Dinge herrschen laesst. Es ist vielmehr ein Erschaffen, welches das Nichstein schlechthin ausschliesst von denjenigen Dingen, die ewig bestehen koennen." In other words, what *can* be eternal, *must* be eternal.

27. See Ibn Rushd, *Tahāfut at-Tahāfut*, 421, and L. Strauss, *Farabi's Plato*, 390 ff., on what may be al-Farabi's esoteric teaching in this matter.

28. Al-Farabi mentions it first in an enumeration of problems troubling his contemporaries (*Philosophische Abhandlungen*, 1).

29. *EI*, vol. 1, 305.

30. Al-Farabi, *Philosophische Abhandlungen*, 22 ff.; see also note 15 above and Ibn Rushd's testimony in his *Tahāfut at-Tahāfut*, 164.

31. Al-Farabi, *Philosophische Abhandlungen*, 83; see also 87. Elsewhere (25) al-Farabi claims that, far from denying *creatio ex nihilo*, Plato and Aristotle had been the first to establish it, and that they had shown that the world, created from nothing (25, l. 17, and 23, ll. 15–16: lā ʿan shayʾ, 26, ll. 19–20: ʿan shayʾ and lā ilā shayʾ; for this term in its connection with Kalām teaching, see H. A. Wolfson, *JQR* 36, 389), had to return to nothing.

32. I am indebted to Leo Strauss for his confirmation of the exoteric character of al-Farabi's *Concordance*. I am also grateful to him for calling my attention to his article "Maimunis Vorsehungslehre," *MGWJ* (1937), and P. Kraus, "Plotin chez les Arabes," *Bulletin de l'Institut d'Egypte* 23 (1940–41), 269 ff., and for his many other valuable suggestions.

33. This problem concerning the relation between the will of God and the rationality of things has a parallel in the field of ethics strikingly formulated by Plato: "Do the gods love what is right because it is right, or is it right because the gods love it?" (*Euthyphron* 10a).

34. Some would not even admit any limitations to God's freedom due to the law of contradiction. See, for example, the Ash'arite statement "it is He who renders things compulsory or necessary. Therefore nothing is necessary or compulsory for Him," in ash-Shahrastāni, *Book of Religious and Philosophical Sects*, ed. Cureton (London, 1846) vol. 1, 73.

35. Cf. Al-Juwayni's testimony: "The old Mu'tazilites generally . . . were of the opinion that the 'thing' was (1) the existing (2) the nonexisting whose existence is thinkable," quoted in M. Schreiner, *ZDMG* 52, pp. 496 ff. According to ash-Shahrastāni, the Mu'tazilite ash-Shahhām (d. 880) "first asserted that the nonexistent was a thing, an essence and a reality and claimed for it the relations of existence, e.g., the subsistence of the accidents in the substance" (ash-Shahrastāni, Kitāb Nihāyatu 'l-Iqdām fi 'ilmi 'l-Kalām, ed. and trans. A. Guillaume [London, 1934], 60). Most Mu'tazilites, with the notable exception of as-Salihi, agreed that the nonexistent was *something*. Their chief reason for this position was the wish to make the rationality of the world independent of the act of creation and the will

of God. Whether their more orthodox opponents were justified in claiming that the "correct conclusion . . . (of the Mu'tazilite position) is that Allah creates one thing from another" (Al-Baghdadi, *Moslem Schisms and Sects*, part 1, trans. K. C. Seelye [New York, 1920], 118) is still a matter of dispute in which we cannot here engage (see Wolfson, 371 ff.). The important point is that they certainly *meant* to preserve *creatio ex nihilo.* See Mas'udi's testimony: "All Mu'tazilites agree that God is *creator ex nihilo*" (mubdiᶜ lā min shayᵓ, *Praries d'Or*, Paris, 1871, vol. 6, 20).

36. See Al-Hasani: "If the nonexistent could not be known, . . . it could not be brought into existence" (quoted by A. Biram, *Die Atomistische Substanzlehre aus dem Buch der Streitfragen zwischen Basrensern und Baghdadensern*, Leiden, 1902, 34). This view, if applied to divine creation, conflicts not only with the view of the more orthodox theologians, but equally with that held by pure Neoplatonists; cf. "*Theology of Aristotle*," 169: "The objects of thought must be within Him or outside Him. If they were outside Him, they would exist before He created them. . . . We claim: it must not be said that the Creator thought things first and then created them; for it is He who brought forth thought."

37. Ash-Shahrastāni, *Kitāb Nihāyatu*, 62; also see Biram, *Die Atomistische Substanzlehre*, 32: "A thing's essence never ceases to be essence, for by essence we mean that which can be known and signified."

38. See note 8 above.

39. "Simply possible" in the sense that it may "not-be" or be other than it is even when those *general* causes are considered as given which eternally and necessarily govern the universe. *All* things are necessary if their *specific* causes are given as well. See note 4.

40. Al-Farabi, *Philosophische Abhandlungen*, 67.

41. *MN* I 74, sixth argument; cf. Munk, *Le Guide des Egarés*, vol. 1 (Paris, 1856), 429 note 2.

42. See note 37 above.

43. See notes 12, 13, and 14.

44. According to al-Farabi and Ibn Sina, existence is not part of the "constituents" (muqawwimāt) of the thing (al-Farabi, *Philosophische Abhandlungen*, 66; Ibn Sina, *Kitāb al-'ishārāt wat-Tanbihāt*, ed. J. Forget (Leiden, 1892), 17, and *an-Najjāh*, 209, 213), and therefore an accident. Ibn Sina does not regard existence as a pure accident, however, but as a "concomitant" (lāzim) which, in contrast with a pure accident, follows the essence as a whole. Yet it is not a "necessary concomitant" either: "the concomitants which follow the thing without being among its constituents belong to it either (1) through and by itself, as e. g. oddness belongs to the number three, or (2) extrinsically, as e. g. existence belongs to the world" (quoted from the *Logic* by Goichon, *Distinction*, 117 ff.). Also see on this difficult and controversial point Munk, *Guide*, vol. 1, 231 ff. note 1 (historical notes), and E. Gilson, *Le Thomisme*, 5th ed. (Paris, 1944), 56 note 1 (critical notes).

45. On numerous occasions, Ibn Rushd attacks the distinction within one thing between "possibility *per se*" and "necessity *ab alio.*" The fact that he considers it permissible as a purely *logical* distinction (*Tahāfut at-Tahāfut*, 199) proves that he at least believed that al-Farabi and Ibn Sina meant it to be not merely logical.

46. This aspect of Ibn Sina's doctrine is ably and at length discussed by G. Smith, "Avicenna and the Possibles," *New Scholasticism*, vol. 17, 340 ff.

47. For Ibn Sina's struggle to avoid the pure accidentality of existence, see note 44 above. Also see Gilson's criticism of Avicennian "essentialism" in his *Thomisme*, 83 and passim, and *The Spirit of Mediaeval Philosophy* (New York, 1940), 436.

48. In pure Neoplatonism, God is not only, as the "Necessarily Existent," the cause from which all existence emanates; as "the One," He is also (and perhaps primarily) the cause and *conditio sine qua non* of all multiplicity, including that of thought and its objects. Therefore, there is in pure Neoplatonism no such thing as an essence *really* independent of the One. See the thoroughly Neoplatonic "*Theology of Aristotle*," 169: "The objects of thought must be within Him or outside Him. If they were outside Him, they would exist before He created them. . . . We claim: it must not be said that the Creator thought things first and then created them; *for it is He who brought forth thought.*" Purely Neoplatonic distinctions between what a derived being has *per se* and what it has *ab alio* are therefore not identical with the distinction between essence and existence. Cf. Ibn Sina himself: "quod enim respectu suiipsius habet aliud est ab eo quod habet ab alio a se, et ex his duobus acquiritur ei esse *id quod est* et ideo nihil est omnino exspoliatum ab omni eo quod est potentia et possibilitate respectu ipsius nisi necesse esse." (*Opera*, ed. Venet. 1508, *Metaph.* I 8 f. 74 a).

49. Here precisely lies the relevance of Gilson's criticism of Avicennian "essentialism." The similarity of this position to the *Timaeus* is surprising: the ideas which have a metaphysical status wholly independent of God might be described, from the viewpoint of the problems of the *Timaeus*, as "possibles" in the sense that they are *per se* indifferent to the existence of the "copy" (28 c ff., 48e ff., 51b ff.), and by the same token the "existence" of the copy might be called an accident (the problem here becomes different because of Plato's specific doctrine of space, 48 e ff.); again, the created universe possesses "necessity *ab alio*"—a necessity which rests neither in the ideas nor in anything in the universe itself, but in the goodness of God (29e ff., 41a ff.).

50. In his letter to Samuel ibn Tibbon (*JQR*, vol. 25, 379).

51. L. Strauss, *Farabi's Plato*, 357.

52. See L. Strauss, *The Literary Character of the Guide: Essays on Maimonides*, ed. S. Baron (New York, 1941), 39.

53. Strauss's formulation (ibid.): "Maimonides' true science of the law and the *kalām* . . . belong to the same genus, the specific difference between them being that the *kalām* proper is imaginative, whereas that of Maimonides is an intelligent, or enlightened *kalām*."

54. For quotations from the *Guide* in English, Friedlaender's translation is used as a rule, but not invariably.

55. In his *Treatise on Logic*, Maimonides says: "A thing can be possible only with reference to the future, before one of the alternatives is realized; when such a realization takes place, the possibility is removed. When Zayd stands near us, his standing is no longer a possibility but resembles something necessary" (text ed. and trans. by I. Efros and published in the *Proceedings* of the American Academy for Jewish Research, vol. 8 [New York, 1938], 11, 39; also see Efros's introduction, 23 ff. For Ibn Sina, see note 4 above. Ibn Rushd rejects "necessity *ab alio*" in this sense as fully as in the other Avicennian sense (see note 4), unaccepted by Maimonides: "the possible nature is of necessity outside the necessary nature . . . for the possible cannot 'become' necessary" (*Tahāfut at-Tahāfut*, 246). To him, "possibility" is the

capacity of a being for "existing or not existing" (*Epitome*, trans. van den Bergh, 79), due to an inherent element of potentiality. This remains unaltered by the actualization of the possibility.

56. See earlier discussion and note 4 above.

57. *MN* I 52, ed. Munk, vol. 1, f. 60b–61a.

58. See note 13 above.

59. See, e.g., Plotinus, *Enneads*, VI 1, 1–24.

60. *MN* I 73 end, ed. Munk, vol. 1, f. 115b.

61. E.g., *MN* I 73, 75; II 13; III 15. This rationalist conviction Maimonides shares with the bulk of both Muslim and Jewish philosophers; see, e.g., *Die Lehre von der Weltseele bei den Arabern im zehnten Jahrhundert*, trans. F. Dieterici (Leipzig, 1872), 150, and Saadia, *Emunoth ve-Deoth* I 25, II 56, VII 107. We must draw attention here to the strange fact that Maimonides, who had already decided that reason rather than imagination decides whether a thing is possible (*MN* I 73), takes up this question again in *MN* III 15, with very different results. In the former passage he sides with the philosopher who determines possibility by scientific investigation into the nature of things; he sides there against the Mutakallim, to whom anything which can be imagined without contradiction is possible, the laws and properties of nature being but "custom" (minhag) comparable to that of a king for whom it is not customary, but yet possible, to walk through the streets on foot. In *MN* III 15 the question is raised again—and left open! That this contradiction is due to carelessness or incompetence is an absurd assumption (see Strauss, *Literary Character*, as well as Maimonides' style in the chapter quoted in the text, emphasizing the importance he attributes to its content). No doubt the contradiction is intended; to uncover fully Maimonides' own enigmatic position, much close study is still required, which takes into consideration not only the content but also the literary form of all passages dealing with this problem. The problem as it appears to Maimonides may be sketched as follows: in *MN* III 15 he "wonders" whether anything imaginable (without contradiction) may be regarded as possible, a position allowing all kinds of arbitrary doctrines. Yet he cannot simply side with the philosopher who derives what is possible from an investigation into the conditions of possibility (the "potentiality") of actual reality: "the production of a corporeal thing from no matter at all is possible according to us, but impossible according to the philosophers." Does this mean that possibility is to be defined entirely in terms of imagination? Do the laws of nature become "custom" after all? Creation implies the "possibility" of miracles (see earlier discussion), and Maimonides naturally states that that which is impossible even by miracle must be defined in terms of logical contradiction, not of nonconformity with the "custom" of nature (minhag hatevah). *Treatise on Resurrection*, ed. J. Finkel and published in the *Proceedings* of the American Academy for Jewish Research, vol. 8, 30. Maimonides' doctrine of a *physis* deriving from the fiat of divine creation, described in these pages, is the answer to these questions. But the questions raised in *MN* III 15 and the way in which they are raised prove that he fully understands the profound implications of the problem, and that his answer does not fully resolve them. It would be desirable to have this problem studied more thoroughly.

62. See *Treatise on Resurrection*, 36 (dealing with the subject of miracles): "we must refrain from believing in the permanence of something which happens contrary to nature" (nahrib min iʿtiqād dawām amr khārij ʿan al-tabʿ).

63. See esp. *MN* II 17: "Aristotle says that prime matter is eternal, and by referring to the properties of transient things he attempts to prove this statement, and to show that prime matter could not possibly have been produced. He is right; we do not maintain that prime matter has been produced in the same manner as man is produced from the ovum and that it can be destroyed in the same manner as man is reduced to dust. But we believe that God created it from nothing, and that since its creation it has its own properties, *viz.*, that all things are produced of it and again reduced to it, when they cease to exist; that it does not exist without form; and that it is the source of all genesis and destruction. Its genesis is not like that of things produced from it, nor is its destruction like theirs; for it has been created from nothing, and if it should please the Creator, He might reduce it to absolutely nothing."

64. *MN* II 17: "As regards the theory that the heavens contain no opposites, we admit its correctness, but we do not maintain that the production of the heavens has taken place in the same way as that of a horse or an ass, and we do not say that they are like plants and animals which are destructible on account of the opposite element they contain."

65. *MN* II 17: "The same argument we employ as regards the law that a state of potentiality precedes all actual genesis. This law applies to the universe as it exists at present, when everything produced originates in another thing; but nothing perceived with our senses or comprehended with our mind can prove that a thing created from nothing must have been previously in a state of potentiality." See also *MN* III 15: "the creation of corporeal things otherwise than from a substance is possible according to our view, whilst the philosophers say that it is impossible."

66. *MN* II 17; see also *MN* II 13.

67. See note 46 above.

68. Exodus 3:14.

69. See note 55.

70. See, e.g., *MN* II 25.

71. However, the temporal origin of the world does not necessarily imply its destruction: "We do not hold that the universe came into existence like all things in nature, as the result of the laws of nature" (*MN* II 27). Therefore, if the world will be destroyed, it will be not by reason of the laws of nature, according to which indeed the universe will last forever, but by reason of the will of God, who, having created the laws of nature along with nature itself, is free to abrogate them when He sees fit.

72. See, e.g., *MN* III 13.

73. It is true that he exhibits the problems arising from the emanation theory, such as the difficulty of deriving multiplicity from the One, if the principle *De Uno nihil nisi Unum* is accepted (as it must be in emanationism), the difficulty of establishing a link between immaterial and material being, and the insufficient determination of this particular world; he also attempts to show that his own theory ("creation by design") is free from these difficulties (*MN* II 22). With all that, however, he claims not more than that the eternity and necessity of the world cannot be proven (*MN* II introd. prop. xxvi), and even reprimands the *Mutakallimūn* for having tried to represent it as being impossible (ibid.). Correspondingly, he explicitly states that he will show the possibility of *creatio ex nihilo*, but will not attempt to prove it *philosophically* (*MN* II 17 end).

74. See *MN* II 6 end: "The whole difference between Aristotle and ourselves is this: he believes all these beings to be eternal, co-existing with the First Cause as its necessary effect, whereas we believe that all this is created, and that God created the intelligences and put into the spheres the capacity of seeking to become like them, and that He who created the intellects and spheres endowed them with their governing powers." See also *MN* II 13.

75. *MN* II 13, 19–21, III 25 end.

76. *MN* II 20, 21, III 13.

77. *MN* III 25 end.

78. *MN* II 20 end.

79. See, e.g., *STh* I iii qu. 46 art. 1, 2; *ScG* I c. lxxxi, II c. xxiii, xxxi ff., *Quaestiones Disputatae de Potentia Dei*, esp. I qu. III art. 15, 17.

80. That this is not *really* so is evident from the following passage: "We have thus been brought to examine two questions: (1) Is it necessary to assume that the variety of the things in the universe is the result of design and not of fixed laws of nature, or is it not necessary? (2) Assuming that all this is the result of design, does it follow that it has been created after not having existed, or does *creatio ex nihilo* not follow, and has the Being which has determined all this always done so? . . . " (*MN* II 19 end).

81. See Ibn Sina: "The term *qadīm* is used either in respect of essence or in respect of time. (1) The *qadīm* in essence is that whose essence has no principle other than itself to which it owes its being. (2) The *qadīm* in respect of time is that whose duration has no beginning. The term *muḥdath* also has two meanings: (1) it is that whose essence has a principle other than itself to which it owes its being; (2) it is that being which has a beginning in time, there having been a time when it did not exist, a preceding period, already past, in which it was non-existent." (*An-Najjāh*, 218; see further Goichon, *Lexique*, 64 ff., 300 ff.). Maimonides appears to ignore these terminological distinctions: "the philosophers believe in the eternity of the world (qadīmal-ʿālam) and we believe in the creation (ḥuduth)" (*MN* III 25 end, ed. Munk, III f. 57a); "we say that God is *ḥuduth* to indicate that He is not *ḥadith*" (*MN* I 57, ed. Munk, I f. 69b).

82. *Treatise on Logic*, 11, 39.

83. See *MN* II 21: "These philosophers abandoned the term 'necessary result,' but retained the theory of it; they perhaps sought to use a better expression, or to remove an objectionable term. For it is the same thing whether we say in accordance with . . . Aristotle that the universe is the result of the Prime Cause and must be eternal as that Cause is eternal, or in accordance with these philosophers that the universe is the result of the act, design, will, selection, determination of God, but it has always been so, and will always be so; in the same manner as the rising of the sun undoubtedly produces the day, and yet does not precede it. But when we speak of design we do not mean it in this sense; we mean to express by it that the universe is not the 'necessary result' of God's existence, as the effect is the necessary result of the efficient cause; in the latter case the effect cannot be separated from the cause. . . . "

84. It is true that Maimonides appears at first glance to accept Avicennian doctrine when he says that existence is an accident in all beings other than God (*MN* I 57 beginning), but, as in St. Thomas Aquinas (see Gilson, *The Spirit of Mediaeval Philosophy*, 436), that term signifies here only that existence in created beings is not

self-produced, and that it is God who gives to them, and may deprive them of, existence.

85. See earlier discussion and notes 46–49 above.

86. Since philosophically creation can be proved as little as the eternity of the universe; see note 73.

87. *MN* II 2.

88. *MN* II 25.

89. *MN* II 13.

90. See *Treatise on Resurrection*, 31 ff., *MN* II 25: "If we accept the eternity of the universe as taught by Aristotle, that everything in the universe is the result of fixed laws, that nature does not change, and that there is nothing supernatural, we should necessarily be in opposition to the foundation of our religion, we should disbelieve all miracles and signs, and certainly reject all hopes and fears derived from Scripture, unless the miracles are to be explained figuratively."

91. *Treatise on Resurrection*, 31, *MN* II 25: "Accepting creation, we find that miracles are possible, that revelation is possible, and that every difficulty in this question is removed. We might be asked, 'Why has God inspired a certain person and not another? Why has He revealed the Law to one particular nation, and at one particular time? Why has He commanded this, and forbidden that? Why has He shown through a prophet certain particular miracles? What is the object of these laws? And why has He not made the commandments and the prohibitions part of our nature, if it was His object that we should live in accordance with them?' We answer to all these questions: He willed it so; or, His wisdom decided so."

92. *Treatise on Resurrection*, 32.

93. Al-Farabi, *Philosophische Abhandlungen*, 27.

94. See Strauss, *Literary Character*, 37 ff., and note 53 above.

2. Samuel Hirsch and Hegel

This chapter is reprinted from *Studies in Nineteenth Century Jewish Intellectual History*, edited by A. Altmann, vol. II, 171–201 (Cambridge, Mass.: Harvard University Press, 1964), with permission of Harvard University Press.

1. The interpretation of Hegel reflected here must wait for a future study specifically dedicated to Hegel in order to have the detailed documentation it requires. In the absence of such documentation, little purpose is served by mere piecemeal references, which are therefore, for the most part, avoided. [Now see *The Religious Dimension in Hegel's Thought* (Indiana, 1968) —ed.]

2. Karl Barth rightly asks: "Why did Hegel not become for the Protestant world something similar to what Thomas Aquinas was for Roman Catholicism?" (*From Rousseau to Ritschl* [London, 1959], 268). Barth offers a penetrating answer to his own question.

3. The most persistent and most disastrous misunderstanding of post-Kantian German idealists is that they seek to give mere a priori constructions of reality. Their true aim is to comprehend philosophically what in experience is already real. For Hegel in particular, a reality beyond all experience, and merely postulated by philosophical thought, is a mere *caput mortuum*.

4. Hegel's sensitivity to this danger is illustrated by his famous criticism, in the preface of the *Phenomenology*, of Schelling's Absolute, which, because it failed to

preserve difference as well as identity, resembles a "night in which all cows are black" (*The Phenomenology of Mind*, trans. J. B. Baillie, 2nd ed. [London, 1931], 79).

5. See *Philosophy of Right*, preface. This famous remark is often quoted out of context and made to imply that philosophical comprehension marks the end of *all* life which it comprehends. But the context does not necessarily commit Hegel's remark to so sweeping an interpretation. Possibly philosophical comprehension marks the end only of phases of "objective," not of "absolute" spirit: that is, of forms of life rendered finite by a historical setting, not of aesthetic and religious forms of life which transcend such settings.

6. Traces of this view, which permeates Hegel's mature works, are found as early as in his *Glauben und Wissen* (1802), which speaks of a "speculative Good Friday" followed by a speculative resurrection, both of which are to be given "philosophical existence" (*Werke*, ed. H. Glockner, 2nd ed. [Stuttgart, 1941], I, 433). Still earlier writings, not published by Hegel himself, do not yet attribute a speculative life to philosophy. But they also deny that philosophy can comprehend religion. (See *Early Theological Writings*, trans. Knox and Kroner [Chicago, 1948], 313.)

7. For Hegel's account of the Biblical myth of the fall, see, e.g., his shorter *Logic*, no. 24, addition 3, *Werke*, ed. H. Glockner, 3rd ed. [Stuttgart, 1955], VIII, 91ff.

8. While rejecting "theological morality," which regards the right as right because it is the will of God, Kant embraces "moral theology," which regards the right as the will of God because it *is* right and known to be so by autonomous reason. The question as to why, nevertheless, the will of God does not in "moral theology" reduce itself to a redundancy is beyond the scope of the present study.

9. "Not he who believes in a Holy Scripture has true religion, but he who does not require such a Scripture, and indeed could compose one in his own right" (F. D. E. Schleiermacher, *Reden über die Religion*, ed. M. Rade [Berlin, n.d.], 89). It ought to be added that this radical statement appears only in the first edition of the *Addresses*, and also that, while coming close to identifying the voice of God with the voice within, Schleiermacher never quite embraced that view, which is characteristic of romanticism. But Schleiermacher never committed himself completely to the romantic standpoint.

10. For the most recent treatment of Kant's attitude toward Judaism, see H. M. Graupe, "Kant und das Judentum," *Zeitschrift für Religions- und Geistesgeschichte*, 13:308–333 (1961). For Hegel's early image of Judaism, see his *Early Theological Writings*. It is at present fashionable to focus scholarly attention on these early pieces—despite the fact that Hegel himself did not publish them—the purpose of this attention being to discover genetic clues to the mature Hegel. But the "genetic" approach, always dubious in the case of philosophers, is especially so in the case of Hegel. More dubious still—to anyone familiar with Hegel's publishing habits—is the attempt to interpret what Hegel published in terms of what he deliberately left unpublished. It is well known that among German classical philosophers the notion of Judaism as a mere legalistic system is in no small measure traceable to the influence of Spinoza and Moses Mendelssohn. It would seem, however, that this prejudice—and, indeed, the whole treatment of Judaism by these philosophers—has deeper roots, in Christian tendencies in Germany to reject or play down the Old Testament basis of Christianity. This whole subject still awaits adequate exploration.

11. For the best available treatment of this subject, see N. Rotenstreich, "Hegel's

Image of Judaism," *Jewish Social Studies*, 15: 33–52 (1953). Cf. also H. J. Schoeps, "Die Ausserchristlichen Religionen bei Hegel," *Zeitschrift für Religions- und Geistesgeschichte*, 7: 27–33 (1955). An exhaustive treatment of Hegel's concept of Judaism is both more worthwhile and more needed than that of any other German philosopher. But it is also more difficult. It would have to consider Hegel's entire philosophy of religion, if indeed not his philosophy as a whole.

12. K. C. Planck, "Über die religionsphilosophische Stellung des Judentums," *Theologische Jahrbücher*, II (Tübingen, 1843), 430ff. Planck writes: "Die göttliche Heiligkeit tritt im Judentum nicht als jene abstrakte, negative Bestimmung auf, wie bei Hegel, sondern als positive, und eben darum hat auch das Volk, obgleich es der Knecht Jehovahs ist, eine grössere Berechtigung; die Theokratie bezweckt ebenso sehr das Glück des Volkes, wie die Verherrlichung Jehovahs. Hegel dagegen hat die göttliche Heiligkeit nur nach ihrer theoretischen, nicht nach ihrer praktischen Seite gefasst, so wie überall bei ihm dies praktische Moment der Religion gegen das theoretische zurücktreten muss . . . *Das Gesetz und das Bundesverhältnis, worin die Eigentümlichkeit des Judentums besteht, fällt also ganz weg*" (433–434, our italics). Planck further makes the important observation that the treatment of Judaism may be regarded as a test of the whole "speculative principle" not only in the case of Hegel but also in that of Kant and Schleiermacher: "Bei Allen finden wir jene einseitige Trennung des Judentums von dem Christentum, zufolge deren das letztere, obgleich es geschichtlich vermittelt sein soll, doch ebenso sehr wieder aus dem geschichtlichen Zusammenhang herausgerissen ist . . . " (429).

13. This is illustrated by Planck's essay, referred to in note 12. While Planck gives Judaism a higher place in the dialectic than Hegel does, he still allows it to be superseded by Christianity.

14. Hirsch, who was born near Trier, Germany, in 1815, and died in Chicago in 1889, wrote a number of minor works in addition to his *Religionsphilosophie der Juden oder das Prinzip der jüdischen Religionsanschauung und sein Verhältniss zum Heidenthum, Christenthum und zur absoluten Philosophie* (Leipzig, 1842). The latter, however, remained his only systematic philosophical work, though intended to be only the first volume of a projected larger work. The *Religionsphilosophie* will henceforth be referred to as *RJ*. Because the *RJ* is virtually unavailable in non-German libraries we shall, in our notes, quote far more amply from that work than is customary. Hirsch seeks to demonstrate at length (1) that modern philosophy has superseded all premodern philosophy, and (2) that Hegelian philosophy has superseded all pre-Hegelian modern philosophy (*RJ*, 793 ff.). Taking these claims seriously, the interpreter cannot treat the influence upon Hirsch of such thinkers as Kant and Fichte on a par with that of Hegel (as is done, e.g., by J. Guttmann, *Die Philosophie des Judentums* [Munich, 1933], 331, and by M. Wiener, *Jüdische Religion im Zeitalter der Emanzipation* [Berlin, 1933], 132). In the present study, we shall interpret Hirsch as being in primordial confrontation with Hegel, and as falling back, at strategic points in that primordial confrontation, on thinkers other than Hegel for support.

15. To carry out our task we must, in our exposition, depart from Hirsch's own. And we must also refrain from summarizing those of Hirsch's ideas which do not directly concern our issue. Full summaries of the *RJ* are given by the works of Guttmann and Wiener referred to in note 14, and by H. J. Schoeps, *Geschichte der jüdischen Religionsphilosophie der Neuzeit*, I (Berlin, 1935), 93–132.

16. E.g., *RJ*, 15, 28 ff., 94 ff., 460 ff., 509, 564 ff., 584 ff. On the whole, Hirsch accuses the Hegelian school rather than Hegel himself of anti-Jewish prejudice. As for Hegel's own misunderstanding of Judaism, this Hirsch considers as mainly the result of philosophical errors on Hegel's part, above all of the attempt to deny a sharp distinction between pagan error and religious truth (see, e.g., *RJ*, 814 ff.). Hirsch also considers this misunderstanding as having to some extent been caused by Hegel's undue reliance on Philo for his interpretation of Judaism; see *RJ*, 273 and 545: "Von dem Vorwurf Hegels gegen das Judentum, dass hier Gott ein Jenseits sei, ist gerade das Gegenteil wahr. Nur in dem Christentum der Kirche ist Gott so ein Jenseits. Hegel scheint seine ganze Philosophie des Judentums aus Philo geschöpft zu haben. Dieser von ägyptischem Heidentum angesteckt, weiss allerdings nur von so einem jenseitigem Gott, ganz anders aber die heilige Schrift."

17. Hegel contrasts the "sublime" Jewish religion, which "explicitly recognizes as inadequate" the natural "material" in which the Divine manifests itself, with the Greek "religion of beauty," which "reconciles significance with material." In this contrast, to be sure, he shows a lifelong preference for Greek reconciliation. But he also writes: "Wenn man . . . die Entäusserung der Natur bedauert, so muss man zugeben, dass die schöne Vereinigung der Natur und Gottes nur für die Phantasie gilt, nicht für die Vernunft. Denen, die noch so schlecht von der Entgötterung sprechen und jene Identität preisen, wird es doch gewiss schwer sein, an einen Ganges, eine Kuh, ein Meer, einen indischen *oder griechischen* Gott usf. zu glauben. . . . " In this connection, it is a significant fact that, while in Hegel's Berlin lectures of 1824 and 1831 Jewish religion preceded Greek religion in dialectical sequence, the lectures of 1827 reversed this sequence, containing also the assertion that Greek beauty is inferior from a religious point of view to holiness, which first appears in Judaism (*Vorlesungen über die Philosophie der Religion*, ed. G. Lasson [Leipzig, 1925–30], vol. II, part II, 71, 68 ff., 250 ff., 57; the italics are ours).

18. See *RJ*, 517 ff.: "Wir können das Heidentum in zwei Gruppen teilen. Die erste fühlt sich befriedigt in dieser Welt und strebt nicht über sie hinaus; sie kennt nur eine sinnliche, nicht eine geistige Welt. Zu dieser Gruppe gehören die Fetischdiener und die Chinesen, die Vorderasiaten, Griechen und Römer. Die andere Gruppe aber fühlt sich unglücklich in dieser Welt, sucht sie zu entbehren. Die sinnliche Welt erfüllt sie mit Trauer und Schmerz; sie erstrebt eine unsinnliche. Zu dieser gehören die Indier, Buddhadiener, Perser und Ägypter. . . . [Aber die heilige Schrift] ist eben so weit entfernt von dem heidnischen Versenktsein in der Natur, als von der heidnischen Flucht aus derselben. Diese Natur ist gut und vollkommen, nach der Lehre der heiligen Schrift, denn Gott sah Alles, was er gemacht hatte, und es war sehr gut . . . Der Mensch braucht also nicht aus dieser Natur zu fliehen, um Gott zu finden, nicht erst nach dem Tode ist er bei Gott, sondern auf dieser Erde soll er vor Gott wandeln und vollkommen werden. . . . " For more about paganism and Judaism, see sections V and VI of the present essay.

19. As will be seen (sections VI and VII), there is a sense in which, for Hirsch, Judaism and Christianity share absoluteness. Judaism is the "intensive religiosity" which consists of living with the true God Who has entered into Israel's midst, while Christianity is the "extensive religiosity" which consists of the dynamic effort of bringing this God to the pagan world (*RJ*, 440–839). "Absolute religiosity" will be achieved in the Messianic age, in which Christianity will have converted all pa-

ganism within and outside itself, and in which the Jew will obey the true God freely, no longer merely by compulsion (*RJ*, 840–884). But—as will be seen—Hirsch's "absoluteness" cannot be Hegel's, which is comprehensiveness.

20. The most obvious exception is Islam. This is treated by Hegel as only a modification of Judaism, and by Hirsch not at all. Possibly traces of Hegelian influence may still be found in the treatment of Islam in F. Rosenzweig's *Stern der Erlösung* (Frankfurt, 1921).

21. See e.g., *RJ*, 509: "Wer weiss nicht, dass die heilige Schrift immer und über-all mit dem Heidentum in Opposition steht? Doch die neueste Kritik weiss das wirklich nicht. Ihr ist der Jehovakult nur eine Modifikation des persischen Licht-kultus usw. Dieser Kritik muss daher denn auch immer wieder zugemutet werden, dass sie sich bescheide, von den so gering geschätzten Rabbinen noch lernen zu können." (The "most recent criticism" refers to the Hegelian school.) Possibly it is not farfetched to look for similarities between Hirsch's protest against the Biblical critics of his time and the protest of Yehezkel Kaufmann against those of our time (*The Religion of Israel* [Chicago, 1960]).

22. Hirsch's position vis-à-vis trinitarianism is complex but consistent. In the first place, he rejects Christian trinitarianism, as reflecting what he regards as the Pauline relapse into paganism. (See section VII.) In the second place, he rejects, as pantheistic, Hegel's trinitarianism, which he sharply distinguishes from that of the Church. (*RJ*, p. 780: "Nach der kirchlichen Lehre ist nur Gott der Dreieinige. Gott steht jenseits der Welt; die Welt als solche bildet kein Moment in der Drei-einigkeit Gottes und ist für sich auch nicht nach dem Gesetze der Dreieinigkeit ge-gliedert.") But, in the third place, there is a sense in which the true God—Jewish and Christian—must be trinitarian. He is a *living* God: "but all that lives is trini-tarian in the Hegelian sense" (*RJ*, 817). The One God of Hirsch, then, is not Hegel's abstract and lifeless unity. He is One because His life differs from that of the world and because He is real apart from the life of the world. See note 48.

23. Hirsch is enough of a Hegelian to be thoroughly aware of this fact. Thus having criticized Hegel's concept of Judaism he writes: "Aber das ist das Göttliche an der Hegelschen Anforderung, die er an die Philosophie stellt, dass es nirgendwo im System einen Fehler geben kann, den man nicht durch das ganze System fühlen müsste . . . " (*RJ*, 819).

24. See, e.g., *RJ*, xxv ff., 45, 165, 545ff.

25. See, e.g., *RJ*, 385 ff., 603, 786 ff., and esp. xv ff. See also 34: "Das Philoso-phieren ist eben so eine Tätigkeit des Menschen, wie alle anderen Tätigkeiten des Geistes, gehört also mit zur Religion und steht nicht neben oder über ihr. Zu re-ligiösen Erkenntnissen kommt der Mensch zunächst, wie zu anderen Erkenntnis-sen, z. B. zur Sprachbildung durch Anschauung . . . Die Philosophie begreift jene Anschauungen verändert sie aber nicht, wenn sie richtig ist. Nur wenn sie falsch sind, halten sie vor der Philosophie nicht aus: falsch sind sie aber nur durch die Schuld des Menschen, wie sich zeigen wird."

26. *RJ*, 25. Hirsch goes on to say: "Nur endliche Dinge verhalten sich zu einan-der. Endliche Dinge, von denen das Eine hier, das Andere dort steht, haben in gewissem Sinne eine Beziehung auf einander, in anderem wiederum nicht. Deswegen verhalten sie sich zu einander, bleiben aber auch Jedes für sich selbständig. Das Eine ist die Grenze des Anderen. . . . Der Mensch kann daher auch nicht in diesem Sinne in einem Verhältnis zu Gott stehen, denn wo der Mensch ist,

da ist auch Gott. . . . " When we characterize Hirsch's denial of a Divine-human relationship as utterly un-Hegelian, we are not unaware of Hegel's doctrine of true
Infinity, which asserts that the "true Infinite" must be inclusive of the finite, instead
of being related to it in an external relation (see, e.g., his shorter *Logic*, nos. 91–95).
There is, however, a world of difference between Hirsch, who denies the religious
God-man relationship, and Hegel, who interprets it as an internal rather than an
external relationship. We may add in passing that a good many Hegelians on both
right and left have failed to understand this difference.

27. *RJ*, 29–30: "Denn wenn die Religiosität auch nicht ein Verhalten des Menschen zu Gott, sondern nur sein, des Menschen, Verhalten zu sich selbst ausdrückt,
so muss doch der Grund, die Wurzel dieses seines Zu-sich-selbst-Verhaltens Gott
sein. . . . Nur der Mensch ist fähig, das Leben für seine Freiheit hinzugeben. Diese
Macht nun über Alles, diese Harmonie . . . zwischen der menschlichen Freiheit und
dem All, dieses, dass es schlechterdings nichts gibt, was den Menschen zu irgend
etwas zwingen könnte, hat er sich nicht selbst gegeben, noch hat er sie erworben.
Er schaut also über sich ein Wesen, das ihm diese seine Freiheit geschenkt . . . hat.
Dieses Wesen hat ihm diese Macht über Alles gegeben; es muss also selbst das
Allmächtige, das schlechterdings Macht über Alles Habende sein. Dieses Wesen
nennt er Gott."

28. This dilemma, characteristic of both romantic and pragmatic philosophies
of religion, is illustrated in Schleiermacher's *Addresses*, which, having insisted on
the irreducible plurality of true religions—if only they are alive—nevertheless ends
up referring to Christianity as the "religion of religions." The dilemma is also present in present-day pluralistic philosophies, which, comparing religions to players
in an orchestra, each of whom must perform his own individual task, unconsciously
assume the role of conductor.

29. In the light of the exposition given in section I, this assertion requires qualification. To the extent to which religious immediacy retains the distinction between
worshiping man and worshiped God, it experiences freedom as human freedom,
and its primordial choices as for or against God. But to the extent to which religious
immediacy experiences an inner bond between worshiping man and worshiped
God, it no longer experiences freedom as simply human.

30. *RJ*, 449. Because Hirsch considers the issue of sin as the decisive issue between Hegel and himself, it is advisable to quote at least one crucial passage in full:

Dieser Punkt von der Möglichkeit des Bösen, welche als Möglichkeit notwendig ist, um dem Menschen das Moment seiner formalen Freiheit zu erhalten, welche aber auch nur Möglichkeit bleiben und niemals Wirklichkeit
werden soll, jedoch Wirklichkeit werden kann, ist der Angelpunkt, der
Scheideweg, wo wir uns von der neuesten Philosophie durchaus trennen;
ist, wie wir noch sehen werden, der Grundgedanke des Judentums, das Schi-
boleth, woran Judentum im Gegensatz zum Heidentum und im Unter-
schiede vom Christentum einzig und allein zu erkennen ist.

Nach Hegel . . . ist Sünde nur der notwendige Durchgang zum Guten.
Nicht die bloss mögliche Sünde, sondern die wirkliche Sünde ist notwendig,
um zum Guten zu kommen. Im Anfange soll nämlich der Naturzustand
sein. Diesen stellt man sich vor als den seligen Zustand, wo der Mensch eins
mit . . . der Natur, weder vom Guten noch vom Bösen etwas weiss. Er soll

hier ein glückliches Traumleben führen. In diesen kindlichen Naturzustand muss aber der Widerspruch hineinkommen; denn der Mensch soll nicht in dieser Unbefangenheit bleiben. So kommt der Zwiespalt in die menschliche Brust und diesen Zwiespalt, der doch notwendig ist, schaut der Mensch nachher als Folge seiner Schuld, seiner Sünde an. So glaubt der Mensch immer schon gesündigt zu haben, wenn er zum Bewusstsein des Guten und Bösen kommt, oder wenn er sich in diesem Zwiespalt des Naturzustandes findet. Dieses ist die Hegelsche Theorie. Das Böse unterscheidet sich demnach nur insofern vom Guten, dass das Böse das notwendige Mittel ist, um gut zu werden. . . .

Es ist leicht einzusehen, wie die Philosophie auf diese Theorie kommen musste. Die Philosophie will nämlich Alles begreifen. Begreifen heisst aber etwas in seiner Notwendigkeit einsehen. So will sie auch die Notwendigkeit der Sünde einsehen. Sie macht es sich nun leicht, indem sie etwas Sünde nennt, was gar nicht Sünde ist; das aber, was wirklich Sünde ist, völlig ignoriert. . . .

Die Folge dieser Hegelschen Theorie ist der Pantheismus. Es ist überall nur das eine göttliche Leben, welches sich von sich unterscheidet, in der Natur; welches zum Bewusstsein dieses Unterschiedes kommt, im menschlichen Geiste und welches diesen Unterschied dann aufhebt, ebenfalls im menschlichen Geiste. Nach meiner Überzeugung ist Hegel nur zu überwinden, wenn dieser Punkt genau ins Auge gefasst wird. . . .

Es bildet, wie gesagt, die Grundlehre des Judentums, dass die Sünde, nicht bloss als Durchgangspunkt, sondern immerfort, während des ganzen Lebens, möglich ist; dass sie in dieser blossen Möglichkeit von Gott gewollt ist, weil der Mensch sich die Frömmigkeit auf eine freie Weise aneignen soll; dass sie aber in ihrer Wirklichkeit immer zufällig ist, weil der Mensch niemals zu sündigen braucht. (*RJ*, 43–46)

See also, for Hirsch's rejection of Hegel's interpretation of Genesis 2 and 3, *RJ*, 74 ff. Hirsch finds the ultimate source of Hegel's error concerning sin—and indeed possibly of all his errors—in the *Logic*, which, he asserts, confuses finiteness and evil, thus failing to understand the true nature of evil (*RJ*, 826). Committing this confusion, and hence seeking to save evil as partially good instead of rejecting it as totally evil, Hegelianism unwittingly becomes a form of paganism. "Der Hegelianismus ist . . . das sublimierteste Heidentum: dort soll auch die Sünde, der notwendige Widerspruch des endlichen Geistes sein, der alsdann, wie im Heidentum das Naturübel, zu sühnen und aufzuheben ist" (*RJ*, 98).

31. They are reminiscent of the categories in which Kant (in the first part of his *Religion innerhalb der Grenzen der blossen Vernunft*) seeks to understand the choice between good and evil, but also of Schelling, to whose doctrine of evil, understood as fall from God (first stated in his *Philosophie und Religion* of 1804), Hirsch explicitly refers, *RJ*, 107 ff., 110: "Das ist richtig, dass alle Barbarei nur als ein Abfall des Menschen von Gott zu begreifen ist." As for the full development of that doctrine in Schelling's last phase, Hirsch did not know it (*RJ*, 813). Nor could he have known it. Schelling's *Philosophie der Mythologie und Offenbarung* was published only posthumously, in 1857–1858.

32. The fact that, though applying Hegelian dialectic to material mostly borrowed from Hegel, Hirsch's account of paganism can arrive at very different conclusions dramatically highlights a central difficulty in Hegel's whole approach to religious—and not only religious—fact. Hirsch's account—and indeed his work as a whole—ought therefore to have occasioned some soul-searching among contemporary Christian Hegelians. They preferred, however, to ignore him. As Schoeps wryly remarks: "Die theologische Hegelorthodoxie . . . hat Schweigen für der Weisheit besseren Teil gehalten." (See the essay referred to in note 11.)

33. *RJ*, 110 ff., and the whole section on paganism, 105–439.

34. *RJ*, 277.

35. Ibid., 322 ff.

36. Ibid., 382 ff.:

Die Frage kann nicht ausbleiben: Was nützt denn der Nutzen? Und auf diese Frage hat die römische Welt keine Antwort und daher ist sie mit all ihrem Nützlichen unglücklich.

Mit dieser Frage hat sich aber auch das Heidentum überhaupt vollendet. Das Heidentum war davon ausgegangen, dass der Mensch der Natürlichkeit und Sinnlichkeit die Herrschaft gönnte. Alles, was der Sinnlichkeit Einbruch tat, die Stimme des Gewissens nicht ausgenommen, wurde als etwas Feindliches betrachtet und zu überwinden versucht. In Rom ist dieses Ziel erreicht; der Egoismus ist zur vollständigen Herrschaft gekommen; ein Jeder wird da rechtlich in seinem Nutzen und in dem, was dazu dient, denselben zu fördern, geschützt. Nun erkennt der Mensch, dass das, was er erreicht hat, eben nur der Widerspruch und sein Unglück ist. Wozu der Nutzen? Das ist die Frage, die dieses ganze Gebäude umstürzt . . . In Rom wird . . . das Nichts des menschlichen Geistes gewusst. Dieses ist die bodenlose Leerheit, das Unglück als solches, der Ekel vor sich selbst . . . Das gesuchte Glück hat sich zum totalen Unglück verkehrt. Die falsche Voraussetzung des Heidentums, dass der Mensch seiner Natürlichkeit zu folgen habe, hat sich als das Nichtige erwiesen. Resultatlos schliesst die alte Welt . . . Sie weiss nun, dass weder die Natur noch der menschliche Geist Gott sei . . . Alles ist ihr zur Lüge geworden, das ist ihre grausenhafte Erfahrung. Eine neue Religion, ein neues Völkerleben ist dem Menschen zu finden und zu erfinden total unmöglich. Das Heidentum ist mit dem Beginn des römischen Kaiserreichs untergegangen und das reine Nichts ist dem verzweifelten Menschengeschlecht übrig geblieben.

37. Ibid., 385 ff.

38. Ibid., 418 ff., 426 ff., 436 ff.

39. Ibid., 439.

40. Hirsch comments on the Ten Commandments as follows:

. . . es heissen diese Worte [i.e., the first two Commandments] nichts anderes als Gott ist der Herr über alles Natürliche und der Mensch soll in dieser Herrschaft Gott ähnlich werden. Der Mensch soll sich nicht von der Natur abhängig, sondern ihr gegenüber frei wissen und die Natur als zu seinem Dienste bestimmt ansehen. Diese beiden ersten Worte enthalten daher den ganzen Inhalt der Religion, sowohl nach ihrer allgemeinen Seite, insofern alle Menschen den Ruf vernehmen sollen: Gott und nicht die Natur ist Herr, der Mensch soll ähnlich als Herr und nicht als Sklave der Natur leben, als auch nach der besonderen Seite, dass dieser Gott Jisrael zuerst befreit hat dass Jisrael daher auch vor allen Völkern der Freiheit leben soll. Die übrigen acht Worte sind eben nur die in Umrissen gegebene Explikation dieses Inhalts, seine Anwendung auf das Leben . . . Denn der Gedanke, Gott ist Herr, der Mensch ist frei . . . soll nicht bloss gewusst und anerkannt werden, sondern er soll das ganze Leben durchdringen. . . . ” (RJ, 612)

Cf. also *Die Messiaslehre der Juden* (Leipzig, 1843), 114ff.:

Gerade um dieses Heidentum zu vernichten, ist der Herr am Sinai erschienen. . . . Die Wege des Herrn sind die Wunder, die Gott getan, und diese wollen uns belehren, dass nicht, wie der alte und neue Heide, um sündigen zu können, angibt, die Natur Gott ist, sondern dass Gott der Herr ist über die Natur. . . . Aber die Wunder allein haben nicht diese Macht, uns diese Belehrung zu gewähren, so lange nicht der Wächter erweckt ist, uns die Wunder zu deuten. . . . Und damit wir wissen, dass die Propheten nichts Falsches ausgesagt haben von dem Ewigen unserem Gott . . . dazu bedurfte es einer Erscheinung, welche sowohl ein Wunder als die Auslegung eines Wunders war; dazu ist Gott am Sinai erschienen.

41. See, e.g., *RJ*, 386.
42. Ibid., 113, 148.
43. Ibid., 72.
44. Ibid., 455.
45. As might be expected, Hirsch's thought is not free from the tendency to blur or soften the distinction between revelation and natural insight. Yet though admitting the "rationalistic coloring" of his account of revelation he radically rejects its reduction to natural insight. "Man stellt sich von Anfang an eine unmögliche Aufgabe, will man das Wie der Prophetie—hier für jedes Reden Gottes mit dem Menschen genommen—erklären. . . . Der Mensch weiss . . . , dass er dieses Alles nicht aus seinem Innern schöpft, sondern dass er es von aussen her vernimmt. . . . Es muss . . . das Wort Gottes ihm wirklich von aussenher geworden sein, und doch nicht auf die Weise, wie andere Worte für ihn vernehmbar sind . . . ” (Ibid., 478–482). Hirsch even repudiates all Biblical criticism (Ibid., 590 ff.).

Hirsch explicitly asserts that both the life of the Jewish people and the life of mankind are "exposed to the immediate influence of God," and that the purpose of this exposure is in both cases to make man free (Ibid., 863). The central philosophical problem arising from these assertions—how God can force man to make himself free without destroying man's freedom in so doing—is already the basic theme of Kant's philosophy of history; see my article "Kant's Concept of History," *Kantstudien* 48: 381–398 (1956–1957).

46. *RJ*, 880: "[Jisraels] Geschichte muss es belehren, dass, wenn est nicht freiwillig seinen jisraelitischen Beruf erfüllen will, Gott es dazu zwingt."

47. In the preface of the *RJ*, Hirsch defines his philosophical overall objective as follows:

Heute . . . gilt es, gerade die Eigentümlichkeit, die positive Weltanschauung der jüdischen Religion und die Formen, die sie sich gegeben . . . sich . . . zu vergegenwärtigen, nämlich ihre Zeremonien und Gebräuche, in ihrer absoluten Notwendigkeit zu begreifen und wieder im Herzen zur lebendigen Tat zu erheben, aufzubauen, statt einzureissen, zu erhalten, statt preiszugeben, das wahre Judentum auch unserer Seits zu bewähren. Dahin ist es aber noch nicht gekommen, dass man sich hiervon überzeugt hält; erst die wissenschaftliche Nötigung kann zu dieser Einsicht hinführen." (*RJ,* ix–x)

This program is directed, on the one hand, against Mendelssohn's abstract in the name of Hegel's concrete rationalism, and, on the other hand, against Hegel's sublation of religion by philosophy in the name of Hirsch's own preservation. As for the program itself, this claims to be only in part achieved by the *RJ.* Matters such as ritual were to be dealt with in future works which Hirsch never wrote. (See note 14.) What the *RJ* actually claims to have demonstrated is that human freedom— which even without Divine intervention can be actualized—is assured actualization by that intervention. The last sentence of the text of the *RJ* is the following: "Somit hat sich die Religionsphilosophie, oder die Idee der Freiheit erfüllt; sie hat nachgewiesen, wie sich die Freiheit, trotz der möglichen Sünde in der Welt verwirklicht" (*RJ,* 882).

48. See, e.g., *RJ,* 45, 165, and in particular 547:

Es gibt . . . eine Wirklichkeit, oder kann eine geben, die nicht *notwendig,* sondern *absolut zufällig* ist, die durchaus nicht sein sollte und ihr *Nicht-Sein-Sollen* auch in ihrem resultatlosen und kläglichen Ende manifestiert: es gibt also eine Wirklichkeit, oder kann eine geben, die nicht von Gott, von Ihm weder gewirkt noch gewollt ist, sondern die mit Notwendigkeit, von Gott, nur als eine rein *mögliche* gesetzt ist. Die Wirklichkeit, welche sich diese Möglichkeit geben will, *vernichtet* sich selbst, so dass sie rein weggeschafft ist, ohne Resultat zu hinterlassen; sie berührt also das göttliche Leben nicht: *Gottes Leben ist also ein anderes, als das Leben des menschlichen Geistes, der sich immer die falsche Wirklichkeit statt der wahren geben kann;* Gott ist nur so lange dem menschlichen Geiste immanent, als dieser tugendhaft ist; wählt er aber die Sünde, so ist Gott ihm ein Jenseits; er ist von Gott abgefallen. Gott ist ewig und notwendig; aber weil das *Zufällige,* die Sünde, in dieser Welt sich eine Wirklichkeit geben kann, *so ist Gottes Leben nicht das Leben dieser Welt.* . . . (Hirsch's italics)

49. It would appear that Schoeps errs (in the work referred to in note 15) in closely associating Hirsch with thinkers such as Feuerbach. Because his otherwise excellent account views Hirsch in the light of contemporary "postliberal" theology it is too inclined to regard Hirsch as an "anthropologizer" of religion, underestimating his opposition to the anthropologizing left-wing Hegelians. See, e.g., *RJ,* 624: "Gegen diesen Feind [i.e., the left-wing Hegelians] hat das Judentum durchaus gemeinschaftliche Sache mit dem Christentum zu machen; denn beide sind von ihm bedroht. Ist Gott nichts weiter als die Idee der Menschheit, die sich ewig verwirklicht; kann die Religion sich im einzelnen Menschen auch nur eine endliche,

unvollkommene, d.h., nach dieser Philosophie, eine sündhafte Wirklichkeit geben, so hört Juden- und Christentum zu gleicher Zeit auf, Wahrheit zu sein."

50. See *RJ*, e.g., 455, 599 ff., and 607:

Der Inhalt der Prophetie besteht . . . in Wahrheiten, die allerdings jetzt, nachdem dieselbe so lange schon in der Welt gewirkt, angefangen, uns geläufig zu werden, so dass wir philosophisch die Notwendigkeit dieser Wahrheiten, von der Freiheit aller Menschen, von der Gerechtigkeit und Redlichkeit, die sowohl unter den Völkern, wie unter den einzelnen Menschen herrschen soll u.s.w. einzusehen vermögen und an die einstige Verwirklichung dieser Wahrheiten glauben können . . . die aber ohne göttliche Eingebung vor dreitausend Jahren nicht einmal geahnt werden konnten.

This passage differs not inconsiderably from *Die Messiaslehre der Juden*, 136: "Die Offenbarung . . . ist nicht eine göttliche Belehrung über Wahrheiten, deren die Vernunft ohne eine solche Belehrung nicht fähig gewesen wäre: sondern die Offenbarung ist die göttliche Erziehung zu den Wahrheiten, *die die Vernunft niemals hätte vergessen sollen* . . . (our italics). For Lessing's doctrine, see his "The Education of the Human Race," *Lessing's Theological Writings*, ed. H. Chadwick (London, 1956), 82–98. Possibly Hirsch is influenced also by Kant's ideas on moral education. Recognizing that it is lack of moral autonomy which makes moral education *ab extra* necessary, and that this education can be moral only if it leads to autonomy, Kant conceives of moral education as the kind of external influence whose aim is to emancipate the pupil from the need for such influence.

51. Cf. the passage quoted above in note 48, and also *RJ*, 48 ff., 614.

52. *RJ*, 50. Cf. rabbinic passages such as these: "When the Israelites do God's will, they add to the power of God on high. When the Israelites do not do God's will, they, as it were, weaken the great power of God on high" (*Lam. R.* 1:33). " 'Ye are my witnesses, saith the Lord, and I am God' (Isa. xliii 12). That is, when ye are my witnesses, I am God, and when ye are not my witnesses, I am, as it were, not God" (*Midr. Ps.* on Ps. 123:1).

53. *RJ*, 646 ff., esp. 648, 668, 688 ff., 622. To Hirsch's recognition of Jewish-Christian kinship corresponds his unequivocal repudiation of all Christian claims to a message which is new for the Jew—other than the Pauline error. The Christian message is new only for the pagan. See, e.g., ibid., 728 and esp. 702:

Doch bei den Juden konnte der Erfolg [der Verkündigungen der Apostel] nirgends so ungeheuer ausfallen, als sie erwartet hatten. Verkündeten sie bloss von dem Leben ihres Meisters und dass jeder so leben müsse, wie Jesus gelebt habe, um Gott gefällig zu werden, so war dieses den Juden etwas . . . sich selbst Verstehendes: diese hatten das Alles schon so deutlich von Moscheh und den Propheten gelehrt [*sic!*], dass sie das Neue daran nicht finden konnten. Verkündeten aber die neuen Lehrer mehr—was sie Anfangs gewiss nicht taten—dass nur die Taufe auf den Namen Jesu selig mache, dass diese eine magische Kraft besitze, die Seele, wäre sie auch noch so verderbt, von den Sünden rein zu machen, und dass nur die Taufe fähig mache, an dem zu erwartenden Messiasreiche Teil zu nehmen, so war dieses

für die Juden eine solche Subtilität, bei der sie nichts zu denken wussten
und die zu fassen sie daher sich unfähig fühlten.

In a footnote Hirsch adds: "Es ist dieses das ewige Missverständnis des Christen-
tums, dass es glaubt, es habe den Juden etwas Neues zu lehren, während seine
Mission nur an die Heiden gerichtet sein soll. . . . "

54. Hirsch even insists on the messianic Jewish return to Palestine; see the very
title of the nineteenth chapter of his *Messiaslehre der Juden*, "Israels Nationalität und
Rückkehr nach Palestina." He stresses, however, that the future Jewish nationalism
will not be political but spiritual only. This is in connection with a polemic against
those who would grant to Jews full political emancipation only on condition that
they give up Jewish "nationalism" in every form.

55. Ibid., 706.

56. Ibid., 750, 722–767. Hirsch maintains that the Christian belief in Jesus as
the son of God is Judaically unobjectionable in its pre-Pauline form, which—he
thinks—asserts that every human being is potentially, and, if "educated," actually,
the son of God. But in the sense given to it by St. Paul, "verliert der Ausdruck Sohn
Gottes alle ethische Bedeutung; er bezeichnet nicht mehr das vom ethischen Verhalten des Vaters zum Sohne abstrahierte Verhältnis zwischen Gott und Mensch,
sondern muss in einen metaphysiscnphysischen Sinn umgewandelt werden. Gott ist
der Vater Jesu vermöge der Wesensgleichheit, die zwischen beiden stattfindet, und
er ist in diesem Sinne nur der Vater Jesu. Kein anderer Mensch kann sich dieser
Wesensgleichheit mit Gott rühmen, folglich wenn Gott auch noch der Vater der
anderen Menschen genannt wird so ist dieses uneigentlich gemeint" (ibid., 767–
768).

57. Ibid., 776.

58. Ibid., 789, 786 ff.

59. Cf., e.g., ibid., 722: "Das Heidentum war immer und überall Sklaverei,
wie es denn auch ohne Sklaven nirgends bestehen konnte. Das Heidentum kam
nie über das Dilemma hinaus, dass ihm Gott entweder ein abstraktes Jenseits,
wie in Indien, dem Buddhaismus und Ägypten, blieb, oder dass Gott an aller
Zerrissenheit dieser Welt Teil hatte und so zu sagen gottlos war. Die Heiden
waren daher früher wirklich getrennt von Gott und erst in Christo hörten sie
von der göttlichen Natur des Menschen." According to Hirsch, the original achievement of Jesus survives in the subsequent Pauline involvement in paganism. Otherwise Paulinism would be paganism pure and simple. The question arises for Hirsch
as to what, once Protestantism will have emancipated itself from Paulinism, will be
the remaining difference between it and Judaism. Hirsch replies: "Worin besteht
nun der Unterschied zwischen Juden- und Christentum? Einzig und allein darin,
dass im Christentum Alles in der Person Jesu Christi conzentriert wird, der Jude
aber glaubt, dass Jesus nur deshalb das geworden ist, was er war, weil er als Jude
geboren war, und weil er die Torah und die Propheten begriffen hatte und das
sein wollte, was er als Jude sein sollte; dass aber jeder Jude, gerade weil ihm diesel-
ben Antezedentien vorangehen, die Jesus vorangingen:—Teilnahme an der jüdischen Geschichte vermöge seiner Geburt, Torah und Propheten—auch wenn Jesus
nicht existiert hätte, doch dasselbe hätte werden sollen, was Jesus war" (ibid.,
744 ff.).

60. See, e.g., ibid., 443 ff., 794, 835 ff.

3. Hermann Cohen—after Fifty Years

This chapter first appeared as Leo Baeck Memorial Lecture 12 (1969), pp. 3–27. It is reprinted with permission from the Leo Baeck Institute.

1. See Gershom Scholem, "Jews and Germans," *Commentary*, November 1966.
2. Yaakov Fleischmann, "Franz Rosenzweig as a Critic of Zionism," *Conservative Judaism*, Fall 1967, 54.
3. Julius Guttmann, *Philosophies of Judaism* (New York, 1964), 352.
4. "Death is a metaphysical evil on whose cause or possible abolition mystics may brood. It is not a theme for ethics, and hence neither for true religiosity. It is already different with sickness. . . . Poverty becomes the main representative of human misfortune . . . " (Hermann Cohen, *Die Religion der Vernunft aus den Quellen des Judentums* [Leipzig 1919], 156; henceforth cited as RV).
5. See esp. Ernst Bloch, *Das Prinzip Hoffnung* (Frankfurt am Main, 1959).
6. Samuel H. Bergman, *Faith and Reason* (Washington, D.C., 1961), 28.
7. Hermann Cohen, *Deutschtum und Judentum* (Giessen, 1915); reprinted in *Jüdische Schriften*, ed. B. Strauss, 3 vols. (Berlin, 1924). We shall cite from the more readily available *Jüdische Schriften*, henceforth cited as *JS*.
8. *JS* II, 264.
9. *JS* II, 263.
10. *JS* II, 267.
11. *JS* II, 267.
12. *JS* II, 260.
13. *JS* II, 280.
14. In 1910 Cohen had written: "War is the Satan of world history" (*JS* I, 301).
15. *JS* II, 300.
16. *JS* II, 299.
17. *JS* II, 284.
18. *JS* II, 261.
19. *JS* II, 280.
20. *JS* I, 8. Gershom Scholem's essay, already referred to (note 1), amply illustrates that dreamlike unrealism concerning Jewish and German existence was by no means confined to Cohen. Moreover, it shows quite clearly that those such as Cohen must be quite sharply distinguished from those who ask us to believe—in the name of the prophets, who indeed did not wish Israel to be a people like all other peoples—that "the original meaning of the Jewish idea is the absorption of this people by other peoples." What is so terrible about this statement is not that it has been so devastatingly refuted by history, but that it never signified anything except a perversion whereby Christian ideas—rejected by Jews unto their dying breath—now present themselves as the demand of the greatest Jewish minds (*JS* I, 38).
21. In this section we refer only to Cohen's philosophical works prior to *RV*. For this latter work, see section V.
22. Hermann Cohen, *Kant Begründung der Ethik* (Berlin, 1877). We quote from the 2nd ed. (1910), henceforth cited as *KBE*.
23. *KBE*, 279.

24. See my article "Kant's Concept of History," *Kant-Studien*, 1956–1957, pp. 281–298.

25. *KBE*, 343.

26. *KBE*, 346. See also Hermann Cohen, *Ethik des reinen Willens* (Berlin, 1904; 2nd ed., 1907, henceforth cited as *ErW*), 454: "I must in my moral labor . . . remain wholly independent of and unworried by the question of success." This had been Fichte's doctrine. Kant himself, in contrast, had been led from morality to religion precisely by the purported impossibility of remaining indifferent to the consequences of morally motivated actions.

27. *KBE*, 272.

28. *KBE*, 348.

29. *KBE*, 352.

30. *KBE*, 351.

31. *KBE*, 365 ff.

32. *JS* I, xxxii ff.

33. *ErW*, 407.

34. *ErW*, 395.

35. *ErW*, 391.

36. *ErW*, 118.

37. *ErW*, 402 ff.

38. *ErW*, 321.

39. *ErW*, 405.

40. *ErW*, 399.

41. *ErW*, 409.

42. *ErW*, 87.

43. *ErW*, 410 ff.

44. *ErW*, 454. See note 26 above.

45. *ErW*, 89.

46. *ErW*, 452.

47. *JS* I, xix.

48. See note 3.

49. See note 20.

50. *ErW*, 452, 449 ff.

51. *JS* I, xlv ff.; see also Bergman, *Faith and Reason*, 43 ff.

52. Guttmann, *Philosophies of Judaism*, 360 ff., and esp. Alexander Altmann, "Hermann Cohens Begriff der Korrelation," in *Zwei Welten* (Tel Aviv, 1962), 377–399. Altmann's article is entirely devoted to the issue we presently touch on.

53. *JS* I, xli.

54. *RV*, 194.

55. *RV*, 187.

56. Hermann Cohen, *Der Begriff der Religion im System der Philosophie* (Giessen, 1915), 134.

57. Ibid.

58. This agreement has largely been produced by Altmann's most thorough treatment of the subject.

59. Altmann, "Hermann Cohens Begriff der Korrelation," 397 ff.

60. Quoted in Walter Goldstein, *Hermann Cohen* (Jerusalem, 1963), 9 ff.

61. Ibid., 5.

4. Martin Buber's Concept of Revelation

This chapter is reprinted from *The Philosophy of Martin Buber*, ed. Paul A. Schilpp and Maurice Friedman (La Salle, Ill.: Open Court, 1967; Library of Living Philosophers no. 12), with permission from Open Court Publishing Company.

1. Martin Buber, *I and Thou* (Edinburgh, 1957), 109.
2. See chap. 1 in this volume.
3. While Judah Hallevi is hardly an empiricist in any precise sense of the term, there is some justification in applying this term to a thinker who frowned on efforts to support the Jewish religion through metaphysical speculation, pointing instead to the testimony of those who had been present at Mount Sinai.
4. Martin Buber recognizes with the utmost clarity that C. G. Jung's "religion of pure psychic immanence," for example, is nothing but a "translation of post-Kantian idealism into psychology" (*Eclipse of God*, Harper Torchbook, 78 ff). We might add that the translation is rather less impressive than the original product, cf. E. L. Fackenheim, "Schelling's Philosophy of Religion," *University of Toronto Quarterly*, 22 (Toronto, 1952), 1ff.
5. For the transcendental kind of idealism there is an idea of God but not an existing God, while for the ontological kind the existing God becomes fully real only in human experience. Kant and Hegel do not wholly fit into either of these classes.
6. Buber clearly recognizes the criticism which asserts that "religion has never been anything but an intrapsychic process whose products are 'projected' on a plane in itself fictitious but vested with reality by the soul"; and that, therefore, "every alleged colloquy with the divine was only a soliloquy, or rather a conversation between various strata of the self." See his *Eclipse of God*, 13. In recognizing the criticism, Buber also recognizes the task confronting those who would answer it.
7. Martin Buber, *Drei Reden ueber das Judentum* (Frankfurt, 1920), 71. For a full account of Buber's early thought, see Maurice S. Friedman, *Martin Buber: The Life of Dialogue* (New York, 1955), 27–53.
8. See Martin Buber, *Between Man and Man* (Boston, 1955), 22 ff., and *I and Thou*, 115 ff.
9. It is obvious that some of the above remarks apply only in the case of relations which are *I-Thou* relations from the standpoint of both partners, such as inter-human relations.
10. This is why Buber can call *I-Thou* knowledge "higher than reason" (*ueber-vernuenftig*) rather than irrational, *I and Thou*, p. 49. The implications of Buber's term are too many to be considered here.
11. Buber, *I and Thou*, 81, my italics. See also his *Eclipse of God*, 3, 123.
12. *Eclipse of God*, 13.
13. See note 8.
14. *I and Thou*, 80 ff.
15. Ibid., 84. See also Martin Buber, *Israel and the World* (New York, 1948), 22: "He who imagines that He knows and holds the mystery fast can no longer face it as his *Thou*."
16. *I and Thou*, 11.
17. *Eclipse of God*, 135; *Between Man and Man*, 18.
18. See Martin Buber, *Moses* (Oxford and London, 1946), 188, and a letter from

Buber to Franz Rosenzweig published in Rosenzweig, *On Jewish Learning* (New York, 1955), 111 ff.

19. *Israel and the World*, 209. Perhaps Buber's most explicit statement on the Torah is found in his *Two Types of Faith* (London, 1951), 93.

20. *Between Man and Man*, 15.

21. Exodus 3:14. Cf. Buber's commentaries, *Israel and the World*, 23, *Moses*, 52 ff., and *The Prophetic Faith* (New York, 1949), 28 ff.

22. *Between Man and Man*, 15.

23. *I and Thou*, 75, 112.

24. Ibid., 80.

25. Ibid., 75.

26. This point is most clearly brought out in Buber's comments on Biblical miracles, e.g., *Moses*, 77: "The real miracle means that in the astonishing experience of the event the current system of cause and effect becomes, as it were, transparent and permits a glimpse of the sphere in which the sole power, not restricted by any other, is at work." See also *The Prophetic Faith*, 46, and *Israel and Palestine* (London, 1952), 26: "wherever the action of nature as well as spirit is perceived as a gift, revelation takes place."

27. *I and Thou*, 81.

28. *Between Man and Man*, 56, my italics.

29. *The Prophetic Faith*, 164 ff., my italics.

30. See *I and Thou*, esp. 119.

31. See *Two Types of Faith*, 168 and many other passages. But it would appear that Buber has not wholly decided his stand on this last, and in an age of manifest "eclipse of God" most troubling, question; see, e.g., Martin Buber, *At the Turning* (New York, 1952), 61 ff.

32. *I and Thou*, 95.

33. Ibid., 96.

34. *Between Man and Man*, 12.

35. *Eclipse of God*, 135.

36. *Between Man and Man*, 68.

37. *The Prophetic Faith*, 164.

38. *Eclipse of God*, 135.

39. *I and Thou*, 117.

40. *Between Man and Man*, 69.

41. Our reasons for omitting this aspect of Buber's thought—which includes his interpretation of Judaism—are first, as indicated, that this transcends the mere abstract *concept* of revelation; secondly, the fact that it is treated by other contributors to *The Philosophy of Martin Buber*. We by no means suggest that the aspects of Buber's thought here treated are more important than those omitted.

42. *Israel and the World*, 98. See also Buber's incisive criticism of the thought of C. G. Jung, *Eclipse of God*, 78–92, 133–137.

43. "Religion and Philosophy," *Eclipse of God*, 27–46.

44. "*I-It* finds its highest concentration and illumination in philosophical knowledge," *Eclipse of God*, 45. Consequently, Buber argues in this essay, philosophy deals in abstractions in which existential reality is lost. Its objects are mere "constructions" and "objectifications." Presumably philosophy is unaware of these limitations. For it either fails to discover God among its objects or else mistakes Him for a mere

object. Could it look for Him among objects, or mistake Him for an object, if it knew that objects are only "constructions" or "objectifications"? See earlier discussion.

45. See note 44.

46. *Eclipse of God*, 50.

47. The philosopher most instructive on this fundamental problem is Schelling, who, in his *Philosophie der Mythologie und Offenbarung, Werke* 11–14 (Stuttgart und Augsburg, 1856–1861), distinguishes between a "positive" philosophy, which is based on a commitment, and a "negative" philosophy, which is a dialectical argument for this commitment. See E. L. Fackenheim, "Schelling's Conception of Positive Philosophy," *Review of Metaphysics*, 7, no.4 (1954): 563–582.

48. We confine ourselves to a single but crucially important example. Buber asserts that revelation is "the inexpressible confirmation of meaning. Meaning is assured. Nothing can any longer be meaningless. The question about the meaning of life is no longer there. But were it there, it would not have to be answered," *I and Thou*, 110. Buber clearly teaches that the question about the meaning of life *is* there prior to the meeting with the divine *Thou*. He also clearly teaches that it cannot be answered—or rather removed—by anything but the meeting with the divine *Thou*. For, every other *I-Thou* relation being incomplete (*I and Thou*, 99), man's "sense of *Thou* cannot be satiated till he finds the endless *Thou*," (*I and Thou*, 80). All this implies that, prior to the commitment to the dialogue with God, it is possible to point to the commitment to this dialogue, indicating at least something of what it would mean should such a dialogue take place. It follows that the concepts of religion, revelation, and the divine *Thou* are at least not *wholly* derived from the actuality of the divine-human dialogue.

5. Martin Buber

This chapter appeared first in *Midstream* (1974), pp. 46–56. It is reprinted with permission from the Theodor Herzl Foundation.

1. Milton Himmelfarb, ed., *The Condition of Jewish Belief* (New York, 1966). The symposium originally appeared in *Commentary*, August 1966.

2. This is the tripartite division of Martin Buber, *Werke* (Munich and Heidelberg, 1962). An additional volume of Jewish writings appeared under different auspices.

3. Ibid., vol. II, 7 (italics added).

4. This is too large an issue to be dealt with here. Buber at least recognized the problem; see, e.g., *The Philosophy of Martin Buber*, ed. A. Schilpp and Maurice Friedman (La Salle, Ill., 1967), 725 ff.

5. *Werke*, vol. I, 136 (italics added).

6. Ibid., 548.

7. Ibid., 143.

8. Ibid., 160.

9. Martin Buber, *Moses* (London, 1946), 105.

10. Ibid.

11. Ibid, 17.

12. *The Writings of Martin Buber*, ed. W. Herberg (New York, 1956), 239, 242.

13. Ibid., 242.

6. The Systematic Role of the Matrix (Existence) and Apex (Yom Kippur) of Jewish Religious Life in Rosenzweig's *Star of Redemption*

This chapter is reprinted from *Der Philosoph Franz Rosenzweig (1886–1929): Internationaler Kongress—Kassel 1986*, vol. 2, ed. Wolfdietrich Schmied-Kowarzik (Munich: Karl Alber, 1988), pp. 567–75, with permission from Verlag Karl Alber.

1. See Franz Rosenzweig, *Kleinere Schriften* (Berlin, 1937), 373–398 (henceforth cited as *Kl. Schr.*) For the theme of this essay, albeit in a quite different context, see also my *To Mend The World*, (New York, 1982), 58–100.

2. Franz Rosenzweig, *The Star of Redemption*, trans. William W. Hallo (New York, 1971) (henceforth cited as *Star*).

3. *Kl. Schr.*, 398.

4. I use both terms for Rosenzweig's *Bewährung*, since the connotations of the English "verification" are too scientific-theoretical, whereas "confirmation," with overtones of testimony or commitment, taken by itself, seems to be too subjective and divorced from objective truth. Using a play on words, Rosenzweig alludes to a new theory of knowledge of which *Bewährung der Wahrheit* (Truth) will be the "basic notion" (*Kl. Schr.* 395).

5. In a letter to Ernst Simon, dated 18 September 1924, Rosenzweig writes: "I am regarded as the 'Jewish fanatic,' and yet I have written the first unfanatical Jewish book I know of (that is to say, Jewish and yet unfanatical, unfanatical and yet Jewish)"; *Briefe* (Berlin, 1935), 510.

6. On this subject, see further *To Mend The World*, 66, 73 ff.

7. *Kl. Schr.*, 376.

8. See *Kl. Schr.*, 378.

9. Rosenzweig writes: "Finis philosophiae? . . . But I do not think it will be as bad as that. Rather at the very point at which philosophy has indeed reached its end with its thinking (*Denken*), experiencing philosophy (*erfahrende Philosophie*) can begin" (*Kl. Schr.*, 379).

10. Rosenzweig writes that the "point" of Part One is "to teach only this, that none of these great basic concepts of philosophical thinking [i.e., God, World, Man] can be reduced to another" (*Kl. Schr.*, 379).

11. For my critique of both the doctrine of self-authenticating religious experiences and the view that Martin Buber subscribes to (or implies in) that doctrine, see my *Encounters between Judaism and Modern Philosophy* (New York, 1980), chap. 1. For a fuller account than the following one of Rosenzweig's rejection of the doctrine, see *To Mend The World*, 68 ff.

12. See *The Correspondence of Spinoza*, ed. A. Wolf (London, 1928), 350–355.

13. *Kl. Schr.*, 386.

14. *Kl. Schr.*, 374.

15. *Star*, 156, citing *Song of Songs*, 8: 6.

16. This is the subtitle of the *Herzbuch*.

17. *Star*, 342.

7. Leo Strauss and Modern Judaism

This chapter is reprinted from *The Claremont Review of Books* 4 (1985): 21–23, with permission from the Claremont Institute for the Study of Statesmanship and Political Philosophy.

1. This is a revision of a lecture delivered on March 26, 1985, at the Faculty House of the Claremont Colleges for the Claremont chapter of Pi Sigma Alpha, the national political science honors society.

2. Emil Fackenheim, *To Mend the World: Foundations of Future Jewish Thought* (New York, 1982).

3. The book has been published in the United States as Leo Strauss, *Philosophy and Law*, trans. Fred Baumann (Philadelphia, 1987); it has also been translated by Eve Adler (Albany, 1995).

4. Leo Strauss, "Jerusalem and Athens: Some Preliminary Reflections," *Studies in Platonic Political Philosophy* (Chicago, 1983), 147–73.

5. Leo Strauss, "Preface to the English Translation," *Spinoza's Critique of Religion* (New York, 1965), 2.

8. Pinchas Peli as a Jewish Philosopher

This chapter will appear in *Sefer Zikkaron le Pinchas Peli* (Beer Sheva: Beer Sheva University Press, forthcoming). It is printed here with permission from Beer Sheva University Press.

1. The reference to Kierkegaard, Heidegger, and even Hegel is obvious. Not so that to Kant. For whereas it is well known that Kant's moral-religious faith is not knowledge, not well known is that it is based not on an "it is certain" but an "I am certain." See my essay "Immanuel Kant" in *Nineteenth Century Religious Thought in the West*, ed. Smart, Clayton, Sherry and Katz (New York, 1985), vol. 1, 17–40.

2. G. W. F. Hegel, *Early Theological Writings* (Chicago, 1948), 255. The mature Hegel abandoned this view but not because his "Reason" had turned against inspiration but because it had, so he held, incorporated and superseded it.

3. Pinchas Peli, "Where Was God during the Holocaust," *Jerusalem Post*, April 15 and 22, 1983.

4. See Martin Buber, *At the Turning* (New York, 1952), chap. 3.

5. See part one of the *Post* article, p. 5.

6. Pinchas Peli, *Torah Today* (Washington, D.C., 1987), 8.

7. *Israel: The Religious Dimension* (The Jewish Orientation Fellowship, n.d.) is based on papers delivered at the national conventions of the Rabbinical Council of America and the Rabbinical Assembly, both in 1969. *The Future of Israel* (which also contains an essay by Hans Morgenthau) is reproduced from the *Proceedings of the Rabbinical Assembly*, 1974.

8. *Torah Today*, 28.

9. Ibid., 52.

10. Ibid., 59.

11. Ibid., 67.

12. Ibid., 69 ff.

13. Ibid., 71.

14. Ibid., 72.
15. Ibid., 96.

Introduction to Part II

1. See chap. 6.
2. Also, in a sense, in the essay on Strauss, chap. 7.
3. See *The Jewish Thought of Emil Fackenheim* and esp. *To Mend the World.*

9. Holocaust

This chapter is reprinted from *Contemporary Jewish Religious Thought,* ed. Arthur A. Cohen and Paul Mendes-Flohr (New York: Scribner's, 1987), pp. 399–408, with permission from Macmillan Publishing Company.

1. See the warnings voiced by Yehuda Bauer.
2. Monés Sperber, . . . *Than a Tear in the Sea* (1967), xiii.
3. Quoted in *The Yellow Spot: The Extermination of the Jews in Germany* (1936), 47.
4. Hitler, *Mein Kampf,* trans. R. Mannheim (1943), 60.
5. In a debate with Yaacov Herzog. See Yaacov Herzog, *A People That Dwells Alone* (1975), 31.
6. K. D. Bracher, *The German Dictatorship* (1971), 430.
7. Isaac Deutscher, *The Non-Jewish Jew* (1968), 163 ff.
8. A statement by Hans Jonas, made to Ernst Simon as reported in the latter's "Revisionist History of the Jewish Catastrophe," *Judaism,* 12, no. 4 (Summer 1963), 395.
9. See esp. Martin Heidegger's *Sein und Zeit* (1935), sec. II, chap. 1.
10. Theodor Adorno, *Negative Dialektik* (1966), 354 ff.
11. Primo Levi, *Survival in Auschwitz,* trans. Stuart Woolf (1959), 82.
12. See, e.g., Hannah Arendt, *Eichmann in Jerusalem: A Report on the Banality of Evil* (1977).
13. Franklin Littell, *The Crucifixion of the Jews* (1975).
14. Arthur A. Cohen, *The Tremendum* (1981).
15. Emil L. Fackenheim, *To Mend the World: Foundations of Future Jewish Thought* (1982).
16. Dietrich Bonhoeffer as quoted in *The German Church Struggle and the Holocaust,* ed. Franklin H. Littell and Hubert G. Locke (1974), 288.
17. Johann Baptist Metz in *Gott Nach Auschwitz* (1979), 124 ff., 139 ff.
18. H. H. Henrix, F. M. Marquardt, M. Stoehr, all in personal conversation with this writer. The formulation is Henrix's.
19. The German Lutheran theologian Martin Wittenberg, as quoted in *Auschwitz als Herausforderung für Juden und Christen,* ed. G. B. Ginzel (1980), 566.
20. See Maimonides in his *Responsum on Martyrdom.*
21. A celebrated and much-quoted dictum by the German Jewish poet Heinrich Heine.

10. The Holocaust and Philosophy

This chapter was published in *Journal of Philosophy* 82, 10 (1985), pp. 505–14. It appears here with the permission of the *Journal of Philosophy*.

1. New York, 1948.

2. Leo Strauss, preface to the English edition of *Spinoza's Critique of Religion*, reprinted in Judah Goldin, ed., *The Jewish Expression* (New York, 1970), 347.

3. In a debate with Yaacov Herzog. See Herzog, *A People That Dwells Alone* (London, 1975), 31.

4. *The German Dictatorship* (New York, 1969), esp. chap. 8.

5. *The Foot of Pride* (Boston, 1950), 211.

6. Gitta Sereny, *Into That Darkness* (London, 1974), 101.

7. Cited by Joachim C. Fest, *Hitler* (New York, 1975), 212.

8. Hitler, *Mein Kampf*, trans. Ralph Manheim (Boston, 1943), 325, 365.

9. See his magisterial *Destruction of the European Jews* (Chicago, 1961).

10. In private conversation with this writer.

11. Cited by Herbert Luethy, "Der Fuehrer," in N. Podhoretz, ed., *The Commentary Reader* (New York, 1966), 64.

12. *Survival in Auschwitz*, trans. S. Woolf (New York, 1959), 82, italics added.

13. *Negative Dialektik* (Frankfurt, 1975), 355; my translation, italics added.

14. Referred to in Hannah Arendt, *Eichmann in Jerusalem* (New York, 1977), 135; analyzed in *To Mend the World*, 270 ff.

15. H. Hoehne, *The Order of the Death's Head* (London, 1972), 301 ff.

16. See esp. *Eichmann in Jerusalem*, and R. Feldman, ed., *The Jew as Pariah* (New York, 1978), 251.

17. Luethy, "Der Fuehrer," 65. Luethy's brilliant essay is worth more than many a whole Hitler biography.

18. I have tried to grasp and to capture the idolatrous compact between *Volk* and *Fuehrer*, manifested most clearly in the endless yet empty *Sieg Heils* of the Nuremberg *Parteitage*, in "Idolatry as a Modern Possibility," *Encounters between Judaism and Modern Philosophy* (New York, 1980), 171–198, esp. 192–195.

11. Philosophical Reflections on Claude Lanzmann's *Shoah*

This chapter first appeared in *Faith and Freedom*, ed. Richard Lebowitz (Oxford: Pergamon Press, 1987), pp. 9–15. It is printed here with permission from Pergamon Press.

12. Holocaust and *Weltanschauung*

This chapter is reprinted from *Holocaust and Genocide Studies* 3, 2 (1988), pp. 197–208, with permission from Oxford University Press.

1. See chap. 10.

2. The prize surely goes to Treblinka Kommandant Franz Stangl. When asked why they had murdered the Jews, Stangl replied that they wanted their money—as if the victims had not already been stripped naked! When asked about the point

of all the humiliation and cruelty, if murder was to follow anyway, he replied that it was to condition the murderers—as if these needed the conditioning! See Gitta Sereny, *Into That Darkness* (London, 1974), 101. See also the author's *To Mend the World* (New York, 1982), 214, henceforth cited as *TMW*.

3. Since this document is published and cited in many places, no reference is needed. For the meaning of the German word *das Judentum*, see note 20 below.

4. The best brief account of this theory is C. G. Hempel, "The Function of General Laws in History," conveniently available in *Readings in Philosophical Analysis*, ed. H. Feigl and W. Sellars (New York, 1949), 459–471.

5. I have little doubt that, as the decades wear on, the "why" of the Holocaust will become less rather than more intelligible, with the consequence that the "madness explanation" may keep gaining ground. But since a twelve-year-long collective madness is plainly absurd, the belief may also gain ground that the Holocaust did not happen because it could not have happened.

6. See esp. William Dray, *Laws and Explanation in History* (London, 1957).

7. See R. G. Collingwood. *The Idea of History* (London, 1946), part 5.

8. David Irving's thesis in *Hitler's War* (New York, 1977), to the effect that Hitler ordered the deportation of Jews but not their mass murder, was never to be taken seriously. (See *TMW*, 245.) It is refuted by Gerald Fleming's *Hitler and the Final Solution* (Berkeley, 1984). In Nazi Germany a direct *Führerbefehl* superseded all else, Hitler-inspired laws included.

9. No further reference is needed than to the "secret" (but now well-known) Himmler address to the S.S. murderers, in which he praises them for having done the deed, while yet remaining *anstaendig* (decent). See *TMW*, 185 ff.

10. See *TMW*, 270 ff.

11. See note 9.

12. Autonomy, as defined by Kant, does not require a person to legislate to himself but only, in the case where a law is given by another, to approve of it as though he himself were the legislator. Hence only the robots and sadists among the murderers can be dismissed as persons lacking in autonomy. The case of the "idealists" among the S.S., such as Eichmann and Himmler until he became *treulos* (also dismissed on these grounds by such as Bruno Bettelheim), is more complex than is fancied in the textbooks of pre-Nazi Vienna. See *TMW*, 226–230.

13. See note 17.

14. The thesis, put forward in Hermann Rauschning's *Die Revolution des Nihilismus* (1938) as well as his *Gespräche mit Hitler* (1940), is ably discussed in Eberhard Jäckel, *Hitlers Weltanschauung* (Tübingen, 1969), 13 ff.

15. Any notion to the contrary is a fabrication or, more correctly, "nice" propaganda spread by people who (fairly enough) feel uncomfortable about the singledout condition of Jews in Nazi Germany. That condition, however, was a fact. The Nazis viewed Slavs as *Menschentiere*, to be decimated and, when opportune, worked to death. But there still is a difference between these "human animals" and Jewish "vermin" fit only for "extermination."

16. In the book cited in note 14.

17. Adolf Hitler, *Mein Kampf*, trans. Ralph Manheim (Boston, 1943), 22. (The German word *Weltanschauung* is translated incorrectly as "philosophy.") When throughout this essay I speak of the "extremity that showed forth the truth" of the

"why" of the Holocaust—indeed, I would claim, of Nazism as a whole—I do no more than put Hitler's claim to a "granite"-like *Weltanschauung* to the pragmatic test.

18. Hitler, *Mein Kampf*, 55 ff.

19. In the book virtually every aspect of the *Weltanschauung* turns out to be subject to opportunistic modification or even abrogation—except *das Judentum*, treated in chap. 3.

20. In Hegel the term *das Judentum* denotes an honest (if debatable) philosophical definition of the "essence" of the Jewish religion. A perversion already sets in with Marx, for whom this "essence" is meant to encompass the "existence" of the "real" Jew, whose "God" is "money." (Marx sees no need for gathering data about either the financial or mental condition of the poverty-ridden Jews of tsarist Russia.) The perversion is complete when *das Judentum* becomes the inborn character of the "real" Jew. With Marx that Jew can still escape *das Judentum*, as was done by Marx himself. This is cut off by the Nazi *Weltanschauung* for young and old, rich and poor, the most as well as the least religious.

21. Saul Friedländer quotes Albert Speer as follows: "New York in a hurricane of fire. He described the skyscrapers being turned into gigantic burning torches, collapsing upon one another, the glow of the exploding city illuminating the dark sky." One page later Friedländer quotes Ernst Jünger, a right-wing, militaristic, but anti-Nazi writer reacting to applause given to an 18 December 1944 Hitler speech: "The frenetic applause that accompanied his appearance was the agreement for self-destruction, a highly nihilistic act." See Friedländer, *Reflections of Nazism* (New York, 1984), 70–71.

22. See Dietrich Eckart, *Der Bolschewismus von Moses bis Lenin: Zwiegespräch zwischen Adolf Hitler und Mir* (Munich, 1924).

23. Hitler, *Mein Kampf*, 65.

24. See *Religion in Geschichte und Gegenwart*, 2nd edition, vol. 5, 1845.

25. "The all-shatterer"—a nickname given to Kant by those who understand him as shattering not only this or that metaphysical doctrine but the whole discipline of metaphysics, as harking back to the Greeks.

26. In his *Phänomenologie des Geistes*.

27. In his *Erste Einleitung in die Wissenschaftslehre*. Fichte was a rabid antisemite, but this does not enter into our present reflections.

28. In his *Reden über die Religion*.

29. In his *System des Transzendentalen Idealismus*.

30. For a brief account of this important but complex subject, see Robert G. L. Waite's excellent *Adolf Hitler—the Psychopathic God* (New York, 1977), 99 ff.

31. This is a vast subject in its own right, the exploration of which is not attempted here. A small but insufficient attempt is my essay "Philosophical Reflections on Antisemitism," in *Antisemitism*, ed. Michael Curtis (Boulder, 1986), 21–38.

32. This Waite believes about Hitler; see his *Adolf Hitler*, 85.

33. See, e.g., Alvin Rosenfeld, *Imagining Hitler* (Bloomington, 1985).

34. The furthest Martin Heidegger ever came in his *Denken* about Nazism was to dissipate it into a flattened-out loss of Being. See *TMW*, 147–190. The furthest Ernst Nolte comes in his *Denken* is to dissipate it into but one of three "faces" of fascism, and fascism itself into a flattened-out revolt against transcendence. See Nolte, *Three Faces of Fascism* (New York, 1965). As for the Holocaust, this is acknowledged

by Nolte but viewed as of no philosophical significance. In Heidegger's *Denken* it does not appear at all.

Introduction to Part III

1. It is referred to in Emil Fackenheim, *To Mend the World*, but not used.

2. For this information, see Emil Fackenheim, *Encounters between Judaism and Modern Philosophy*; the essays in Fackenheim, *The Jewish Return into History*; and *The Jewish Thought of Emil Fackenheim*.

3. See also the final, autobiographical pieces reprinted in *The Jewish Thought of Emil Fackenheim*.

13. What is Jewish Philosophy?

This chapter will appear in *Jewish Philosophy in the Academy*, ed. Emil L. Fackenheim and Raphael Jospe (Associated University Presses, forthcoming). It appears here with the permission of Fairleigh Dickinson University Press.

1. Yirmiyahu Yovel, *Spinoza v-kofrim acherim* (Tel Aviv, 1988). [*Spinoza and Other Heretics*, 2 vols. (Princeton, 1989).—ed.]

2. In Tertullian, *On Prescription against Heretics*, chap. 7 (quoted by E. Gilson). On this subject, see Gilson, *Reason and Revelation in the Middle Ages* (New York, 1946), chap. 1.

3. St. Thomas Aquinas, *Summa Theologica* I Qu.1 article 8.

4. See Franz Rosenzweig, "Atheistische Theologie," in *Kleinere Schriften* (Berlin, 1937), 285. The essay is an attack on a "theology" "atheistic" in appeasing "paganism" through "hostility to Revelation." "Atheistische Theologie" was written in 1914, soon after Rosenzweig's celebrated decision against conversion to Christianity and for remaining a Jew: he had rediscovered Revelation in Judaism.

5. Carl Gebhard in the preface to his German edition of Spinoza's *Theologico-Political Treatise* (Leipzig, 1922), xiv ff.

6. Moses Mendelssohn, *Jerusalem and Other Jewish Writings*, trans. and ed. Alfred Jospe (New York, 1969), 104.

7. Ibid.

8. *Herrn Carl Bonnets . . . philosophische Untersuchung der Beweise fuer das Christentum . . . herausgegeben von Johann Caspar Lavater* (Zurich, 1769), 4–5. Cited in Alexander Altmann, *Moses Mendelssohn* (Tuscaloosa, 1973), 209.

9. For a brief statement on Kierkegaard as a modern theologian of Revelation, see my *What is Judaism?* (New York, 1987), 26–27.

10. On my Jewish encounter with Kant and Kierkegaard, see Emil Fackenheim, *Encounters between Judaism and Modern Philosophy* (New York, 1973), chap. 2.

11. Martin Buber, *Eclipse of God* (New York, 1957), 73.

12. John Wisdom, in *Logic and Language*, ed. Antony Flew (New York, 1965), 194–216.

13. Ibid., 213.

14. See note 10.

15. See Fackenheim, *Encounters*, chap. 1.

16. See *Der Philosoph Franz Rosenzweig (1886–1929)*, 2 vols., ed. Wolfdietrich Schmied-Kowarzik (Munich, 1988).

17. On this subject, see further my 1993 lecture at the Martin Luther Universitaet of my native city of Halle, reproduced in English translation as the preface to the third edition of *To Mend the World* (Bloomington, 1994).

18. Further on my views on Hegel, see Emil Fackenheim, *The Religious Dimension in Hegel's Thought* (Chicago, 1982); *Encounters*, chap. 3; and *To Mend the World*, chap. 3.

14. Jewish Philosophy in the Academy

This chapter was first published in *Midstream* (August–September 1987), pp. 19–22. It is reprinted here with permission from the Theodor Herzl Foundation.

15. The 614th Commandment Reconsidered

This chapter was first published in *Reform Judaism* 22, no. 1 (1993), pp. 18–20. It is reprinted with permission from the Union of American Hebrew Congregations.

16. A Political Philosophy for the State of Israel

This chapter was first published in *Jerusalem Center for Public Affairs* (1988), pp. 1–18. It is reprinted with permission from the International Center for University Teaching of Jewish Civilization, Jerusalem.

1. Found in the preface to Hegel's *Philosophy of Right.*

2. Frantz Fanon, *The Wretched of the Earth* (New York, 1966). This book was first published in French in 1961.

3. Article 4 of this document asserts that the "Palestinian identity" is an "inherent characteristic, transmitted from parents to children"; article 6, that only those Jews who resided in Palestine prior to "the beginning of the Zionist invasion" will be "considered Palestinians"; article 9, that "armed struggle is the only way to liberate Palestine"; article 20, that Jews, unlike Palestinians, are without national identity and "are citizens of the states to which they belong." The concluding article (33) reads as follows: "This charter shall not be amended save by vote of the majority of two-thirds of the total membership of the National Congress of the Palestine Liberation Organization, taken at a special session convened for that purpose."

In connection with the current unrest in the territories, Yassir Arafat has been interviewed several times, and made what the interviewers considered positive noises when asked whether he would be willing to make peace with Israel. But to my knowledge not a single interviewer has had either the knowledge or the courage to so much as mention the Covenant.

4. The relevant parts of this debate may conveniently be found in Paul R. Mendes-Flohr and Jehuda Reinharz, eds., *The Jew in the Modern World* (New York, 1980), 448–453.

5. This allusion is to the title of Theodor Herzl's famous Zionist novel.

6. This allusion is to the Israeli self-categorization into *dati* (i.e., Orthodox) and *lo dati* (i.e., everyone else). The historical factors generating this bifurcation are beyond the scope of this essay.

7. For the Law of Return and the most important legal problems and decisions

arising from it, see Oscar Kraines, *The Impossible Dilemma: Who Is a Jew in the State of Israel?* (New York, 1976).

8. See *Mishneh Torah*, book 14, chapter 12. Being the deep thinker he is, Maimonides is, of course, aware of the limitations of his philosophical assertions. Hence, having stated that images such as Isaiah's of the lion eating straw (Isa. 11:7) are only metaphors and imply no setting aside of the laws of nature, he goes on to write: "In the days of King Messiah the full meaning of those metaphors and their allusions will become clear to all."

17. Pillars of Zionism

This chapter was first published in *Midstream* (December 1992), pp. 13–15. It is reprinted with permission from the Theodor Herzl Foundation.

18. A Retrospective of My Thought

This chapter will appear in *Jewish Philosophy in the Academy*, ed. Emil L. Fackenheim and Raphael Jospe (Associated University Presses, forthcoming). It appears here with the permission of Fairleigh Dickinson University Press.

1. See Emil Fackenheim, *To Mend the World* (New York, 1982, 1989), part II, chaps. 3 and 4; also see chap. 6 in this volume.

2. Most recently by E. B. Borowitz, *Renewing the Covenant* (New York, 1991), 79 f.

3. On the unique internment operation of which German Jews such as myself were victims, see Eric Koch, *Deemed Suspect: A Wartime Blunder* (Toronto, 1980). On Canada's immigration policy for Jewish refugees between 1933 and 1948, see Irving Abella and Harold Troper, *None Is Too Many* (Toronto, 1982).

4. See, for example, Emil Fackenheim, *Metaphysics and Historicity* (Milwaukee, 1961).

5. *The Religious Dimension in Hegel's Thought* (Chicago, 1982; first published in 1967) is the work it took me ten years to write. On Hegel's middle, see esp. the crucial chap. 4.

6. For my Jewish thought in relation to Hegel's broken middle, see Emil Fackenheim, *Encounters between Judaism and Modern Philosophy* (New York, 1980; first published in 1973), chap. 3, and *To Mend the World*, chap. 3.

7. See chap. 16 in this volume.

8. See Friedrich Schleiermacher, *On Religion: Speeches to Its Cultured Despisers*, trans. and ed. Richard Crouter (New York, 1988), 211.

9. See *To Mend the World*, part IV, chap. 8.

10. The best known of the previous ones is Emil Fackenheim, "Jewish Faith and the Holocaust: A Fragment," *Commentary*, August 1968, 30–36. See also "The Development of My Thought," *Religious Studies Review*, July 1987, 204–206.

11. See Emil Fackenheim, *The Jewish Bible after the Holocaust: A Re-reading* (Bloomington, 1990), 87 ff.

12. See my book of this title, published by Schocken in 1978.

13. G. W. F. Hegel, *Enzyklopaedie der philosophischen Wissenschaften*, no. 237.

Index

Index

EMIL L. FACKENHEIM, a leading contemporary Jewish philosopher and theologian, is University Professor and Professor Emeritus of Philosophy at the University of Toronto and Fellow of the Institute of Contemporary Jewry at the Hebrew University of Jerusalem. His many books include *The Religious Dimension in Hegel's Thought, God's Presence in History, Encounters between Judaism and Modern Philosophy, The Jewish Bible after the Holocaust: A Re-reading*, and *To Mend the World: Foundations of Post-Holocaust Jewish Thought.*

MICHAEL L. MORGAN is Professor of Philosophy and Jewish Studies at Indiana University in Bloomington. He is the author of *Platonic Piety: Philosophy and Ritual in Fourth Century Athens* and *Dilemmas in Modern Jewish Thought: The Dialectics of Revelation and History* and editor of *The Jewish Thought of Emil Fackenheim* and *Classics in Moral and Political Theory.* His articles on Jewish philosophy, the history of philosophy, and other topics have appeared in various scholarly journals.